STUDENT SOLUTIONS MANUAL

DIFFERENTIAL EQUATIONS AND BOUNDARY VALUE PROBLEMS

COMPUTING AND MODELING

SECOND EDITION

C. HENRY EDWARDS
DAVID E. PENNEY

Prentice Hall

Upper Saddle River, NJ 07458

Executive Editor: George Lobell
Supplement Editor: Melanie Van Benthuysen
Special Projects Manager: Barbara A. Murray
Production Editor: Wendy A. Perez
Supplement Cover Manager: Paul Gourhan
Supplement Cover Designer: PM Workshop Inc.
Manufacturing Buyer: Lisa McDowell

Printed in the United States of America

10 9 8 7 6 5 4 3 2 1

ISBN 0-13-093128-4

Prentice-Hall International (UK) Limited, London
Prentice-Hall of Australia Pty. Limited, Sydney
Prentice-Hall Canada, Inc., Toronto
Prentice-Hall Hispanoamericana, S.A., Mexico
Prentice-Hall of India Private Limited, New Delhi
Pearson Education Asia Pte. Ltd., Singapore
Prentice-Hall of Japan, Inc., Tokyo
Editora Prentice-Hall do Brazil, Ltda., Rio de Janeiro

CONTENTS

PREFACE

This is a solutions manual to accompany the textbook **DIFFERENTIAL EQUATIONS AND BOUNDARY VALUE PROBLEMS: Computing and Modeling** (2nd edition, 2000) by C. Henry Edwards and David E. Penney. We include solutions to most of the odd-numbered problems in the text.

Our goal is to support learning of the subject of elementary differential equations in every way that we can. We therefore invite comments and suggested improvements for future printings of this manual, as well as advice regarding features that might be added to increase its usefulness in subsequent editions. Additional supplementary material can be found at our textbook Web site listed below.

Henry Edwards & David Penney

`hedwards@math.uga.edu`
`dpenney@math.uga.edu`

`www.prenhall.com/edwards`

CHAPTER 1

FIRST-ORDER DIFFERENTIAL EQUATIONS

SECTION 1.1

DIFFERENTIAL EQUATIONS AND MATHEMATICAL MODELING

The main purpose of Section 1.1 is simply to introduce the basic notation and terminology of differential equations, and to show the student what is meant by a solution of a differential equation. Also, the use of differential equations in the mathematical modeling of real-world phenomena is outlined.

Problems 1-12 are routine verifications by direct substitution of the suggested solutions into the given differential equations. We include here just some typical examples of such verifications.

3.   If $y_1 = \cos 2x$ and $y_2 = \sin 2x$, then $y_1' = -2\sin 2x$ and $y_2' = 2\cos 2x$ so

$$y_1'' = -4\cos 2x = -4\,y_1 \quad \text{and} \quad y_2'' = -4\sin 2x = -4\,y_2.$$

Thus $y_1'' + 4\,y_1 = 0$ and $y_2'' + 4\,y_2 = 0$.

5.   If $y = e^x - e^{-x}$, then $y' = e^x + e^{-x}$ so $y' - y = \left(e^x + e^{-x}\right) - \left(e^x - e^{-x}\right) = 2e^{-x}$. Thus $y' = y + 2e^{-x}$.

11.   If $y = y_1 = x^{-2}$ then $y' = -2x^{-3}$ and $y'' = 6x^{-4}$, so

$$x^2 y'' + 5x\,y' + 4y = x^2\left(6x^{-4}\right) + 5x\left(-2x^{-3}\right) + 4\left(x^{-2}\right) = 0.$$

If $y = y_2 = x^{-2}\ln x$ then $y' = x^{-3} - 2x^{-3}\ln x$ and $y'' = -5x^{-4} + 6x^{-4}\ln x$, so

$$x^2 y'' + 5x\,y' + 4y = x^2\left(-5x^{-4} + 6x^{-4}\ln x\right) + 5x\left(x^{-3} - 2x^{-3}\ln x\right) + 4\left(x^{-2}\ln x\right)$$
$$= \left(-5x^{-2} + 5x^{-2}\right) + \left(6x^{-2} - 10x^{-2} + 4x^{-2}\right)\ln x = 0.$$

13.   Substitution of $y = e^{rx}$ into $3y' = 2y$ gives the equation $3r\,e^{rx} = 2e^{rx}$ that simplifies to $3r = 2$. Thus $r = 2/3$.

15. Substitution of $y = e^{rx}$ into $y'' + y' - 2y = 0$ gives the equation $r^2 e^{rx} + r e^{rx} - 2e^{rx} = 0$ that simplifies to $r^2 + r - 2 = (r+2)(r-1) = 0$. Thus $r = -2$ or $r = 1$.

The verifications of the suggested solutions in Problems 17-36 are similar to those in Problems 1-12. We illustrate the determination of the value of C only in some typical cases.

17. $C = 2$

19. If $y(x) = Ce^x - 1$ then $y(0) = 5$ gives $C - 1 = 5$, so $C = 6$.

21. $C = 7$

23. If $y(x) = \frac{1}{4}x^5 + Cx^{-2}$ then $y(2) = 1$ gives the equation $\frac{1}{4} \cdot 32 + C \cdot \frac{1}{8} = 1$ with solution $C = -56$.

25. If $y(x) = \tan(x^2 + C)$ then $y(0) = 1$ gives the equation $\tan C = 1$. Hence one value of C is $C = \pi/4$ (as is this value plus any integral multiple of π).

27. $y' = x + y$

29. If $m = y'$ is the slope of the tangent line and m' is the slope of the normal line at (x, y), then the relation $mm' = -1$ yields $m' = 1/y' = (y-1)/(x-0)$. Solution for y' then gives the differential equation $(1 - y)y' = x$.

31. The slope of the line through (x, y) and $(-y, x)$ is $y' = (x-y)/(-y-x)$, so the differential equation is $(x+y)y' = y-x$.

In Problems 32-36 we get the desired differential equation when we replace the "time rate of change" of the dependent variable with its derivative, the word "is" with the $=$ sign, the phrase "proportional to" with k, and finally translate the remainder of the given sentence into symbols.

33. $dv/dt = kv^2$

35. $dN/dt = k(P - N)$

37. $y(x) = 1$ or $y(x) = x$

39. $y(x) = x^2$

41. $y(x) = e^x/2$

43. **(a)** $y(10) = 10$ yields $10 = 1/(C-10)$, so $C = 101/10$.

(b)   There is no such value of C, but the constant function $y(x) \equiv 0$ satisfies the conditions $y' = y^2$ and $y(0) = 0$.

(c)   It is obvious visually that one and only one solution curve passes through each point (a, b) of the xy-plane, so it follows that there exists a unique solution to the initial value problem $y' = y^2$, $y(a) = b$.

SECTION 1.2

INTEGRALS AS GENERAL AND PARTICULAR SOLUTIONS

This section introduces **general solutions** and **particular solutions** in the very simplest situation — a differential equation of the form $y' = f(x)$ — where only direct integration and evaluation of the constant of integration are involved. Students should review carefully the elementary concepts of velocity and acceleration, as well as the fps and mks unit systems.

1.   Integration of $y' = 2x + 1$ yields $y(x) = \int (2x + 1) \, dx = x^2 + x + C$. Then substitution of $x = 0$, $y = 3$ gives $3 = 0 + 0 + C = C$, so $y(x) = x^2 + x + 3$.

3.   Integration of $y' = \sqrt{x}$ yields $y(x) = \int \sqrt{x} \, dx = \frac{2}{3} x^{3/2} + C$. Then substitution of $x = 4$, $y = 0$ gives $0 = \frac{16}{3} + C$, so $y(x) = \frac{2}{3}(x^{3/2} - 8)$.

5.   Integration of $y' = (x + 2)^{-1/2}$ yields $y(x) = \int (x + 2)^{-1/2} \, dx = 2\sqrt{x + 2} + C$. Then substitution of $x = 2$, $y = -1$ gives $-1 = 2 \cdot 2 + C$, so $y(x) = 2\sqrt{x + 2} - 5$.

7.   Integration of $y' = 10/(x^2 + 1)$ yields $y(x) = \int 10/(x^2 + 1) \, dx = 10 \tan^{-1} x + C$. Then substitution of $x = 0$, $y = 0$ gives $0 = 10 \cdot 0 + C$, so $y(x) = 10 \tan^{-1} x$.

9.   Integration of $y' = 1/\sqrt{1 - x^2}$ yields $y(x) = \int 1/\sqrt{1 - x^2} \, dx = \sin^{-1} x + C$. Then substitution of $x = 0$, $y = 0$ gives $0 = 0 + C$, so $y(x) = \sin^{-1} x$.

11.   If $a(t) = 50$ then $v(t) = \int 50 \, dt = 50t + v_0 = 50t + 10$. Hence

$$x(t) = \int (50t + 10) \, dt = 25t^2 + 10t + x_0 = 25t^2 + 10t + 10.$$

13.   If $a(t) = 3t$ then $v(t) = \int 3t \, dt = \frac{3}{2}t^2 + v_0 = \frac{3}{2}t^2 + 5$. Hence

$$x(t) = \int (\tfrac{3}{2}t^2 + 5)\,dt = \tfrac{1}{2}t^3 + 5t + x_0 = \tfrac{1}{2}t^3 + 5t.$$

15. If $a(t) = 2t+1$ then $v(t) = \int (2t+1)\,dt = t^2 + t + v_0 = t^2 + t - 7$. Hence

$$x(t) = \int (t^2 + t - 7)\,dt = \tfrac{1}{3}t^3 + \tfrac{1}{2}t - 7t + x_0 = \tfrac{1}{3}t^3 + \tfrac{1}{2}t - 7t + 4.$$

17. If $a(t) = (t+1)^{-3}$ then $v(t) = \int (t+1)^{-3}\,dt = -\tfrac{1}{2}(t+1)^{-2} + C = -\tfrac{1}{2}(t+1)^{-2} + \tfrac{1}{2}$ (taking $C = \tfrac{1}{2}$ so that $v(0) = 0$). Hence

$$x(t) = \int \left[-\tfrac{1}{2}(t+1)^{-2} + \tfrac{1}{2} \right] dt = \tfrac{1}{2}(t+1)^{-1} + \tfrac{1}{2}t + C = \tfrac{1}{2}\left[(t+1)^{-1} + t - 1 \right]$$

(taking $C = -\tfrac{1}{2}$ so that $x(0) = 0$).

19. $v = -9.8t + 49$, so the ball reaches its maximum height $(v = 0)$ after $t = 5$ seconds. Its maximum height then is $y(5) = -4.9(5)^2 + 49(5) = 122.5$ meters.

21. $a = -10$ m/s^2 and $v_0 = 100$ km/h ≈ 27.78 m/s, so $v = -10t + 27.78$, and hence $x(t) = -5t^2 + 27.78t$. The car stops when $v = 0$, $t \approx 2.78$, and thus the distance traveled before stopping is $x(2.78) \approx 38.59$ meters.

23. $a = -9.8$ m/s2 so $v = -9.8\,t - 10$ and

$$y = -4.9\,t^2 - 10\,t + y_0.$$

The ball hits the ground when $y = 0$ and

$$v = -9.8\,t - 10 = -60,$$

so $t \approx 5.10$ s. Hence

$$y_0 = 4.9(5.10)^2 + 10(5.10) \approx 178.57 \text{ m}.$$

25. Integration of $dv/dt = 0.12\,t^3 + 0.6\,t$, $v(0) = 0$ gives $v(t) = 0.3\,t^2 + 0.04\,t^3$. Hence $v(10) = 70$. Then integration of $dx/dt = 0.3\,t^2 + 0.04\,t^3$, $x(0) = 0$ gives $x(t) = 0.1\,t^3 + 0.04\,t^4$, so $x(10) = 200$. Thus after 10 seconds the car has gone 200 ft and is traveling at 70 ft/sec.

27. If $a = -20$ m/sec^2 and $x_0 = 0$ then the car's velocity and position at time t are given by

$$v = -20t + v_0, \qquad x = -10\,t^2 + v_0t.$$

It stops when $v = 0$ (so $v_0 = 20t$), and hence when

$$x = 75 = -10\,t^2 + (20t)t = 10\,t^2.$$

Thus $t = \sqrt{7.5}$ sec so

$$v_0 = 20\sqrt{7.5} \approx 54.77 \text{ m/sec} \approx 197 \text{ km/hr}.$$

29. If $v_0 = 0$ and $y_0 = 20$ then

$$v = -at \quad \text{and} \quad y = -\tfrac{1}{2}at^2 + 20.$$

Substitution of $t = 2$, $y = 0$ yields $a = 10 \text{ ft/sec}^2$. If $v_0 = 0$ and $y_0 = 200$ then

$$v = -10t \quad \text{and} \quad y = -5t^2 + 200.$$

Hence $y = 0$ when $t = \sqrt{40} = 2\sqrt{10}$ sec and $v = -20\sqrt{10} \approx -63.25 \text{ ft/sec}$.

31. If $v_0 = 0$ and $y_0 = h$ then the stone's velocity and height are given by

$$v = -gt, \quad y = -0.5\,gt^2 + h.$$

Hence $y = 0$ when $t = \sqrt{2h/g}$ so

$$v = -g\sqrt{2h/g} = -\sqrt{2gh}\,.$$

33. We use units of miles and hours. If $x_0 = v_0 = 0$ then the car's velocity and position after t hours are given by
$$v = at, \quad x = \tfrac{1}{2}t^2.$$

Since $v = 60$ when $t = 5/6$, the velocity equation yields $a = 72 \text{ mi/hr}^2$. Hence the distance traveled by 12:50 pm is

$$x = (0.5)(72)(5/6)^2 = 25 \text{ miles}.$$

35. Integration of $y' = (9/v_s)(1 - 4x^2)$ yields

$$y = (3/v_s)(3x - 4x^3) + C,$$

and the initial condition $y(-1/2) = 0$ gives $C = 3/v_s$. Hence the swimmer's trajectory is
$$y(x) = (3/v_s)(3x - 4x^3 + 1).$$

Substitution of $y(1/2) = 1$ now gives $v_s = 6$ mph.

SLOPE FIELDS AND SOLUTION CURVES

As pointed out in the textbook, the instructor may choose to delay covering Section 1.3 until later in Chapter 1. However, before proceeding to Chapter 2, it is important that students come to grips at some point with the question of the existence of a unique solution of a differential equation — and realize that it makes no sense to look for the solution without knowing in advance that it exists. The instructor may prefer to combine existence and uniqueness by simplifying the statement of the existence-uniqueness theorem as follows:

Suppose that the function $f(x, y)$ and the partial derivative $\partial f / \partial y$ are both continuous in some neighborhood of the point (a, b). Then the initial value problem

$$\frac{dy}{dx} = f(x, y), \qquad y(a) = b$$

has a unique solution in some neighborhood of the point a.

Slope fields and geometrical solution curves are introduced in this section as a concrete aid in visualizing solutions and existence-uniqueness questions. Solution curves corresponding to the slope fields in Problems 1–10 are shown in the answers section of the textbook and will not be duplicated here.

11. Each isocline $x - 1 = C$ is a vertical straight line.

13. Each isocline $y^2 = C \geq 0$, that is, $y = \sqrt{C}$ or $y = -\sqrt{C}$, is a horizontal straight line.

15. Each isocline $y/x = C$, or $y = Cx$, is a straight line through the origin.

17. Each isocline $xy = C$ is a rectangular hyperbola that opens along the line $y = x$ if $C > 0$, along $y = -x$ if $C < 0$.

19. Each isocline $y - x^2 = C$, or $x^2 = y - C$, is a translated parabola that opens along the y–axis.

21. Because both $f(x, y) = 2x^2y^2$ and $\partial f / \partial y = 4x^2y$ are continuous everywhere, the existence-uniqueness theorem of Section 1.3 in the textbook guarantees the existence of a unique solution in some neighborhood of $x = 1$.

23. Both $f(x, y) = y^{1/3}$ and $\partial f / \partial y = (1/3)y^{-2/3}$ are continuous near $(0, 1)$, so the theorem guarantees the existence of a unique solution in some neighborhood of $x = 0$.

25. $f(x, y) = (x - y)^{1/2}$ is not continuous at $(2, 2)$ because it is not even defined if $y > x$. Hence the theorem guarantees neither existence nor uniqueness in any neighborhood of the point $x = 2$.

27. Both $f(x, y) = (x - 1/y$ and $\partial f / \partial y = -(x - 1)/y^2$ are continuous near $(0, 1)$, so the theorem guarantees both existence and uniqueness of a solution in some neighborhood of $x = 0$.

29. Both $f(x, y) = \ln(1 + y^2)$ and $\partial f / \partial y = 2y/(1 + y^2)$ are continuous near $(0, 0)$, so the theorem guarantees the existence of a unique solution near $x = 0$.

31. If $f(x, y) = -(1 - y^2)^{1/2}$ then $\partial f / \partial y = y(1 - y^2)^{-1/2}$ is not continuous when $y = 1$, so the theorem does not guarantee uniqueness.

35. The isoclines of $y' = y/x$ are the straight lines $y = Cx$ through the origin, and $y' = C$ at points of $y = Cx$, so it appears that these same straight lines are the solution curves of $xy' = y$. Then we observe that there is

    (i)   a unique one of these lines through any point not on the y-axis;
    (ii)   no such line through any point on the y-axis other than the origin; and
    (iii)   infinitely many such lines through the origin.

SECTION 1.4

SEPARABLE EQUATIONS AND APPLICATIONS

Of course it should be emphasized to students that the possibility of separating the variables is the first one you look for. The general concept of natural growth and decay is important for all differential equations students, but the particular applications in this section are optional. Torricelli's law in the form of Equation (24) in the text leads to some nice concrete examples and problems.

1. $\quad \displaystyle\int \frac{dy}{y} = -\int 2x\,dx; \quad \ln y = -x^2 + c; \quad y(x) = e^{-x^2+c} = Ce^{-x^2}$

3. $\quad \displaystyle\int \frac{dy}{y} = \int \sin x\,dx; \quad \ln y = -\cos x + c; \quad y(x) = e^{-\cos x + c} = Ce^{-\cos x}$

5. $\quad \displaystyle\int \frac{dy}{\sqrt{1-y^2}} = \int \frac{dx}{2\sqrt{x}}; \quad \sin^{-1} y = \sqrt{x} + C; \quad y(x) = \sin\left(\sqrt{x} + C\right)$

7. $\int \dfrac{dy}{y^{1/3}} = \int 4x^{1/3}\,dx; \quad \tfrac{3}{2}y^{2/3} = 3x^{4/3}+\tfrac{3}{2}C; \quad y(x) = \left(2x^{4/3}+C\right)^{3/2}$

9. $\int \dfrac{dy}{y} = \int \dfrac{2\,dx}{1-x^2} = \int\left(\dfrac{1}{1+x}+\dfrac{1}{1-x}\right)dx \qquad \text{(partial fractions)}$

$\ln y = \ln(1+x)-\ln(1-x)+\ln C; \quad y(x) = C\dfrac{1+x}{1-x}$

11. $\int \dfrac{dy}{y^3} = \int x\,dx; \quad -\dfrac{1}{2y^2} = \dfrac{x^2}{2}-\dfrac{C}{2}; \quad y(x) = \left(C-x^2\right)^{-1/2}$

13. $\int \dfrac{y^3\,dy}{y^4+1} = \int \cos x\,dx; \quad \tfrac{1}{4}\ln\left(y^4+1\right) = \sin x + C$

15. $\int\left(\dfrac{2}{y^2}-\dfrac{1}{y^4}\right)dy = \int\left(\dfrac{1}{x}-\dfrac{1}{x^2}\right)dx; \quad -\dfrac{2}{y}+\dfrac{1}{3y^3} = \ln|x|+\dfrac{1}{x}+C$

17. $y' = 1+x+y+xy = (1+x)(1+y)$

$\int \dfrac{dy}{1+y} = \int(1+x)\,dx; \quad \ln|1+y| = x+\tfrac{1}{2}x^2+C$

19. $\int \dfrac{dy}{y} = \int e^x\,dx; \quad \ln y = e^x + \ln C; \quad y(x) = C\exp(e^x)$

$y(0)=2e$ implies $C=2$ so $y(x) = 2\exp(e^x)$

21. $\int 2y\,dy = \int \dfrac{x\,dx}{\sqrt{x^2-16}}; \quad y^2 = \sqrt{x^2-16}+C$

$y(5)=2$ implies $C=1$ so $y^2 = 1+\sqrt{x^2-16}$

23. $\int \dfrac{dy}{2y-1} = \int dx; \quad \tfrac{1}{2}\ln(2y-1) = x+\tfrac{1}{2}\ln C; \quad 2y-1 = Ce^{2x}$

$y(1)=1$ implies $C=e^{-2}$ so $y(x) = \tfrac{1}{2}\left(1+e^{2x-2}\right)$

25. $\int \dfrac{dy}{y} = \int\left(\dfrac{1}{x}+2x\right); \quad \ln y = \ln x+x^2+\ln C; \quad y(x) = Cx\exp(x^2)$

$y(1)=1$ implies $C=e^{-1}$ so $y(x) = x\exp(x^2-1)$

27. $\int e^y \, dy = \int 6e^{2x} \, dx; \quad e^y = 3e^{2x} + C; \quad y(x) = \ln\left(3e^{2x} + C\right)$

$y(0) = 0$ implies $C = -2$ so $y(x) = \ln\left(3e^{2x} - 2\right)$

29. The population growth rate is $k = \ln(30000/25000)/10 \approx 0.01823$, so the population of the city t years after 1960 is given by $P(t) = 25000\,e^{0.01823t}$. The expected year 2000 population is then $P(40) = 25000\,e^{0.01823 \times 40} \approx 51840$.

31. As in the textbook discussion of radioactive decay, the number of ^{14}C atoms after t years is given by $N(t) = N_0\,e^{-0.0001216\,t}$. Hence we need only solve the equation $\frac{1}{6}N_0 = N_0\,e^{-0.0001216\,t}$ for $t = (\ln 6)/0.0001216 \approx 14735$ years to find the age of the skull.

33. The amount in the account after t years is given by $A(t) = 5000\,e^{0.08t}$. Hence the amount in the account after 18 years is given by $A(20) = 5000\,e^{0.08 \times 20} \approx 21{,}103.48$ dollars.

35. To find the decay rate of this drug in the dog's blood stream, we solve the equation $\frac{1}{2} = e^{-5k}$ (half-life 5 hours) for $k = (\ln 2)/5 \approx 0.13863$. Thus the amount in the dog's bloodstream after t hours is given by $A(t) = A_0\,e^{-0.13863t}$. We therefore solve the equation $A(1) = A_0\,e^{-0.13863} = 50 \times 45 = 2250$ for $A_0 \approx 2585$ mg, the amount to anesthetize the dog properly.

37. Taking $t = 0$ when the body was formed and $t = T$ now, the amount $Q(t)$ of ^{238}U in the body at time t (in years) is given by $Q(t) = Q_0 e^{-kt}$, where $k = (\ln 2)/(4.51 \times 10^9)$. The given information tells us that

$$\frac{Q(T)}{Q_0 - Q(T)} = 0.9.$$

After substituting $Q(T) = Q_0 e^{-kT}$, we solve readily for $e^{kT} = 19/9$, so $T = (1/k)\ln(19/9) \approx 4.86 \times 10^9$. Thus the body was formed approximately 4.86 billion years ago.

39. Because $A = 0$ the differential equation reduces to $T' = kT$, so $T(t) = 25e^{-kt}$. The fact that $T(20) = 15$ yields $k = (1/20)\ln(5/3)$, and finally we solve

$$5 = 25e^{-kt} \quad \text{for} \quad t = (\ln 5)/k \approx 63 \text{ min.}$$

41. **(a)** The light intensity at a depth of x meters is given by $I(x) = I_0 e^{-1.4x}$. We solve the equation $I(x) = I_0 e^{-1.4x} = \frac{1}{2} I_0$ for $x = (\ln 2)/1.4 \approx 0.495$ meters.

(b) At depth 10 meters the intensity is $I(10) = I_0 e^{-1.4 \times 10} \approx (8.32 \times 10^{-7}) I_0$.

(c) We solve the equation $I(x) = I_0 e^{-1.4x} = 0.01 I_0$ for $x = (\ln 100)/1.4 \approx 3.29$ meters.

43. **(a)** $A' = rA + Q$

(b) The solution of the differential equation with $A(0) = 0$ is given by

$$rA + Q = Q e^{rt}.$$

When we substitute $A = 40$ (thousand), $r = 0.11$, and $t = 18$, we find that $Q = 0.70482$, that is, $704.82 per year.

45. The cake's temperature will be $100°$ after 66 min 40 sec; this problem is just like Example 6 in the text.

47. If $N(t)$ denotes the number of people (in thousands) who have heard the rumor after t days, then the initial value problem is

$$N' = k(100 - N), \quad N(0) = 0$$

and we are given that $N(7) = 10$. When we separate variables ($dN/(100 - N) = k\,dt$) and integrate, we get $\ln(100 - N) = -kt + C$, and the initial condition $N(0) = 0$ gives $C = \ln 100$. Then $100 - N = 100 e^{-kt}$, so $N(t) = 100(1 - e^{-kt})$. We substitute $t = 7$, $N = 10$ and solve for the value $k = \ln(100/90)/7 \approx 0.01505$. Finally, 50 thousand people have heard the rumor after $t = (\ln 2)/k \approx 46.05$ days.

49. With $A = \pi(3)^2$ and $a = \pi(1/12)^2$, and taking $g = 32$ ft/sec^2, Equation (20) reduces to $162 y' = -\sqrt{y}$. The solution such that $y = 9$ when $t = 0$ is given by $324\sqrt{y} = -t + 972$. Hence $y = 0$ when $t = 972$ sec $= 16$ min 12 sec.

51. The solution of $y' = -k\sqrt{y}$ is given by

$$2\sqrt{y} = -kt + C.$$

The initial condition $y(0) = h$ (the height of the cylinder) yields $C = 2\sqrt{h}$. Then substitution of $t = T$, $y = 0$ gives $k = (2\sqrt{h})/T$. It follows that

$$y = h(1 - t/T)^2.$$

If r denotes the radius of the cylinder, then

$$V(y) = \pi r^2 y = \pi r^2 h(1-t/T)^2 = V_0(1-t/T)^2.$$

53. (a) Since $x^2 = by$, the cross-sectional area is $A(y) = \pi x^2 = \pi by$. Hence the equation $A(y)y' = -a\sqrt{2gy}$ reduces to the differential equation

$$y^{1/2}y' = -k = -(a/\pi b)\sqrt{2g}$$

with the general solution

$$(2/3)y^{3/2} = -kt + C.$$

The initial condition $y(0) = 4$ gives $C = 16/3$, and then $y(1) = 1$ yields $k = 14/3$. It follows that the depth at time t is

$$y(t) = (8 - 7t)^{2/3}.$$

(b) The tank is empty after $t = 8/7$ hr, that is, at 1:08:34 p.m.

(c) We see above that $k = (a/\pi b)\sqrt{2g} = 14/3$. Substitution of $a = \pi r^2$, $b = 1$, $g = (32)(3600)^2$ ft/hr^2 yields $r = (1/60)\sqrt{7/12}$ ft ≈ 0.15 in for the radius of the bottom-hole.

55. $A(y) = \pi(8y - y^2)$ as in Example 7 in the text, but now $a = \pi/144$ in Equation (24), so the initial value problem is

$$18(8y - y^2)y' = -\sqrt{y}, \qquad y(0) = 8.$$

We seek the value of t when $y = 0$. The answer is $t \approx 869$ sec $= 14$ min 29 sec.

57. (a) As in Example 8, the initial value problem is

$$\pi(8y - y^2)\frac{dy}{dt} = -\pi k\sqrt{y}, \qquad y(0) = 4$$

where $k = 0.6 r^2 \sqrt{2g} = 4.8 r^2$. Integrating and applying the initial condition just in the Example 8 solution in the text, we find that

$$\frac{16}{3}y^{3/2} - \frac{2}{5}y^{5/2} = -kt + \frac{448}{15}.$$

When we substitute $y = 2$ (ft) and $t = 1800$ (sec, that is, 30 min), we find that $k \approx 0.009469$. Finally, $y = 0$ when

$$t = \frac{448}{15k} \approx 3154 \text{ sec} = 53 \text{ min } 34 \text{ sec}.$$

Thus the tank is empty at 1:53:34 pm.

(b) The radius of the bottom-hole is

$$r = \sqrt{k/4.8} \approx 0.04442 \text{ ft} \approx 0.53 \text{ in, thus about a half inch.}$$

59. Let $t = 0$ at the time of death. Then the solution of the initial value problem

$$T' = k(70 - T), \qquad T(0) = 98.6$$

is

$$T(t) = 70 + 28.6e^{-kt}.$$

If $t = a$ at 12 noon, then we know that

$$T(t) = 70 + 28.6e^{-ka} = 80,$$

$$T(a+1) = 70 + 28.6e^{-k(a+1)} = 75.$$

Hence

$$28.6e^{-ka} = 10 \quad \text{and} \quad 28.6e^{-ka}e^{-k} = 5.$$

It follows that $e^{-k} = 1/2$, so $k = \ln 2$. Finally the first of the previous two equations yields

$$a = (\ln 2.86)/(\ln 2) \approx 1.516 \text{ hr} \approx 1 \text{ hr } 31 \text{ min},$$

so the death occurred at 10:29 a.m.

61. Let $t = 0$ when it began to snow, and $t = t_0$ at 7:00 a.m. Let x denote distance along the road, with $x = 0$ where the snowplow begins at 7:00 a.m. If $y = ct$ is the snow depth at time t, w is the width of the road, and $v = dx/dt$ is the plow's velocity, then "plowing at a constant rate" means that the product wyv is constant. Hence our differential equation is of the form

$$k\frac{dx}{dt} = \frac{1}{t}.$$

The solution with $x = 0$ when $t = t_0$ is

$$t = t_0 e^{kx}.$$

We are given that $x = 4$ when $t = t_0 + 1$ and $x = 7$ when $t = t_0 + 2$, so it follows that

$$t_0 + 1 = t_0 e^{4k} \quad \text{and} \quad t_0 + 2 = t_0 e^{7k}$$

at 8 a.m. and 9 a.m., respectively. Elimination of t_0 gives the equation

$$2e^{4k} - e^{7k} - 1 = 0,$$

which we solve numerically for $k = 0.08276$. Using this value, we finally solve one of the preceding pair of equations for $t_0 = 2.5483$ hr ≈ 2 hr 33 min. Thus it began to snow at 4:27 a.m.

SECTION 1.5

LINEAR FIRST-ORDER EQUATIONS

1. $\rho = \exp\left(\int 1\,dx\right) = e^x; \quad D_x\left(y \cdot e^x\right) = 2e^x; \quad y \cdot e^x = 2e^x + C; \quad y(x) = 2 + Ce^{-x}$

   $y(0) = 0$ implies $C = -2$ so $y(x) = 2 - 2e^{-x}$

3. $\rho = \exp\left(\int 3\,dx\right) = e^{3x}; \quad D_x\left(y \cdot e^{3x}\right) = 2x; \quad y \cdot e^{3x} = x^2 + C; \quad y(x) = (x^2 + C)e^{-3x}$

5. $\rho = \exp\left(\int (2/x)\,dx\right) = e^{2\ln x} = x^2; \quad D_x\left(y \cdot x^2\right) = 3x^2; \quad y \cdot x^2 = x^3 + C$

   $y(x) = x + C/x^2; \quad y(1) = 5$ implies $C = 4$ so $y(x) = x + 4/x^2$

7. $\rho = \exp\left(\int (1/2x)\,dx\right) = e^{(\ln x)/2} = \sqrt{x}; \quad D_x\left(y \cdot \sqrt{x}\right) = 5; \quad y \cdot \sqrt{x} = 5x + C$

   $y(x) = 5\sqrt{x} + C/\sqrt{x}$

9. $\rho = \exp\left(\int (-1/x)\,dx\right) = e^{-\ln x} = 1/x; \quad D_x\left(y \cdot 1/x\right) = 1/x; \quad y \cdot 1/x = \ln x + C$

   $y(x) = x\ln x + Cx; \quad y(1) = 7$ implies $C = 7$ so $y(x) = x\ln x + 7x$

11. $\rho = \exp\left(\int (1/x - 3)\,dx\right) = e^{\ln x - 3x} = xe^{-3x}$; $\quad D_x\left(y \cdot xe^{-3x}\right) = 0$; $\quad y \cdot xe^{-3x} = C$

$y(x) = Cx^{-1}e^{3x}$; $\quad y(1) = 0$ implies $C = 0$ so $y(x) \equiv 0$ (constant)

13. $\rho = \exp\left(\int 1\,dx\right) = e^x$; $\quad D_x\left(y \cdot e^x\right) = e^{2x}$; $\quad y \cdot e^x = \frac{1}{2}e^{2x} + C$

$y(x) = \frac{1}{2}e^x + Ce^{-x}$; $\quad y(0) = 1$ implies $C = \frac{1}{2}$ so $y(x) = \frac{1}{2}e^x + \frac{1}{2}e^{-x}$

15. $\rho = \exp\left(\int 2x\,dx\right) = e^{x^2}$; $\quad D_x\left(y \cdot e^{x^2}\right) = xe^{x^2}$; $\quad y \cdot e^{x^2} = \frac{1}{2}e^{x^2} + C$

$y(x) = \frac{1}{2} + Ce^{-x^2}$; $\quad y(0) = -2$ implies $C = -\frac{5}{2}$ so $y(x) = \frac{1}{2} - \frac{5}{2}e^{-x^2}$

17. $\rho = \exp\left(\int 1/(1+x)\,dx\right) = e^{\ln(1+x)} = 1 + x$; $\quad D_x\left(y \cdot (1+x)\right) = \cos x$; $\quad y \cdot (1+x) = \sin x + C$

$y(x) = \dfrac{C + \sin x}{1 + x}$; $\quad y(0) = 1$ implies $C = 1$ so $y(x) = \dfrac{1 + \sin x}{1 + x}$

19. $\rho = \exp\left(\int \cot x\,dx\right) = e^{\ln(\sin x)} = \sin x$; $\quad D_x\left(y \cdot \sin x\right) = \sin x \cos x$

$y \cdot \sin x = \frac{1}{2}\sin^2 x + C$; $\quad y(x) = \frac{1}{2}\sin x + C\csc x$

21. $\rho = \exp\left(\int (-3/x)\,dx\right) = e^{-3\ln x} = x^{-3}$; $\quad D_x\left(y \cdot x^{-3}\right) = \cos x$; $\quad y \cdot x^{-3} = \sin x + C$

$y(x) = x^3 \sin x + Cx^3$; $\quad y(2\pi) = 0$ implies $C = 0$ so $y(x) = x^3 \sin x$

23. $\rho = \exp\left(\int (2 - 3/x)\,dx\right) = e^{2x - 3\ln x} = x^{-3}e^{2x}$; $\quad D_x\left(y \cdot x^{-3}e^{2x}\right) = 4e^{2x}$

$y \cdot x^{-3}e^{2x} = 2e^{2x} + C$; $\quad y(x) = 2x^3 + Cx^3e^{-2x}$

25. First we calculate

$$\int \frac{3x^3\,dx}{x^2 + 1} = \int \left[3x - \frac{3x}{x^2 + 1}\right]dx = \frac{3}{2}\left[x^2 - \ln(x^2 + 1)\right].$$

It follows that $\rho = (x^2 + 1)^{-3/2}\exp(3x^2/2)$ and thence that

$$D_x\left(y \cdot (x^2 + 1)^{-3/2}\exp(3x^2/2)\right) = 6x(x^2 + 4)^{-5/2},$$
$$y \cdot (x^2 + 1)^{-3/2}\exp(3x^2/2) = -2(x^2 + 4)^{-3/2} + C,$$
$$y(x) = -2\exp(3x^2/2) + C(x^2 + 1)^{3/2}\exp(-3x^2/2).$$

Finally, $y(0) = 1$ implies that $C = 3$ so the desired particular solution is

$$y(x) = -2\exp(3x^2/2) + 3(x^2+1)^{3/2}\exp(-3x^2/2).$$

27. With $x' = dx/dy$, the differential equation is $x' - x = ye^y$. Then with y as the independent variable we calculate

$$\rho(y) = \exp\left(\int(-1)\,dy\right) = e^{-y}; \quad D_y\left(x \cdot e^{-y}\right) = y$$

$$x \cdot e^{-y} = \tfrac{1}{2}y^2 + C; \quad x(y) = \left(\tfrac{1}{2}y^2 + C\right)e^y$$

29. $\rho = \exp\left(\int(-2x)\,dx\right) = e^{-x^2}; \quad D_x\left(y \cdot e^{-x^2}\right) = e^{-x^2}; \quad y \cdot e^{-x^2} = C + \int_0^x e^{-t^2}\,dt$

$$y(x) = e^{-x^2}\left(C + \tfrac{\sqrt{\pi}}{2}\operatorname{erf}(x)\right)$$

31. **(a)** $y_c' = Ce^{-\int P\,dx}(-P) = -Py_c$, so $y_c' + Py_c = 0$.

(b) $y_p' = (-P)e^{-\int P\,dx} \cdot \left[\int\left(Qe^{\int P\,dx}\right)dx\right] + e^{-\int P\,dx} \cdot Qe^{\int P\,dx} = -Py_p + Q$

33. The amount $x(t)$ of salt (in kg) after t seconds satisfies the differential equation $x' = -x/200$, so $x(t) = 100e^{-t/200}$. Hence we need only solve the equation $10 = 100e^{-t/200}$ for $t = 461$ sec $= 7$ min 41 sec (approximately).

35. The only difference from the Example 4 solution in the textbook is that $V = 1640$ km^3 and $r = 410$ km^3/yr for Lake Ontario, so the time required is

$$t = \frac{V}{r}\ln 4 = 4\ln 4 \approx 5.5452 \text{ years.}$$

37. The volume of brine in the tank after t min is $V(t) = 100 + 2t$ gal, so the initial value problem is

$$\frac{dx}{dt} = 5 - \frac{3x}{100 + 2t}, \qquad x(0) = 50.$$

The integrating factor $\rho(t) = (100 + 2t)^{3/2}$ leads to the solution

$$x(t) = (100 + 2t) - \frac{50000}{(100 + 2t)^{3/2}}.$$

such that $x(0) = 50$. The tank is full after $t = 150$ min, at which time $x(150) = 393.75$ lb.

39. **(a)** The initial value problem

$$\frac{dx}{dt} = -\frac{x}{10}, \qquad x(0) = 100$$

for Tank 1 has solution $x(t) = 100\,e^{-t/10}$. Then the initial value problem

$$\frac{dy}{dt} = \frac{x}{10} - \frac{y}{10} = 10\,e^{-t/10} - \frac{y}{10}, \qquad y(0) = 0$$

for Tank 2 has solution $y(t) = 10t\,e^{-t/10}$.

(b) The maximum value of y occurs when

$$y'(t) = 10\,e^{-t/10} - t\,e^{-t/10} = 0$$

and thus when $t = 10$. We find that $y_{max} = y(10) = 100e^{-1} \approx 36.79$ gal.

41. **(a)** $A'(t) = 0.06A + 0.12S = 0.06A + 3.6\,e^{0.05t}$

(b) The solution with $A(0) = 0$ is

$$A(t) = 360(e^{0.06\,t} - e^{0.05\,t}),$$

so $A(40) \approx 1308.283$ thousand dollars.

43. The solution of the initial value problem $y' = x - y$, $y(-5) = y_0$ is

$$y(x) = x - 1 + (y_0 + 6)e^{-x-5}.$$

Substituting $x = 5$, we therefore solve the equation $4 + (y_0 + 6)e^{-10} = y_1$ with $y_1 = 3.998, 3.999, 4, 4.001, 4.002$ for the desired initial values $y_0 = -50.0529, -28.0265, -6.0000, 16.0265, 38.0529$, respectively.

SECTION 1.6

SUBSTITUTION METHODS AND EXACT EQUATIONS

It is traditional for every elementary differential equations text to include the particular types of equations that are found in this section. However, no one of them is vitally important solely in its own right. Their real purpose (at this point in the course) is to familiarize students with the technique of transforming a differential equation by substitution. The subsection on airplane flight trajectories (together with Problems 56–59) is optional material and may be omitted if the instructor desires.

The differential equations in Problems 1–15 are homogeneous, so we make the substitutions

$$v = \frac{y}{x}, \qquad y = vx, \qquad \frac{dy}{dx} = v + x\frac{dv}{dx}.$$

For each problem we give the differential equation in x, $v(x)$, and $v' = dv/dx$ that results, together with the principal steps in its solution.

1. $\quad x(v+1)v' = -(v^2 + 2v - 1); \quad \displaystyle\int \frac{2(v+1)\,dv}{v^2 + 2v - 1} = -\int 2x\,dx; \quad \ln(v^2 + 2v - 1) = -2\ln x + \ln C$

$\quad\quad x^2(v^2 + 2v - 1) = C; \quad y^2 + 2xy - x^2 = C$

3. $\quad xv' = 2\sqrt{v}; \quad \displaystyle\int \frac{dv}{2\sqrt{v}} = \int \frac{dx}{x}; \quad \sqrt{v} = \ln x + C; \quad y = x(\ln x + C)^2$

5. $\quad x(v+1)v' = -2v^2; \quad \displaystyle\int \left(\frac{1}{v} + \frac{1}{v^2}\right)dv = -\int \frac{2\,dx}{x}; \quad \ln v - \frac{1}{v} = -2\ln x + C$

$\quad\quad \ln y - \ln x - \dfrac{x}{y} = -2\ln x + C; \quad \ln(xy) = C + \dfrac{x}{y}$

7. $\quad xv^2 v' = 1; \quad \displaystyle\int 3v^2\,dv = \int \frac{3\,dx}{x}; \quad v^3 = 3\ln x + C; \quad y^3 = x^3(3\ln x + C)$

9. $\quad xv' = v^2; \quad -\displaystyle\int \frac{dv}{v^2} = -\int \frac{dx}{x}; \quad \frac{1}{v} = -\ln x + C; \quad x = y(C - \ln x)$

11. $\quad x(1-v^2)v' = v + v^3; \quad \displaystyle\int \frac{1-v^2}{v^3 + v}\,dv = \int \frac{dx}{x}; \quad \int \left(\frac{1}{v} - \frac{2v}{v^2 + 1}\right)dv = \int \frac{dx}{x}$

$\quad\quad \ln v - \ln(v^2 + 1) = \ln x + \ln C; \quad v = Cx(v^2 + 1); \quad y = C(x^2 + y^2)$

13. $\quad xv' = \sqrt{v^2 + 1}; \quad \displaystyle\int \frac{dv}{\sqrt{v^2 + 1}} = \int \frac{dx}{x}; \quad \ln\left(v + \sqrt{v^2 + 1}\right) = \ln x + \ln C$

$\quad\quad v + \sqrt{v^2 + 1} = Cx; \quad y + \sqrt{x^2 + y^2} = Cx^2$

15. $x(v+1)v' = -2(v^2+2v);$ $\int \dfrac{2(v+1)dv}{v^2+2v} = -\int \dfrac{4\,dx}{x};$ $\ln(v^2+2v) = -4\ln x + \ln C$

$v^2+2v = C/x^4;$ $x^2y^2+2x^3y = C$

17. $v = 4x + y;$ $v' = v^2 + 4;$ $x = \int \dfrac{dv}{v^2+4} = \dfrac{1}{2}\tan^{-1}\dfrac{v}{2} + \dfrac{C}{2}$

$v = 2\tan(2x-C);$ $y = 2\tan(2x-C) - 4x$

Problems 19–25 are Bernoulli equations. For each, we indicate the appropriate substitution as specified in Equation (10) of this section, the resulting linear differential equation in v, its integrating factor ρ, and finally the resulting solution of the original Bernoulli equation.

19. $v = y^{-2};$ $v' - 4v/x = -10/x^2;$ $\rho = 1/x^4;$ $y^2 = x/(Cx^5+2)$

21. $v = y^{-2};$ $v' + 2v = -2;$ $\rho = e^{2x};$ $y^2 = 1/(Ce^{-2x}-1)$

23. $v = y^{-1/3};$ $v' - 2v/x = -1;$ $\rho = x^{-2};$ $y^3 = 1/(x+Cx^2)$

25. $v = y^3;$ $v' + 3v/x = 3/\sqrt{1+x^4};$ $\rho = x^3;$ $y^3 = (C+3\sqrt{1+x^4})/(2x^3)$

27. The substitution $v = y^3$ yields the linear equation $xv' - v = 3x^4$ with integrating factor $\rho = 1/x.$ Solution: $y = (x^4 + Cx)^{1/3}$

29. The substitution $v = \sin y$ yields the homogeneous equation $2xv\,v' = 4x^2 + v^2.$ Solution: $\sin^2 y = 4x^2 - Cx$

Each of the differential equations in Problems 31–42 is of the form $M\,dx + N\,dy = 0,$ and the exactness condition $\partial M/\partial y = \partial N/\partial x$ is routine to verify. For each problem we give the principal steps in the calculation corresponding to the method of Example 9 in this section.

31. $F = \int(2x+3y)\,dx = x^2+3xy+g(y);$ $F_y = 3x+g'(y) = 3x+2y = N$

$g'(y) = 2y;$ $g(y) = y^2;$ $x^2+3xy+y^2 = C$

33. $F = \int(3x^2+2y^2)\,dx = x^3+xy^2+g(y);$ $F_y = 4xy+g'(y) = 4xy+6y^2 = N$

$g'(y) = 6y^2;$ $g(y) = 2y^3;$ $x^3+2xy^2+2y^3 = C$

35. $F = \int(x^3+y/x)\,dx = \tfrac{1}{4}x^4+y\ln x+g(y);$ $F_y = \ln x+g'(y) = y^2+\ln x = N$

$g'(y) = y^2; \quad g(y) = \frac{1}{3}y^3; \qquad \frac{1}{4}x^3 + \frac{1}{3}y^2 + y\ln x = C$

37. $F = \int(\cos x + \ln y)\,dx = \sin x + x\ln y + g(y); \quad F_y = x/y + g'(y) = x/y + e^y = N$

$g'(y) = e^y; \quad g(y) = e^y; \qquad \sin x + x\ln y + e^y = C$

39. $F = \int(3x^2 y^3 + y^4)\,dx = x^3 y^3 + x y^4 + g(y);$

$F_y = 3x^3 y^2 + 4xy^3 + g'(y) = 3x^3 y^2 + y^4 + 4xy^3 = N$

$g'(y) = y^4; \quad g(y) = \frac{1}{5}y^5; \qquad x^3 y^3 + xy^4 + \frac{1}{5}y^5 = C$

41. $F = \int\left(\frac{2x}{y} - \frac{3y^2}{x^4}\right)dx = \frac{x^2}{y} + \frac{y^2}{x^3} + g(y);$

$F_y = -\frac{x^2}{y^2} + \frac{2y}{x^3} + g'(y) = -\frac{x^2}{y^2} + \frac{2y}{x^3} + \frac{1}{\sqrt{y}} = N$

$g'(y) = \frac{1}{\sqrt{y}}; \quad g(y) = 2\sqrt{y}; \qquad \frac{x^2}{y} + \frac{y^2}{x^3} + 2\sqrt{y} = C$

43. The substitution $v = ax + by + c, \; y = (v - ax - c)/b$ in $y' = F(ax + by + c)$ yields the separable differential equation $(dv/dx - a)/b = F(v)$, that is, $dv/dx = a + bF(v)$.

45. If $v = \ln y$ then $y = e^v$ so $y' = e^v v'$. Hence the given equation transforms to $e^v v' + P(x) e^v = Q(x) v e^v$. Cancellation of the factor e^v then yields the linear differential equation $v' - Q(x)v = P(x)$.

47. The substitution $x = u - 1, \; y = v - 2$ yields the homogeneous equation

$$\frac{dv}{du} = \frac{u - v}{u + v}.$$

The substitution $v = pu$ leads to

$$\ln u = -\int\frac{(p+1)\,dp}{(p^2 + 2p - 1)} = -\frac{1}{2}\left[\ln\left(p^2 + 2p - 1\right) - \ln C\right].$$

We thus obtain the implicit solution

$$u^2\left(p^2 + 2p - 1\right) = C$$

$$u^2 \left(\frac{v^2}{u^2} + 2\frac{v}{u} - 1 \right) = v^2 + 2uv - u^2 = C$$

$$(y+2)^2 + 2(x+1)(y+2) - (x+1)^2 = C$$

$$y^2 + 2xy - x^2 + 2x + 6y = C.$$

49. The substitution $v = x - y$ yields the separable equation $v' = 1 - \sin v$. With the aid of the identity

$$\frac{1}{1 - \sin v} = \frac{1 + \sin v}{\cos^2 v} = \sec^2 v + \sec v \tan v$$

we obtain the solution

$$x = \tan(x - y) + \sec(x - y) + C.$$

51. If we substitute $y = y_1 + 1/v$, $y' = y_1' - v'/v^2$ (primes denoting differentiation with respect to x) into the Riccati equation $y' = Ay^2 + By + C$ and use the fact that $y_1' = Ay_1^2 + By_1 + C$, then we immediately get the linear differential equation $v' + (B + 2Ay_1)v = -A$.

In Problems 52 and 53 we outline the application of the method of Problem 51 to the given Riccati equation.

53. The substitution $y = x + 1/v$ yields the trivial linear equation $v' = -1$ with immediate solution $v(x) = C - x$. Hence the general solution of our Riccati equation is given by $y(x) = x + 1/(C - x)$.

55. Clearly the line $y = Cx - C^2/4$ and the tangent line at $(C/2, C^2/4)$ to the parabola $y = x^2$ both have slope C.

57. With $a = 100$ and $k = 1/10$, Equation (19) in the text is

$$y = 50[(x/100)^{9/10} - (x/100)^{11/10}].$$

The equation $y'(x) = 0$ then yields

$$(x/100)^{1/10} = (9/11)^{1/2},$$

so it follows that

$$y_{max} = 50[(9/11)^{9/2} - (9/11)^{11/2}] \approx 3.68 \text{ mi.}$$

59. **(a)** With $a = 100$ and $k = w/v_0 = 2/4 = 1/2$, the solution given by equation (19) in the textbook is $y(x) = 50[(x/100)^{1/2} - (x/100)^{3/2}]$. The fact that $y(0) = 0$ means that this trajectory goes through the origin where the tree is located.

(b)   With $k = 4/4 = 1$ the solution is $y(x) = 50[1 - (x/100)^2]$ and we see that the swimmer hits the bank at a distance $y(0) = 50$ north of the tree.

(c)   With $k = 6/4 = 1$ the solution is $y(x) = 50[(x/100)^{-1/2} - (x/100)^{5/2}]$. This trajectory is asymptotic to the positive x-axis, so we see that the swimmer never reaches the west bank of the river.

CHAPTER 1 Review Problems

The main objective of this set of review problems is practice in the identification of the different types of first-order differential equations discussed in this chapter. In each of Problems 1-36 we identify the type of the given equation and indicate an appropriate method of solution.

1.   If we write the equation in the form $y' - (3/x)y = x^2$ we see that it is *linear* with integrating factor $\rho = x^{-3}$. The method of Section 1.5 then yields the general solution $y = x^3(C + \ln x)$.

3.   This equation is *homogeneous*. The substitution $y = vx$ of Equation (8) in Section 1.6 leads to the general solution $y = x/(C - \ln x)$.

5.   We write this equation in the *separable* form $y'/y^2 = (2x - 3)/x^4$. Then separation of variables and integration as in Section 1.4 yields the general solution $y = C \exp[(1 - x)/x^3]$.

7.   If we write the equation in the form $y' + (2/x)y = 1/x^3$ we see that it is *linear* with integrating factor $\rho = x^2$. The method of Section 1.5 then yields the general solution $y = x^{-2}(C + \ln x)$.

9.   If we write the equation in the form $y' + (2/x)y = 6x\sqrt{y}$ we see that it is a *Bernoulli equation* with $n = 1/2$. The substitution $v = y^{-1/2}$ of Eq. (10) in Section 1.6 then yields the general solution $y = (x^2 + C/x)^2$.

11.   This equation is *homogeneous*. The substitution $y = vx$ of Equation (8) in Section 1.6 leads to the general solution $y = x/(C - 3\ln x)$.

13.   We write this equation in the *separable* form $y'/y^2 = 5x^4 - 4x$. Then separation of variables and integration as in Section 1.4 yields the general solution $y = 1/(C + 2x^2 - x^5)$.

15. This is a *linear* differential equation with integrating factor $\rho = e^{3x}$. The method of Section 1.5 yields the general solution $y = (x^3 + C)e^{-3x}$.

17. We note that $D_y\left(e^x + y e^{xy}\right) = D_x\left(e^y + x e^{xy}\right) = e^{xy} + xy e^{xy}$, so the given equation is *exact*. The method of Example 9 in Section 1.6 yields the implicit general solution $e^x + e^y + e^{xy} = C$.

19. We write this equation in the *separable* form $y'/y^2 = \left(2 - 3x^5\right)/x^3$. Then separation of variables and integration as in Section 1.4 yields the general solution $y = x^2 / (x^5 + Cx^2 + 1)$.

21. If we write the equation in the form $y' + \left(1/(x+1)\right)y = 1/(x^2 - 1)$ we see that it is *linear* with integrating factor $\rho = x+1$. The method of Section then 1.5 yields the general solution $y = [C + \ln(x - 1)] / (x + 1)$.

23. We note that $D_y\left(e^y + y\cos x\right) = D_x\left(x e^y + \sin x\right) = e^y + \cos x$, so the given equation is *exact*. The method of Example 9 in Section 1.6 yields the implicit general solution $x e^y + y \sin x = C$

25. If we write the equation in the form $y' + \left(2/(x+1)\right)y = 3$ we see that it is *linear* with integrating factor $\rho = (x+1)^2$. The method of Section 1.5 then yields the general solution $y = x + 1 + C(x + 1)^{-2}$.

27. If we write the equation in the form $y' + (1/x)y = -x^2 y^4 /3$ we see that it is a *Bernoulli equation* with $n = 4$. The substitution $v = y^{-3}$ of Eq. (10) in Section 1.6 then yields the general solution $y = x^{-1}(C + \ln x)^{-1/3}$.

29. If we write the equation in the form $y' + \left(1/(2x+1)\right)y = (2x+1)^{1/2}$ we see that it is *linear* with integrating factor $\rho = (2x+1)^{1/2}$. The method of Section 1.5 then yields the general solution $y = (x^2 + x + C)(2x + 1)^{-1/2}$.

31. $dy/(y+7) = 3x^2 dx$ is separable; $y' + 3x^2 y = 21x^2$ is linear.

33. $(3x^2 + 2y^2)dx + 4xy\,dy = 0$ is exact; $y' = -\frac{1}{4}(3x/y + 2y/x)$ is homogeneous.

35. $dy/(y+1) = 2x\,dx/\left(x^2 + 1\right)$ is separable; $y' - \left(2x/(x^2 + 1)\right)y = 2x/(x^2 + 1)$ is linear.

CHAPTER 2

MATHEMATICAL MODELS
AND NUMERICAL METHODS

SECTION 2.1

POPULATION MODELS

Section 2.1 introduces the first of the two major classes of mathematical models studied in the textbook, and is a prerequisite to the discussion of equilibrium solutions and stability in Section 2.2.

In Problems 1-4 we outline the derivation of the desired particular solution.

1. Noting that $x > 5$ because $x(0) = 8$, we write

$$\int \frac{dx}{x(x-5)} = \int (-3)\, dt; \qquad \int \left(\frac{1}{x} - \frac{1}{x-5} \right) dx = \int 15\, dt$$

$$\ln x - \ln(x-5) = 15t + \ln C; \qquad \frac{x}{x-5} = C\, e^{15t}$$

$$x(0) = 8 \text{ implies } C = 8/3; \qquad 3x = 8(x-5)\, e^{15t}$$

$$x(t) = \frac{-40\, e^{15t}}{3 - 8\, e^{15t}} = \frac{40}{8 - 3\, e^{-15t}}.$$

3. Noting that $x > 7$ because $x(0) = 11$, we write

$$\int \frac{dx}{x(x-7)} = \int (-4)\, dt; \qquad \int \left(\frac{1}{x} - \frac{1}{x-7} \right) dx = \int 28\, dt$$

$$\ln x - \ln(x-7) = 28t + \ln C; \qquad \frac{x}{x-7} = C\, e^{28t}$$

$$x(0) = 11 \text{ implies } C = 11/4; \qquad 4x = 11(x-17)\, e^{28t}$$

$$x(t) = \frac{-77\, e^{28t}}{4 - 11 e^{28t}} = \frac{77}{11 - 4\, e^{-28t}}$$

5. Substitution of $P(0) = 100$ and $P'(0) = 20$ into $P' = k\sqrt{P}$ yields $k = 2$, so the differential equation is $P' = 2\sqrt{P}$. Separation of variables and integration, $\int dP/2\sqrt{P} = \int dt$, gives $\sqrt{P} = t + C$. Then $P(0) = 100$ implies $C = 10$, so $P(t) = (t + 10)^2$. Hence the number of rabbits after one year is $P(12) = 484$.

7. **(a)** Starting with $dP/dt = k\sqrt{P}$, $dP/dt = k\sqrt{P}$, we separate the variables and integrate to get $P(t) = (kt/2 + C)^2$. Clearly $P(0) = P_0$ implies $C = \sqrt{P_0}$.

   (b) If $P(t) = (kt/2 + 10)^2$, then $P(6) = 169$ implies that $k = 1$. Hence $P(t) = (t/2 + 10)^2$, so there are 256 fish after 12 months.

9. **(a)** If the birth and death rates both are proportional to P^2 and $\beta > \delta$, then Eq. (1) in this section gives $P' = kP^2$ with k positive. Separating variables and integrating as in Problem 8, we find that $P(t) = 1/(C - kt)$. The initial condition $P(0) = P_0$ then gives $C = 1/P_0$, so $P(t) = 1/(1/P_0 - kt) = P_0/(1 - kP_0 t)$.

   (b) If $P_0 = 6$ then $P(t) = 6/(1 - 6kt)$. Now the fact that $P(10) = 9$ implies that $k = 180$, so $P(t) = 6/(1 - t/30) = 180/(30 - t)$. Hence it is clear that $P \to \infty$ as $t \to 30$ (doomsday).

11. If we write $P' = bP(a/b - P)$ we see that $M = a/b$. Hence

$$\frac{B_0 P_0}{D_0} = \frac{(aP_0)P_0}{bP_0^2} = \frac{a}{b} = M.$$

Note also (for Problems 12 and 13) that $a = B_0/P_0$ and $b = D_0/P_0^2 = k$.

13. The relations in Problem 11 give $k = 1/2400$ and $M = 180$. The solution is $P(t) = 43200/(240 - 60e^{-3t/80})$. We find that $P = 1.05M$ after about 44.22 months.

15. The relations in Problem 14 give $k = 1/1000$ and $M = 90$. The solution is $P(t) = 9000/(100 - 10e^{9t/100})$. We find that $P = 10M$ after about 24.41 months.

17. The only difference is that, if $P > M$, then

$$\int \frac{dP}{M - P} = -\ln|M - P| = -\ln(P - M)$$

so integration of the separated equation yields

$$\frac{P}{P-M} = A e^{kMt}.$$

This gives $A = P_0/(P_0 - M)$, so each side of the equation preceding Equation (4) in this section is simply multiplied by -1, and the result in Equation (4) is unchanged.

19. **(a)** $x' = 0.8x - 0.004x^2 = 0.004x(200 - x)$, so the maximum amount that will dissolve is $M = 200$ g.

(b) With $M = 200$, $P_0 = 50$, and $k = 0.004$, Equation (4) in the text yields the solution

$$x(t) = \frac{10000}{50 + 150 e^{-0.08t}}.$$

Substituting $x = 100$ on the left, we solve for $t = 1.25 \ln 3 \approx 1.37$ sec.

21. Proceeding as in Example 4 in the text, we solve the equations

$$25.00k(M - 25.00) = 3/8, \qquad 47.54k(M - 47.54) = 1/2$$

for $M = 100$ and $k = 0.0002$. Then Equation (4) gives the population function

$$P(t) = \frac{2500}{25 + 75e^{-0.02t}}.$$

We find that $P = 75$ when $t = 50 \ln 9 \approx 110$, that is, in 2035 A. D.

23. We are given that
$$P' = kP^2 - 0.01P,$$

and the fact that $P = 200$ and $P' = 2$ when $t = 0$ implies that $k = 0.0001$, so

$$P' = 10^{-4}(P^2 - P).$$

The solution with $P(0) = 200$ is $P(t) = 100/\left(1 - 0.5 e^{0.01t}\right)$.

(a) $P = 1000$ when $t = 100 \ln(9/5) \approx 58.78$.

(b) $P \to \infty$ as $t \to 100 \ln 2 \approx 69.31$

25. The equation is separable, so we have

$$\int \frac{dP}{P} = \int \beta_0 e^{-\alpha t} dt, \quad \text{so} \quad \ln P = -\frac{\beta_0}{\alpha} e^{-\alpha t} + C.$$

The initial condition $P(0) = P_0$ gives $C = \ln P_0 + \beta_0/\alpha$, so

$$P(t) = P_0 \exp\left[\frac{\beta_0}{\alpha}\left(1 - e^{-\alpha t}\right)\right].$$

27.   Any way you look at it, you should see that, the larger the parameter $k > 0$ is, the faster the logistic population $P(t)$ approaches its limiting population M.

In Problems 29 and 30 we give just the values of k and M calculated using Eqs. (ii) and (iii) in Problem 28 above, the resulting logistic solution, and the predicted year 2000 population.

29. $k = 0.0000668717$ and $M = 338.027$, so $P(t) = \dfrac{25761.7}{76.212 + 261.815 e^{-0.0226045 t}}$,

predicting $P = 192.525$ in the year 2000.

SECTION 2.2

EQUILIBRIUM SOLUTIONS AND STABILITY

In Problems 1-12 we identify the stable and unstable critical points as well as the funnels and spouts along the equilibrium solutions. In each problem the indicated solution satisfying $x(0) = x_0$ is derived fairly routinely by separation of variables. In some cases, various signs in the solution depend on the initial value, and we give a typical solution.

1.   Unstable critical point: $x = 4$
       Spout: Along the equilibrium solution $x(t) = 4$

       Solution: If $x_0 > 4$ then

$$\int \frac{dx}{x-4} = \int dt; \quad \ln(x-4) = t + C; \quad C = \ln(x_0 - 4)$$

$$x - 4 = (x_0 - 4)e^t; \quad x(t) = 4 + (x_0 - 4)e^t$$

3.   Stable critical point: $x = 0$
       Unstable critical point: $x = 4$
       Funnel: Along the equilibrium solution $x(t) = 0$
       Spout: Along the equilibrium solution $x(t) = 4$

       Solution: If $x_0 > 4$ then

$$\int 4\,dt = \int \frac{4\,dx}{x(x-4)} = \int \left(\frac{1}{x-4} - \frac{1}{x}\right)dx$$

$$4t + C = \ln\frac{x-4}{x}; \quad C = \ln\frac{x_0-4}{x_0}$$

$$4t = \ln\frac{x_0(x-4)}{x(x_0-4)}; \quad e^{4t} = \frac{x_0(x-4)}{x(x_0-4)}$$

$$x(t) = \frac{4x_0}{x_0+(4-x_0)e^{4t}}$$

5. Stable critical point: $x = -2$
Unstable critical point: $x = 2$
Funnel: Along the equilibrium solution $x(t) = -2$
Spout: Along the equilibrium solution $x(t) = 2$

Solution: If $x_0 > 2$ then

$$\int 4\,dt = \int \frac{4\,dx}{x^2-4} = \int\left(\frac{1}{x-2} - \frac{1}{x+2}\right)dx$$

$$4t + C = \ln\frac{x-2}{x+2}; \quad C = \ln\frac{x_0-2}{x_0+2}$$

$$4t = \ln\frac{(x-2)(x_0+2)}{(x+2)(x_0-2)}; \quad e^{4t} = \frac{(x-2)(x_0+2)}{(x+2)(x_0-2)}$$

$$x(t) = \frac{2\left[(x_0+2)+(x_0-2)e^{4t}\right]}{(x_0+2)-(x_0-2)e^{4t}}$$

7. Critical point: $x = 2$

This single critical point is *semi-stable*, meaning that solutions with $x_0 > 2$ go to infinity as t increases, while solutions with $x_0 < 2$ approach 2.

Solution: If $x_0 > 2$ then

$$\int \frac{-dx}{(x-2)^2} = \int(-1)\,dt; \quad \frac{1}{x-2} = -t+C; \quad C = \frac{1}{x_0-2}$$

$$\frac{1}{x-2} = -t + \frac{1}{x_0-2} = \frac{1-t(x_0-2)}{x_0-2}$$

$$x(t) = 2 + \frac{x_0-2}{1-t(x_0-2)} = \frac{x_0(2t-1)-4t}{tx_0-2t-1}$$

9. Stable critical point: $x = 1$
Unstable critical point: $x = 4$
Funnel: Along the equilibrium solution $x(t) = 1$

Spout: Along the equilibrium solution $x(t) = 4$

Solution: If $x_0 > 4$ then

$$\int 3\,dt \;=\; \int \frac{3\,dx}{(x-4)(x-1)} \;=\; \int \left(\frac{1}{x-4} - \frac{1}{x-1}\right) dx$$

$$3t + C \;=\; \ln\frac{x-4}{x-1}; \quad C \;=\; \ln\frac{x_0-4}{x_0-1}$$

$$3t \;=\; \ln\frac{(x-4)(x_0-1)}{(x-1)(x_0-4)}; \quad e^{3t} \;=\; \frac{(x-4)(x_0-1)}{(x-1)(x_0-4)}$$

$$x(t) \;=\; \frac{4(1-x_0)+(x_0-4)e^{3t}}{(1-x_0)+(x_0-4)e^{3t}}$$

11.   Unstable critical point: $x = 1$
Spout: Along the equilibrium solution $x(t) = 1$

Solution: $$\int \frac{-2\,dx}{(x-1)^3} \;=\; \int (-2)\,dt; \quad \frac{1}{(x-1)^2} \;=\; -2t + \frac{1}{(x_0-1)^2}$$

13.   **(a)**   If $k = -a^2$ where $h > 0$ then $kx - x^3 = -a^2 x - x^3 = -x(a^2+x^2)$ is positive if $x < 0$, negative if $x > 0$, and is 0 only if $x = 0$.

(b)   If $k = +a^2$ where $h > 0$ then $kx - x^3 = +a^2 x - x^3 = -x(x+a)(x-a)$ is positive if $x < -a$, negative if $-a < x < 0$, positive if $0 < x < a$, and negative if $x > a$.

15.   If $x_0 > M$ then

$$\int kM\,dt \;=\; \int \frac{M\,dx}{x(x-M)} \;=\; \int \left(\frac{1}{x-M} - \frac{1}{x}\right) dx$$

$$kM\,t + C \;=\; \ln\frac{x-M}{x}; \quad C \;=\; \ln\frac{x_0-M}{x_0}$$

$$kM\,t \;=\; \ln\frac{x_0(x-M)}{x(x_0-M)}; \quad e^{kMt} \;=\; \frac{x_0(x-M)}{x(x_0-M)}$$

$$x(t) \;=\; \frac{Mx_0}{x_0 + (M-x_0)e^{kMt}}$$

17.   **(i)**   In the first alternative form that is given, all of the coefficients within parentheses are positive if $H < x_0 < N$. Hence it is obvious that $x(t) \to N$ as $t \to \infty$.

(ii) In the second alternative form that is given, all of the coefficients within parentheses are positive if $x_0 < H$. Hence the denominator is initially equal to $N - H > 0$, but decreases as t increases, and reaches the value 0 when

$$t = \frac{1}{N-H} \ln \frac{N-x_0}{H-x_0} > 0.$$

19. Separation of variables in the differential equation $x' = -k\left((x-a)^2 + b^2\right)$ yields

$$x(t) = a - b \tan\left(bk\,t + \tan^{-1} \frac{a-x_0}{b} \right).$$

It therefore follows that $x(t)$ goes to minus infinity in a finite period of time.

21. This is simply a matter of analyzing the signs of x' in the cases $x < a$, $a < x < b$, $b < x < c$, and $c > x$.

SECTION 2.3

ACCELERATION-VELOCITY MODELS

This section consists of three essentially independent subsections that can be studied separately: resistance proportional to velocity, resistance proportional to velocity-squared, and inverse-square gravitational acceleration.

1. Equation: $v' = k(250 - v)$, $v(0) = 0$, $v(10) = 100$

Solution: $\displaystyle\int \frac{(-1)\,dv}{250-v} = -\int k\,dt;\quad \ln(250-v) = -kt + \ln C,$

$v(0) = 0$ implies $C = 250$; $\quad v(t) = 250(1 - e^{-kt})$

$v(10) = 100$ implies $k = \frac{1}{10}\ln(250/150) \approx 0.0511$;

Answer: $v = 200$ when $t = -(\ln 50/250)/k \approx 31.5$ sec

3. Equation: $v' = -kv$, $v(0) = 40$; $v(10) = 20 \quad x' = v$, $x(0) = 0$

Solution: $v(t) = 40\,e^{-kt}$ with $k = (1/10)\ln 2$

$x(t) = (40/k)(1 - e^{-kt})$

Answer: $x(\infty) = \lim_{t\to\infty}(40/k)(1 - e^{-kt}) = 40/k = 400/\ln 2 \approx 577$ ft

5.   Equation: $v' = -kv, \quad v(0) = 40; \quad v(10) = 20 \quad x' = v, \quad x(0) = 0$

        Solution: $v = \dfrac{40}{1+40kt} \quad$ (as in Problem 3)

$$v(10) = 20 \text{ implies } 40k = 1/10, \text{ so } v(t) = \frac{400}{10+t}$$

$$x(t) = 400 \ln[(10+t)/10]$$

        Answer: $x(60) = 400 \ln 7 \approx 778$ ft

7.   Equation: $v' = 10 - 0.1v, \quad x(0) = v(0) = 0$

        (a) $\displaystyle\int \frac{-0.1\,dv}{10-0.1v} = \int(-0.1)\,dt; \quad \ln(10-0.1v) = -t/10 + \ln C$

$$v(0) = 0 \text{ implies } C = 10; \quad \ln\big[(10-0.1v)/10\big] = -t/10$$

$$v(t) = 100(1 - e^{-t/10}); \quad v(\infty) = 100 \text{ ft/sec} \quad \text{(limiting velocity)}$$

        (b) $x(t) = 100t - 1000(1 - e^{-t/10})$

$$v = 90 \text{ ft/sec when } t = 23.0259 \text{ sec and } x = 1402.59 \text{ ft}$$

9.   The solution of the initial value problem

$$1000\,v' = 5000 - 100\,v, \qquad v(0) = 0$$

        is

$$v(t) = 50(1 - e^{-t/10}).$$

Hence, as $t \to \infty$, we see that $v(t)$ approaches $v_{max} = 50$ ft/sec ≈ 34 mph.

11.   If the paratrooper's terminal velocity was 100 mph $= 440/3$ ft/sec, then Equation (7) in the text yields $\rho = 12/55$. Then we find by solving Equation (9) numerically with $y_0 = 1200$ and $v_0 = 0$ that $y = 0$ when $t \approx 12.5$ sec. Thus the newspaper account is inaccurate.

Given the hints and integrals provided in the text, Problems 13-16 are fairly straightforward (and fairly tedious) integration problems.

17.   To solve the initial value problem $v' = -9.8 - 0.0011v^2, \quad v(0) = 49$ we write

$$\int \frac{dv}{9.8 + 0.0011v^2} = -\int dt; \quad \int \frac{0.010595\,dv}{1 + (0.010595\,v)^2} = -\int 0.103827\,dt$$

$$\tan^{-1}(0.010595\,v) = -0.103827\,t + C; \quad v(0) = 49 \text{ implies } C = 0.478854$$

$$v(t) = 94.3841 \tan(0.478854 - 0.103827\,t)$$

Integration with $y(0) = 0$ gives

$$y(t) = 108.468 + 909.052 \, \ln(\cos(0.478854 - 0.103827\,t)).$$

We solve $v(0) = 0$ for $t = 4.612$, and then calculate $y(4.612) = 108.468$.

19. Equation: $\quad v' = 4 - (1/400)v^2, \quad v(0) = 0$

Solution: $\quad \displaystyle\int \frac{dv}{4 - (1/400)v^2} = \int dt; \quad \int \frac{(1/40)\,dv}{1 - (v/40)^2} = \int \frac{1}{10}\,dt$

$$\tanh^{-1}(v/40) = t/10 + C; \quad C = 0; \quad v(t) = 40 \tanh(t/10)$$

Answer: $\quad v(10) \approx 30.46 \text{ ft/sec}, \quad v(\infty) = 40 \text{ ft/sec}$

21. Equation: $\quad v' = -g - \rho v^2, \quad v(0) = v_0, \quad y(0) = 0$

Solution: $\quad \displaystyle\int \frac{dv}{g + \rho v^2} = -\int dt; \quad \int \frac{\sqrt{\rho/g}\,dv}{1 + \left(\sqrt{\rho/g}\,v\right)^2} = -\int \sqrt{g\rho}\,dt;$

$$\tan^{-1}\left(\sqrt{\rho/g}\,v\right) = -\sqrt{g\rho}\,t + C; \quad v(0) = v_0 \text{ implies } C = \tan^{-1}\left(\sqrt{\rho/g}\,v_0\right)$$

$$v(t) = -\sqrt{\frac{g}{\rho}}\,\tan\left(t\sqrt{g\rho} - \tan^{-1}\left(v_0\sqrt{\frac{\rho}{g}}\right)\right)$$

We solve $v(t) = 0$ for $t = \dfrac{1}{\sqrt{g\rho}}\tan^{-1}\left(v_0\sqrt{\dfrac{\rho}{g}}\right)$ and substitute in Eq. (17) for $y(t)$:

$$y_{\max} = \frac{1}{\rho}\ln\left|\frac{\cos\left(\tan^{-1}v_0\sqrt{\rho/g} - \tan^{-1}v_0\sqrt{\rho/g}\right)}{\cos\left(\tan^{-1}v_0\sqrt{\rho/g}\right)}\right|$$

$$= \frac{1}{\rho}\ln\left(\sec\left(\tan^{-1}v_0\sqrt{\rho/g}\right)\right) = \frac{1}{\rho}\ln\sqrt{1 + \frac{\rho v_0^2}{g}}$$

$$y_{\max} = \frac{1}{2\rho}\ln\left(1 + \frac{\rho v_0^2}{g}\right)$$

23. Before opening parachute:

$$v' = -32 + 0.00075\,v^2, \quad v(0) = 0, \quad y(0) = 10000$$

$$v(t) = -206.559\,\tanh(0.154919\,t) \quad v(30) = -206.521 \;\; \text{ft/sec}$$

$$y(t) = 10000 - 1333.33\,\ln(\cosh(0.154919\,t)), \quad y(30) = 4727.30 \;\; \text{ft}$$

After opening parachute:

$$v' = -32 + 0.075\,v^2, \quad v(0) = -206.521, \quad y(0) = 4727.30$$

$$v(t) = -20.6559\,\tanh(1.54919\,t + 0.00519595)$$

$$y(t) = 4727.30 - 13.3333\,\ln(\cosh(1.54919\,t + 0.00519595))$$

$$y = 0 \;\; \text{when} \;\; t = 229.304$$

Thus she opens her parachute after 30 sec at a height of 4727 feet, and the total time of descent is $30 + 229.304 = 259.304$ sec, about 4 minutes and 19.3 seconds.

25. We get the desired formula when we set $v = 0$ in Eq. (23) and solve for r.

27. Integration of $v\dfrac{dv}{dy} = -\dfrac{GM}{(y+R)^2}, \;\; y(0) = 0, \; v(0) = v_0$ gives

$$\frac{1}{2}v^2 \;=\; \frac{GM}{y+R} - \frac{GM}{R} + \frac{1}{2}v_0^2$$

which simplifies to the desired formula for v^2. Then substitution of $G = 6.6726\times10^{-11}$, $M = 5.975\times10^{24}$ kg, $R = 6.378\times10^6$ m, $v = 0$, and $v_0 = 1$ yields an equation that we easily solve for $y = 51427.3$, that is, about 51.427 km.

SECTION 2.4

NUMERICAL APPROXIMATION: EULER'S METHOD

In each of Problems 1-10 we also give first the iterative formula of Euler's method. These iterations are readily implemented, either manually or with a computer system or graphing calculator (as we illustrate in Problem 1). We give in each problem a table showing the approximate values obtained, as well as the corresponding values of the exact solution.

1. For the differential equation $y' = f(x, y)$ with $f(x, y) = -y$, the iterative formula of Euler's method is $y_{n+1} = y_n + h(-y_n)$, and the exact solution is $y(x) = 2\,e^{-x}$. The TI-83 screen on the left shows a graphing calculator implementation of this iterative formula.

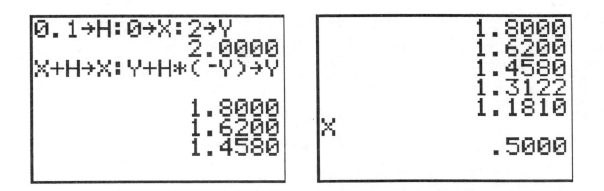

After the variables are initialized (in the first line), and the formula is entered, each press of the enter key carries out an additional step. The screen on the right above shows the results of 5 steps from $x = 0$ to $x = 0.5$ with step size $h = 0.1$ — winding up with $y(0.5) \approx 1.1810$ — and we see the approximate values shown in the second row of the table below. We get the values shown in the next row if we start afresh with $h = 0.05$ and record every other approximation that is obtained.

x	0.0	0.1	0.2	0.3	0.4	0.5
y with $h=0.1$	2.0000	1.8000	1.6200	1.4580	1.3122	1.1810
y with $h=0.05$	2.0000	1.8050	1.6290	1.4702	1.3258	1.1975
y actual	2.0000	1.8097	1.6375	1.4816	1.3406	1.2131

3.   Iterative formula: $y_{n+1} = y_n + h(y_n + 1)$

      Exact solution: $y(x) = 2e^x - 1$

x	0.0	0.1	0.2	0.3	0.4	0.5
y with $h=0.1$	1.0000	1.2000	1.4200	1.6620	1.9282	2.2210
y with $h=0.05$	1.0000	1.2050	1.4310	1.6802	1.9549	2.2578
y actual	1.0000	1.2103	1.4428	1.6997	1.9837	2.2974

5.   Iterative formula: $y_{n+1} = y_n + h(y_n - x_n - 1)$

      Exact solution: $y(x) = 2 + x - e^x$

x	0.0	0.1	0.2	0.3	0.4	0.5
y with $h=0.1$	1.0000	1.0000	0.9900	0.9690	0.9359	0.8895
y with $h=0.05$	1.0000	0.9975	0.9845	0.9599	0.9225	0.8711
y actual	1.0000	0.9948	0.9786	0.9501	0.9082	0.8513

7.   Iterative formula: $y_{n+1} = y_n + h(-3x_n^2 y_n)$

      Exact solution: $y(x) = 3 \exp(-x^3)$

x	0.0	0.1	0.2	0.3	0.4	0.5
y with $h=0.1$	3.0000	3.0000	2.9910	2.9551	2.8753	2.7373
y with $h=0.05$	3.0000	2.9989	2.9843	2.9386	2.8456	2.6930
y actual	3.0000	2.9970	2.9761	2.9201	2.8140	2.6475

9. Iterative formula: $\quad y_{n+1} = y_n + h(1 + y_n^2)/4$

Exact solution: $\quad y(x) = \tan[(x + \pi)/4]$

x	0.0	0.1	0.2	0.3	0.4	0.5
y with $h=0.1$	1.0000	1.0500	1.1026	1.1580	1.2165	1.2785
y with $h=0.05$	1.0000	1.0506	1.1039	1.1602	1.2197	1.2828
y actual	1.0000	1.0513	1.1054	1.1625	1.2231	1.2874

The tables of approximate and actual values called for in Problems 11–16 were produced using the following MATLAB script (appropriately altered for each problem).

```
% Section 2.4, Problems 11-16
x0 = 0;     y0 = 1;
% first run:
h = 0.01;
x = x0;   y = y0;   y1 = y0;
for   n = 1:100
    y = y + h*(y-2);
    y1 = [y1,y];
    x = x + h;
    end
% second run:
h = 0.005;
x = x0;   y = y0;   y2 = y0;
for   n = 1:200
    y = y + h*(y-2);
    y2 = [y2,y];
    x = x + h;
    end
% exact values
x = x0 : 0.2 : x0+1;
ye = 2 - exp(x);
% display table
ya = y2(1:40:201);
err = 100*(ye-ya)./ye;
[x; y1(1:20:101); ya; ye; err]
```

11.   The iterative formula of Euler's method is $y_{n+1} = y_n + h(y_n - 2)$, and the exact solution is $y(x) = 2 - e^x$. The resulting table of approximate and actual values is

x	0.0	0.2	0.4	0.6	0.8	1.0
y ($h=0.01$)	1.0000	0.7798	0.5111	0.1833	−0.2167	−0.7048
y ($h=0.005$)	1.0000	0.7792	0.5097	0.1806	−0.2211	−0.7115
y actual	1.0000	0.7786	0.5082	0.1779	−0.2255	−0.7183
error	0%	−0.08%	−0.29%	−1.53%	1.97%	0.94%

13. Iterative formula: $\quad y_{n+1} = y_n + 2hx_n^3/y_n$

Exact solution: $\quad y(x) = (8 + x^4)^{1/2}$

x	1.0	1.2	1.4	1.6	1.8	2.0
y ($h=0.01$)	3.0000	3.1718	3.4368	3.8084	4.2924	4.8890
y ($h=0.005$)	3.0000	3.1729	3.4390	3.8117	4.2967	4.8940
y actual	3.0000	3.1739	3.4412	3.8149	4.3009	4.8990
error	0%	0.03%	0.06%	0.09%	0.10%	0.10%

15. Iterative formula: $\quad y_{n+1} = y_n + h(3 - 2y_n/x_n)$

Exact solution: $\quad y(x) = x + 4/x^2$

x	2.0	2.2	2.4	2.6	2.8	3.0
y ($h=0.01$)	3.0000	3.0253	3.0927	3.1897	3.3080	3.4422
y ($h=0.005$)	3.0000	3.0259	3.0936	3.1907	3.3091	3.4433
y actual	3.0000	3.0264	3.0944	3.1917	3.3102	3.4444
error	0%	0.019%	0.028%	0.032%	0.033%	0.032%

The tables of approximate values called for in Problems 17-24 were produced using a MATLAB script similar to the one listed preceding the Problem 11 solution above.

17.

x	0.0	0.2	0.4	0.6	0.8	1.0
y ($h=0.1$)	0.0000	0.0010	0.0140	0.0551	0.1413	0.2925
y ($h=0.02$)	0.0000	0.0023	0.0198	0.0688	0.1672	0.3379
y ($h=0.004$)	0.0000	0.0026	0.0210	0.0717	0.1727	0.3477
y ($h=0.0008$)	0.0000	0.0027	0.0213	0.0723	0.1738	0.3497

These data that $y(1) \approx 0.35$, in contrast with Example 4 in the text, where the initial condition is $y(0) = 1$.

In Problems 18-24 we give only the final approximate values of y obtained using Euler's method with step sizes $h = 0.1$, $h = 0.02$, $h = 0.004$, and $h = 0.0008$.

19. With $x_0 = 0$ and $y_0 = 1$, the approximate values of $y(2)$ obtained are:

h	0.1	0.02	0.004	0.0008
y	6.1831	6.3653	6.4022	6.4096

21. With $x_0 = 1$ and $y_0 = 2$, the approximate values of $y(2)$ obtained are:

h	0.1	0.02	0.004	0.0008
y	2.8508	2.8681	2.8716	2.8723

23. With $x_0 = 0$ and $y_0 = 0$, the approximate values of $y(1)$ obtained are:

h	0.1	0.02	0.004	0.0008
y	1.2262	1.2300	1.2306	1.2307

25. With step sizes $h = 0.15$, $h = 0.03$, and $h = 0.006$ we get the following results:

x	y with $h=0.15$	y with $h=0.03$	y with $h=0.006$
-1.0	1.0000	1.0000	1.0000
-0.7	1.0472	1.0512	1.0521
-0.4	1.1213	1.1358	1.1390
-0.1	1.2826	1.3612	1.3835
$+0.2$	0.8900	1.4711	0.8210
$+0.5$	0.7460	1.2808	0.7192

While the values for $h = 0.15$ alone are not conclusive, a comparison of the values of y for all three step sizes with $x > 0$ suggests some anomaly in the transition from negative to positive values of x.

27. With step sizes $h = 0.1$ and $h = 0.01$ we get the following results:

x	y with $h = 0.1$	y with $h = 0.01$
0.0	1.0000	1.0000
0.1	1.2000	1.2200
0.2	1.4428	1.4967
.	.	.
.	.	.
.	.	.
0.7	4.3460	6.4643
0.8	5.8670	11.8425
0.9	8.3349	39.5010

Clearly there is some difficulty near $x = 0.9$.

SECTION 2.5

A CLOSER LOOK AT THE EULER METHOD

In each of Problems 1-10 we give first the predictor formula for u_{n+1}, next the improved Euler corrector for y_{n+1} and the exact solution. These predictor-corrector iterations are readily implemented, either manually or with a computer system or graphing calculator (as we illustrate in Problem 1). We give in each problem a table showing the approximate values obtained, as well as the corresponding values of the exact solution.

```
0.1→H:0→X:2→Y
            2.0000
Y-H*Y→U:Y+(H/2)*
(-Y-U)→Y
            1.8100
            1.6381
            1.4824
```

```
Y-H*Y→U:Y+(H/2)*
(-Y-U)→Y
            1.8100
            1.6381
            1.4824
            1.3416
            1.2142
```

1. $u_{n+1} = y_n + h(-y_n)$

    $y_{n+1} = y_n + (h/2)[-y_n - u_{n+1}]$

    $y(x) = 2e^{-x}$

    The TI-83 screen on the left above shows a graphing calculator implementation of this iteration. After the variables are initialized (in the first line), and the formulas are entered, each press of the enter key carries out an additional step. The screen on the right shows the results of 5 steps from $x = 0$ to $x = 0.5$ with step size $h = 0.1$ — winding up with $y(0.5) \approx 1.2142$ — and we see the approximate values shown in the second row of the table below.

x	0.0	0.1	0.2	0.3	0.4	0.5
y with $h=0.1$	2.0000	1.8100	1.6381	1.4824	1.3416	1.2142
y actual	2.0000	1.8097	1.6375	1.4816	1.3406	1.2131

3. $u_{n+1} = y_n + h(y_n + 1)$

    $y_{n+1} = y_n + (h/2)[(y_n + 1) + (u_{n+1} + 1)]$

    $y(x) = 2e^x - 1$

x	0.0	0.1	0.2	0.3	0.4	0.5
y with $h=0.1$	1.0000	1.2100	1.4421	1.6985	1.9818	2.2949
y actual	1.0000	1.2103	1.4428	1.6997	1.9837	2.2974

5. $u_{n+1} = y_n + h(y_n - x_n - 1)$

$y_{n+1} = y_n + (h/2)[(y_n - x_n - 1) + (u_{n+1} - x_n - h - 1)]$

$y(x) = 2 + x - e^x$

x	0.0	0.1	0.2	0.3	0.4	0.5
y with $h=0.1$	1.0000	0.9950	0.9790	0.9508	0.9091	0.8526
y actual	1.0000	0.9948	0.9786	0.9501	0.9082	0.8513

7. $u_{n+1} = y_n - 3x_n^2 y_n h$

$y_{n+1} = y_n - (h/2)[3x_n^2 y_n + 3(x_n + h)^2 u_{n+1}]$

$y(x) = 3 \exp(-x^3)$

x	0.0	0.1	0.2	0.3	0.4	0.5
y with $h=0.1$	3.0000	2.9955	2.9731	2.9156	2.8082	2.6405
y actual	3.0000	2.9970	2.9761	2.9201	2.8140	2.6475

9. $u_{n+1} = y_n + h(1 + y_n^2)/4$

$y_{n+1} = y_n + h[1 + y_n^2 + 1 + (u_{n+1})^2]/8$

$y(x) = \tan[(x + \pi)/4]$

x	0.0	0.1	0.2	0.3	0.4	0.5
y with $h=0.1$	1.0000	1.0513	1.1053	1.1625	1.2230	1.2873
y actual	1.0000	1.0513	1.1054	1.1625	1.2231	1.2874

The results given below for Problems 11-16 were computed using the following MATLAB script.

```
% Section 2.5, Problems 11-16
x0 = 0;   y0 = 1;
% first run:
h = 0.01;
x = x0;   y = y0;   y1 = y0;
for  n = 1:100
   u = y + h*f(x,y);                    %predictor
   y = y + (h/2)*(f(x,y)+f(x+h,u));   %corrector
   y1 = [y1,y];
   x = x + h;
   end
% second run:
h = 0.005;
```

```
x = x0;  y = y0;   y2 = y0;
for  n = 1:200
   u = y + h*f(x,y);                    %predictor
   y = y + (h/2)*(f(x,y)+f(x+h,u));    %corrector
   y2 = [y2,y];
   x = x + h;
end
% exact values
x = x0 : 0.2 : x0+1;

ye = g(x);
% display table
ya = y2(1:40:201);
err = 100*(ye-ya)./ye;
x = sprintf('%10.5f',x), sprintf('\n');
y1 = sprintf('%10.5f',y1(1:20:101)), sprintf('\n');
ya = sprintf('%10.5f',ya), sprintf('\n');
ye = sprintf('%10.5f',ye), sprintf('\n');
err = sprintf('%10.5f',err), sprintf('\n');
table = [x; y1; ya; ye; err]
```

For each problem the differential equation $y' = f(x, y)$ and the known exact solution $y = g(x)$ are stored in the files **f.m** and **g.m** — for instance, the files

```
function  yp = f(x,y)
yp = y-2;

function ye = g(x,y)
ye = 2-exp(x);
```

for Problem 11. (The exact solutions for Problems 11-16 here are given in the solutions for Problems 11-16 in Section 2.4.)

11.

x	0.0	0.2	0.4	0.6	0.8	1.0
y (h=0.01)	1.00000	0.77860	0.50819	0.17790	−0.22551	−0.71824
y (h=0.005)	1.00000	0.77860	0.50818	0.17789	−0.22553	−0.71827
y actual	1.00000	0.77860	0.50818	0.17788	−0.22554	−0.71828
error	0.000%	−0.000%	−0.001%	−0.003%	0.003%	0.002%

13.

x	1.0	1.2	1.4	1.6	1.8	2.0
y (h=0.01)	3.00000	3.17390	3.44118	3.81494	4.30091	4.89901
y (h=0.005)	3.00000	3.17390	3.44117	3.81492	4.30089	4.89899
y actual	3.00000	3.17389	3.44116	3.81492	4.30088	4.89898
error	0.0000%	−0.0001%	−0.0001%	0.0001%	−0.0002%	−0.0002%

15.

x	2.0	2.2	2.4	2.6	2.8	3.0
y (h=0.01)	3.000000	3.026448	3.094447	3.191719	3.310207	3.444448
y (h=0.005)	3.000000	3.026447	3.094445	3.191717	3.310205	3.444445
y actual	3.000000	3.026446	3.094444	3.191716	3.310204	3.444444
error	0.00000%	−0.00002%	−0.00002%	−0.00002%	−0.00002%	−0.00002%

17.   With $h = \ \ 0.1$: $y(1) \approx 0.35183$
With $h = \ \ 0.02$: $y(1) \approx 0.35030$
With $h = \ 0.004$: $y(1) \approx 0.35023$
With $h = 0.0008$: $y(1) \approx 0.35023$

The table of numerical results is

x	y with h = 0.1	y with h = 0.02	y with h = 0.004	y with h = 0.0008
0.0	0.00000	0.00000	0.00000	0.00000
0.2	0.00300	0.00268	0.00267	0.00267
0.4	0.02202	0.02139	0.02136	0.02136
0.6	0.07344	0.07249	0.07245	0.07245
0.8	0.17540	0.17413	0.17408	0.17408
1.0	0.35183	0.35030	0.35023	0.35023

In Problems 18-24 we give only the final approximate values of y obtained using the improved Euler method with step sizes $h = 0.1$, $h = 0.02$, $h = 0.004$, and $h = 0.0008$.

19.   With $h = \ \ 0.1$: $y(2) \approx 6.40834$
With $h = \ \ 0.02$: $y(2) \approx 6.41134$
With $h = \ 0.004$: $y(2) \approx 6.41147$
With $h = 0.0008$: $y(2) \approx 6.41147$

21.   With $h = \ \ 0.1$: $y(2) \approx 2.87204$
With $h = \ \ 0.02$: $y(2) \approx 2.87245$
With $h = \ 0.004$: $y(2) \approx 2.87247$
With $h = 0.0008$: $y(2) \approx 2.87247$

23.   With $h = \ \ 0.1$: $y(1) \approx 1.22967$
With $h = \ \ 0.02$: $y(1) \approx 1.23069$
With $h = \ 0.004$: $y(1) \approx 1.23073$
With $h = 0.0008$: $y(1) \approx 1.23073$

In the solutions for Problems 25 and 26 we illustrate the following general MATLAB ode solver.

```
function  [t,y] = ode(method, yp, t0,b, y0, n)
%   [t,y] = ode(method, yp, t0,b, y0, n)
%   calls the method described by 'method' for the
%   ODE 'yp' with function header
%
%                 y' = yp(t,y)
%
%   on the interval  [t0,b]  with initial (column)
%   vector  y0.  Choices for method are 'euler',
%   'impeuler', 'rk' (Runge-Kutta), 'ode23', 'ode45'.
%   Results are saved at the endPoints of n subintervals,
%   that is, in steps of length  h = (b - t0)/n.  The
%   result  t  is an (n+1)-column vector from b to t1,
%   while  y  is a matrix with  n+1  rows (one for each
%   t-value) and one column for each dependent variable.

h = (b - t0)/n;              % step size
t = t0 : h : b;
t = t';                            % col. vector of t-values
y = y0';                     % 1st row of result matrix
for  i = 2 : n+1             % for i=2 to i=n+1
   t0 = t(i-1);              % old t
   t1 = t(i);                   % new t
   y0 = y(i-1,:)';              % old y-row-vector
   [T,Y] = feval(method, yp, t0,t1, y0);
   y = [y;Y'];                   % adjoin new y-row-vector
end
```

To use the improved Euler method, we call as **'method'** the following function.

```
function [t,y] = impeuler(yp, t0,t1, y0)
%
%   [t,y] = impeuler(yp, t0,t1, y0)
%   Takes one improved Euler step for
%
%        y' = yprime( t,y ),
%
%   from t0  to  t1  with initial value  the
%   column vector  y0.

h = t1 - t0;
k1 = feval( yp, t0, y0        );
k2 = feval( yp, t1, y0 + h*k1 );
k  = (k1 + k2)/2;
t = t1;
y = y0 + h*k;
```

25.   Here our differential equation is described by the MATLAB function

```
function  vp = vpbolt1(t,v)
vp = -0.04*v - 9.8;
```

Then the commands

```
n = 50;
[t1,v1] = ode('impeuler','vpbolt1',0,10,49,n);
n = 100;
[t2,v2] = ode('impeuler','vpbolt1',0,10,49,n);
t = (0:10)';
ve = 294*exp(-t/25)-245;
[t, v1(1:5:51), v2(1:10:101), ve]
```

generate the table

t	with $n = 50$	with $n = 100$	actual v
0	49.0000	49.0000	49.0000
1	37.4722	37.4721	37.4721
2	26.3964	26.3963	26.3962
3	15.7549	15.7547	15.7546
4	5.5307	5.5304	5.5303
5	-4.2926	-4.2930	-4.2932
6	-13.7308	-13.7313	-13.7314
7	-22.7989	-22.7994	-22.7996
8	-31.5115	-31.5120	-31.5122
9	-39.8824	-39.8830	-39.8832
10	-47.9251	-47.9257	-47.9259

We notice first that the final two columns agree to 3 decimal places (each difference being than 0.0005). Scanning the $n = 100$ column for sign changes, we suspect that $v = 0$ (at the bolt's apex) occurs just after $t = 4.5$ sec. Then interpolation between $t = 4.5$ and $t = 4.6$ in the table

```
[t2(40:51),v2(40:51)]
```

```
3.9000    6.5345
4.0000    5.5304
4.1000    4.5303
4.2000    3.5341
4.3000    2.5420
4.4000    1.5538
4.5000    0.5696
4.6000   -0.4108
4.7000   -1.3872
4.8000   -2.3597
4.9000   -3.3283
5.0000   -4.2930
```

indicates that $t = 4.56$ at the bolt's apex. Finally, interpolation in

```
[t2(95:96),v2(95:96)]
```

```
                    9.4000   -43.1387
                    9.5000   -43.9445
```

gives the impact velocity $v(9.41) \approx -43.22$ m/s.

SECTION 2.6

THE RUNGE-KUTTA METHOD

The actual solutions in Problems 1-10 are the same as those given in the solutions for Problems 1-10 (respectively) in Section 2.4. Each problem can be solved with a "template" of computations like those listed in Problem 1. We include a table showing the slope values k_1, k_2, k_3, k_4 and the *xy*-values at the ends of two successive steps of size $h = 0.25$.

1. To make the first step of size $h = 0.25$ we start with the function defined by

```
f[x_, y_] := -y
```

and the initial values

```
x = 0;      y = 2;      h = 0.25;
```

and then perform the calculations

```
k1 = f[x, y]
k2 = f[x + h/2, y + h*k1/2]
k3 = f[x + h/2, y + h*k2/2]
k4 = f[x + h, y + h*k3]
y  = y + h/6*(k1 + 2*k2 + 2*k3 + k4)
x  = x + h
```

in turn. Here we are using Mathematica notation that translates transparently to standard mathematical notation describing the corresponding manual computations. A repetition of this same block of calculations carries out a second step of size $h = 0.25$. The following table lists the intermediate and final results obtained in these two steps.

k_1	k_2	k_3	k_4	x	Approx. y	Actual y
−2	−1/75	−1.78125	−1.55469	0.25	1.55762	1.55760
−1.55762	−1.36292	−1.38725	−1.2108	0.5	1.21309	1.21306

3.

k_1	k_2	k_3	k_4	x	Approx. y	Actual y
2	2.25	2.28125	2.57031	0.25	1.56803	1.56805
2.56803	2.88904	2.92916	3.30032	0.5	2.29740	2.29744

5.

k_1	k_2	k_3	k_4	x	Approx. y	Actual y
0	−0.125	−0.14063	−0.28516	0.25	0.96598	0.96597
−28402	−0.44452	−0.46458	−0.65016	0.5	0.85130	0.85128

7.

k_1	k_2	k_3	k_4	x	Approx. y	Actual y
0	−0.14063	−0.13980	−0.55595	0.25	2.95347	2.95349
−0.55378	−1.21679	−1.18183	−1.99351	0.5	2.6475	2.64749

9.

k_1	k_2	k_3	k_4	x	Approx. y	Actual y
0.5	0.53223	0.53437	0.57126	0.25	1.13352	1.13352
0.57122	0.61296	0.61611	0.66444	0.5	1.28743	1.28743

The results given below for Problems 11–16 were computed using the following MATLAB script.

```
% Section 2.6, Problems 11-16
x0 = 0;  y0 = 1;
% first run:
h = 0.2;
x = x0;  y = y0;  y1 = y0;
for  n = 1:5
   k1 = f(x,y);
   k2 = f(x+h/2,y+h*k1/2);
   k3 = f(x+h/2,y+h*k2/2);
   k4 = f(x+h,y+h*k3);
   y = y +(h/6)*(k1+2*k2+2*k3+k4);
   y1 = [y1,y];
   x = x + h;
   end
% second run:
h = 0.1;
x = x0;  y = y0;  y2 = y0;
for  n = 1:10
   k1 = f(x,y);
   k2 = f(x+h/2,y+h*k1/2);
   k3 = f(x+h/2,y+h*k2/2);
   k4 = f(x+h,y+h*k3);
   y = y +(h/6)*(k1+2*k2+2*k3+k4);
   y2 = [y2,y];
   x = x + h;
end
% exact values
x = x0 : 0.2 : x0+1;
ye = g(x);
% display table
y2 = y2(1:2:11);
```

```
err = 100*(ye-y2)./ye;
x = sprintf('%10.6f',x), sprintf('\n');
y1 = sprintf('%10.6f',y1), sprintf('\n');
y2 = sprintf('%10.6f',y2), sprintf('\n');
ye = sprintf('%10.6f',ye), sprintf('\n');
err = sprintf('%10.6f',err), sprintf('\n');
table = [x;y1;y2;ye;err]
```

For each problem the differential equation $y' = f(x, y)$ and the known exact solution $y = g(x)$ are stored in the files **f.m** and **g.m** — for instance, the files

```
function  yp = f(x,y)
yp = y-2;

function ye = g(x,y)
ye = 2-exp(x);
```

for Problem 11. (The exact solutions for Problems 11-16 here are given in the solutions for Problems 11-16 in Section 2.4.)

11.

x	0.0	0.2	0.4	0.6	0.8	1.0
y (h=0.2)	1.000000	0.778600	0.508182	0.177894	−0.225521	−0.718251
y (h=0.1)	1.000000	0.778597	0.508176	0.177882	−0.225540	−0.718280
y actual	1.000000	0.778597	0.508175	0.177881	−0.225541	−0.718282
error	0.00000%	−0.00002%	−0.00009%	−0.00047%	−0.00061%	−0.00029%

13.

x	1.0	1.2	1.4	1.6	1.8	2.0
y (h=0.2)	3.000000	3.173896	3.441170	3.814932	4.300904	4.899004
y (h=0.1)	3.000000	3.173894	3.441163	3.814919	4.300885	4.898981
y actual	3.000000	3.173894	3.441163	3.814918	4.300884	4.898979
error	0.00000%	−0.00001%	−0.00001%	−0.00002%	−0.00003%	−0.00003%

15.

x	2.0	2.2	2.4	2.6	2.9	3.0
y (h=0.2)	3.000000	3.026448	3.094447	3.191719	3.310207	3.444447
y (h=0.1)	3.000000	3.026446	3.094445	3.191716	3.310204	3.444445
y actual	3.000000	3.026446	3.094444	3.191716	3.310204	3.444444
error	0.000000%	−0.000004%	−0.000005%	−0.000005%	−0.000005%	−0.000004%

17.   With $h = 0.2$: $y(1) \approx 0.350258$
     With $h = 0.1$: $y(1) \approx 0.350234$
     With $h = 0.05$: $y(1) \approx 0.350232$
     With $h = 0.025$: $y(1) \approx 0.350232$

The table of numerical results is

x	y with h = 0.2	y with h = 0.1	y with h = 0.05	y with h = 0.025
0.0	0.000000	0.000000	0.000000	0.000000
0.2	0.002667	0.002667	0.002667	0.002667
0.4	0.021360	0.021359	0.021359	0.021359
0.6	0.072451	0.072448	0.072448	0.072448
0.8	0.174090	0.174081	0.174080	0.174080
1.0	0.350258	0.350234	0.350232	0.350232

In Problems 18-24 we give only the final approximate values of y obtained using the Runge-Kutta method with step sizes $h = 0.2$, $h = 0.1$, $h = 0.05$, and $h = 0.025$.

19. With $h = 0.2$: $y(2) \approx 6.411464$
     With $h = 0.1$: $y(2) \approx 6.411474$
     With $h = 0.05$: $y(2) \approx 6.411474$
     With $h = 0.025$: $y(2) \approx 6.411474$

21. With $h = 0.2$: $y(2) \approx 2.872467$
     With $h = 0.1$: $y(2) \approx 2.872468$
     With $h = 0.05$: $y(2) \approx 2.872468$
     With $h = 0.025$: $y(2) \approx 2.872468$

23. With $h = 0.2$: $y(1) \approx 1.230735$
     With $h = 0.1$: $y(1) \approx 1.230731$
     With $h = 0.05$: $y(1) \approx 1.230731$
     With $h = 0.025$: $y(1) \approx 1.230731$

In the solutions for Problems 25 and 26 we use the general MATLAB solver **ode** that was listed prior to the Problem 25 solution in Section 2.5. To use the Runge-Kutta method, we call as **'method'** the following function.

```
function [t,y] = rk(yp, t0,t1, y0)

%   [t, y] = rk(yp, t0, t1, y0)
%   Takes one Runge-Kutta step for
%
%        y' = yp( t,y ),
%
%   from t0  to  t1  with initial value  the
%   column vector  y0.
h = t1 - t0;
k1 = feval(yp, t0        , y0            );
k2 = feval(yp, t0 + h/2, y0 + (h/2)*k1 );
k3 = feval(yp, t0 + h/2, y0 + (h/2)*k2 );
```

```
k4 = feval(yp, t0 + h    ,y0 +     h *k3 );
k  = (1/6)*(k1 + 2*k2 + 2*k3 + k4);
t  = t1;
y  = y0 + h*k;
```

25.   Here our differential equation is described by the MATLAB function

```
function  vp = vpbolt1(t,v)
vp = -0.04*v - 9.8;
```

Then the commands

```
n = 100;
[t1,v1] = ode('rk','vpbolt1',0,10,49,n);
n = 200;
[t2,v] = ode('rk','vpbolt1',0,10,49,n);
t = (0:10)';
ve = 294*exp(-t/25)-245;
[t, v1(1:n/20:1+n/2), v(1:n/10:n+1), ve]
```

generate the table

t	with $n = 100$	with $n = 200$	actual v
0	49.0000	49.0000	49.0000
1	37.4721	37.4721	37.4721
2	26.3962	26.3962	26.3962
3	15.7546	15.7546	15.7546
4	5.5303	5.5303	5.5303
5	-4.2932	-4.2932	-4.2932
6	-13.7314	-13.7314	-13.7314
7	-22.7996	-22.7996	-22.7996
8	-31.5122	-31.5122	-31.5122
9	-39.8832	-39.8832	-39.8832
10	-47.9259	-47.9259	-47.9259

We notice first that the final three columns agree to the 4 displayed decimal places. Scanning the last column for sign changes in v, we suspect that $v = 0$ (at the bolt's apex) occurs just after $t = 4.5$ sec. Then interpolation between $t = 4.55$ and $t = 4.60$ in the table

```
[t2(91:95),v(91:95)]
```

```
4.5000     0.5694
4.5500     0.0788
4.6000    -0.4109
4.6500    -0.8996
4.7000    -1.3873
```

indicates that $t = 4.56$ at the bolt's apex. Now the commands

```
y = zeros(n+1,1);
h = 10/n;
for j = 2:n+1
   y(j) = y(j-1) + v(j-1)*h +
                  0.5*(-.04*v(j-1) - 9.8)*h^2;
end
ye = 7350*(1 - exp(-t/25)) - 245*t;
[t, y(1:n/10:n+1), ye]
```

generate the table

t	Approx y	Actual y
0	0	0
1	43.1974	43.1976
2	75.0945	75.0949
3	96.1342	96.1348
4	106.7424	106.7432
5	107.3281	107.3290
6	98.2842	98.2852
7	79.9883	79.9895
8	52.8032	52.8046
9	17.0775	17.0790
10	−26.8540	−26.8523

We see at least 2-decimal place agreement between approximate and actual values of y. Finally, interpolation between $t = 9$ and $t = 10$ here suggests that $y = 0$ just after $t = 9.4$. Then interpolation between $t = 9.40$ and $t = 9.45$ in the table

```
[t2(187:191),y(187:191)]
```

9.3000	4.7448
9.3500	2.6182
9.4000	0.4713
9.4500	−1.6957
9.5000	−3.8829

indicates that the bolt is aloft for about 9.41 seconds.

CHAPTER 3

LINEAR EQUATIONS OF HIGHER ORDER

SECTION 3.1

INTRODUCTION: SECOND-ORDER LINEAR EQUATIONS

In this section the central ideas of the theory of linear differential equations are introduced and illustrated concretely in the context of **second-order** equations. These key concepts include superposition of solutions (Theorem 1), existence and uniqueness of solutions (Theorem 2), linear independence, the Wronskian (Theorem 3), and general solutions (Theorem 4). This discussion of second-order equations serves as preparation for the treatment of nth order linear equations in Section 3.2. Although the concepts in this section may seem somewhat abstract to students, the problems set is quite tangible and largely computational.

In each of Problems 1-16 the verification that y_1 and y_2 satisfy the given differential equation is a routine matter. As in Example 2, we then impose the given initial conditions on the general solution $y = c_1 y_1 + c_2 y_2$. This yields two linear equations that determine the values of the constants c_1 and c_2.

1. Imposition of the initial conditions $y(0) = 0$, $y'(0) = 5$ on the general solution $y(x) = c_1 e^x + c_2 e^{-x}$ yields the two equations $c_1 + c_2 = 0$, $c_1 - c_2 = 0$ with solution $c_1 = 5/2$, $c_2 = -5/2$. Hence the desired particular solution is $y(x) = 5(e^x - e^{-x})/2$.

3. Imposition of the initial conditions $y(0) = 3$, $y'(0) = 8$ on the general solution $y(x) = c_1 \cos 2x + c_2 \sin 2x$ yields the two equations $c_1 = 3$, $2c_2 = 8$ with solution $c_1 = 3$, $c_2 = 4$. Hence the desired particular solution is $y(x) = 3 \cos 2x + 4 \sin 2x$.

5. Imposition of the initial conditions $y(0) = 1$, $y'(0) = 0$ on the general solution $y(x) = c_1 e^x + c_2 e^{2x}$ yields the two equations $c_1 + c_2 = 1$, $c_1 + 2c_2 = 0$ with solution $c_1 = 2$, $c_2 = -1$. Hence the desired particular solution is $y(x) = 2e^x - e^{2x}$.

7. Imposition of the initial conditions $y(0) = -2$, $y'(0) = 8$ on the general solution $y(x) = c_1 + c_2 e^{-x}$ yields the two equations $c_1 + c_2 = -2$, $-c_2 = 8$ with solution $c_1 = 6$, $c_2 = -8$. Hence the desired particular solution is $y(x) = 6 - 8e^{-x}$.

9. Imposition of the initial conditions $y(0) = 2$, $y'(0) = -1$ on the general solution $y(x) = c_1 e^{-x} + c_2 x e^{-x}$ yields the two equations $c_1 = 2$, $-c_1 + c_2 = -1$ with solution $c_1 = 2$, $c_2 = 1$. Hence the desired particular solution is $y(x) = 2e^{-x} + xe^{-x}$.

11. Imposition of the initial conditions $y(0) = 0$, $y'(0) = 5$ on the general solution $y(x) = c_1 e^x \cos x + c_2 e^x \sin x$ yields the two equations $c_1 = 0$, $c_1 + c_2 = 5$ with solution $c_1 = 0$, $c_2 = 5$. Hence the desired particular solution is $y(x) = 5e^x \sin x$.

13. Imposition of the initial conditions $y(1) = 3$, $y'(1) = 1$ on the general solution $y(x) = c_1 x + c_2 x^2$ yields the two equations $c_1 + c_2 = 3$, $c_1 + 2c_2 = 1$ with solution $c_1 = 5$, $c_2 = -2$. Hence the desired particular solution is $y(x) = 5x - 2x^2$.

15. Imposition of the initial conditions $y(1) = 7$, $y'(1) = 2$ on the general solution $y(x) = c_1 x + c_2 x \ln x$ yields the two equations $c_1 = 7$, $c_1 + c_2 = 2$ with solution $c_1 = 7$, $c_2 = -5$. Hence the desired particular solution is $y(x) = 7x - 5x \ln x$.

17. If $y = c/x$ then $y' + y^2 = -c/x^2 + c^2/x^2 = c(c-1)/x^2 \neq 0$ unless either $c = 0$ or $c = 1$.

19. If $y = 1 + \sqrt{x}$ then $yy'' + (y')^2 = (1 + \sqrt{x})(-x^{-3/2}/4) + (x^{-1/2}/2)^2 = -x^{-3/2}/4 \neq 0$.

21. Linearly independent, because $x^3 = +x^2|x|$ if $x > 0$, whereas $x^3 = -x^2|x|$ if $x < 0$.

23. Linearly independent, because $f(x) = +g(x)$ if $x > 0$, whereas $f(x) = -g(x)$ if $x < 0$.

25. $f(x) = e^x \sin x$ and $g(x) = e^x \cos x$ are linearly independent, because $f(x) = k\,g(x)$ would imply that $\sin x = k \cos x$, whereas $\sin x$ and $\cos x$ are linearly independent.

27. Let $L[y] = y'' + py' + qy$. Then $L[y_c] = 0$ and $L[y_p] = f$, so

$$L[y_c + y_p] = L[y_c] + [y_p] = 0 + f = f.$$

29. There is no contradiction because if the given differential equation is divided by x^2 to get the form in Equation (8) in the text, then the resulting functions $p(x) = -4/x$ and $q(x) = 6/x^2$ are not continuous at $x = 0$.

31. $W(y_1, y_2) = -2x$ vanishes at $x = 0$, whereas if y_1 and y_2 were (linearly independent) solutions of an equation $y'' + py' + qy = 0$ with p and q both continuous on an open interval I containing $x = 0$, then Theorem 3 would imply that $W \neq 0$ on I.

In Problems 33-42 we give the characteristic equation, its roots, and the corresponding general solution.

33. $r^2 - 3r + 2 = 0$; $r = 1, 2$; $y(x) = c_1 e^x + c_2 e^{2x}$

35. $r^2 + 5r = 0$; $r = 0, -5$; $y(x) = c_1 + c_2 e^{-5x}$

37. $2r^2 - r - 2 = 0$; $r = 1, -1/2$; $y(x) = c_1 e^{-x/2} + c_2 e^x$

39. $4r^2 + 4r + 1 = 0$; $r = -1/2, -1/2$; $y(x) = (c_1 + c_2 x)e^{-x/2}$

41. $6r^2 - 7r - 20 = 0$; $r = -4/3, 5/2$; $y(x) = c_1 e^{-4x/3} + c_2 e^{5x/2}$

In Problems 43-48 we first write and simplify the equation with the indicated characteristic roots, and then write the corresponding differential equation.

43. $(r - 0)(r + 10) = r^2 + 10r = 0$; $y'' + 10y' = 0$

45. $(r + 10)(r + 10) = r^2 + 20r + 100 = 0$; $y'' + 20y' + 100y = 0$

47. $(r - 0)(r - 0) = r^2 = 0$; $y'' = 0$

49. The solution curve with $y(0) = 1$, $y'(0) = 6$ is $y(x) = 8e^{-x} - 7e^{-2x}$. We find that $y'(x) = 0$ when $x = \ln(7/4)$ so $e^{-x} = 4/7$ and $e^{-2x} = 16/49$. It follows that $y(\ln(7/4)) = 16/7$, so the high point on the curve is $(\ln(7/4)), 16/7) \approx (0.56, 2.29)$, which looks consistent with Fig. 3.1.6.

SECTION 3.2

GENERAL SOLUTIONS OF LINEAR EQUATIONS

Students should check each of Theorems 1 through 4 in this section to see that, in the case $n = 2$, it reduces to the corresponding theorem in Section 3.1. Similarly, the computational problems for this section largely parallel those for the previous section. By the end of Section 3.2 students should understand that, although we do not prove the existence-uniqueness theorem now, it provides the basis for everything we do with linear differential equations.

The linear combinations listed in Problems 1-6 were discovered "by inspection" — that is, by trial and error.

1. $(5/2)(2x) + (-8/3)(3x^2) + (-1)(5x - 8x^2) = 0$

3. $(1)(0) + (0)(\sin x) + (0)(e^x) = 0$

5. $(1)(17) + (-34)(\cos^2 x) + (17)(\cos 2x) = 0$, because $2\cos^2 x = 1 + \cos 2x$.

7. $W = \begin{vmatrix} 1 & x & x^2 \\ 0 & 1 & 2x \\ 0 & 0 & 2 \end{vmatrix} = 2$ is nonzero everywhere.

9. $W = e^x(\cos^2 x + \sin^2 x) = e^x \neq 0$

11. $W = x^3 e^{2x}$ is nonzero if $x \neq 0$.

In each of Problems 13–20 we first form the general solution

$$y(x) = c_1 y_1(x) + c_2 y_2(x) + c_3 y_3(x),$$

then calculate $y'(x)$ and $y''(x)$, and finally impose the given initial conditions to determine the values of the coefficients c_1, c_2, c_3.

13.   Imposition of the initial conditions $y(0) = 1,\ y'(0) = 2,\ y''(0) = 0$ on the general solution $y(x) = c_1 e^x + c_2 e^{-x} + c_3 e^{-2x}$ yields the three equations

$$c_1 + c_2 + c_3 = 1, \quad c_1 - c_2 - 2c_3 = 2, \quad c_1 + c_2 + 4c_3 = 0$$

with solution $c_1 = 4/3,\ c_2 = 0,\ c_3 = -1/3$. Hence the desired particular solution is given by $y(x) = (4e^x - e^{-2x})/3$.

15.   Imposition of the initial conditions $y(0) = 2,\ y'(0) = 0,\ y''(0) = 0$ on the general solution $y(x) = c_1 e^x + c_2 x e^x + c_3 x^2 e^{3x}$ yields the three equations

$$c_1 = 2, \quad c_1 + c_2 = 0, \quad c_1 + 2c_2 + 2c_3 = 0$$

with solution $c_1 = 2,\ c_2 = -2,\ c_3 = 1$. Hence the desired particular solution is given by $y(x) = (2 - 2x + x^2)e^x$.

17.   Imposition of the initial conditions $y(0) = 3,\ y'(0) = -1,\ y''(0) = 2$ on the general solution $y(x) = c_1 + c_2 \cos 3x + c_3 \sin 3x$ yields the three equations

$$c_1 + c_2 = 3, \quad 3c_3 = -1, \quad -9c_2 = 2$$

with solution $c_1 = 29/9,\ c_2 = -2/9,\ c_3 = -1/3$. Hence the desired particular solution is given by $y(x) = (29 - 2\cos 3x - 3\sin 3x)/9$.

19. Imposition of the initial conditions $y(1) = 6$, $y'(1) = 14$, $y''(1) = 22$ on the general solution $y(x) = c_1 x + c_2 x^2 + c_3 x^3$ yields the three equations

$$c_1 + c_2 + c_3 = 6, \qquad c_1 + 2c_2 + 3c_3 = 14, \qquad 2c_2 + 6c_3 = 22$$

with solution $c_1 = 1$, $c_2 = 2$, $c_3 = 3$. Hence the desired particular solution is given by $y(x) = x + 2x^2 + 3x^3$.

In each of Problems 21–24 we first form the general solution

$$y(x) = y_c(x) + y_p(x) = c_1 y_1(x) + c_2 y_2(x) + y_p(x),$$

then calculate $y'(x)$, and finally impose the given initial conditions to determine the values of the coefficients c_1 and c_2.

21. Imposition of the initial conditions $y(0) = 2$, $y'(0) = -2$ on the general solution $y(x) = c_1 \cos x + c_2 \sin x + 3x$ yields the two equations $c_1 = 2$, $c_2 + 3 = -2$ with solution $c_1 = 2$, $c_2 = -5$. Hence the desired particular solution is given by $y(x) = 2 \cos x - 5 \sin x + 3x$.

23. Imposition of the initial conditions $y(0) = 3$, $y'(0) = 11$ on the general solution $y(x) = c_1 e^{-x} + c_2 e^{3x} - 2$ yields the two equations $c_1 + c_2 - 2 = 3$, $-c_1 + 3c_2 = 11$ with solution $c_1 = 1$, $c_2 = 4$. Hence the desired particular solution is given by $y(x) = e^{-x} + 4e^{3x} - 2$.

25. $L[y] = L[y_1 + y_2] = L[y_1] + L[y_2] = f + g$

27. The equations

$$c_1 + c_2 x + c_3 x^2 = 0, \qquad c_2 + 2c_3 x + 0, \qquad 2c_3 = 0$$

(the latter two obtained by successive differentiation of the first one) evidently imply — by substituting $x = 0$ — that $c_1 = c_2 = c_3 = 0$.

29. If $c_0 e^{rx} + c_1 x e^{rx} + \cdots + c_n x^n e^{rx} = 0$, then division by e^{rx} yields

$$c_0 + c_1 x + \cdots + c_n x^n = 0,$$

so the result of Problem 28 applies.

31. **(a)** Substitution of $x = a$ in the differential equation gives $y''(a) = -p\, y'(a) - q(a)$.

(b) If $y(0) = 1$ and $y'(0) = 0$, then the equation $y'' - 2y' - 5y = 0$ implies that $y''(0) = 2y'(0) + 5y(0) = 5$.

33.   This follows from the fact that

$$\begin{vmatrix} 1 & 1 & 1 \\ a & b & c \\ a^2 & b^2 & c^2 \end{vmatrix} = (b-a)(c-b)(c-a).$$

SECTION 3.3

HOMOGENEOUS EQUATIONS WITH CONSTANT COEFFICIENTS

This is a purely computational section devoted to the single most widely applicable type of higher order differential equations — linear ones with constant coefficients. In Problems 1-20, we write first the characteristic equation and its list of roots, then the corresponding general solution of the given differential equation. Explanatory comments are included only when the solution of the characteristic equation is not routine.

1. $r^2 - 4 = (r-2)(r+2) = 0;$ $r = -2, 2;$ $y(x) = c_1 e^{2x} + c_2 e^{-2x}$

3. $r^2 + 3r - 10 = (r+5)(r-2) = 0;$ $r = -5, 2;$ $y(x) = c_1 e^{2x} + c_2 e^{-5x}$

5. $r^2 + 6r + 9 = (r+3)^2 = 0;$ $r = -3, -3;$ $y(x) = c_1 e^{-3x} + c_2 x e^{-3x}$

7. $4r^2 - 12r + 9 = (2r-3)^2 = 0;$ $r = -3/2, -3/2;$ $y(x) = c_1 e^{3x/2} + c_2 x e^{3x/2}$

9. $r^2 + 8r + 25 = 0;$ $r = \left(-8 \pm \sqrt{-36}\right)/2 = -4 \pm 3i;$ $y(x) = e^{-4x}(c_1 \cos 3x + c_2 \sin 3x)$

11. $r^4 - 8r^3 + 16r^2 = r^2(r-4)^2 = 0;$ $r = 0, 0, 4, 4;$ $y(x) = c_1 + c_2 x + c_3 e^{4x} + c_4 x e^{4x}$

13. $9r^3 + 12r^2 + 4r = r(3r+2)^2 = 0;$ $r = 0, -2/3, -2/3$
$y(x) = c_1 + c_2 e^{-2x/3} + c_3 x e^{-2x/3}$

15. $4r^4 - 8r^2 + 16 = (r^2 - 4)^2 = (r-2)^2(r+2)^2 = 0;$ $r = 2, 2, -2, -2$
$y(x) = c_1 e^{2x} + c_2 x e^{2x} + c_3 e^{-2x} + c_4 x e^{-2x}$

17. $6r^4 + 11r^2 + 4 = (2r^2 + 1)(3r^2 + 4) = 0;$ $r = \pm i/\sqrt{2}, \pm 2i/\sqrt{3},$

$$y(x) = c_1 \cos(x/\sqrt{2}) + c_2 \sin(x/\sqrt{2}) + c_3 \cos(2x/\sqrt{3}) + c_4 \sin(2x/\sqrt{3})$$

19. $r^3 + r^2 - r - 1 = r(r^2 - 1) + (r^2 - 1) = (r-1)(r+1)^2 = 0; \quad r = 1, -1, -1;$

$$y(x) = c_1 e^x + c_2 e^{-x} + c_3 x e^{-x}$$

21. Imposition of the initial conditions $y(0) = 7$, $y'(0) = 11$ on the general solution $y(x) = c_1 e^x + c_2 e^{3x}$ yields the two equations $c_1 + c_2 = 7$, $c_1 + 3c_2 = 11$ with solution $c_1 = 5$, $c_2 = 2$. Hence the desired particular solution is $y(x) = 5e^x + 2e^{3x}$.

23. Imposition of the initial conditions $y(0) = 3$, $y'(0) = 1$ on the general solution $y(x) = e^{3x}(c_1 \cos 4x + c_2 \sin 4x)$ yields the two equations $c_1 = 3$, $3c_1 + 4c_2 = 1$ with solution $c_1 = 3$, $c_2 = -2$. Hence the desired particular solution is $y(x) = e^{3x}(3 \cos 4x - 2 \sin 4x)$.

25. Imposition of the initial conditions $y(0) = -1$, $y'(0) = 0$, $y''(0) = 1$ on the general solution $y(x) = c_1 + c_2 x + c_3 e^{-2x/3}$ yields the three equations

$$c_1 + c_3 = -1, \quad c_2 - 2c_3/3 = 0, \quad 4c_3/9 = 1$$

with solution $c_1 = -13/4$, $c_2 = 3/2$, $c_3 = 9/4$. Hence the desired particular solution is $y(x) = (-13 + 6x + 9e^{-2x/3})/4$.

27. First we spot the root $r = 1$. Then long division of the polynomial $r^3 + 3r^2 - 4$ by $r - 1$ yields the quadratic factor $r^2 + 4r + 4 = (r+2)^2$ with roots $r = -2, -2$. Hence the general solution is $y(x) = c_1 e^x + c_2 e^{-2x} + c_3 x e^{-2x}$.

29. First we spot the root $r = -3$. Then long division of the polynomial $r^3 + 27$ by $r + 3$ yields the quadratic factor $r^2 - 3r + 9$ with roots $r = 3(1 \pm i\sqrt{3})/2$. Hence the general solution is $y(x) = c_1 e^{-3x} + e^{3x/2}[c_2 \cos(3x\sqrt{3}/2) + c_3 \sin(3x\sqrt{3}/2)]$.

31. The characteristic equation $r^3 + 3r^2 + 4r - 8 = 0$ has the evident root $r = 1$, and long division then yields the quadratic factor $r^2 + 4r + 8 = (r+2)^2 + 4$ corresponding to the complex conjugate roots $-2 \pm 2i$. Hence the general solution is

$$y(x) = c_1 e^x + e^{-2x}(c_2 \cos 2x + c_3 \sin 2x).$$

33. Knowing that $y = e^{3x}$ is one solution, we divide the characteristic polynomial $r^3 + 3r^2 - 54$ by $r - 3$ and get the quadratic factor

$$r^2 + 6r + 18 = (r+3)^2 + 9.$$

Hence the general solution is $y(x) = c_1e^{3x} + e^{-3x}(c_2\cos 3x + c_3\sin 3x)$.

35. The fact that $y = \cos 2x$ is one solution tells us that $r^2 + 4$ is a factor of the characteristic polynomial

$$6r^4 + 5r^3 + 25r^2 + 20r + 4.$$

Then long division yields the quadratic factor $6r^2 + 5r + 1 = (3r+1)(2r+1)$ with roots $r = -1/2, -1/3$. Hence the general solution is

$$y(x) = c_1e^{-x/2} + c_2e^{-x/3} + c_3\cos 2x + c_4\sin 2x$$

37. The characteristic equation is $r^4 - r^3 = r^3(r-1) = 0$, so the general solution is $y(x) = A + Bx + Cx^2 + De^x$. Imposition of the given initial conditions yields the equations

$$A + D = 18, \quad B + D = 12, \quad 2C + D = 13, \quad D = 7$$

with solution $A = 11$, $B = 5$, $C = 3$, $D = 7$. Hence the desired particular solution is

$$y(x) = 11 + 5x + 3x^2 + 7e^x.$$

39. $(r-2)^3 = r^3 - 6r^2 + 12r - 8$, so the differential equation is

$$y''' - 6y'' + 12y' - 8y = 0.$$

41. $(r^2 + 4)(r^2 - 4) = r^4 - 16$, so the differential equation is $y^{(4)} - 16y = 0$.

45. The characteristic polynomial is the quadratic polynomial of Problem 44(b). Hence the general solution is

$$y(x) = c_1e^{-ix} + c_2e^{3ix} = c_1(\cos x - i\sin x) + c_2(\cos 3x + i\sin 3x).$$

47. The characteristic roots are $r = \pm\sqrt{-2 + 2i\sqrt{3}} = \pm(1 + i\sqrt{3})$ so the general solution is

$$y(x) = c_1e^{(1+i\sqrt{3})x} + c_2e^{-(1+i\sqrt{3})x} = c_1e^x\left(\cos\sqrt{3}\,x + i\sin\sqrt{3}\,x\right) + c_2e^{-x}\left(\cos\sqrt{3}\,x - i\sin\sqrt{3}\,x\right)$$

49. The general solution is $y = Ae^{2x} + Be^{-x} + C\cos x + D\sin x$. Imposition of the given initial conditions yields the equations

$$A + B + C \qquad = 0$$
$$2A - B \qquad + D = 0$$
$$4A + B - C \qquad = 0$$
$$8A - B \qquad - D = 30$$

that we solve for $A = 2$, $B = -5$, $C = 3$, and $D = -9$. Thus

$$y(x) = 2e^{2x} - 5e^{-x} + 3 \cos x - 9 \sin x.$$

SECTION 3.4

Mechanical Vibrations

In this section we discuss four types of free motion of a mass on a spring — undamped, underdamped, critically damped, and overdamped. However, the undamped and underdamped cases — in which actual oscillations occur — are emphasized because they are both the most interesting and the most important cases for applications.

1. Frequency: $\omega_0 = \sqrt{k/m} = \sqrt{16/4} = 2$ rad/sec $= 1/\pi$ Hz
Period: $P = 2\pi/\omega_0 = 2\pi/2 = \pi$ sec

3. The spring constant is $k = 15$ N/0.20 m $= 75$ N/m. The solution of $3x'' + 75x = 0$ with $x(0) = 0$ and $x'(0) = -10$ is $x(t) = -2 \sin 5t$. Thus the amplitude is 2 m; the frequency is $\omega_0 = \sqrt{k/m} = \sqrt{75/3} = 5$ rad/sec $= 2.5/\pi$ Hz ; and the period is $2\pi/5$ sec.

5. The gravitational acceleration at distance R from the center of the earth is $g = GM/R^2$. According to Equation (6) in the text the (circular) frequency ω of a pendulum is given by $\omega^2 = g/L = GM/R^2L$, so its period is $p = 2\pi/\omega = 2\pi R\sqrt{L/GM}$.

7. The period equation $p = 3960\sqrt{100.10} = (3960 + x)\sqrt{100}$ yields $x \approx 1.9795$ mi $\approx$ 10,450 ft for the altitude of the mountain.

11. The fact that the buoy weighs 100 lb means that $mg = 100$ so $m = 100/32$ slugs. The weight of water is 62.4 lb/ft^3, so the $F = ma$ equation of Problem 10 is

$$(100/32)x'' = 100 - 62.4\pi r^2 x.$$

It follows that the buoy's circular frequency ω is given by

$$\omega^2 = (32)(62.4\pi)r^2/100.$$

But the fact that the buoy's period is $p = 2.5$ sec means that $\omega = 2\pi/2.5$. Equating these two results yields $r \approx 0.3173$ ft ≈ 3.8 in.

13. **(a)** The characteristic equation $10r^2 + 9r + 2 = (5r+2)(2r+1) = 0$ has roots $r = -2/5, -1/2$. When we impose the initial conditions $x(0) = 0$, $x'(0) = 5$ on the general solution $x(t) = c_1 e^{-2t/5} + c_2 e^{-t/2}$ we get the particular solution

$$x(t) = 50\left(e^{-2t/5} - e^{-t/2}\right).$$

(b) The derivative $x'(t) = 25e^{-t/2} - 20e^{-2t/5} = 5e^{-2t/5}\left(5e^{-t/10} - 4\right) = 0$ when $t = 10\ln(5/4) \approx 2.23144$. Hence the mass's farthest distance to the right is given by $x(10\ln(5/4)) = 512/125 = 4.096$.

15. The characteristic equation $(1/2)r^2 + 3r + 4 = 0$ has roots $r = -2, -4$. When we impose the initial conditions $x(0) = 2$, $x'(0) = 0$ on the general solution $x(t) = c_1 e^{-2t} + c_2 e^{-4t}$ we get the particular solution $x(t) = 4e^{-2t} - 2e^{-4t}$ that describes overdamped motion.

17. The characteristic equation $r^2 + 8r + 16 = 0$ has roots $r = -4, -4$. When we impose the initial conditions $x(0) = 5$, $x'(0) = -10$ on the general solution $x(t) = (c_1 + c_2 t)e^{-4t}$ we get the particular solution $x(t) = (5 + 10t)e^{-4t}$ that describes critically damped motion.

19. The characteristic equation $4r^2 + 20r + 169 = 0$ has roots $r = -5/2 \pm 6i$. When we impose the initial conditions $x(0) = 4$, $x'(0) = 16$ on the general solution $x(t) = e^{-5t/2}\left(A\cos 6t + B\sin 6t\right)$ we get the particular solution

$$x(t) = e^{-5t/2}[4\cos 6t + (13/3)\sin 2t] \approx (1/3)\sqrt{313}\, e^{-5t/2}\cos(6t - 0.8254)$$

that describes underdamped motion.

21. The characteristic equation $r^2 + 10r + 125 = 0$ has roots $r = -5 \pm 10i$. When we impose the initial conditions $x(0) = 6$, $x'(0) = 50$ on the general solution $x(t) = e^{-5t}\left(A\cos 10t + B\sin 10t\right)$ we get the particular solution

$$x(t) = e^{-5t}(6\cos 10t + 8\sin 10t) \approx 10\, e^{-5t}\cos(10t - 0.9273)$$

that describes underdamped motion.

23. **(a)** With $m = 100$ slugs we get $\omega = \sqrt{k/100}$. But we are given that

$$\omega = (80 \text{ cycles/min})(2\pi)(1 \text{ min/60 sec}) = 8\pi/3,$$

and equating the two values yields $k \approx 7018$ lb/ft.

(b)   With $\omega_1 = 2\pi(78/60)$ sec^{-1}, Equation (21) in the text yields $c \approx 372.31$ lb/(ft/sec). Hence $p = c/2m \approx 1.8615$. Finally $e^{-pt} = 0.01$ gives $t \approx 2.47$ sec.

31.   The binomial series

$$(1+x)^\alpha = 1 + \alpha x + \frac{\alpha(\alpha-1)}{2!}x^2 + \frac{\alpha(\alpha-1)(\alpha-2)}{3!}x^3 + \cdots$$

converges if $|x| < 1$. (See, for instance, Section 11.8 of Edwards and Penney, *Calculus with Analytic Geometry*, 5th edition, Prentice Hall, 1998.) With $\alpha = 1/2$ and $x = -c^2/4mk$ in Eq. (21) of Section 3.4 in this text, the binomial series gives

$$\omega_1 = \sqrt{\omega_0^2 - p^2} = \sqrt{\frac{k}{m} - \frac{c^2}{4m^2}} = \sqrt{\frac{k}{m}}\sqrt{1 - \frac{c^2}{4mk}}$$

$$= \sqrt{\frac{k}{m}}\left(1 - \frac{c^2}{8mk} - \frac{c^4}{128m^2k^2} - \cdots\right) \approx \omega_0\left(1 - \frac{c^2}{8mk}\right).$$

33.   If $x_1 = x(t_1)$ and $x_2 = x(t_2)$ are two successive local maxima, then $\omega_1 t_2 = \omega_1 t_1 + 2\pi$ so

$$x_1 = C\exp(-pt_1)\cos(\omega_1 t_1 - \alpha),$$

$$x_2 = C\exp(-pt_2)\cos(\omega_1 t_2 - \alpha) = C\exp(-pt_2)\cos(\omega_1 t_1 - \alpha).$$

Hence $x_1/x_2 = \exp[-p(t_1 - t_2)]$, and therefore

$$\ln(x_1/x_2) = -p(t_1 - t_2) = 2\pi p/\omega_1.$$

35.   The characteristic equation $r^2 + 2r + 1 = 0$ has roots $r = -1, -1$. When we impose the initial conditions $x(0) = 0$, $x'(1) = 0$ on the general solution $x(t) = (c_1 + c_2 t)e^{-t}$ we get the particular solution $x_1(t) = te^{-t}$.

37.   The characteristic equation $r^2 + 2r + (1 + 10^{-2n}) = 0$ has roots $r = -1 \pm 10^{-n}i$. When we impose the initial conditions $x(0) = 0$, $x'(1) = 0$ on the general solution

$$x(t) = e^{-t}\left[A\cos\left(10^{-n}t\right) + B\sin\left(10^{-n}t\right)\right]$$

we get the equations $c_1 = 0$, $-c_1 + 10^{-n}c_2 = 1$ with solution $c_1 = 0$, $c_2 = 10^n$. This gives the particular solution $x_3(t) = 10^n e^{-t}\sin(10^{-n}t)$.

SECTION 3.5

NONHOMOGENEOUS EQUATIONS AND
THE METHOD OF UNDETERMINED COEFFICIENTS

The method of undetermined coefficients is based on "educated guessing". If we can guess correctly the **form** of a particular solution of a nonhomogeneous linear equation with constant coefficients, then we can determine the particular solution explicitly by substitution in the given differential equation. It is pointed out at the end of Section 3.5 that this simple approach is not always successful — in which case the method of variation of parameters is available if a complementary function is known. However, undetermined coefficients *does* turn out to work well with a surprisingly large number of the nonhomogeneous linear differential equations that arise in elementary scientific applications.

In each of Problems 1-20 we give first the form of the trial solution y_{trial}, then the equations in the coefficients we get when we substitute y_{trial} into the differential equation and collect like terms, and finally the resulting particular solution y_p.

1. $y_{\text{trial}} = A e^{3x}$; $25A = 1$; $y_p = (1/25)e^{3x}$

3. $y_{\text{trial}} = A\cos 3x + B\sin 3x$; $-15A - 3B = 0,\ 3A - 15B = 2$;
$y_p = (\cos 3x - 5\sin 3x)/39$

5.   First we substitute $\sin^2 x = (1 - \cos 2x)/2$ on the right-hand side of the differential equation. Then:

$y_{\text{trial}} = A + B\cos 2x + C\sin 2x$, $A = 1/2,\ -3B + 2C = -1/2,\ -2B - 3C = 0$;
$y_p = (13 + 3\cos 2x - 2\sin 2x)/26$

7.   First we substitute $\sinh x = (e^x - e^{-x})/2$ on the right-hand side of the differential equation. Then:

$y_{\text{trial}} = A e^x + B e^{-x}$; $-3A = 1/2,\ -3B = -1/2$; $y_p = (e^{-x} - e^x)/6 = -(1/3)\sinh x$

9.   First we note that e^x is part of the complementary function $y_c = c_1 e^x + c_2 e^{-3x}$. Then:

$y_{\text{trial}} = A + x(B + Cx)e^x$; $-3A = 0,\ 4B + 2C = 0,\ 8C = 1$;
$y_p = -(1/3) + (2x^2 - x)e^x/16$.

11.   First we note the duplication with the complementary function

$y_c = c_1 x + c_2\cos 2x + c_3\sin 2x$. Then:

$y_{\text{trial}} = x(A + Bx)$; $4A = -1,\ 8B = 3$; $y_p = (3x^2 - 2x)/8$

13. $y_{trial} = e^x(A\cos x + B\sin x);$ $7A + 4B = 0,\ -4A + 7B = 1;$
  $y_p = e^x(7\sin x - 4\cos x)/65$

15. This is something of a trick problem. We cannot solve the characteristic equation $r^5 + 5r^4 - 1 = 0$ to find the complementary function, but we can see that it contains no constant term (why?). Hence the trial solution $y_{trial} = A$ leads immediately to the particular solution $y_p = -17$.

17. First we note the duplication with the complementary function $y_c = c_1\cos x + c_2\sin x$. Then:

$$y_{trial} = x[(A + Bx)\cos x + (C + Dx)\sin x];$$
$$2B + 2C = 0,\ 4D = 1, -2A + 2D = 1, -4B = 0;$$
$$y_p = (x^2\sin x - x\cos x)/4$$

19. First we note the duplication with the part $c_1 + c_2x$ of the complementary function (which corresponds to the factor r^2 of the characteristic polynomial). Then:

$$y_{trial} = x^2(A + Bx + Cx^2);\qquad 4A + 12B = -1,\ 12B + 48C = 0,\ 24C = 3;$$
$$y_p = (10x^2 - 4x^3 + x^4)/8$$

In Problems 21-30 we list first the complementary function y_c, then the initially proposed trial function y_i, and finally the actual trial function y_p in which duplication with the complementary function has been eliminated.

21. $y_c = e^x(c_1\cos x + c_2\sin x);$ $y_i = e^x(A\cos x + B\sin x)$
  $y_p = x \cdot e^x(A\cos x + B\sin x)$

23. $y_c = c_1\cos x + c_2\sin x;$ $y_i = (A + Bx)\cos 2x + (C + Dx)\sin 2x$
  $y_p = x \cdot [(A + Bx)\cos 2x + (C + Dx)\sin 2x]$

25. $y_c = c_1 e^{-x} + c_2 e^{-2x};$ $y_i = (A + Bx)e^{-x} + (C + Dx)e^{-2x}$
  $y_p = x \cdot (A + Bx)e^{-x} + x \cdot (C + Dx)e^{-2x}$

27. $y_c = (c_1\cos x + c_2\sin x) + (c_3\cos 2x + c_3\sin 2x)$
  $y_i = (A\cos x + B\sin x) + (C\cos 2x + D\sin 2x)$
  $y_p = x \cdot [(A\cos x + B\sin x) + (C\cos 2x + D\sin 2x)]$

29. $y_c = (c_1 + c_2x + c_3x^2)e^x + c_4 e^{2x} + c_5 e^{-2x};$ $y_i = (A + Bx)e^x + C e^{2x} + D e^{-2x}$

$$y_p = x^3 \cdot (A + Bx)e^x + x \cdot (Ce^{2x}) + x \cdot (De^{-2x})$$

In Problems 31-40 we list first the complementary function y_c, the trial solution y_{tr} for the method of undetermined coefficients, and the corresponding general solution $y_g = y_c + y_p$ where y_p results from determining the coefficients in y_{tr} so as to satisfy the given nonhomogeneous differential equation. Then we list the linear equations obtained by imposing the given initial conditions, and finally the resulting particular solution $y(x)$.

31. $y_c = c_1 \cos 2x + c_2 \sin 2x;$ $y_{tr} = A + Bx;$ $y_g = c_1 \cos 2x + c_2 \sin 2x + x/2 ;$

$c_1 = 1, \quad 2c_2 + 1/2 = 2; \quad y(x) = \cos 2x + (3/4)\sin 2x + x/2$

33. $y_c = c_1 \cos 3x + c_2 \sin 3x;$ $y_{tr} = A\cos 2x + B\sin 2x$

$y_g = c_1 \cos 3x + c_2 \sin 3x + (1/5)\sin 2x$

$c_1 = 1, \quad 3c_2 + 2/5 = 0; \quad y(x) = (15\cos 3x - 2\sin 3x + 3\sin 2x)/15$

35. $y_c = e^x (c_1 \cos x + c_2 \sin x);$ $y_{tr} = A + Bx$

$y_g = e^x (c_1 \cos x + c_2 \sin x) + 1 + x/2$

$c_1 + 1 = 3, \quad c_1 + c_2 + 1/2 = 0; \quad y(x) = e^x (4\cos x - 5\sin x)/2 + 1 + x/2$

37. $y_c = c_1 + c_2 e^x + c_3 x e^x;$ $y_{tr} = x \cdot (A) + x^2 \cdot (B + Cx)e^x$

$y_g = c_1 + c_2 e^x + c_3 x e^x + x - x^2 e^x /2 + x^3 e^x /6$

$c_1 + c_2 = 0, \quad c_2 + c_3 + 1 = 0, \quad c_2 + 2c_3 - 1 = 1$

$y(x) = 4 + x + e^x (-24 + 18x - 3x^2 + x^3)/6$

39. $y_c = c_1 + c_2 x + c_3 e^{-x};$ $y_{tr} = x^2 \cdot (A + Bx) + x \cdot (Ce^{-x})$

$y_g = c_1 + c_2 x + c_3 e^{-x} - x^2 /2 + x^3 /6 + xe^{-x}$

$c_1 + c_3 = 1, \quad c_2 - c_3 + 1 = 0, \quad c_3 - 3 = 1$

$y(x) = (-18 + 18x - 3x^2 + x^3)/6 + (4 + x)e^{-x}$

41.   The trial solution $y_{tr} = A + Bx + Cx^2 + Dx^3 + Ex^4 + Fx^5$ leads to the equations

$$2A - B - 2C - 6D + 24E = 0$$
$$-2B - 2C - 6D - 24E + 120F = 0$$
$$-2C - 3D - 12E - 60F = 0$$
$$-2D - 4E - 20F = 0$$
$$-2E - 5F = 0$$
$$-2F = 8$$

that are readily solve by back-substitution. The resulting particular solution is

$$y(x) = -255 - 450x + 30x^2 + 20x^3 + 10x^4 - 4x^5$$

43. **(a)** $\cos 3x + i \sin 3x = (\cos x + i \sin x)^3$
$$= \cos^3 x + 3i \cos^2 x \sin x - 3 \cos x \sin^2 x - i \sin^3 x$$

When we equate real parts we get the equation

$$\cos^3 x - 3(\cos x)(1 - \cos^2 x) = 4 \cos^3 x - 3 \cos x$$

and readily solve for $\cos^3 x = \frac{3}{4} \cos x + \frac{1}{4} \cos 3x$. The formula for $\sin^3 x$ is derived similarly by equating imaginary parts in the first equation above.

(b) Upon substituting the trial solution $y_p = A \cos x + B \sin x + C \cos 3x + D \sin 3x$ in the differential equation $y'' + 4y = \frac{3}{4} \cos x + \frac{1}{4} \cos 3x$, we find that $A = 1/4, B = 0$, $C = -1/20, D = 0$. The resulting general solution is

$$y(x) = c_1 \cos 2x + c_2 \sin 2x + (1/4)\cos x - (1/20)\cos 3x.$$

45. We substitute

$$\sin^4 x = (1 - \cos 2x)^2 / 4$$
$$= (1 - 2\cos 2x + \cos^2 2x)/4 = (3 - 4\cos 2x + \cos 4x)/8$$

on the right-hand side of the differential equation, and then substitute the trial solution $y_p = A\cos 2x + B\sin 2x + C\cos 4x + D\sin 4x + E$. We find that $A = -1/10, B = 0$, $C = -1/56, D = 0, E = 1/24$. The resulting general solution is

$$y = c_1 \cos 3x + c_2 \sin 3x + 1/24 - (1/10)\cos 2x - (1/56)\cos 4x.$$

In Problems 47-49 we list the independent solutions y_1 and y_2 of the associated homogeneous equation, their Wronskian $W = W(y_1, y_2)$, the coefficient functions

$$u_1(x) = -\int \frac{y_2(x)f(x)}{W(x)}\,dx \quad \text{and} \quad u_2(x) = \int \frac{y_1(x)f(x)}{W(x)}\,dx$$

in the particular solution $y_p = u_1 y_1 + u_2 y_2$ of Eq. (32) in the text, and finally y_p itself.

47. $\quad y_1 = e^{-2x}, \qquad\qquad y_2 = e^{-x}, \qquad\qquad W = e^{-3x}$

$\quad\quad u_1 = -(4/3)e^{3x}, \qquad u_2 = 2e^{2x},$

$\quad\quad y_p = (2/3)e^{x}$

49. $\quad y_1 = e^{2x}, \qquad\qquad y_2 = xe^{2x}, \qquad\qquad W = e^{4x}$

$\quad\quad u_1 = -x^2, \qquad\qquad u_2 = 2x,$

$\quad\quad y_p = x^2 e^{2x}$

51. $\quad y_1 = \cos 2x, \qquad y_2 = \sin 2x, \qquad W = 2$

Liberal use of trigonometric sum and product identities yields

$\quad\quad u_1 = (\cos 5x - 5\cos x)/20, \qquad u_1 = (\sin 5x - 5\sin x)/20$

$\quad\quad y_p = -(1/4)(\cos 2x \cos x - \sin 2x \sin x) + (1/20)(\cos 5x \cos 2x + \sin 5x \sin 2x)$

$\quad\quad\quad = -(1/5)\cos 3x \ \ (!)$

53. $\quad y_1 = \cos 3x, \qquad\qquad y_2 = \sin 3x, \qquad\qquad W = 3$

$\quad\quad u_1' = -(2/3)\tan 3x, \qquad\qquad u_2' = 2/3$

$\quad\quad y_p = (2/9)[3x \sin 3x + (\cos 3x)\ln|\cos 3x|]$

55. $\quad y_1 = \cos 2x, \qquad\qquad y_2 = \sin 2x, \qquad\qquad W = 2$

$\quad\quad u_1' = -(1/2)\sin^2 x \sin 2x = -(1/4)(1 - \cos 2x)\sin 2x$

$\quad\quad u_2' = (1/2)\sin^2 x \cos 2x = (1/4)(1 - \cos 2x)\cos 2x$

$\quad\quad y_p = (1 - x\sin 2x)/8$

57. With $y_1 = x$, $y_2 = x^{-1}$, and $f(x) = 72x^3$, Equations (31) in the text take the form

$$x u_1' + x^{-1} u_2' = 0,$$
$$u_1' - x^{-2} u_2' = 72x^3.$$

Upon multiplying the second equation by x and then adding, we readily solve first for

$$u_1' = 36x^3, \quad \text{so} \quad u_1 = 9x^4$$

and then

$$u_2' = -x^2 u_1' = -36x^5, \quad \text{so} \quad u_2 = -6x^6.$$

Then it follows that

$$y_p = y_1 u_1 + y_2 u_2 = (x)(9x^4) + (x^{-1})(-6x^6) = 3x^5.$$

59. $y_1 = x^2,$ $y_2 = x^2 \ln x,$

$W = x^3,$ $f(x) = x^2$

$u_1' = -x \ln x,$ $u_2' = x$

$y_p = x^4/4$

61. $y_1 = \cos(\ln x),$ $y_2 = \sin(\ln x),$ $W = 1/x,$

$f(x) = (\ln x)/x^2$

$u_1 = (\ln x)\cos(\ln x) - \sin(\ln x)$

$u_2 = (\ln x)\sin(\ln x) + \cos(\ln x)$

$y_p = \ln x$ (!)

63.   This is simply a matter of solving the equations in (31) for the derivatives

$$u_1' = -\frac{y_2(x)f(x)}{W(x)} \quad \text{and} \quad u_2' = \frac{y_1(x)f(x)}{W(x)},$$

integrating each, and then substituting the results in (32).

SECTION 3.6

FORCED OSCILLATIONS AND RESONANCE

1.   Trial of $x = A \cos 2t$ yields the particular solution $x_p = 2 \cos 2t$. (Can you see that — because the differential equation contains no first-derivative term — there is no need to include a $\sin 2t$ term in the trial solution?) Hence the general solution is

$$x(t) = c_1 \cos 3t + c_2 \sin 3t + 2 \cos 2t.$$

The initial conditions imply that $c_1 = -2$ and $c_2 = 0$, so $x(t) = 2 \cos 2t - 2 \cos 3t$.

3.   First we apply the method of undetermined coefficients — with trial solution

$x = A\cos 5t + B\sin 5t$ — to find the particular solution

$$x_p = (3/15)\cos 5t + (4/15)\sin 5t$$

$$= \frac{1}{3}\left[\frac{3}{5}\cos 5t + \frac{4}{5}\sin 5t\right] = \frac{1}{3}\cos(5t - \beta)$$

where $\beta = \tan^{-1}(4/3) \approx 0.9273$. Hence the general solution is

$$x(t) = c_1\cos 10t + c_2\sin 10t + (3/15)\cos 5t + (4/15)\sin 5t.$$

The initial conditions $x(0) = 25$, $x'(0) = 0$ now yield $c_1 = 372/15$ and $c_2 = -2/15$, so the part of the solution with frequency $\omega = 10$ is

$$x_c = (1/15)(372\cos 10t - 2\sin 10t) =$$

$$= \frac{\sqrt{138388}}{15}\left[\frac{372}{\sqrt{138388}}\cos 10t - \frac{2}{\sqrt{138388}}\sin 10t\right]$$

$$= \frac{\sqrt{138388}}{15}\cos(10t - \alpha)$$

where $\alpha = 2\pi - \tan^{-1}(1/186) \approx 6.2778$ is a fourth-quadrant angle.

5.   Substitution of the trial solution $x = C\cos\omega t$ gives $C = F_0/(k - m\omega^2)$. Then imposition of the initial conditions $x(0) = x_0$, $x'(0) = 0$ on the general solution

$$x(t) = c_1\cos\omega_0 t + c_2\sin\omega_0 t + C\cos\omega t \quad \text{(where } \omega_0 = \sqrt{k/m}\text{)}$$

gives the particular solution $x(t) = (x_0 - C)\cos\omega_0 t + C\cos\omega t$.

In Problems 7-10 we give first the trial solution x_p involving undetermined coefficients A and B, then the equations that determine these coefficients, and finally the resulting steady periodic solution x_{sp}.

7. $x_p = A\cos 3t + B\sin 3t;$ $-5A + 12B = 0,$ $12A + 5B = 0$

$$x_{sp}(t) = -\frac{50}{169}\cos 3t + \frac{120}{169}\sin 3t = \frac{10}{13}\left(-\frac{5}{13}\cos 3t + \frac{12}{13}\sin 3t\right) = \frac{10}{13}\cos(3t - \alpha)$$

$\alpha = \pi - \tan^{-1}(12/5) \approx 1.9656$ (2nd quadrant angle)

9. $x_p = A\cos 10t + 10\sin 5t;$ $-199A + 20B = 0,$ $-20A - 199B = 3$

$$x_{sp}(t) = -\frac{60}{40001}\cos 10t - \frac{597}{40001}\sin 10t$$

$$= \frac{3}{\sqrt{40001}}\left(-\frac{20}{\sqrt{40001}}\cos 10t - \frac{199}{\sqrt{40001}}\sin 10t\right) = \frac{3}{\sqrt{40001}}\cos(10t - \alpha)$$

$$\alpha = \pi + \tan^{-1}(199/20) \approx 4.6122 \quad \text{(3rd quadrant angle)}$$

Each solution in Problems 11-14 has two parts. For the first part, we give first the trial solution x_p involving undetermined coefficients A and B, then the equations that determine these coefficients, and finally the resulting steady periodic solution x_{sp}. For the second part, we give first the general solution $x(t)$ involving the coefficients c_1 and c_2 in the transient solution, then the equations that determine these coefficients, and finally the resulting transient solution x_{tr}.

11. $x_p = A\cos 3t + B\sin 3t;$ $-4A + 12B = 10,$ $12A + 4B = 0$

$$x_{sp}(t) = -\frac{1}{4}\cos 3t + \frac{3}{4}\sin 3t = \frac{\sqrt{10}}{4}\left(-\frac{1}{\sqrt{10}}\cos 3t + \frac{3}{\sqrt{10}}\sin 3t\right) = \frac{\sqrt{10}}{4}\cos(3t - \alpha)$$

$$\alpha = \pi - \tan^{-1}(3) \approx 1.8925 \quad \text{(2nd quadrant angle)}$$

$$x(t) = e^{-2t}\left(c_1\cos t + c_2\sin t\right) + x_{sp}(t); \quad c_1 - 1/4 = 0, \quad -2c_1 + c_2 + 9/4 = 0$$

$$x_{tr}(t) = e^{-2t}\left(\frac{1}{4}\cos t - \frac{7}{4}\sin t\right) = \frac{\sqrt{50}}{4}\left(\frac{1}{\sqrt{50}}\cos t - \frac{7}{\sqrt{50}}\sin t\right) = \frac{\sqrt{50}}{4}\cos(t - \beta)$$

$$\beta = 2\pi - \tan^{-1}(7) \approx 4.8543 \quad \text{(4th quadrant angle)}$$

13. $x_p = A\cos 10t + B\sin 10t;$ $-94A + 20B = 3,$ $20A + 94B = 0$

$$x_{sp}(t) = -\frac{141}{4618}\cos 10t + \frac{30}{4618}\sin 10t$$

$$= \frac{3\sqrt{2309}}{4618}\left(-\frac{47}{\sqrt{2309}}\cos 10t + \frac{10}{\sqrt{2309}}\sin 10t\right) = \frac{3}{2\sqrt{2309}}\cos(10t - \alpha)$$

$$\alpha = \pi - \tan^{-1}(10/47) \approx 2.9320 \quad \text{(2nd quadrant angle)}$$

$$x(t) = e^{-t}\left(c_1\cos t\sqrt{5} + c_2\sin t\sqrt{5}\right) + x_{sp}(t);$$

$$c_1 - 141/4618 = 10, \quad -c_1 + \sqrt{5}\,c_2 + 150/2309 = 0$$

$$x_{tr}(t) = \frac{e^{-t}}{4618\sqrt{5}}\left(46321\sqrt{5}\cos t\sqrt{5} + 46021\sin t\sqrt{5}\right)$$

$$= 3\sqrt{\frac{309083}{23090}}\, e^{-t} \cos\left(t\sqrt{5}-\beta\right) \approx 10.9761\, e^{-t} \cos\left(t\sqrt{5}-\beta\right)$$

$$\beta = \tan^{-1}(46321\sqrt{5}/46021) \approx 1.1527 \quad \text{(1st quadrant angle)}$$

In Problems 15-18 we substitute $x(t) = A(\omega)\cos\omega t + B(\omega)\sin\omega t$ into the differential equation $mx'' + cx' + kx = F_0 \cos\omega t$ with the given numerical values of m, c, k, and F_0. We give first the equations in A and B that result upon collection of coefficients of $\cos\omega t$ and $\sin\omega t$, and then the values of $A(\omega)$ and $B(\omega)$ that we get by solving these equations. Finally, $C = \sqrt{A^2 + B^2}$ gives the amplitude of the resulting forced oscillations as a function of the forcing frequency ω.

15.　$(2-\omega^2)A + 2\omega B = 2, \quad -2\omega A + (2-\omega^2)B = 0$

$$A = 2(2-\omega^2)/(4+\omega^4), \quad B = 4\omega/(4+\omega^4)$$

$C(\omega) = 2/\sqrt{4+\omega^4}$ begins with $C(0) = 1$ and steadily decreases as ω increases. Hence there is no practical resonance frequency.

17.　$(45-\omega^2)A + 6\omega B = 50, \quad -6\omega A + (45-\omega^2)B = 0$

$$A = 50(45-\omega^2)/(2025-54\omega^2+\omega^4), \quad B = 300\omega/(2025-54\omega^2+\omega^4)$$

$C(\omega) = 50/\sqrt{2025-54\omega^2+\omega^4}$ so, to find its maximum value, we calculate the derivative

$$C'(\omega) = \frac{-100\,\omega(-27+\omega^2)}{(2025-54\omega^2+\omega^4)^{3/2}}.$$

Hence the practical resonance frequency (where the derivative vanishes) is $\omega = \sqrt{27} = 3\sqrt{3}$.

19.　$m = 100/32$ slugs and $k = 1200$ lb/ft, so the critical frequency is $\omega_0 = \sqrt{k/m}$ $= \sqrt{384}$ rad/sec $= \sqrt{384}/2\pi \approx 3.12$ Hz.

21.　If θ is the angular displacement from the vertical, then the (essentially horizontal) displacement of the mass is $x = L\theta$, so twice its total energy (KE + PE) is

$$m(x')^2 + kx^2 + 2mgh = mL^2(\theta')^2 + kL^2\theta^2 + 2mgL(1 - \cos\theta) = C.$$

Differentiation, substitution of $\theta \approx \sin\theta$, and simplification yields

$$\theta'' + (k/m + g/L)\theta = 0$$

so

$$\omega_0 = \sqrt{k/m + g/L}.$$

23. **(a)** In ft-lb-sec units we have $m = 1000$ and $k = 10000$, so $\omega_0 = \sqrt{10}$ rad/sec ≈ 0.50 Hz.

(b) We are given that $\omega = 2\pi/2.25 \approx 2.79$ rad/sec, and the equation $mx'' + kx = F(t)$ simplifies to

$$x'' + 10x = (1/4)\omega^2 \sin \omega t.$$

When we substitute $x(t) = A \sin \omega t$ we find that the amplitude is

$$A = \omega^2/4(10 - \omega^2) \approx 0.8854 \text{ ft} \approx 10.63 \text{ in.}$$

25. Substitution of the trial solution $x = A \cos \omega t + B \sin \omega t$ in the differential equation, and then collection of coefficients as usual yields the equations

$$\left(k - m\omega^2\right)A + \left(c\omega\right)B = 0, \quad -\left(c\omega\right)A + \left(k - m\omega^2\right)B = F_0$$

with coefficient determinant $\Delta = \left(k - m\omega^2\right)^2 + \left(c\omega\right)^2$ and solution $A = -\left(c\omega\right)F_0/\Delta$, $B = \left(k - m\omega^2\right)F_0/\Delta$. Hence

$$x(t) = \frac{F_0}{\sqrt{\Delta}}\left[\frac{k - m\omega^2}{\sqrt{\Delta}}\sin \omega t - \frac{c\omega}{\sqrt{\Delta}}\cos \omega t\right] = C\sin\left(\omega t - \alpha\right),$$

where $C = F_0/\sqrt{\Delta}$ and $\sin \alpha = c\omega/\sqrt{\Delta}$, $\cos \alpha = \left(k - m\omega^2\right)/\sqrt{\Delta}$.

27. The derivative of $C(\omega) = F_0/\sqrt{\left(k - m\omega^2\right)^2 + \left(c\omega\right)^2}$ is given by

$$C'(\omega) = -\frac{\omega F_0}{2}\frac{(c^2 - 2km) + 2(m\omega)^2}{\left[\left(k - m\omega^2\right)^2 + \left(c\omega\right)^2\right]^{3/2}}.$$

(a) Therefore, if $c^2 \geq 2km$, it is clear from the numerator that $C'(\omega) < 0$ for all ω, so $C(\omega)$ steadily decreases as ω increases.

(b) But if $c^2 < 2km$, then the numerator (and hence $C'(\omega)$) vanishes when $\omega = \omega_m = \sqrt{k/m - c^2/2m^2} < \sqrt{k/m} = \omega_0$. Calculation then shows that

$$C''(\omega_m) = \frac{16F_0 m^3(c^2 - 2km)}{c^3\left(4km - c^2\right)^{3/2}} < 0,$$

so it follows from the second-derivative test that $C(\omega_m)$ is a local maximum value.

29. We need only substitute $E_0 = ac\omega$ and $F_0 = ak$ in the result of Problem 26.

SECTION 3.7

ELECTRICAL CIRCUITS

1. With $E(t) \equiv 0$ we have the simple exponential equation $5I' + 25I = 0$ whose solution with $I(0) = 4$ is $I(t) = 4e^{-5t}$.

3. Now the differential equation is $5I' + 25I = 100 \cos 60t$. Substitution of the trial solution

$$I_p = A \cos 60t + B \sin 60t$$

yields

$$I_p = 4(\cos 60t + 12 \sin 60t)/145.$$

The complementary function is $I_c = ce^{-5t}$; the solution with $I(0) = 0$ is

$$I(t) = 4(\cos 60t + 12 \sin 60t - e^{-5t})/145.$$

5. The linear equation $I' + 10I = 50 e^{-10t}\cos 60t$ has integrating factor $\rho = e^{10t}$. The resulting general solution is $I(t) = e^{-10t}\left[(5/6)\sin 60t + C\right].]$ To satisfy the initial condition $I(0) = 0$, we take $C = 0$ and get $I(t) = (5/6)e^{-10t}\sin 60t$.

7. **(a)** The linear differential equation $RQ' + (1/C)Q = E_0$ has integrating factor $\rho = e^{t/RC}$. The resulting solution with $Q(0) = 0$ is $Q(t) = E_0 C(1 - e^{-t/RC})$. Then $I(t) = Q'(t) = (E_0/R)e^{-t/RC}$.

(b) These solutions make it obvious that $\lim_{t \to \infty} Q(t) = E_0 C$ and $\lim_{t \to \infty} I(t) = 0$.

9. Substitution of the trial solution $Q = A\cos 120t + B\sin 120t$ into the differential equation $200Q' + 4000Q = 100\cos 120t$ yields the equations

$$4000A + 24000B = 100, \quad -24000A + 4000B = 0$$

with solution $A = 1/1480$, $B = 3/740$. The complementary function is $Q_c = ce^{-20t}$, and imposition of the initial condition $Q(0) = 0$ yields the solution $Q(t) = (\cos 120t + 6\sin 120t - e^{-20t})/1480$. The current function is then $I(t) = Q'(t) = (36\cos 120t - 6\sin 120t + e^{-20t})/74$. Thus the steady-periodic current is

$$I_{sp} = \frac{6}{74}(6\cos 120t - \sin 120t)$$

$$= \frac{6\sqrt{37}}{74}\left(\frac{6}{\sqrt{37}}\cos 120t - \frac{1}{\sqrt{37}}\sin 120t\right) = \frac{3}{\sqrt{37}}\cos(120t - \alpha),$$

so the steady-state amplitude is $3/\sqrt{37}$.

In Problems 11-16, we give first the trial solution $I_p = A\cos\omega t + B\sin\omega t$, then the equations in A and B that we get upon substituting this trial solution into the RLC equation $LI'' + RI' + (1/C)I = E'(t)$, and finally the resulting steady periodic solution.

11. $I_p = A\cos 2t + B\sin 2t; \qquad A + 6B = 10, \quad -6A + B = 0$

$$I_{sp}(t) = \frac{10}{37}\cos 2t + \frac{60}{37}\sin 2t = \frac{10}{\sqrt{37}}\left(\frac{1}{\sqrt{37}}\cos 2t + \frac{6}{\sqrt{37}}\sin 2t\right) = \frac{10}{\sqrt{37}}\sin(2t - \delta)$$

$$\delta = 2\pi - \tan^{-1}(1/6) \approx 6.1180 \quad \text{(4th quadrant angle)}$$

13. $I_p = A\cos 5t + B\sin 5t; \qquad 3A - 2B = 0, \quad 2A + 3B = 20$

$$I_{sp}(t) = \frac{40}{13}\cos 5t + \frac{60}{13}\sin 5t = \frac{20}{\sqrt{13}}\left(\frac{2}{\sqrt{13}}\cos 5t + \frac{3}{\sqrt{13}}\sin 5t\right) = \frac{20}{\sqrt{13}}\sin(5t - \delta)$$

$$\delta = 2\pi - \tan^{-1}(2/3) \approx 5.6952 \quad \text{(4th quadrant angle)}$$

15. $I_p = A\cos 60\pi t + B\sin 60\pi t;$

$$(1000 - 36\pi^2)A + 30\pi B = 33\pi, \quad 15\pi A - (500 - 18\pi^2)B = 0$$

$$A = \frac{33\pi(250 - 9\pi^2)}{250000 - 17775\pi^2 + 324\pi^4}, \quad B = \frac{495\pi^2}{2(250000 - 17775\pi^2 + 324\pi^4)}$$

$$I_{sp}(t) \approx I_0\sin(60\pi t - \delta); \quad I_0 = \frac{33\pi}{2\sqrt{250000 - 17775\pi^2 + 324\pi^4}} \approx 0.1591$$

$$\delta = 2\pi - \tan^{-1}\left(\frac{500 - 18\pi^2}{15\pi}\right) \approx 4.8576$$

In each of Problems 17-22, the first step is to substitute the given RLC parameters, the initial values $I(0)$ and $Q(0)$, and the voltage $E(t)$ into Eq. (16) and solve for the remaining initial value

$$I'(0) = \frac{1}{L}\left[E(0) - RI(0) - (1/C)Q(0)\right]. \qquad (*)$$

17. With $I(0) = 0$ and $Q(0) = 5$, Equation (*) gives $I'(0) = -75$. The solution of the RLC equation $2I'' + 16I' + 50I = 0$ with these initial conditions is $I(t) = -25e^{-4t}\sin 3t$.

19. Now our differential equation to solve is

$$2I'' + 60I' + 400I = -1000e^{-10t}.$$

We find the particular solution $I_p = -50t\, e^{-10t}$ by substituting the trial solution $At\, e^{-10t}$; the general solution is

$$I(t) = c_1 e^{-10t} + c_2 e^{-20t} - 50t\, e^{-10t}.$$

The initial conditions are $I(0) = 0$ and $I'(0) = -150$, the latter found by substituting $L = 2, R = 60, 1/C = 400, I(0) = 0, Q(0) = 1$, and $E(0) = 100$ into Equation (*). Imposition of these initial values on the general solution above yields the equations $c_1 + c_2 = 0, -10c_1 - 20c_2 - 50 = -150$ with solution $c_1 = -10, c_2 = 10$. Thus we get the solution

$$I(t) = 10e^{-20t} - 10e^{-10t} - 50te^{-10t}.$$

21. The differential equation $10I'' + 20I' + 100I = -1000\sin 5t$ has transient solution

$$I_{tr}(t) = e^{-t}\left(c_1 \cos 3t + c_2 \sin 3t\right),$$

and in Problem 13 we found the steady periodic solution

$$I_{sp}(t) = \frac{20}{13}\left(2\cos 5t + 3\sin 5t\right).$$

When we impose the initial conditions $I(0) = 0, I'(0) = -10$ on the general solution $I(t) = I_{tr}(t) + I_{sp}(t),$ we get the equations

$$c_1 + 40/13 = 0, \quad -c_1 + 3c_2 + 300/13 = -10$$

with solution $c_1 = -40/13, c_2 = -470/39.$

23. The LC equation $LI'' + (1/C)I = 0$ has general solution $I(t) = c_1 \cos \omega_0 t + c_2 \sin \omega_0 t$ with critical frequency $\omega_0 = 1/\sqrt{LC}$.

25. According to Eq. (8) in the text, the amplitude of the steady periodic current is $E_0 / \sqrt{R^2 + (\omega L - 1/\omega C)^2}$. Because the radicand in the denominator is a sum of squares, it is obvious that the denominator is least when $\omega L - 1/\omega C = 0$, that is, when $\omega = 1/\sqrt{LC}$.

SECTION 3.8

ENDPOINT PROBLEMS AND EIGENVALUES

The material on eigenvalues and endpoint problems in Section 3.8 can be considered optional at this point in a first course. It will not be needed until we discuss boundary value problems in the last three sections of Chapter 9 and in Chapter 10. However, after the concentration thus far on initial value problems, the inclusion of this section can give students a view of a new class of problems that have diverse and important applications (as illustrated by the subsection on the whirling string). If Section 3.8 is not covered at this point in the course, then it can be inserted just prior to Section 9.5.

1. If $\lambda = 0$ then $y'' = 0$ implies that $y(x) = A + Bx$. The endpoint conditions $y'(0) = 0$ and $y(1) = 0$ yield $B = 0$ and $A = 0$, respectively. Hence $\lambda = 0$ is *not* an eigenvalue.

If $\lambda = \alpha^2 > 0$, then the general solution of $y'' + \alpha^2 y = 0$ is

$$y(x) = A \cos \alpha x + B \sin \alpha x,$$

so

$$y'(x) = -A\alpha \sin \alpha x + B\alpha \cos \alpha x.$$

Then $y'(0) = 0$ yields $B = 0$, so $y(x) = A \cos \alpha x$. Next $y(1) = 0$ implies that $\cos \alpha = 0$, so α is an odd multiple of $\pi/2$. Hence the positive eigenvalues are $\{(2n - 1)^2 \pi^2 / 4\}$ with associated eigenfunctions $\{\cos(2n - 1)\pi x/2\}$ for $n = 1, 2, 3, \cdots$.

3. Much as in Problem 1 we see that $\lambda = 0$ is not an eigenvalue. Suppose that $\lambda = \alpha^2 > 0$, so

$$y(x) = A \cos \alpha x + B \sin \alpha x.$$

Then the conditions $y(-\pi) = y(\pi) = 0$ yield

$$A \cos \alpha\pi + B \sin \alpha\pi = 0,$$

$$A \cos \alpha\pi - B \sin \alpha\pi = 0.$$

It follows that

$$A \cos \alpha\pi = 0 = B \sin \alpha\pi.$$

Hence either $A = 0$ and $B \neq 0$ with $\alpha\pi$ an even multiple of $\pi/2$, or $A \neq 0$ and $B = 0$ with $\alpha\pi$ an odd multiple of $\pi/2$. Thus the eigenvalues are $\{n^2/4\}$ for n a positive integer, and the nth eigenfunction is $y_n(x) = \cos(nx/2)$ if n is odd, $y_n(x) = \sin(nx/2)$ if n is even.

5.　　If $\lambda = \alpha^2 > 0$ and

$$y(x) = A \cos \alpha x + B \sin \alpha x,$$

$$y'(x) = -A\alpha \sin \alpha x + B\alpha \cos \alpha x$$

then the conditions $y(-2) = y'(2) = 0$ yield

$$A \cos 2\alpha - B \sin 2\alpha = 0,$$

$$-A \sin 2\alpha + B \cos 2\alpha = 0.$$

It follows either that $A = B$ and $\cos 2\alpha = \sin 2\alpha$, or that $A = -B$ and $\cos 2\alpha = -\sin 2\alpha$. The former occurs if

$$2\alpha = \pi/4, 5\pi/4, 9\pi/4, \cdots,$$

the latter if

$$2\alpha = 3\pi/4, 7\pi/4, 11\pi/4, \cdots.$$

Hence the nth eigenvalue is

$$\lambda_n = \alpha_n^2 = (2n-1)^2\pi^2/64$$

for $n = 1, 2, 3, \cdots$, and the associated eigenfunction is

$$y_n(x) = \cos \alpha_n x + \sin \alpha_n x \quad (n \text{ odd})$$

or

$$y_n(x) = \cos \alpha_n x - \sin \alpha_n x \quad (n \text{ even}).$$

7.　　**(a)**　　If $\lambda = 0$ and $y(x) = A + Bx$, then $y(0) = A = 0$, so $y(x) = Bx$. But then $y(1) + y'(1) = 2B = 0$, so $A = B = 0$ and $\lambda = 0$ is not an eigenvalue.

(b)　　If $\lambda = \alpha^2 > 0$ and $y(x) = A \cos \alpha x + B \sin \alpha x$, then $y(0) = A = 0$ so $y(x) = B \sin \alpha x$. Hence

$$y(1) + y'(1) = B(\sin \alpha + \alpha \cos \alpha) = 0.$$

so α must be a positive root of the equation $\tan \alpha = -\alpha$.

9.   If $y'' + \lambda y = 0$ and $\lambda = -\alpha^2 < 0$, then

$$y(x) = Ae^{\alpha x} + Be^{-\alpha x}.$$

Then $y(0) = A + B = 0$, so $B = -A$ and therefore

$$y(x) = A(e^{\alpha x} - e^{-\alpha x}).$$

Hence

$$y'(L) = A\alpha(e^{\alpha L} + e^{-\alpha L}) = 0.$$

But $\alpha \neq 0$ and $e^{\alpha L} + e^{-\alpha L} > 0$, so $A = 0$. Thus $\lambda = -\alpha^2$ is not an eigenvalue.

11.   If $\lambda = -\alpha^2 < 0$, then the general solution of $y'' + \lambda y = 0$ is
$y(x) = A\cosh \alpha x + B \sinh \alpha x$. Then $y'(0) = 0$ implies that $B = 0$, so $y(x) = \cosh \alpha x$
(or a nonzero multiple thereof). Next,

$$y(1) + y'(1) = \cosh \alpha + \alpha \sinh \alpha = 0$$

implies that $\tanh \alpha = -1/\alpha$. But the graph of $y = \tanh \alpha$ lies in the first and third
quadrants, while the graph of $y = -1/\alpha$ lies in the second and fourth quadrants. It
follows that the only solution of $\tanh \alpha = -1/\alpha$ is $\alpha = 0$, and hence that our
eigenvalue problem has no negative eigenvalues.

13.   **(a)**   With $\lambda = 1$, the general solution of $y'' + 2y' + y = 0$ is

$$y(x) = Ae^{-x} + Bxe^{-x}.$$

But then $y(0) = A = 0$ and $y(1) = e^{-1}(A + B) = 0$. Hence $\lambda = 1$ is not an
eigenvalue.

(b)   If $\lambda < 1$, then the equation $y'' + 2y' + \lambda y = 0$ has characteristic equation
$r^2 + 2r + \lambda = 0$. This equation has the two distinct real roots $\left(-2 \pm \sqrt{4 - 4\lambda}\right)/2$; call
them r and s. Then the general solution is

$$y(x) = Ae^{rx} + Be^{sx},$$

and the conditions $y(0) = y(1) = 0$ yield the equations

$$A + B = 0, \quad Ae^r + Be^s = 0.$$

If $A, B \neq 0$, then it follows that $e^r = e^s$. But $r \neq s$, so there is no eigenvalue $\lambda < 1$.

(c)   If $\lambda > 1$ let $\lambda - 1 = \alpha^2$, so $\lambda = 1 + \alpha^2$. Then the characteristic equation

$$r^2 + 2r + \lambda = (r+1)^2 + \alpha^2 = 0$$

has roots $-1 \pm \alpha i$, so

$$y(x) = e^{-x}(A \cos \alpha x + B \sin \alpha x).$$

Now $y(0) = A = 0$, so $y(x) = Ae^{-x} \sin \alpha x$. Next, $y(1) = Ae^{-1} \sin \alpha = 0$, so $\alpha = n\pi$ with n an integer. Thus the nth positive eigenvalue is $\lambda_n = n^2\pi^2 + 1$. Because $\lambda = \alpha^2 + 1$, the eigenfunction associated with λ_n is

$$y_n(x) = e^{-x} \sin n\pi x.$$

15.   **(a)**   The endpoint conditions are

$$y(0) = y'(0) = y''(L) = y^{(3)}(L) = 0.$$

With these conditions, four successive integrations as in Example 5 yield the indicated shape function $y(x)$.

(b)   The maximum value y_{max} of $y(x)$ on the closed interval $[0, L]$ must occur either at an interior point where $y'(x) = 0$ or at one of the endpoints $x = 0$ and $x = L$. Now

$$y'(x) = k(4x^3 - 12Lx^2 + 12L^2x) = 4kx(x^2 - 3Lx + 3L^2)$$

where $k = w/24EI$, and the quadratic factor has no real zero. Hence $x = 0$ is the only zero of $y'(x)$. But $y(0) = 0$, so it follows that $y_{max} = y(L)$.

17.   If $y(x) = k(x^4 - 2Lx^3 + L^3x)$ with $k = w/24EI$, then

$$y'(x) = k(4x^3 - 6Lx^2 + L^3) = 0$$

has the solution $x = L/2$ that we can verify by inspection. Now long division of the cubic $4x^3 - 6Lx^2 + L^3$ by $2x - L$ yields the quadratic factor $2x^2 - 2Lx - L^2$ whose zeros $\left(2L \pm \sqrt{12L^2}\right)/4 = \left(1 \pm \sqrt{3}\right)L/2$ both lie outside the interval $[0, L]$. Thus $x = L/2$ is, indeed, the only zero of $y'(x) = 0$ in this interval.

CHAPTER 4

INTRODUCTION TO SYSTEMS OF DIFFERENTIAL EQUATIONS

This chapter bridges the gap between the treatment of a single differential equation in Chapters 1-3 and the comprehensive treatment of linear and nonlinear systems in Chapters 5-6. It also is designed to offer some flexibility in the treatment of linear systems, depending on the background in linear algebra that students are assumed to have — Sections 4.1 and 4.2 can stand alone as a very brief introduction to linear systems without the use of linear algebra and matrices. The final Section 4.3 of this chapter extends to systems the numerical approximation techniques of Chapter 2.

SECTION 4.1

FIRST-ORDER SYSTEMS AND APPLICATIONS

1. Let $x_1 = x$ and $x_2 = x_1' = x'$, so $x_2' = x'' = -7x - 3x' + t^2$.

Equivalent system:

$$x_1' = x_2, \qquad x_2' = -7x_1 - 3x_2 + t^2$$

3. Let $x_1 = x$ and $x_2 = x_1' = x'$, so $x_2' = x'' = \left[\left(1 - t^2 \right) x - tx' \right] / t^2$.

Equivalent system:

$$x_1' = x_2, \qquad t^2 x_2' = (1 - t^2)x_1 - tx_2$$

5. Let $x_1 = x$, $x_2 = x_1' = x'$, $x_3 = x_2' = x''$, so $x_3' = x''' = \left(x' \right)^2 + \cos x$.

Equivalent system:

$$x_1' = x_2, \qquad x_2' = x_3, \qquad x_3' = x_2^2 + \cos x_1$$

7. Let $x_1 = x$, $x_2 = x_1' = x'$, $y_1 = y$, $y_2 = y_1' = y'$ so $x_2' = x'' = -kx / (x^2 + y^2)^{3/2}$,
$y_2' = y'' = -ky / (x^2 + y^2)^{3/2}$.

Equivalent system:

$$x_1' = x_2, \qquad x_2' = -kx_1 / \left(x_1^2 + y_1^2 \right)^{3/2}$$

$$y_1' = y_2, \qquad y_2' = -ky_1 / \left(x_1^2 + y_1^2 \right)^{3/2}$$

9. Let $x_1 = x$, $x_2 = x_1' = x'$, $y_1 = y$, $y_2 = y_1' = y'$, $z_1 = z$, $z_2 = z_1' = z'$, so
    $x_2' = x'' = 3x - y + 2z$, $y_2' = y'' = x + y - 4z$, $z_2' = z'' = 5x - y - z$.

    Equivalent system:

    $$x_1' = x_2, \qquad x_2' = 3x_1 - y_1 + 2z_1$$

    $$y_1' = y_2, \qquad y_2' = x_1 + y_1 - 4z_1$$

    $$z_1' = z_2, \qquad z_2' = 5x_1 - y_1 - z_1$$

11. The computation $x'' = y' = -x$ yields the single linear second-order equation
    $x'' + x = 0$ with characteristic equation $r^2 + 1 = 0$ and general solution

    $$x(t) = A \cos t + B \sin t.$$

    Then the original first equation $y = x'$ gives

    $$y(t) = B \cos t - A \sin t.$$

13. The computation $x'' = -2y' = -4x$ yields the single linear second-order equation
    $x'' + 4x = 0$ with characteristic equation $r^2 + 4 = 0$ and general solution

    $$x(t) = A \cos 2t + B \sin 2t.$$

    Then the original first equation $y = -x'/2$ gives

    $$y(t) = -B \cos 2t + A \sin 2t.$$

    Finally, the condition $x(0) = 1$ implies that $A = 1$, and then the condition $y(0) = 0$
    gives $B = 0$. Hence the desired particular solution is given by

    $$x(t) = \cos 2t, \qquad y(t) = \sin 2t.$$

15. The computation $x'' = y'/2 = -4x$ yields the single linear second-order equation
    $x'' + 4x = 0$ with characteristic equation $r^2 + 4 = 0$ and general solution

    $$x(t) = A \cos 2t + B \sin 2t.$$

    Then the original first equation $y = 2x'$ gives

    $$y(t) = 4B \cos 2t - 4A \sin 2t.$$

17. The computation $x'' = y' = 6x - y = 6x - x'$ yields the single linear second-order
    equation $x'' + x' - 6x = 0$ with characteristic equation $r^2 + r - 6 = 0$ and characteristic
    roots $r = -3$ and 2, so the general solution

$$x(t) = A e^{-3t} + B e^{2t}.$$

Then the original first equation $y = x'$ gives

$$y(t) = -3A e^{-3t} + 2B e^{2t}.$$

Finally, the initial conditions

$$x(0) = A + B = 1, \quad y(0) = -3A + 2B = 2$$

imply that $A = 0$ and $B = 1$, so the desired particular solution is given by

$$x(t) = e^{2t}, \qquad y(t) = 2 e^{2t}.$$

19.   The computation $x'' = -y' = -13x - 4y = -13x + 4x'$ yields the single linear second-order equation $x'' - 4x' + 13x = 0$ with characteristic equation $r^2 - 4r + 13 = 0$ and characteristic roots $r = 2 \pm 3i$, hence the general solution is

$$x(t) = e^{2t}(A \cos 3t + B \sin 3t).$$

The initial condition $x(0) = 0$ then gives $A = 0$, so $x(t) = B e^{2t} \sin 3t$. Then the original first equation $y = -x'$ gives

$$y(t) = -e^{2t}(3B \cos 3t + 2B \sin 3t).$$

Finally, the initial condition $y(0) = 3$ gives $B = -1$, so the desired particular solution is given by

$$x(t) = -e^{2t} \sin 3t, \qquad y(t) = e^{2t}(3 \cos 3t + 2 \sin 3t).$$

21.   **(a)**   Substituting the general solution found in Problem 11 we get

$$\begin{aligned} x^2 + y^2 &= (A \cos t + B \sin t)^2 + (B \cos t - A \sin t)^2 \\ &= (A^2 + B^2)(\cos^2 t + \sin^2 t) = A^2 + B^2 \\ x^2 + y^2 &= C^2, \end{aligned}$$

the equation of a circle of radius $C = (A^2 + B^2)^{1/2}$.

(b)   Substituting the general solution found in Problem 12 we get

$$x^2 - y^2 = (Ae^t + Be^{-t})^2 - (Ae^t - Be^{-t})^2 = 4AB,$$

the equation of a hyperbola.

23.   When we solve Equations (20) and (21) in the text for e^{-t} and e^{2t} we get

$$2x - y = 3Ae^{-t} \text{ and } \quad x + y = 3Be^{2t}.$$

Hence

$$(2x - y)^2(x + y) = (3Ae^{-t})^2(3Be^{2t}) = 27A^2B = C.$$

Clearly $y = 2x$ or $y = -x$ if $C = 0$, and expansion gives the equation $4x^3 - 3xy^2 + y^3 = C$.

25. Looking at Fig. 4.1.12 in the text, we see that

$$my_1'' = -T\sin\theta_1 + T\sin\theta_2 \approx -T\tan\theta_1 + T\tan\theta_2 = -Ty_1/L + T(y_2 - y_1)/L,$$

$$my_2'' = -T\sin\theta_2 - T\sin\theta_3 \approx -T\tan\theta_2 - T\tan\theta_3 = -T(y_2 - y_1)/L - Ty_2/L.$$

We get the desired equations when we multiply each of these equations by L/T and set $k = mL/T$.

27. We apply Kirchhoff's law to each loop in Figure 4.1.14 in the text, and immediately get the equations

$$2(I_1' - I_2') + 50I_1 = 100\sin 60t, \quad 2(I_2' - I_1') + 25I_2 = 0.$$

29. If θ is the polar angular coordinate of the point (x, y) and we write $F = k/(x^2 + y^2) = k/r^2$, then Newton's second law gives

$$mx'' = -F\cos\theta = -(k/r^2)(x/r) = -kx/r^3,$$
$$my'' = -F\sin\theta = -(k/r^2)(y/r) = -ky/r^3,$$

31. If $\mathbf{r} = (x, y, z)$ is the particle's position vector, then Newton's law $m\mathbf{r}'' = \mathbf{F}$ gives

$$m\mathbf{r}'' = q\,\mathbf{v} \times \mathbf{B} = q\begin{vmatrix} \mathbf{i} & \mathbf{j} & \mathbf{k} \\ x' & y' & z' \\ 0 & 0 & B \end{vmatrix} = +qBy'\mathbf{i} - qBx'\mathbf{j} = qB(-y', x', 0).$$

SECTION 4.2

THE METHOD OF ELIMINATION

1. The second differential equation $y' = 2y$ has the exponential solution

$$y(t) = c_2 e^{2t}.$$

Substitution in the first differential equation gives the linear first-order equation $x' + x = 3c_2 e^{2t}$ with integrating factor $\rho = e^t$. Solution of this equation in the usual way gives

$$x(t) = e^{-t}\left(c_1 + c_2 e^{3t}\right) = c_1 e^{-t} + c_2 e^{2t}.$$

3.   From the first differential equation we get $y = (3x + x')/2$, so $y' = (3x' + x'')/2$. Substitution of these expressions for y and y' into the second differential equation yields the second-order equation

$$x'' - x' + 6x = 0$$

with general solution

$$x(t) = c_1 e^{-2t} + c_2 e^{3t}.$$

Substitution in $y = (3x + x')/2$ now yields

$$y(t) = \tfrac{1}{2}c_1 e^{-2t} + 3c_2 e^{3t}.$$

Imposition of the initial conditions $x(0) = 0$, $y(0) = 2$ now gives the equations $c_1 + c_2 = 0$, $c_1/2 + 3c_2 = 0$ with solution $c_1 = -4/5$, $c_2 = 4/5$. These coefficients give the desired particular solution

$$x(t) = 4(e^{3t} - e^{-2t})/5, \qquad y(t) = 2(6e^{3t} - e^{-2t})/5.$$

5.   Substitution of $y = -(x' + 3x)/4$ and $y' = -(x'' + 3x')/4$ — from the first equation — into the second equation yields the second-order equation $x'' + 2x' + 5x = 0$ with general solution

$$x(t) = e^{-t}\left(c_1 \cos 2t + c_2 \sin 2t\right).$$

Substitution of this solution in $y = -(x' + 3x)/4$ gives

$$y(t) = \frac{1}{2}e^{-t}\left[-(c_1 + c_2)\cos 2t + (c_1 - c_2)\sin 2t\right].$$

7.   Substitution of $y = x' - 4x - 2t$ and $y' = x'' - 4x' - 2$ — from the first equation — into the second equation yields the nonhomogeneous second-order equation $x'' - 5x' + 6x = 2 - 2t$. Substitution of the trial solution $x_p = A + Bt$ yields $A = 1/18$, $B = -1/3$ so $x_p = 1/18 - t/3$. Hence the general solution for x is

$$x(t) = c_1 e^{2t} + c_2 e^{3t} - t/3 + 1/18.$$

Substitution in $y = x' - 4x - 2t$ now yields

$$y(t) = -2c_1e^{2t} - c_2e^{3t} - 2t/3 - 5/9.$$

9.   Substitution of $y = (-x' + 2x + 2\sin 2t)/3$ and $y' = (-x'' + 2x' + 4\cos 2t)/3$ — from the first equation — into the second equation yields the second-order equation $x'' - x = 7\cos 2t + 4\sin 2t$ with general solution

$$x(t) = c_1e^{-t} + c_2e^{t} - \frac{1}{5}(7\cos 2t + 4\sin 2t).$$

Substitution in $y = (-x' + 2x + 2\sin 2t)/3$ now yields

$$y(t) = c_1e^{-t} + \frac{1}{3}c_2e^{t} - \frac{1}{5}(2\cos 2t + 4\sin 2t).$$

Imposition of the initial conditions $x(0) = 3$, $y(0) = 2$ now gives the equations $c_1 = 3$, $-c_1/3 + c_2/3 = 2$ with solution $c_1 = 3$, $c_2 = 9$. These coefficients give the desired particular solution

$$x(t) = e^{-2t}(3\cos 3t + 9\sin 3t), \qquad y(t) = e^{-2t}(2\cos 3t - 4\sin 3t).$$

11.   First we solve the given equations for the normal-form first-order equations

$$x' = 3x - 9y + e^{-t} + 2e^{t},$$
$$y' = 2x - 3y + e^{-t}/2 + 3e^{t}/2.$$

Substitution of $y = (-x' + 3x + e^{-t} + 2e^{t})/9$ and $y' = (-x'' + 3x' - e^{-t} + 2e^{t})/9$ — from the first equation — into the second equation yields the nonhomogeneous second-order equation $x'' + 9x = (5e^{-t} + 11e^{t})/2$. Substitution of the trial solution $x_p = Ae^{-t} + Be^{t}$ yields $A = -1/4$, $B = -11/20$ so $x_p = -e^{-t}/4 - 11e^{t}/20$. Hence the general solution for x is

$$x(t) = c_1\cos 3t + c_2\sin 3t - \frac{1}{4}e^{-t} - \frac{11}{20}e^{t}.$$

Substitution in $y = (-x' + 3x + e^{-t} + 2e^{t})/9$ now yields

$$y(t) = \frac{1}{3}(c_1 - c_2)\cos 3t + \frac{1}{3}(c_1 + c_2)\sin 3t + \frac{1}{2}e^{-t} + \frac{8}{5}e^{t}.$$

13.   The first equation yields $y = (x'' + 5x)/2$, so $y'' = (x^{(4)} + 5x'')/2$. Substitution in the second equation yields

$$x^{(4)} + 13x'' + 36x = 0.$$

The characteristic equation is $r^4 + 13r^2 + 36 = (r^2 + 4)(r^2 + 9) = 0$, so the general solution for x is

$$x(t) = a_1 \cos 2t + a_2 \cos 2t + b_1 \cos 3t + b_2 \sin 3t.$$

Substitution in $y = (x'' + 5x)/2$ now gives

$$y(t) = \frac{1}{2}a_1 \cos 2t + \frac{1}{2}a_2 \cos 2t - 2b_1 \cos 3t - 2b_2 \sin 3t.$$

15. If we write the given differential equations in operator notation as

$$(D^2 - 2)x - 3Dy = 0$$
$$3Dx + (D^2 - 2)y = 0,$$

we see that the system has operational determinant

$$(D^2 - 2)^2 + 9D^2 = D^4 + 5D^2 + 4 = (D^2 + 1)(D^2 + 4).$$

Therefore (as in Example 3) we see that x satisfies the fourth-order differential equation $(D^2 + 1)(D^2 + 4)x = 0$ with characteristic equation $(r^2 + 1)(r^2 + 4) = 0$ and general solution

$$x(t) = a_1 \cos t + a_2 \sin t + b_1 \cos 2t + b_2 \sin 2t.$$

Similarly, the general solution for y is of the form

$$y(t) = c_1 \cos t + c_2 \sin t + d_1 \cos 2t + d_2 \sin 2t.$$

Now, substitution of these two general solutions in the first equation $x'' - 3y' - 2x = 0$ and collection of coefficients gives

$$(-3a_1 - 3c_2)\cos t + (3c_1 - 3a_2)\sin t + (-6b_1 - 6d_2)\cos 2t + (3d_1 - 3b_2)\sin 2t = 0.$$

Thus we see finally that $c_1 = a_2$, $c_2 = -a_1$, $d_1 = b_2$, $d_2 = -b_1$. Hence

$$y(t) = a_2 \cos t - a_1 \sin t + b_2 \cos 2t - b_1 \sin 2t.$$

17. If we write the given equations in the operational form

$$(D^2 - 3D - 2)x + (D^2 - D + 2)y = 0,$$
$$(2D^2 - 9D - 4)x + (3D^2 - 2D + 6)y = 0$$

we see (thinking of the operational determinant) that x satisfies a homogeneous fourth-order equation with characteristic equation

$$\left(r^2 - 3r - 2\right)\left(3r^2 - 2r + 6\right) - \left(r^2 - r + 2\right)\left(2r^2 - 9r - 4\right)$$
$$= r^4 - 3r^2 - 4 = \left(r^2 + 1\right)\left(r^2 - 4\right) = \left(r^2 + 1\right)(r+2)(r-2) = 0.$$

Hence the general solution for x is

$$x(t) = a_1 \cos t + a_2 \sin t + b_1 e^{-2t} + b_2 e^{2t},$$

and, similarly, the general solution for y is

$$y(t) = c_1 \cos t + c_2 \sin t + d_1 e^{-2t} + d_2 e^{2t}.$$

To determine the relations between the arbitrary constants in these two general solutions, we substitute them in the first of the original differential equations and get

$$\left(-a_1 \cos t - a_2 \sin t + 4b_1 e^{-2t} + 4b_2 e^{2t}\right) + \left(-c_1 \cos t - c_2 \sin t + 4d_1 e^{-2t} + 4d_2 e^{2t}\right) +$$
$$\left(3a_1 \sin t - 3a_2 \cos t + 6b_1 e^{-2t} - 6b_2 e^{2t}\right) + \left(c_1 \sin t - c_2 \cos t + 2d_1 e^{-2t} - 2d_2 e^{2t}\right) +$$
$$\left(-2a_1 \cos t - 2a_2 \sin t - 2b_1 e^{-2t} - 2b_2 e^{2t}\right) + \left(+2c_1 \cos t + 2c_2 \sin t + 2d_1 e^{-2t} + 2d_2 e^{2t}\right) = 0$$

If we collect coefficients of the trigonometric and exponential terms we get the equations

$$\begin{array}{ll} -3a_1 - 3a_2 + c_1 - c_2 = 0, & \qquad 8b_1 + 8d_1 = 0, \\ 3a_1 - 3a_2 + c_1 + c_2 = 0 & \qquad -4b_2 + 4d_2 = 0. \end{array}$$

and

The first two of these equations imply that $c_1 = -3a_2$ and $c_2 = 3a_1$, while the latter two give $d_1 = -b_1$, $d_2 = b_2$. We therefore see finally that

$$y(t) = -3a_2 \cos t + 3a_1 \sin t - b_1 e^{-2t} + b_2 e^{2t}.$$

19. The operational determinant of the given system is

$$L = \begin{vmatrix} D-4 & 2 & 0 \\ 4 & D-4 & 2 \\ 0 & 4 & D-4 \end{vmatrix} = D^3 - 12D^2 + 32D,$$

so x, y, and z all satisfy a third-order homogeneous linear differential equation with characteristic equation $r^3 - 12r^2 + 32r = r(r-4)(r-8) = 0$. The corresponding general solutions are

$$x(t) = a_1 + a_2 e^{4t} + a_3 e^{8t}, \quad y(t) = b_1 + b_2 e^{4t} + b_3 e^{8t}, \quad z(t) = c_1 + c_2 e^{4t} + c_3 e^{8t}.$$

If we substitute $x(t)$ and $y(t)$ in the first differential equation $x' = 4x - 2y$ and collect coefficients of like terms, we find quickly that $b_1 = 2a_1$, $b_2 = 0$, and $b_3 = -2a_3$. Similarly, we find by substitution in the other two equations that $c_1 = 2a_1$, $c_2 = -2a_2$, and $c_3 = 2a_3$. Thus y and z are given by

$$y(t) = 2a_1 - 2a_3 e^{8t} \quad \text{and} \quad z(t) = 2a_1 - 2a_2 e^{4t} + 2a_3 e^{8t}.$$

21. $L_1 L_2 = L_2 L_1$ because both sides simplify to the same thing upon multiplying out and collecting terms in the usual fashion of polynomial algebra. This "works" because different powers of D commute — that is, $D^i D^j = D^j D^i$ because $D^i(D^j x) = D^{i+j} x = D^j(D^i x)$.

23. Subtraction of the two equations yields $x + y = e^{-2t} - e^{-3t}$. We then verify readily that any two differentiable functions $x(t)$ and $y(t)$ satisfying this condition will constitute a solution of the given system, which thus has infinitely many solutions.

25. Infinitely many solutions, because any solution of the second equation also satisfies the first equation (because it is $D + 2$ times the second one).

27. Subtraction of the second equation from the first one gives $x + y = e^{-t}$. Then substitution in the second equation yields

$$x(t) = D^2(x + y) = e^{-t}.$$

It follows that $y(t) \equiv 0$, so there are *no* arbitrary constants.

29. Addition of the two given equations yields $D^2 x = e^{-t}$, so $x(t) = e^{-t} + a_1 t + a_2$. Then the second equation gives $D^2 y = a_1 t + a_2$, so

$$y(t) = (1/6)a_1 t^3 + (1/2)a_2 t^2 + a_3 t + a_4.$$

Thus there are *four* arbitrary constants.

31. Substitution of $I_2 = (I_1' + 25I_1 - 50)/25$ and $I_2' = (I_1'' + 25I_1')/25$ — from the first equation — into the second equation yields the second-order equation $3I_1'' + 30I_1' + 125I_1 = 250$ with general solution

$$I_1(t) = 2 + e^{-5t}\left[c_1 \cos\left(5t\sqrt{6}/3\right) + c_2 \sin\left(5t\sqrt{6}/3\right)\right].$$

Substitution in $I_2 = (I_1' + 25I_1 - 50)/25$ now yields

$$I_2(t) = \frac{1}{15}e^{-5t}\left[\left(12c_1 + \sqrt{6}\,c_2\right)\cos\left(5t\sqrt{6}/3\right) + \left(12c_2 - \sqrt{6}\,c_1\right)\sin\left(5t\sqrt{6}/3\right)\right].$$

Imposition of the initial conditions $I_1(0) = 0$, $I_2(0) = 0$ now gives the equations $c_1 + 2 = 0$, $4c_1/5 + \sqrt{6}\,c_2/15 = 0$ with solution $c_1 = -2$, $c_2 = 4\sqrt{6}$. These coefficients give the desired particular solution

$$I_1(t) = 2 + e^{-5t}\left[-2\cos\left(5t\sqrt{6}/3\right) + 4\sqrt{6}\sin\left(5t\sqrt{6}/3\right)\right],$$

$$I_2(t) = \frac{20}{\sqrt{6}}e^{-5t}\sin\left(5t\sqrt{6}/3\right).$$

33. To solve the system
$$I_1' = -20(I_1 - I_2), \qquad I_2' = 40(I_1 - I_2)$$
we first note that $I_2' = -2I_1'$, so $I_2 = -2I_1 + K$. Then $K = 2I_1(0) + I_2(0) = 2(2) + 0 = 4$, so $I_2' = -2I_1'$, so $I_2 = -2I_1 + 4$. Substitution of this into the first equation gives the simple first-order linear equation $I_1' + 60I_1 = 80$ with general solution $I_1(t) = 4/3 + ce^{-60t}$. The initial condition $I_1(0) = 2$ gives $c = 2/3$, so

$$I_1(t) = \frac{2}{3}\left(2 + e^{-60t}\right), \qquad I_2(t) = \frac{4}{3}\left(1 - e^{-60t}\right).$$

35. The two given equations yield

$$mx^{(3)} = qBy'' = -q^2B^2x'/m,$$

so $x^{(3)} + \omega^2 x' = 0$. The general solution is

$$x(t) = A\cos\omega t + B\sin\omega t + C.$$

Now $x'(0) = 0$ implies $B = 0$, and then $x(0) = r_0$ gives $A + C = r_0$. Next,

$$\omega y' = x'' = -A\omega^2\cos\omega t,$$

so $y'(0) = -\omega r_0$ implies $A = r_0$, hence $C = 0$. It now follows readily that the trajectory is the circle

$$x(t) = r_0\cos\omega t, \qquad y(t) = -r_0\sin\omega t.$$

37.   **(a)**   If we set $m_1 = 2$, $m_2 = 1/2$, $k_1 = 75, k_2 = 25$ in Eqs. (3) of Section 4.1, we get the system $2x'' = -100x + 25y$, $\frac{1}{2}y'' = 25x - 25y$ with operational determinant $D^4 + 100D^2 + 1875 = (D^2 + 25)(D^2 + 75)$. Hence the general form of the solution is

$$x(t) = a_1 \cos 5t + a_2 \sin 5t + b_1 \cos 5t\sqrt{3} + b_2 \sin 5t\sqrt{3},$$
$$y(t) = c_1 \cos 5t + c_2 \sin 5t + d_1 \cos 5t\sqrt{3} + d_2 \sin 5t\sqrt{3}.$$

Upon substitution in either differential equation we see that $c_1 = 2a_1$, $c_2 = 2a_2$ and $d_1 = -2b_1$, $d_2 = -2b_2$. This gives

$$x(t) = a_1 \cos 5t + a_2 \sin 5t + b_1 \cos 5t\sqrt{3} + b_2 \sin 5t\sqrt{3},$$
$$y(t) = 2a_1 \cos 5t + 2a_2 \sin 5t - 2b_1 \cos 5t\sqrt{3} - 2b_2 \sin 5t\sqrt{3}.$$

(b)   In the natural mode with frequency $\omega_1 = 5$ the masses move in the same direction, while in the natural mode with frequency $\omega_2 = 5\sqrt{3}$ they move in opposite directions. In each case the amplitude of the motion of m_2 is twice that of m_1.

39.   The system has operational determinant is $8D^4 + 40D^2 + 32 = 8(D^2 + 1)(D^2 + 4)$. Hence the general form of the solution is

$$x(t) = a_1 \cos t + a_2 \sin t + b_1 \cos 2t + b_2 \sin 2t,$$
$$y(t) = c_1 \cos t + c_2 \sin t + d_1 \cos 2t + d_2 \sin 2t.$$

Upon substitution in either differential equation we see that $c_1 = 2a_1$, $c_2 = 2a_2$ and $d_1 = -b_1$, $d_2 = -b_2$. This gives

$$x(t) = a_1 \cos t + a_2 \sin t + b_1 \cos 2t + b_2 \sin 2t,$$
$$y(t) = 2a_1 \cos t + 2a_2 \sin t - b_1 \cos 2t - b_2 \sin 2t.$$

In the natural mode with frequency $\omega_1 = 1$ the masses move in the same direction, with the amplitude of motion of the second mass twice that of the first mass. In the natural mode with frequency $\omega_2 = 2$ they move in opposite directions with the same amplitude of motion.

41.   The system has operational determinant is $D^4 + 10D^2 + 9 = (D^2 + 1)(D^2 + 9)$. Hence the general form of the solution is

$$x(t) = a_1 \cos t + a_2 \sin t + b_1 \cos 3t + b_2 \sin 3t,$$
$$y(t) = c_1 \cos t + c_2 \sin t + d_1 \cos 3t + d_2 \sin 3t.$$

Upon substitution in either differential equation we see that $c_1 = a_1$, $c_2 = a_2$ and $d_1 = -b_1$, $d_2 = -b_2$. This gives

$$x(t) = a_1 \cos t + a_2 \sin t + b_1 \cos 3t + b_2 \sin 3t,$$
$$y(t) = a_1 \cos t + a_2 \sin t - b_1 \cos 3t - b_2 \sin 3t.$$

In the natural mode with frequency $\omega_1 = 1$ the masses move in the same direction, while in the natural mode with frequency $\omega_2 = 3$ they move in opposite directions. In each case the amplitudes of motion of the two masses are equal.

43. The system has operational determinant is $D^4 + 6D^2 + 5 = (D^2 + 1)(D^2 + 5)$. Hence the general form of the solution is

$$x(t) = a_1 \cos t + a_2 \sin t + b_1 \cos t\sqrt{5} + b_2 \sin t\sqrt{5},$$
$$y(t) = c_1 \cos t + c_2 \sin t + d_1 \cos t\sqrt{5} + d_2 \sin t\sqrt{5}.$$

Upon substitution in either differential equation we see that $c_1 = a_1$, $c_2 = a_2$ and $d_1 = -b_1$, $d_2 = -b_2$. This gives

$$x(t) = a_1 \cos t + a_2 \sin t + b_1 \cos t\sqrt{5} + b_2 \sin t\sqrt{5},$$
$$y(t) = a_1 \cos t + a_2 \sin t - b_1 \cos t\sqrt{5} - b_2 \sin t\sqrt{5}.$$

In the natural mode with frequency $\omega_1 = 1$ the masses move in the same direction, while in the natural mode with frequency $\omega_2 = \sqrt{5}$ they move in opposite directions. In each case the amplitudes of motion of the two masses are equal.

45. The system has operational determinant is $2D^4 + 20D^2 + 32 = 2(D^2 + 2)(D^2 + 8)$. Hence the general form of the solution is

$$x(t) = a_1 \cos t\sqrt{2} + a_2 \sin t\sqrt{2} + b_1 \cos t\sqrt{8} + b_2 \sin t\sqrt{8},$$
$$y(t) = c_1 \cos t\sqrt{2} + c_2 \sin t\sqrt{2} + d_1 \cos t\sqrt{8} + d_2 \sin t\sqrt{8}.$$

Upon substitution in either differential equation we see that $c_1 = a_1$, $c_2 = a_2$ and $d_1 = -b_1/2$, $d_2 = -b_2/2$. This gives

$$x(t) = a_1 \cos t\sqrt{2} + a_2 \sin t\sqrt{2} + b_1 \cos t\sqrt{8} + b_2 \sin t\sqrt{8},$$
$$y(t) = a_1 \cos t\sqrt{2} + a_2 \sin t\sqrt{2} - \tfrac{1}{2}b_1 \cos t\sqrt{8} - \tfrac{1}{2}b_2 \sin t\sqrt{8}.$$

In the natural mode with frequency $\omega_1 = \sqrt{2}$ the two masses move in the same direction with equal amplitudes of oscillation. In the natural mode with frequency $\omega_2 = \sqrt{8} = 2\sqrt{2}$ the two masses move in opposite directions with the amplitude of m_2 being half that of m_1.

47. **(a)** Looking at Fig. 4.2.7 in the text, we see that the first spring is stretched by x, the second spring is stretched by $y - x$, the third spring is stretched by $z - y$, and the fourth spring is compressed by z. Hence Newton's second law gives $mx'' = -k(x) + k(y - x)$, $my'' = -k(y - x) + k(z - y)$, and $mz'' = -k(z - y) - k(z)$.

(b) The operational determinant is

$$(D^2 + 2)[(D^2 + 2)^2 - 1] + [-(D^2 + 2)] = (D^2 + 2)[(D^2 + 2)^2 - 2],$$

and the characteristic equation $(r^2 + 2)[(r^2 + 2)^2 - 2] = 0$ has roots $\pm i\sqrt{2}$ and $\pm i\sqrt{2 \pm \sqrt{2}}$.

SECTION 4.3

NUMERICAL METHODS FOR SYSTEMS

In Problems 1-8 we first write the given system in the form $x' = f(t, x, y)$, $y' = g(t, x, y)$. Then we use the template

$$h = 0.1; \quad t_1 = t_0 + h$$
$$x_1 = x_0 + h f(t_0, x_0, y_0); \quad y_1 = y_0 + h g(t_0, x_0, y_0)$$
$$x_2 = x_1 + h f(t_1, x_1, y_1); \quad y_2 = y_1 + h g(t_1, x_1, y_1)$$

(with the given values of t_0, x_0, and y_0) to calculate the Euler approximations $x_1 \approx x(0.1)$, $y_1 \approx y(0.1)$ and $x_2 \approx x(0.2)$, $y_2 \approx y(0.2)$ in part (a). We give these approximations and the actual values $x_{act} = x(0.2)$, $y_{act} = y(0.2)$ in tabular form. We use the template

$$h = 0.2; \quad t_1 = t_0 + h$$
$$u_1 = x_0 + h f(t_0, x_0, y_0); \quad v_1 = y_0 + h g(t_0, x_0, y_0)$$
$$x_1 = x_0 + \tfrac{1}{2}h\big[f(t_0, x_0, y_0) + f(t_1, u_1, v_1)\big]$$
$$y_1 = y_0 + \tfrac{1}{2}h\big[g(t_0, x_0, y_0) + g(t_1, u_1, v_1)\big]$$

to calculate the improved Euler approximations $u_1 \approx x(0.2)$, $u_1 \approx y(0.2)$ and $x_1 \approx x(0.2)$, $y_1 \approx y(0.2)$ in part (b). We give these approximations and the actual values $x_{act} = x(0.2)$, $y_{act} = y(0.2)$ in tabular form. We use the template

$$h = 0.2;$$
$$F_1 = f(t_0, x_0, y_0); \quad G_1 = g(t_0, x_0, y_0)$$
$$F_2 = f(t_0 + \tfrac{1}{2}h, x_0 + \tfrac{1}{2}hF_1, y_0 + \tfrac{1}{2}hG_1); \quad G_2 = g(t_0 + \tfrac{1}{2}h, x_0 + \tfrac{1}{2}hF_1, y_0 + \tfrac{1}{2}hG_1)$$
$$F_3 = f(t_0 + \tfrac{1}{2}h, x_0 + \tfrac{1}{2}hF_2, y_0 + \tfrac{1}{2}hG_2); \quad G_3 = g(t_0 + \tfrac{1}{2}h, x_0 + \tfrac{1}{2}hF_2, y_0 + \tfrac{1}{2}hG_2)$$
$$F_4 = f(t_0 + h, x_0 + hF_3, y_0 + hG_3); \quad G_4 = g(t_0 + h, x_0 + hF_3, y_0 + hG_3)$$
$$x_1 = x_0 + \frac{h}{6}(F_1 + 2F_2 + 2F_3 + F_4); \quad y_1 = y_0 + \frac{h}{6}(G_1 + 2G_2 + 2G_3 + G_4)$$

to calculate the intermediate slopes and Runge-Kutta approximations $x_1 \approx x(0.2)$, $y_1 \approx y(0.2)$ for part (c). Again, we give the results in tabular form.

1. **(a)**

x_1	y_1	x_2	y_2	x_{act}	y_{act}
0.4	2.2	0.88	2.5	1.0034	2.6408

(b)

u_1	v_1	x_1	y_1	x_{act}	y_{act}
0.8	2.4	0.96	2.6	1.0034	2.6408

(c)

F_1	G_1	F_2	G_2	F_3	G_3	F_4	G_4
4	2	4.8	3	5.08	3.26	6.32	4.684

x_1	y_1	x_{act}	y_{act}				
1.0027	2.6401	1.0034	2.6408				

3. **(a)**

x_1	y_1	x_2	y_2	x_{act}	y_{act}
1.7	1.5	2.81	2.31	3.6775	2.9628

(b)

u_1	v_1	x_1	y_1	x_{act}	y_{act}
2.4	2	3.22	2.62	3.6775	2.9628

(c)

F_1	G_1	F_2	G_2	F_3	G_3	F_4	G_4
7	5	11.1	8.1	13.57	9.95	23.102	17.122

x_1	y_1	x_{act}	y_{act}				
3.6481	2.9407	3.6775	2.9628				

5. **(a)**

x_1	y_1	x_2	y_2	x_{act}	y_{act}
0.9	3.2	−0.52	2.92	−0.5793	2.4488

(b)

u_1	v_1	x_1	y_1	x_{act}	y_{act}
−0.2	3.4	−0.84	2.44	−0.5793	2.4488

(c)

F_1	G_1	F_2	G_2	F_3	G_3	F_4	G_4
−11	2	−14.2	−2.8	−12.44	−3.12	−12.856	−6.704

x_1	y_1	x_{act}	y_{act}				
−0.5712	2.4485	−0.5793	2.4488				

7. **(a)**

x_1	y_1	x_2	y_2	x_{act}	y_{act}
2.5	1.3	3.12	1.68	3.2820	1.7902

(b)

u_1	v_1	x_1	y_1	x_{act}	y_{act}
3	1.6	3.24	1.76	3.2820	1.7902

(c)

F_1	G_1	F_2	G_2	F_3	G_3	F_4	G_4
5	3	6.2	3.8	6.48	4	8.088	5.096

x_1	y_1	x_{act}	y_{act}				
3.2816	1.7899	3.2820	1.7902				

In Problems 9–11 we use the same Runge-Kutta template as in part (c) of Problems 1-8 above, and give both the Runge-Kutta approximate values with step sizes $h = 0.1$ and $h = 0.05$, and also the actual values.

9.   With $h = 0.1$: $x(1) \approx 3.99261,$ $y(1) \approx 6.21770$
   With $h = 0.05$: $x(1) \approx 3.99234,$ $y(1) \approx 6.21768$
   Actual values: $x(1) \approx 3.99232,$ $y(1) \approx 6.21768$

11.   With $h = 0.1$: $x(1) \approx -0.05832,$ $y(1) \approx 0.56664$
   With $h = 0.05$: $x(1) \approx -0.05832,$ $y(1) \approx 0.56665$
   Actual values: $x(1) \approx -0.05832,$ $y(1) \approx 0.56665$

13.   With $y = x'$ we want to solve numerically the initial value problem

$$x' = y, \qquad\qquad x(0) = 0$$

$$y' = -32 - 0.04y, \qquad y(0) = 288.$$

When we run Program RK2DIM with step size $h = 0.1$ we find that the change of sign in the velocity v occurs as follows:

t	x	v
7.6	1050.2	+2.8
7.7	1050.3	−0.4

Thus the bolt attains a maximum height of about 1050 feet in about 7.7 seconds.

15. With $y = x'$, and with x in miles and t in seconds, we want to solve numerically the initial value problem

$$x' = y$$

$$y' = -95485.5/(x^2 + 7920x + 15681600)$$

$$x(0) = 0, \qquad\qquad y(0) = 1.$$

We find (running RK2DIM with $h = 1$) that the projectile reaches a maximum height of about 83.83 miles in about 168 sec = 2 min 48 sec.

16. We first defined the MATLAB function

```
function  xp  =   fnball(t,x)
%  Defines the baseball system
%       x1'  =  x'  =  x3,   x3'  =   -cvx'
%       x2'  =  y'  =  x4,   x4'  =   -cvy'- g
%  with air resistance coefficient c.

g   =   32;
c   =   0.0025;
xp  =   x;
v   =   sqrt(x(3).^2) + x(4).^2);
xp(1)   =     x(3);
xp(2)   =     x(4);
xp(3)   =   -c*v*x(3);
xp(4)   =   -c*v*x(4) - g;
```

Then, using the n-dimensional program **rkn** with step size 0.1 and initial data corresponding to the indicated initial inclination angles, we got the following results:

Angle	Time	Range
40	5.0	352.9
45	5.4	347.2
50	5.8	334.2

We have listed the time to the nearest tenth of a second, but have interpolated to find the range in feet.

17. The data in Problem 16 indicate that the range increases when the initial angle is decreased below 45°. The further data

Angle	Range
41.0	352.1
40.5	352.6
40.0	352.9
39.5	352.8
39.0	352.7
35.0	350.8

indicate that a maximum range of about 353 ft is attained with $\alpha \approx 40°$.

19. First we run program **rkn** (with $h = 0.1$) with $v_0 = 250$ ft/sec and obtain the following results:

t	x	y
5.0	457.43	103.90
6.0	503.73	36.36

Interpolation gives $x = 494.4$ when $y = 50$. Then a run with $v_0 = 255$ ft/sec gives the following results:

t	x	y
5.5	486.75	77.46
6.0	508.86	41.62

Finally a run with $v_0 = 253$ ft/sec gives these results:

t	x	y
5.5	484.77	75.44
6.0	506.82	39.53

Now $x \approx 500$ ft when $y = 50$ ft. Thus Babe Ruth's home run ball had an initial velocity of 253 ft/sec.

21. A run of program **rkn** with $h = 0.1$ indicates that the projectile has a range of about 21,400 ft ≈ 4.05 mi and a flight time of about 46 sec. It attains a maximum height of about 8970 ft in about 17.5 sec. At time $t \approx 23$ sec it has its minimum velocity of about 368 ft/sec. It hits the ground ($t \approx 46$ sec) at an angle of about 77° with a velocity of about 518 ft/sec.

CHAPTER 5

LINEAR SYSTEMS OF DIFFERENTIAL EQUATIONS

Along with Chapter 4, this chapter is designed to offer considerable flexibility in the treatment of linear systems, depending on the background in linear algebra that students are assumed to have. Sections 4.1 and 4.2 of the previous chapter can stand alone as a brief introduction to linear systems without the use of linear algebra and matrices. But this chapter employs the notation and terminology of elementary linear algebra. For ready reference and review, Section 5.1 includes a complete and self-contained account of the needed background of determinants, matrices, and vectors. The additional linear algebra that is needed in subsequent sections is introduced along the way.

SECTION 5.1

MATRICES AND LINEAR SYSTEMS

The first half-dozen pages of this section are devoted to a review of matrix notation and terminology. With students who've had some prior exposure to matrices and determinants, this review material can be skimmed rapidly. In this event serious study of the section can begin with the subsections on matrix-valued functions and first-order linear systems. About all that's actually needed for this purpose is some acquaintance with determinants, with matrix multiplication and inverse matrices, and with the fact that a square matrix is invertible if and only if its determinant is nonzero.

1.   **(a)** $2\mathbf{A} + 3\mathbf{B} = \begin{bmatrix} 4 & -6 \\ 8 & 14 \end{bmatrix} + \begin{bmatrix} 9 & -12 \\ 15 & 3 \end{bmatrix} = \begin{bmatrix} 13 & -18 \\ 23 & 17 \end{bmatrix}$

     (b) $3\mathbf{A} - 2\mathbf{B} = \begin{bmatrix} 6 & -9 \\ 12 & 21 \end{bmatrix} - \begin{bmatrix} 6 & -8 \\ 10 & 2 \end{bmatrix} = \begin{bmatrix} 0 & -1 \\ 2 & 19 \end{bmatrix}$

     (c) $\mathbf{AB} = \begin{bmatrix} -9 & -11 \\ 47 & -9 \end{bmatrix}$ **(d)** $\mathbf{BA} = \begin{bmatrix} -10 & -37 \\ 14 & -8 \end{bmatrix}$

3. $\mathbf{AB} = \begin{bmatrix} -1 & 8 \\ 46 & -1 \end{bmatrix};$ $\mathbf{BA} = \begin{bmatrix} 11 & -12 & 14 \\ -14 & 0 & 7 \\ 0 & 8 & -13 \end{bmatrix}$

The products **Ax** and **By** are not defined, because in neither case is the number of columns of the first factor equal to the number of rows of the second factor.

5.   **(a)** $7A + 4B = \begin{bmatrix} 21 & 14 & -7 \\ 0 & 28 & 21 \\ -35 & 14 & 49 \end{bmatrix} + \begin{bmatrix} 0 & -12 & 8 \\ 4 & 16 & -12 \\ 8 & 20 & -4 \end{bmatrix} = \begin{bmatrix} 21 & 2 & 1 \\ 4 & 44 & 9 \\ -27 & 34 & 45 \end{bmatrix}$

     (b) $3A - 5B = \begin{bmatrix} 9 & 6 & -3 \\ 0 & 12 & 9 \\ -15 & 6 & 21 \end{bmatrix} - \begin{bmatrix} 0 & -15 & 10 \\ 5 & 20 & -15 \\ 10 & 25 & -5 \end{bmatrix} = \begin{bmatrix} 9 & 21 & -13 \\ -5 & -8 & 24 \\ -25 & -19 & 26 \end{bmatrix}$

     (c) $AB = \begin{bmatrix} 0 & -6 & 1 \\ 10 & 31 & -15 \\ 16 & 58 & -23 \end{bmatrix}$

     (d) $BA = \begin{bmatrix} -10 & -8 & 5 \\ 18 & 12 & -10 \\ 11 & 22 & 6 \end{bmatrix}$

     (e) $A - tI = \begin{bmatrix} 3 & 2 & -1 \\ 0 & 4 & 3 \\ -5 & 2 & 7 \end{bmatrix} - \begin{bmatrix} t & 0 & 0 \\ 0 & t & 0 \\ 0 & 0 & t \end{bmatrix} = \begin{bmatrix} 3-t & 2 & -1 \\ 0 & 4-t & 3 \\ -5 & 2 & 7-t \end{bmatrix}$

7. $\det(AB) = 0 = 0 \cdot 0 = \det(A) \cdot \det(B)$

9. $(AB)' = \begin{bmatrix} t - 4t^2 + 6t^3 & t + t^2 - 4t^3 + 8t^4 \\ 3t + t^3 - t^4 & 4t^2 + t^3 + t^4 \end{bmatrix}' = \begin{bmatrix} 1 - 8t + 18t^2 & 1 + 2t - 12t^2 + 32t^3 \\ 3 + 3t^2 - 4t^3 & 8t + 3t^2 + 4t^3 \end{bmatrix}$

$A'B + AB' = \begin{bmatrix} 1 & 2 \\ 3t^2 & -\dfrac{1}{t^2} \end{bmatrix} \begin{bmatrix} 1-t & 1+t \\ 3t^2 & 4t^3 \end{bmatrix} + \begin{bmatrix} t & 2t-1 \\ t^3 & \dfrac{1}{t} \end{bmatrix} \begin{bmatrix} -1 & 1 \\ 6t & 12t^2 \end{bmatrix}$

$= \begin{bmatrix} 1 - t + 6t^2 & 1 + t + 8t^3 \\ -3 + 3t^2 - 3t^3 & -4t + 3t^2 + 3t^3 \end{bmatrix} + \begin{bmatrix} -7t + 12t^2 & t - 12t^2 + 24t^3 \\ 6 - t^3 & 12t + t^3 \end{bmatrix}$

$= \begin{bmatrix} 1 - 8t + 18t^2 & 1 + 2t - 12t^2 + 32t^3 \\ 3 + 3t^2 - 4t^3 & 8t + 3t^2 + 4t^3 \end{bmatrix}$

11. $\mathbf{x} = \begin{bmatrix} x \\ y \end{bmatrix}$, $P(t) = \begin{bmatrix} 0 & -3 \\ 3 & 0 \end{bmatrix}$, $\mathbf{f}(t) = \begin{bmatrix} 0 \\ 0 \end{bmatrix}$

13. $\mathbf{x} = \begin{bmatrix} x \\ y \end{bmatrix}$, $\quad \mathbf{P}(t) = \begin{bmatrix} 2 & 4 \\ 5 & -1 \end{bmatrix}$, $\quad \mathbf{f}(t) = \begin{bmatrix} 3e^t \\ -t^2 \end{bmatrix}$

15. $\mathbf{x} = \begin{bmatrix} x \\ y \\ z \end{bmatrix}$, $\quad \mathbf{P}(t) = \begin{bmatrix} 0 & 1 & 1 \\ 1 & 0 & 1 \\ 1 & 1 & 0 \end{bmatrix}$, $\quad \mathbf{f}(t) = \begin{bmatrix} 0 \\ 0 \\ 0 \end{bmatrix}$

17. $\mathbf{x} = \begin{bmatrix} x \\ y \\ z \end{bmatrix}$, $\quad \mathbf{P}(t) = \begin{bmatrix} 3 & -4 & 1 \\ 1 & 0 & -3 \\ 0 & 6 & -7 \end{bmatrix}$, $\quad \mathbf{f}(t) = \begin{bmatrix} t \\ t^2 \\ t^3 \end{bmatrix}$

19. $\mathbf{x} = \begin{bmatrix} x_1 \\ x_2 \\ x_3 \\ x_4 \end{bmatrix}$, $\quad \mathbf{P}(t) = \begin{bmatrix} 0 & 1 & 0 & 0 \\ 0 & 0 & 2 & 0 \\ 0 & 0 & 0 & 3 \\ 4 & 0 & 0 & 0 \end{bmatrix}$, $\quad \mathbf{f}(t) = \begin{bmatrix} 0 \\ 0 \\ 0 \\ 0 \end{bmatrix}$

21. $W(t) = \begin{vmatrix} 2e^t & e^{2t} \\ -3e^t & -e^{2t} \end{vmatrix} = e^{3t} \neq 0$

$$\mathbf{x}_1' = \begin{bmatrix} 2e^t \\ -3e^t \end{bmatrix}' = \begin{bmatrix} 2e^t \\ -3e^t \end{bmatrix} = \begin{bmatrix} 4 & 2 \\ -3 & -1 \end{bmatrix}\begin{bmatrix} 2e^t \\ -3e^t \end{bmatrix} = \mathbf{A}\mathbf{x}_1$$

$$\mathbf{x}_2' = \begin{bmatrix} e^{2t} \\ -e^{2t} \end{bmatrix}' = \begin{bmatrix} 2e^{2t} \\ -2e^{2t} \end{bmatrix} = \begin{bmatrix} 4 & 2 \\ -3 & -1 \end{bmatrix}\begin{bmatrix} e^{2t} \\ -e^{2t} \end{bmatrix} = \mathbf{A}\mathbf{x}_2$$

$$\mathbf{x}(t) = c_1\mathbf{x}_1 + c_2\mathbf{x}_2 = c_1\begin{bmatrix} 2e^t \\ -3e^t \end{bmatrix} + c_2\begin{bmatrix} e^{2t} \\ -e^{2t} \end{bmatrix} = \begin{bmatrix} 2c_1e^t + c_2e^{2t} \\ -3c_1e^t - c_2e^{2t} \end{bmatrix}$$

In most of Problems 22-30, we omit the verifications of the given solutions. In each case, this is simply a matter of calculating both the derivative $\mathbf{x}_i'$ of the given solution vector and the product $\mathbf{A}\mathbf{x}_i$ (where $\mathbf{A}$ is the coefficient matrix in the given differential equation) to verify that $\mathbf{x}_i' = \mathbf{A}\mathbf{x}_i$ (just as in the verification of the solutions $\mathbf{x}_1$ and $\mathbf{x}_2$ in Problem 21 above).

23. $W(t) = \begin{vmatrix} e^{2t} & e^{-2t} \\ e^{2t} & 5e^{-2t} \end{vmatrix} = 4 \neq 0$

$$\mathbf{x}(t) = c_1\mathbf{x}_1 + c_2\mathbf{x}_2 = c_1\begin{bmatrix} 1 \\ 1 \end{bmatrix}e^{2t} + c_2\begin{bmatrix} 1 \\ 5 \end{bmatrix}e^{-2t} = \begin{bmatrix} c_1e^{2t} + c_2e^{-2t} \\ c_1e^{2t} + 5c_2e^{-2t} \end{bmatrix}$$

25. $W(t) = \begin{vmatrix} 3e^{2t} & e^{-5t} \\ 2e^{2t} & 3e^{-5t} \end{vmatrix} = 7e^{-3t} \neq 0$

$$\mathbf{x}(t) = c_1\mathbf{x}_1 + c_2\mathbf{x}_2 = c_1\begin{bmatrix} 3e^{2t} \\ 2e^{2t} \end{bmatrix} + c_2\begin{bmatrix} e^{-5t} \\ 3e^{-5t} \end{bmatrix} = \begin{bmatrix} 3c_1e^{2t} + c_2e^{-5t} \\ 2c_1e^{2t} + 3c_2e^{-5t} \end{bmatrix}$$

27. $W(t) = \begin{vmatrix} e^{2t} & e^{-t} & 0 \\ e^{2t} & 0 & e^{-t} \\ e^{2t} & -e^{-t} & -e^{-t} \end{vmatrix} = 3 \neq 0$

$$\mathbf{x}(t) = c_1\mathbf{x}_1 + c_2\mathbf{x}_2 + c_3\mathbf{x}_3 = c_1\begin{bmatrix} 1 \\ 1 \\ 1 \end{bmatrix}e^{2t} + c_2\begin{bmatrix} 1 \\ 0 \\ -1 \end{bmatrix}e^{-t} + c_3\begin{bmatrix} 0 \\ 1 \\ -1 \end{bmatrix}e^{-t} = \begin{bmatrix} c_1e^{2t} + c_2e^{-t} \\ c_1e^{2t} + c_3e^{-t} \\ c_1e^{2t} - c_2e^{-t} - c_3e^{-t} \end{bmatrix}$$

$$\mathbf{x}_1' = \begin{bmatrix} 2 \\ 2 \\ 2 \end{bmatrix}e^t = \begin{bmatrix} 0 & 1 & 1 \\ 1 & 0 & 1 \\ 1 & 1 & 0 \end{bmatrix}\begin{bmatrix} 1 \\ 1 \\ 1 \end{bmatrix}e^t = \mathbf{A}\mathbf{x}_1$$

$$\mathbf{x}_2' = \begin{bmatrix} -1 \\ 0 \\ 1 \end{bmatrix}e^{-t} = \begin{bmatrix} 0 & 1 & 1 \\ 1 & 0 & 1 \\ 1 & 1 & 0 \end{bmatrix}\begin{bmatrix} 1 \\ 0 \\ -1 \end{bmatrix}e^{-t} = \mathbf{A}\mathbf{x}_2$$

$$\mathbf{x}_3' = \begin{bmatrix} 0 \\ -1 \\ 1 \end{bmatrix}e^t = \begin{bmatrix} 0 & 1 & 1 \\ 1 & 0 & 1 \\ 1 & 1 & 0 \end{bmatrix}\begin{bmatrix} 0 \\ 1 \\ -1 \end{bmatrix}e^{-t} = \mathbf{A}\mathbf{x}_3$$

29. $W(t) = \begin{vmatrix} 3e^{-2t} & e^t & e^{3t} \\ -2e^{-2t} & -e^t & -e^{3t} \\ 2e^{-2t} & e^t & 0 \end{vmatrix} = e^{2t} \neq 0$

$$\mathbf{x}(t) = c_1\mathbf{x}_1 + c_2\mathbf{x}_2 + c_3\mathbf{x}_3 = c_1\begin{bmatrix} 3 \\ -2 \\ 2 \end{bmatrix}e^{-2t} + c_2\begin{bmatrix} 1 \\ -1 \\ 1 \end{bmatrix}e^t + c_3\begin{bmatrix} 1 \\ -1 \\ 0 \end{bmatrix}e^{3t} = \begin{bmatrix} 3c_1e^{-2t} + c_2e^t + c_3e^{3t} \\ -2c_1e^{-2t} - c_2e^t - c_3e^{3t} \\ 2c_1e^{-2t} + c_2e^t \end{bmatrix}$$

In Problems 31-34 (and similarly in Problems 35-40) we give first the scalar components $x_1(t)$ and $x_2(t)$ of a general solution, then the equations in the coefficients c_1 and c_2 that are obtained when the given initial conditions are imposed, and finally the resulting particular solution of the given system.

31. $\quad x_1(t) = c_1e^{3t} + 2c_2e^{-2t}, \quad x_2(t) = 3c_1e^{3t} + c_2e^{-2t}$

$\quad c_1 + 2c_2 = 0, \qquad 3c_1 + c_2 = 5$

$\quad x_1(t) = 2e^{3t} - 2e^{-2t}, \quad x_2(t) = 6e^{3t} - e^{-2t}$

33. $\quad x_1(t) = c_1e^{3t} + c_2e^{2t}, \quad x_2(t) = -c_1e^{3t} - 2c_2e^{2t}$

$\quad c_1 + c_2 = 11, \qquad -c_1 - 2c_2 = -7$

$\quad x_1(t) = 15e^{3t} - 4e^{2t}, \quad x_2(t) = -15e^{3t} + 8e^{2t}$

35. $\quad x_1(t) = 2c_1e^t - 2c_2e^{3t} + 2c_3e^{5t}, \quad x_2(t) = 2c_1e^t - 2c_3e^{5t}, \quad x_3(t) = c_1e^t + c_2e^{3t} + c_3e^{5t}$

$\quad 2c_1 - 2c_2 + 2c_3 = 0, \qquad 2c_1 - 2c_3 = 0, \qquad c_1 + c_2 + c_3 = 4$

$\quad x_1(t) = 2e^t - 4e^{3t} + 2e^{5t}, \quad x_2(t) = 2e^t - 2e^{5t}, \quad x_3(t) = e^t + 2e^{3t} + e^{5t}$

37. $\quad x_1(t) = 3c_1e^{-2t} + c_2e^t + c_3e^{3t}, \quad x_2(t) = -2c_1e^{-2t} - c_2e^t - c_3e^{3t}, \quad x_3(t) = 2c_1e^{-2t} + c_2e^t$

$\quad 3c_1 + c_2 + c_3 = 1, \qquad -2c_1 - c_2 - c_3 = 2, \qquad 2c_1 + c_2 = 3$

$\quad x_1(t) = 9e^{-2t} - 3e^t - 5e^{3t}, \quad x_2(t) = -6e^{-2t} + 3e^t + 5e^{3t}, \quad x_3(t) = 6e^{-2t} - 3e^t$

39. $\quad x_1(t) = c_1e^{-t} + c_4e^t, \quad x_2(t) = c_3e^t, \quad x_3(t) = c_2e^{-t} + 3c_4e^t, \quad x_4(t) = c_1e^{-t} - 2c_3e^t$

$\quad c_1 + c_4 = 1, \qquad c_3 = 1, \qquad c_2 + 3c_4 = 1, \qquad c_1 - 2c_3 = 1$

$\quad x_1(t) = 3e^{-t} - 2e^t, \quad x_2(t) = e^t, \quad x_3(t) = 7e^{-t} - 6e^t, \quad x_4(t) = 3e^{-t} - 2e^t$

41. (a) $\mathbf{x}_2 = t\mathbf{x}_1$, so neither is a constant multiple of the other.

(b) $W(\mathbf{x}_1, \mathbf{x}_2) = 0$, whereas Theorem 2 would imply that $W \neq 0$ if $\mathbf{x}_1$ and $\mathbf{x}_2$ were independent solutions of a system of the indicated form.

43. Suppose $W(a) = x_{11}(a)x_{22}(a) - x_{12}(a)x_{21}(a) = 0$. Then the coefficient determinant of the homogeneous linear system $c_1x_{11}(a) + c_2x_{12}(a) = 0$, $c_1x_{21}(a) + c_2x_{22}(a) = 0$ vanishes. The system therefore has a non-trivial solution $\{c_1, c_2\}$ such that $c_1\mathbf{x}_1(a) + c_2\mathbf{x}_2(a) = 0$. Then $\mathbf{x}(t) = c_1\mathbf{x}_1(t) + c_2\mathbf{x}_2(t)$ is a solution of $\mathbf{x}' = \mathbf{Px}$ such that $\mathbf{x}(a) = 0$. It therefore follows (by uniqueness of solutions) that $\mathbf{x}(t) \equiv 0$, that is, $c_1\mathbf{x}_1(t) + c_2\mathbf{x}_2(t) \equiv 0$ with c_1 and c_2 not both zero. Thus the solution vectors $\mathbf{x}_1$ and $\mathbf{x}_2$ are linearly dependent.

45. Suppose that $c_1\mathbf{x}_1(t) + c_2\mathbf{x}_2(t) + \cdots + c_n\mathbf{x}_n(t) \equiv 0$. Then the ith scalar component of this vector equation is $c_1x_{i1}(t) + c_2x_{i2}(t) + \cdots + c_nx_{in}(t) \equiv 0$. Hence the fact that the scalar functions $x_{i1}(t), x_{i2}(t), \cdots, x_{in}(t)$ are linear linearly independent implies that

$c_1 = c_2 = \cdots \ c_n = 0$. Consequently the vector functions $\mathbf{x}_1(t), \mathbf{x}_2(t), \cdots, \mathbf{x}_n(t)$ are linearly independent.

SECTION 5.2

THE EIGENVALUE METHOD FOR HOMOGENEOUS LINEAR SYSTEMS

In each of Problems 1-16 we give the characteristic equation, the eigenvalues λ_1 and λ_2 of the coefficient matrix of the given system, the corresponding equations determining the associated eigenvectors $\mathbf{v}_1 = [a_1 \ \ b_1]^T$ and $\mathbf{v}_2 = [a_2 \ \ b_2]^T$, these eigenvectors, and the resulting scalar components $x_1(t)$ and $x_2(t)$ of a general solution $\mathbf{x}(t) = c_1 \mathbf{v}_1 e^{\lambda_1 t} + c_2 \mathbf{v}_2 e^{\lambda_2 t}$ of the system.

1. Characteristic equation $\quad \lambda^2 - 2\lambda - 3 = 0$

Eigenvalues $\quad \lambda_1 = -1$ and $\lambda_2 = 3$

Eigenvector equations $\begin{bmatrix} 2 & 2 \\ 2 & 2 \end{bmatrix} \begin{bmatrix} a_1 \\ b_1 \end{bmatrix} = \begin{bmatrix} 0 \\ 0 \end{bmatrix}$ and $\begin{bmatrix} -2 & 2 \\ 2 & -2 \end{bmatrix} \begin{bmatrix} a_2 \\ b_2 \end{bmatrix} = \begin{bmatrix} 0 \\ 0 \end{bmatrix}$

Eigenvectors $\mathbf{v}_1 = [1 \ \ -1]^T$ and $\mathbf{v}_2 = [1 \ \ 1]^T$

$x_1(t) = c_1 e^{-t} + c_2 e^{3t}, \quad x_2(t) = -c_1 e^{-t} + c_2 e^{3t}$

3. Characteristic equation $\quad \lambda^2 - 5\lambda - 6 = 0$

Eigenvalues $\quad \lambda_1 = -1$ and $\lambda_2 = 6$

Eigenvector equations $\begin{bmatrix} 4 & 4 \\ 3 & 3 \end{bmatrix} \begin{bmatrix} a_1 \\ b_1 \end{bmatrix} = \begin{bmatrix} 0 \\ 0 \end{bmatrix}$ and $\begin{bmatrix} -3 & 4 \\ 3 & -4 \end{bmatrix} \begin{bmatrix} a_2 \\ b_2 \end{bmatrix} = \begin{bmatrix} 0 \\ 0 \end{bmatrix}$

Eigenvectors $\mathbf{v}_1 = [1 \ \ -1]^T$ and $\mathbf{v}_2 = [4 \ \ 3]^T$

$x_1(t) = c_1 e^{-t} + 4c_2 e^{6t}, \quad x_2(t) = -c_1 e^{-t} + 3c_2 e^{6t}$

The equations

$$x_1(0) = c_1 + 4c_2 = 1$$
$$x_2(0) = -c_1 + 3c_2 = 1$$

yield $c_1 = -1/7$ and $c_2 = 2/7$, so the desired particular solution is given by

$$x_1(t) = (-e^{-t} + 8e^{6t})/7, \quad x_2(t) = (\ e^{-t} + 6e^{6t})/7.$$

5.   Characteristic equation $\lambda^2 - 4\lambda - 5 = 0$

Eigenvalues $\lambda_1 = -1$ and $\lambda_2 = 5$

Eigenvector equations $\begin{bmatrix} 7 & -7 \\ 1 & -1 \end{bmatrix}\begin{bmatrix} a_1 \\ b_1 \end{bmatrix} = \begin{bmatrix} 0 \\ 0 \end{bmatrix}$ and $\begin{bmatrix} 1 & -7 \\ 1 & -7 \end{bmatrix}\begin{bmatrix} a_2 \\ b_2 \end{bmatrix} = \begin{bmatrix} 0 \\ 0 \end{bmatrix}$

Eigenvectors $\mathbf{v}_1 = \begin{bmatrix} 1 & 1 \end{bmatrix}^T$ and $\mathbf{v}_2 = \begin{bmatrix} 7 & 1 \end{bmatrix}^T$

$x_1(t) = c_1 e^{-t} + 7c_2 e^{5t}, \quad x_2(t) = c_1 e^{-t} + c_2 e^{5t}$

7.   Characteristic equation $\lambda^2 + 8\lambda - 9 = 0$

Eigenvalues $\lambda_1 = 1$ and $\lambda_2 = -9$

Eigenvector equations $\begin{bmatrix} -4 & 4 \\ 6 & -6 \end{bmatrix}\begin{bmatrix} a_1 \\ b_1 \end{bmatrix} = \begin{bmatrix} 0 \\ 0 \end{bmatrix}$ and $\begin{bmatrix} 6 & 4 \\ 6 & 4 \end{bmatrix}\begin{bmatrix} a_2 \\ b_2 \end{bmatrix} = \begin{bmatrix} 0 \\ 0 \end{bmatrix}$

Eigenvectors $\mathbf{v}_1 = \begin{bmatrix} 1 & 1 \end{bmatrix}^T$ and $\mathbf{v}_2 = \begin{bmatrix} 2 & -3 \end{bmatrix}^T$

$x_1(t) = c_1 e^{t} + 2c_2 e^{-9t}, \quad x_2(t) = c_1 e^{t} - 3c_2 e^{-9t}$

9.   Characteristic equation $\lambda^2 + 16 = 0$

Eigenvalue $\lambda = 4i$

Eigenvector equation $\begin{bmatrix} 2-4i & -5 \\ 4 & -2-4i \end{bmatrix}\begin{bmatrix} a \\ b \end{bmatrix} = \begin{bmatrix} 0 \\ 0 \end{bmatrix}$

Eigenvector $\mathbf{v} = \begin{bmatrix} 5 & 2-4i \end{bmatrix}^T$

The real and imaginary parts of

$$\mathbf{x}(t) = \mathbf{v}e^{4it} = \begin{bmatrix} 5\cos 4t + 5i\sin 4t \\ (2\cos 4t + 4\sin 4t) + i(2\sin 4t - 4\cos 4t) \end{bmatrix}$$

yield the general solution

$$x_1(t) = 5c_1\cos 4t + 5c_2\sin 4t$$
$$x_2(t) = c_1(2\cos 4t + 4\sin 4t) + c_2(2\sin 4t - 4\cos 4t).$$

The initial conditions $x_1(0) = 2$ and $x_2(0) = 3$ give $c_1 = 2/5$ and $c_2 = -11/20$, so the desired particular solution is

$$x_1(t) = 2\cos 4t - (11/4)\sin 4t$$
$$x_2(t) = 3\cos 4t + (1/2)\sin 4t.$$

11.   Characteristic equation $\lambda^2 - 2\lambda + 5 = 0$

Eigenvalue $\lambda = 1 - 2i$

Eigenvector equation $\begin{bmatrix} 2i & -2 \\ 2 & 2i \end{bmatrix} \begin{bmatrix} a \\ b \end{bmatrix} = \begin{bmatrix} 0 \\ 0 \end{bmatrix}$

Eigenvector $\mathbf{v} = [1 \quad i]^T$

The real and imaginary parts of

$$\mathbf{x}(t) = [1 \quad i]^T e^t(\cos 2t - i \sin 2t)$$
$$= e^t [\cos 2t \quad \sin 2t]^T + i e^t [-\sin 2t \quad \cos 2t]^T$$

yield the general solution

$$x_1(t) = e^t(c_1 \cos 2t - c_2 \sin 2t)$$
$$x_2(t) = e^t(c_1 \sin 2t + c_2 \cos 2t).$$

The particular solution with $x_1(0) = 0$ and $x_2(0) = 4$ is obtained with $c_1 = 0$ and $c_2 = 4$, so

$$x_1(t) = -4e^t \sin 2t, \qquad\qquad x_2(t) = 4e^t \cos 2t.$$

13.   Characteristic equation $\lambda^2 - 4\lambda + 13 = 0$

Eigenvalue $\lambda = 2 - 3i$

Eigenvector equation $\begin{bmatrix} 3+3i & -9 \\ 2 & -3-3i \end{bmatrix} \begin{bmatrix} a \\ b \end{bmatrix} = \begin{bmatrix} 0 \\ 0 \end{bmatrix}$

Eigenvector $\mathbf{v} = [3 \quad 1+i]^T$

$$\mathbf{x}(t) = \mathbf{v} e^{(2-3i)t} = e^{2t} \begin{bmatrix} 3\cos 3t - 3i\sin 3t \\ (\cos 3t + \sin 3t) + i(\cos 3t - \sin 3t) \end{bmatrix}$$

$$x_1(t) = 3e^{2t}(c_1 \cos 3t - c_2 \sin 3t)$$
$$x_2(t) = e^{2t}[(c_1 + c_2)\cos 3t + (c_1 - c_2)\sin 3t].$$

15.   Characteristic equation $\lambda^2 - 10\lambda + 41 = 0$

Eigenvalue $\lambda = 5 - 4i$

Eigenvector equation $\begin{bmatrix} 2-4i & -5 \\ 4 & -2-4i \end{bmatrix} \begin{bmatrix} a \\ b \end{bmatrix} = \begin{bmatrix} 0 \\ 0 \end{bmatrix}$

Eigenvector $\mathbf{v} = [5 \quad 2+4i]^T$

$$\mathbf{x}(t) = \mathbf{v} e^{(5-4i)t} = e^{5t} \begin{bmatrix} 5\cos 4t - 5i\sin 4t \\ (2\cos 4t + 4\sin 4t) + i(4\cos 4t - 2\sin 4t) \end{bmatrix}$$

$x_1(t) = 5e^{5t}(c_1\cos 4t - c_2\sin 4t)$

$x_2(t) = e^{5t}[(2c_1 + 4c_2)\cos 4t + (4c_1 - 2c_2)\sin 4t]$

17. Characteristic equation $-\lambda^3 + 15\lambda^2 - 54\lambda = 0$

Eigenvalues $\lambda_1 = 9, \quad \lambda_2 = 6, \quad \lambda_3 = 0$

Eigenvector equations

$$\begin{bmatrix} -5 & 1 & 4 \\ 1 & -2 & 1 \\ 4 & 1 & -5 \end{bmatrix}\begin{bmatrix} a_1 \\ b_1 \\ c_1 \end{bmatrix} = \begin{bmatrix} 0 \\ 0 \\ 0 \end{bmatrix}, \quad \begin{bmatrix} -2 & 1 & 4 \\ 1 & 1 & 1 \\ 4 & 1 & -2 \end{bmatrix}\begin{bmatrix} a_2 \\ b_2 \\ c_2 \end{bmatrix} = \begin{bmatrix} 0 \\ 0 \\ 0 \end{bmatrix}, \quad \begin{bmatrix} 4 & 1 & 4 \\ 1 & 7 & 1 \\ 4 & 1 & 4 \end{bmatrix}\begin{bmatrix} a_3 \\ b_3 \\ c_3 \end{bmatrix} = \begin{bmatrix} 0 \\ 0 \\ 0 \end{bmatrix}$$

Eigenvectors $\mathbf{v}_1 = [1 \quad 1 \quad 1]^T, \quad \mathbf{v}_2 = [1 \quad -2 \quad 1]^T, \quad \mathbf{v}_3 = [1 \quad 0 \quad -1]^T$

$x_1(t) = c_1 e^{9t} + c_2 e^{6t} + c_3$

$x_2(t) = c_1 e^{9t} - 2c_2 e^{6t}$

$x_3(t) = c_1 e^{9t} + c_2 e^{6t} - c_3$

19. Characteristic equation $-\lambda^3 + 12\lambda^2 - 45\lambda + 54 = 0$

Eigenvalues $\lambda_1 = 6, \quad \lambda_2 = 3, \quad \lambda_3 = 3$

Eigenvector equations

$$\begin{bmatrix} -2 & 1 & 1 \\ 1 & -2 & 1 \\ 1 & 1 & -2 \end{bmatrix}\begin{bmatrix} a_1 \\ b_1 \\ c_1 \end{bmatrix} = \begin{bmatrix} 0 \\ 0 \\ 0 \end{bmatrix}, \quad \begin{bmatrix} 1 & 1 & 1 \\ 1 & 1 & 1 \\ 1 & 1 & 1 \end{bmatrix}\begin{bmatrix} a_2 \\ b_2 \\ c_2 \end{bmatrix} = \begin{bmatrix} 0 \\ 0 \\ 0 \end{bmatrix}, \quad \begin{bmatrix} 1 & 1 & 1 \\ 1 & 1 & 1 \\ 1 & 1 & 1 \end{bmatrix}\begin{bmatrix} a_3 \\ b_3 \\ c_3 \end{bmatrix} = \begin{bmatrix} 0 \\ 0 \\ 0 \end{bmatrix}$$

Eigenvectors $\mathbf{v}_1 = [1 \quad 1 \quad 1]^T, \quad \mathbf{v}_2 = [1 \quad -2 \quad 1]^T, \quad \mathbf{v}_3 = [1 \quad 0 \quad -1]^T$

$x_1(t) = c_1 e^{6t} + c_2 e^{3t} + c_3 e^{3t}$

$x_2(t) = c_1 e^{6t} - 2c_2 e^{3t}$

$x_3(t) = c_1 e^{6t} + c_2 e^{3t} - c_3 e^{3t}$

21. Characteristic equation $-\lambda^3 + \lambda = 0$

Eigenvalues $\lambda_1 = 0, \quad \lambda_2 = 1, \quad \lambda_3 = -1$

Eigenvector equations

$$\begin{bmatrix} -4 & 1 & 3 \\ 1 & -2 & 1 \\ 3 & 1 & -4 \end{bmatrix}\begin{bmatrix} a_1 \\ b_1 \\ c_1 \end{bmatrix} = \begin{bmatrix} 0 \\ 0 \\ 0 \end{bmatrix}, \quad \begin{bmatrix} 5 & 0 & -6 \\ 2 & -1 & -2 \\ 4 & -2 & -4 \end{bmatrix}\begin{bmatrix} a_2 \\ b_2 \\ c_2 \end{bmatrix} = \begin{bmatrix} 0 \\ 0 \\ 0 \end{bmatrix}, \quad \begin{bmatrix} 6 & 0 & -6 \\ 2 & 0 & -2 \\ 4 & -2 & -3 \end{bmatrix}\begin{bmatrix} a_3 \\ b_3 \\ c_3 \end{bmatrix} = \begin{bmatrix} 0 \\ 0 \\ 0 \end{bmatrix}$$

Eigenvectors $\mathbf{v}_1 = [6 \ \ 2 \ \ 5]^T, \quad \mathbf{v}_2 = [3 \ \ 1 \ \ 2]^T, \quad \mathbf{v}_3 = [2 \ \ 1 \ \ 2]^T$

$x_1(t) = 6c_1 + 3c_2 e^t + 2c_3 e^{-t}$

$x_2(t) = 2c_1 + c_2 e^t + c_3 e^{-t}$

$x_3(t) = 5c_1 + 2c_2 e^t + 2c_3 e^{-t}$

23. Characteristic equation $-\lambda^3 + 3\lambda^2 + 4\lambda - 12 = 0$

Eigenvalues $\lambda_1 = 2, \ \lambda_2 = -2, \ \lambda_3 = 3$

Eigenvector equations

$$\begin{bmatrix} 1 & 1 & 1 \\ -5 & -5 & -1 \\ 5 & 5 & 1 \end{bmatrix}\begin{bmatrix} a_1 \\ b_1 \\ c_1 \end{bmatrix} = \begin{bmatrix} 0 \\ 0 \\ 0 \end{bmatrix}, \quad \begin{bmatrix} 5 & 1 & 1 \\ -5 & -1 & -1 \\ 5 & 5 & 5 \end{bmatrix}\begin{bmatrix} a_2 \\ b_2 \\ c_2 \end{bmatrix} = \begin{bmatrix} 0 \\ 0 \\ 0 \end{bmatrix}, \quad \begin{bmatrix} 0 & 1 & 1 \\ -5 & -6 & -1 \\ 5 & 5 & 0 \end{bmatrix}\begin{bmatrix} a_3 \\ b_3 \\ c_3 \end{bmatrix} = \begin{bmatrix} 0 \\ 0 \\ 0 \end{bmatrix}$$

Eigenvectors $\mathbf{v}_1 = [1 \ \ -1 \ \ 0]^T, \quad \mathbf{v}_2 = [0 \ \ 1 \ \ -1]^T, \quad \mathbf{v}_3 = [1 \ \ -1 \ \ 1]^T$

$x_1(t) = c_1 e^{2t} \qquad\qquad + c_3 e^{3t}$

$x_2(t) = -c_1 e^{2t} + c_2 e^{-2t} - c_3 e^{3t}$

$x_3(t) = \qquad\qquad - c_2 e^{-2t} + c_3 e^{3t}$

25. Characteristic equation $-\lambda^3 + 4\lambda^2 - 13\lambda = 0$

Eigenvalues $\lambda = 0$ and $2 \pm 3i$

With $\lambda = 1$ the eigenvector equation

$$\begin{bmatrix} 5 & 5 & 2 \\ -6 & -6 & -5 \\ 6 & 6 & 5 \end{bmatrix}\begin{bmatrix} a_1 \\ b_1 \\ c_1 \end{bmatrix} = \begin{bmatrix} 0 \\ 0 \\ 0 \end{bmatrix} \qquad \text{gives eigenvector } \mathbf{v}_1 = [1 \ \ -1 \ \ 0]^T.$$

With $\lambda = 2 + 3i$ we solve the eigenvector equation

$$\begin{bmatrix} 3-3i & 5 & 2 \\ -6 & -8-3i & -5 \\ 6 & 6 & 3-3i \end{bmatrix}\begin{bmatrix} a \\ b \\ c \end{bmatrix} = \begin{bmatrix} 0 \\ 0 \\ 0 \end{bmatrix}$$

to find the complex-valued eigenvector $\mathbf{v} = [1+i \quad -2 \quad 2]^T$. The corresponding complex-valued solution is

$$\mathbf{x}(t) = \mathbf{v}e^{(2+3i)t} = e^{2t}\begin{bmatrix} (\cos 3t - \sin 3t) + i(\cos 3t + \sin 3t) \\ -2\cos 3t - 2i\sin 3t \\ 2\cos 3t + 2i\sin 3t \end{bmatrix}.$$

The scalar components of the resulting general solution are

$$x_1(t) = c_1 + e^{2t}[(c_2 + c_3)\cos 3t + (-c_2 + c_3)\sin 3t]$$

$$x_2(t) = -c_1 + 2e^{2t}(-c_2\cos 3t - c_3\sin 3t)$$

$$x_3(t) = 2e^{2t}(c_2\cos 3t + c_3\sin 3t)$$

27.   The coefficient matrix

$$\mathbf{A} = \begin{bmatrix} -0.2 & 0 \\ 0.2 & -0.4 \end{bmatrix}$$

has characteristic equation $\lambda^2 + 0.6\lambda + 0.08 = 0$ with eigenvalues $\lambda_1 = -0.2$ and $\lambda_2 = -0.4$. We find easily that the associated eigenvectors are $\mathbf{v}_1 = [1 \quad 1]^T$ and $\mathbf{v}_2 = [0 \quad 1]^T$, so we get the general solution

$$x_1(t) = c_1e^{-0.2t}, \qquad x_2(t) = c_1e^{-0.2t} + c_2e^{-0.4t}.$$

The initial conditions $x_1(0) = 15$, $x_2(0) = 0$ give $c_1 = 15$ and $c_2 = -15$, so we get

$$x_1(t) = 15e^{-0.2t}, \qquad x_2(t) = 15e^{-0.2t} - 15e^{-0.4t}.$$

To find the maximum value of $x_2(t)$, we solve the equation $x_2'(t) = 0$ for $t = 5\ln 2$, which gives the maximum value $x_2(5\ln 2) = 3.75$ lb.

29.   The coefficient matrix

$$\mathbf{A} = \begin{bmatrix} -0.2 & 0.4 \\ 0.2 & -0.4 \end{bmatrix}$$

has eigenvalues $\lambda_1 = 0$ and $\lambda_2 = -0.6$, with eigenvectors $\mathbf{v}_1 = [2 \quad 1]^T$ and $\mathbf{v}_2 = [1 \quad -1]^T$ that yield the general solution

$$x_1(t) = 2c_1 + c_2e^{-0.6t}, \qquad x_2(t) = c_1 - c_2e^{-0.6t}.$$

The initial conditions $x_1(0) = 15$, $x_2(0) = 0$ give $c_1 = c_2 = 5$, so we get

$$x_1(t) = 10 + 5e^{-0.6t}, \qquad x_2(t) = 5 - 5e^{-0.6t}.$$

31. The coefficient matrix

$$\mathbf{A} = \begin{bmatrix} -1 & 0 & 0 \\ 1 & -2 & 0 \\ 0 & 2 & -3 \end{bmatrix}$$

has as eigenvalues its diagonal elements $\lambda_1 = -1$, $\lambda_2 = -2$, and $\lambda_3 = -3$. We find readily that the associated eigenvectors are $\mathbf{v}_1 = [1 \ 1 \ 1]^T$, $\mathbf{v}_2 = [0 \ 1 \ 2]^T$, and $\mathbf{v}_3 = [0 \ 0 \ 1]^T$. The resulting general solution is solution is given by

$$x_1(t) = c_1 e^{-t}$$
$$x_2(t) = c_1 e^{-t} + c_2 e^{-2t}$$
$$x_3(t) = c_1 e^{-t} + 2c_2 e^{-2t} + c_3 e^{-3t}.$$

The initial conditions $x_1(0) = 27$, $x_2(0) = x_2(0) = 0$ give $c_1 = c_3 = 27$, $c_2 = -27$, so we get

$$x_1(t) = 27 e^{-t}$$
$$x_2(t) = 27 e^{-t} - 27 e^{-2t}$$
$$x_3(t) = 27 e^{-t} - 54 e^{-2t} + 27 e^{-3t}.$$

The equation $x_3'(t) = 0$ simplifies to the equation

$$3e^{-2t} - 4e^{-t} + 1 = \left(3e^{-t} - 1\right)\left(e^{-t} - 1\right) = 0$$

with positive solution $t_m = \ln 3$. Thus the maximum amount of salt ever in tank 3 is $x_3(\ln 3) = 4$ pounds.

33. The coefficient matrix

$$\mathbf{A} = \begin{bmatrix} -4 & 0 & 0 \\ 4 & -6 & 0 \\ 0 & 6 & -2 \end{bmatrix}$$

has as eigenvalues its diagonal elements $\lambda_1 = -4$, $\lambda_2 = -6$, and $\lambda_3 = -2$. We find readily that the associated eigenvectors are $\mathbf{v}_1 = [-1 \ -2 \ 6]^T$, $\mathbf{v}_2 = [0 \ -2 \ 3]^T$, and $\mathbf{v}_3 = [0 \ 0 \ 1]^T$. The resulting general solution is solution is given by

$$x_1(t) = -c_1 e^{-4t}$$
$$x_2(t) = -2c_1 e^{-4t} - 2c_2 e^{-6t}$$
$$x_3(t) = 6c_1 e^{-4t} + 3c_2 e^{-6t} + c_3 e^{-2t}.$$

The initial conditions $x_1(0) = 45$, $x_2(0) = x_2(0) = 0$ give $c_1 = -45$, $c_2 = 45$, $c_3 = 135$, so we get

$$x_1(t) = 45e^{-4t}$$
$$x_2(t) = 90e^{-4t} - 90e^{-6t}$$
$$x_3(t) = -270e^{-4t} + 135e^{-6t} + 135e^{-2t}.$$

The equation $x_3'(t) = 0$ simplifies to the equation

$$3e^{-4t} - 4e^{-2t} + 1 = \left(3e^{-2t} - 1\right)\left(e^{-2t} - 1\right) = 0$$

with positive solution $t_m = \frac{1}{2}\ln 3$. Thus the maximum amount of salt ever in tank 3 is $x_3(\frac{1}{2}\ln 3) = 20$ pounds.

35. The coefficient matrix

$$\mathbf{A} = \begin{bmatrix} -6 & 0 & 3 \\ 6 & -20 & 0 \\ 0 & 20 & -3 \end{bmatrix}$$

has characteristic equation $-\lambda^3 - 29\lambda^2 - 198\lambda = -\lambda(\lambda - 18)(\lambda - 11) = 0$ with eigenvalues $\lambda_0 = 0$, $\lambda_1 = -18$, and $\lambda_2 = -11$. We find that associated eigenvectors are $\mathbf{v}_0 = [10 \quad 3 \quad 20]^T$, $\mathbf{v}_1 = [-1 \quad -3 \quad 4]^T$, and $\mathbf{v}_2 = [-3 \quad -2 \quad 5]^T$. The resulting general solution is solution is given by

$$x_1(t) = 10c_0 - c_1 e^{-18t} - 3c_2 e^{-11t}$$
$$x_2(t) = 3c_0 - 3c_1 e^{-18t} - 2c_2 e^{-11t}$$
$$x_3(t) = 20c_0 + 4c_1 e^{-18t} + 5c_2 e^{-11t}.$$

The initial conditions $x_1(0) = 33$, $x_2(0) = x_2(0) = 0$ give $c_1 = 1$, $c_2 = 55/7$, $c_3 = -72/7$, so we get

$$x_1(t) = 10 - \frac{1}{7}\left(55e^{-18t} - 216e^{-11t}\right)$$
$$x_2(t) = 3 - \frac{1}{7}\left(165e^{-18t} - 144e^{-11t}\right)$$
$$x_3(t) = 20 + \frac{1}{7}\left(220e^{-18t} - 360e^{-11t}\right).$$

Thus the limiting amounts of salt in tanks 1, 2, and 3 are 10 lb, 3 lb, and 20 lb.

37. The coefficient matrix

$$A = \begin{bmatrix} -1 & 0 & 2 \\ 1 & -3 & 0 \\ 0 & 3 & -2 \end{bmatrix}$$

has characteristic equation $-\lambda^3 - 6\lambda^2 - 11\lambda = 0$ with eigenvalues $\lambda_0 = 0$, $\lambda_1 = -3 - i\sqrt{2}$, and $\lambda_2 = -3 + i\sqrt{2}$., The eigenvector equation

$$\begin{bmatrix} -1 & 0 & 2 \\ 1 & -3 & 0 \\ 0 & 3 & -2 \end{bmatrix}\begin{bmatrix} a \\ b \\ c \end{bmatrix} = \begin{bmatrix} 0 \\ 0 \\ 0 \end{bmatrix}$$

associated with the eigenvalue $\lambda_0 = 0$ yields the associated eigenvector $\mathbf{v}_0 = \begin{bmatrix} 6 & 2 & 3 \end{bmatrix}^T$ and consequently the constant solution $\mathbf{x}_0(t) \equiv \mathbf{v}_0$. Then the eigenvector equation

$$\begin{bmatrix} 2+i\sqrt{2} & 0 & 2 \\ 1 & i\sqrt{2} & 0 \\ 0 & 3 & 1+i\sqrt{2} \end{bmatrix}\begin{bmatrix} a \\ b \\ c \end{bmatrix} = \begin{bmatrix} 0 \\ 0 \\ 0 \end{bmatrix}$$

associated with $\lambda_1 = -3 - i\sqrt{2}$ yields the complex-valued eigenvector $\mathbf{v}_1 = \begin{bmatrix} (-2+i\sqrt{2})/3 & (-1-i\sqrt{2})/3 & 1 \end{bmatrix}^T$. The corresponding complex-valued solution is

$$\mathbf{x}_1(t) = \mathbf{v}_1 e^{(-3-i\sqrt{2})t}$$

$$= \frac{1}{3}e^{-3t}\begin{bmatrix} \left(-2\cos(t\sqrt{2}) + \sqrt{2}\sin(t\sqrt{2})\right) + i\left(\sqrt{2}\cos(t\sqrt{2}) + 2\sin(t\sqrt{2})\right) \\ \left(-\cos(t\sqrt{2}) - \sqrt{2}\sin(t\sqrt{2})\right) + i\left(-\sqrt{2}\cos(t\sqrt{2}) + \sin(t\sqrt{2})\right) \\ 3\cos(t\sqrt{2}) - 3i\sin(t\sqrt{2}) \end{bmatrix}.$$

The scalar components of resulting general solution $\mathbf{x} = c_0\mathbf{x}_0 + c_1\,\mathrm{Re}(\mathbf{x}_1) + c_2\,\mathrm{Im}(\mathbf{x}_1)$ are given by

$$x_1(t) = 6c_0 + \frac{1}{3}e^{-3t}\left[\left(-2c_1 + \sqrt{2}\,c_2\right)\cos(t\sqrt{2}) + \left(\sqrt{2}\,c_1 + 2c_2\right)\sin(t\sqrt{2})\right]$$

$$x_2(t) = 2c_0 + \frac{1}{3}e^{-3t}\left[\left(-c_1 - \sqrt{2}\,c_2\right)\cos(t\sqrt{2}) + \left(-\sqrt{2}\,c_1 + c_2\right)\sin(t\sqrt{2})\right]$$

$$x_3(t) = 3c_0 + e^{-3t}\left[c_1\cos(t\sqrt{2}) - c_2\sin(t\sqrt{2})\right].$$

When we impose the initial conditions $x_1(0) = 55$, $x_2(0) = x_2(0) = 0$ we find that $c_0 = 5$, $c_1 = -15$, and $c_2 = 45/\sqrt{2}$. This finally gives the particular solution

$$x_1(t) = 30 + e^{-3t}\left[25\cos(t\sqrt{2}) + 10\sqrt{2}\sin(t\sqrt{2})\right]$$

$$x_2(t) = 10 - e^{-3t}\left[10\cos(t\sqrt{2}) - \tfrac{25}{2}\sqrt{2}\sin(t\sqrt{2})\right]$$

$$x_3(t) = 15 - e^{-3t}\left[15\cos(t\sqrt{2}) + \tfrac{45}{2}\sqrt{2}\sin(t\sqrt{2})\right].$$

Thus the limiting amounts of salt in tanks 1, 2, and 3 are 30 lb, 10 lb, and 15 lb.

In Problems 38-41 the Maple command **with(linalg):eigenvects(A)**, the Mathematica command **Eigensystem[A]**, or the MATLAB command **[V,D] = eig(A)** can be used to find the eigenvalues and associated eigenvectors of the given coefficient matrix **A**.

39. Characteristic equation: $(\lambda^2 - 1)(\lambda^2 - 4) = 0$

Eigenvalues and associated eigenvectors:

$$\lambda = 1, \qquad \mathbf{v} = [3 \quad -2 \quad 4 \quad 1]^{\mathrm{T}}$$
$$\lambda = -1, \qquad \mathbf{v} = [0 \quad 0 \quad 1 \quad 0]^{\mathrm{T}}$$
$$\lambda = 2, \qquad \mathbf{v} = [0 \quad 1 \quad 0 \quad 0]^{\mathrm{T}}$$
$$\lambda = -2, \qquad \mathbf{v} = [1 \quad -1 \quad 0 \quad 0]^{\mathrm{T}}$$

Scalar solution equations:

$$x_1(t) = 3c_1e^t \qquad\qquad + c_4e^{-2t}$$

$$x_2(t) = -2c_1e^t \qquad + c_3e^{2t} - c_4e^{-2t}$$

$$x_3(t) = 4c_1e^t + c_2e^{-t}$$

$$x_4(t) = c_1e^t$$

41. The eigenvectors associated with the respective eigenvalues $\lambda_1 = -3$, $\lambda_2 = -6$, $\lambda_3 = 10$, and $\lambda_4 = 15$ are

$$\mathbf{v}_1 = [\,1 \quad 0 \quad 0 \quad -1]^{\mathrm{T}}$$
$$\mathbf{v}_2 = [\,0 \quad 1 \quad -1 \quad 0]^{\mathrm{T}}$$
$$\mathbf{v}_3 = [-2 \quad 1 \quad 1 \quad -2]^{\mathrm{T}}$$
$$\mathbf{v}_4 = [\,1 \quad 2 \quad 2 \quad 1]^{\mathrm{T}}.$$

Hence the general solution has scalar component functions

$$x_1(t) = c_1 e^{-3t} \qquad - 2c_3 e^{10t} + c_4 e^{15t}$$
$$x_2(t) = \qquad c_2 e^{-6t} + c_3 e^{10t} + 2c_4 e^{15t}$$
$$x_3(t) = \qquad - c_2 e^{-6t} + c_3 e^{10t} + 2c_4 e^{15t}$$
$$x_4(t) = -c_1 e^{-3t} \qquad - 2c_3 e^{10t} + c_4 e^{15t}.$$

The given initial conditions are satisfied by choosing $c_1 = c_2 = 0$, $c_3 = -1$, and $c_4 = 1$, so the desired particular solution is given by

$$x_1(t) = 2e^{10t} + e^{15t} = x_4(t)$$
$$x_2(t) = -e^{10t} + 2e^{15t} = x_3(t) .$$

SECTION 5.3

SECOND-ORDER SYSTEMS AND MECHANICAL APPLICATIONS

This section uses the eigenvalue method to exhibit realistic applications of linear systems. If a computer system like Maple, Mathematica, MATLAB, or even a TI-85/86/89/92 calculator is available, then a system of more than three railway cars, or a multistory building with four or more floors (as in the project), can be investigated. However, the problems in the text are intended for manual solution.

Problems 1-7 involve the system

$$m_1 x_1'' = -(k_1 + k_2)x_1 + \qquad k_2 x_2$$
$$m_2 x_2'' = \qquad k_2 x_1 - (k_2 + k_3)x_2$$

with various values of m_1, m_2 and k_1, k_2, k_3. In each problem we divide the first equation by m_1 and the second one by m_2 to obtain a second-order linear system $\mathbf{x}'' = \mathbf{A}\mathbf{x}$ in the standard form of Theorem 1 in this section. If the eigenvalues λ_1 and λ_2 are both negative, then the natural (circular) frequencies of the system are $\omega_1 = \sqrt{-\lambda_1}$ and $\omega_2 = \sqrt{-\lambda_2}$, and — according to Eq. (11) in Theorem 1 of this section — the eigenvalues $\mathbf{v}_1$ and $\mathbf{v}_2$ associated with λ_1 and λ_2 determine the natural modes of oscillations at these frequencies.

1.   The matrix $\mathbf{A} = \begin{bmatrix} -2 & 2 \\ 2 & -2 \end{bmatrix}$ has eigenvalues $\lambda_0 = 0$ and $\lambda_1 = -4$ with associated eigenvalues $\mathbf{v}_0 = [1 \quad 1]^{\mathrm{T}}$ and $\mathbf{v}_1 = [1 \quad -1]^{\mathrm{T}}$. Thus we have the special case described in Eq. (12) of Theorem 1, and a general solution is given by

$$x_1(t) = a_1 + a_2 t + b_1 \cos 2t + b_2 \sin 2t,$$
$$x_2(t) = a_1 + a_2 t - b_1 \cos 2t - b_2 \sin 2t.$$

The natural frequencies are $\omega_1 = 0$ and $\omega_2 = 2$. In the degenerate natural mode with "frequency" $\omega_1 = 0$ the two masses move by translation without oscillating. At frequency $\omega_2 = 2$ they oscillate in opposite directions with equal amplitudes.

3. The matrix $\mathbf{A} = \begin{bmatrix} -3 & 2 \\ 1 & -2 \end{bmatrix}$ has eigenvalues $\lambda_1 = -1$ and $\lambda_2 = -4$ with associated eigenvalues $\mathbf{v}_1 = [1 \quad 1]^T$ and $\mathbf{v}_2 = [2 \quad -1]^T$. Hence a general solution is given by

$$x_1(t) = a_1 \cos t + a_2 \sin t + 2b_1 \cos 2t + 2b_2 \sin 2t,$$
$$x_2(t) = a_1 \cos t + a_2 \sin t - b_1 \cos 2t - b_2 \sin 2t.$$

The natural frequencies are $\omega_1 = 1$ and $\omega_2 = 2$. In the natural mode with frequency ω_1, the two masses m_1 and m_2 move in the same direction with equal amplitudes of oscillation. In the natural mode with frequency ω_2 they move in opposite directions with the amplitude of oscillation of m_1 twice that of m_2.

5. The matrix $\mathbf{A} = \begin{bmatrix} -3 & 1 \\ 1 & -3 \end{bmatrix}$ has eigenvalues $\lambda_1 = -2$ and $\lambda_2 = -4$ with associated eigenvalues $\mathbf{v}_1 = [1 \quad 1]^T$ and $\mathbf{v}_2 = [1 \quad -1]^T$. Hence a general solution is given by

$$x_1(t) = a_1 \cos t\sqrt{2} + a_2 \sin t\sqrt{2} + b_1 \cos 2t + b_2 \sin 2t,$$
$$x_2(t) = a_1 \cos t\sqrt{2} + a_2 \sin t\sqrt{2} - b_1 \cos 2t - b_2 \sin 2t.$$

The natural frequencies are $\omega_1 = \sqrt{2}$ and $\omega_2 = 2$. In the natural mode with frequency ω_1, the two masses m_1 and m_2 move in the same direction with equal amplitudes of oscillation. At frequency ω_2 they move in opposite directions with equal amplitudes.

7. The matrix $\mathbf{A} = \begin{bmatrix} -10 & 6 \\ 6 & -10 \end{bmatrix}$ has eigenvalues $\lambda_1 = -4$ and $\lambda_2 = -16$ with associated eigenvalues $\mathbf{v}_1 = [1 \quad 1]^T$ and $\mathbf{v}_2 = [1 \quad -1]^T$. Hence a general solution is given by

$$x_1(t) = a_1 \cos 2t + a_2 \sin 2t + b_1 \cos 4t + b_2 \sin 4t,$$
$$x_2(t) = a_1 \cos 2t + a_2 \sin 2t - b_1 \cos 4t - b_2 \sin 4t.$$

The natural frequencies are $\omega_1 = 2$ and $\omega_2 = 4$. In the natural mode with frequency ω_1, the two masses m_1 and m_2 move in the same direction with equal amplitudes of oscillation. At frequency ω_2 they move in opposite directions with equal amplitudes.

9.   Substitution of the trial solution $x_1 = c_1 \cos 3t$, $x_2 = c_2 \cos 3t$ in the system

$$x_1'' = -3x_1 + 2x_2, \quad 2x_2'' = 2x_1 - 4x_2 + 120\cos 3t$$

yields $c_1 = 3$, $c_2 = -9$, so a general solution is given by

$$x_1(t) = a_1 \cos t + a_2 \sin t + 2b_1 \cos 2t + 2b_2 \sin 2t + 3\cos 3t,$$
$$x_2(t) = a_1 \cos t + a_2 \sin t - b_1 \cos 2t - b_2 \sin 2t - 9\cos 3t.$$

Imposition of the initial conditions $x_1(0) = x_2(0) = x_1'(0) = x_2'(0) = 0$ now yields $a_1 = 5$, $a_2 = 0$, $b_1 = -4$, $b_2 = 0$. The resulting particular solution is

$$x_1(t) = 5\cos t - 8\cos 2t + 3\cos 3t,$$
$$x_2(t) = 5\cos t + 4\cos 2t - 9\cos 3t.$$

We have a superposition of three oscillations, in which the two masses move

- in the same direction with frequency $\omega_1 = 1$ and equal amplitudes;
- in opposite directions with frequency $\omega_2 = 2$ and with the amplitude of motion of m_1 being twice that of m_2;
- in opposite directions with frequency $\omega_3 = 3$ and with the amplitude of motion of m_2 being 3 times that of m_1.

11.   **(a)**   The matrix $\mathbf{A} = \begin{bmatrix} -40 & 8 \\ 12 & -60 \end{bmatrix}$ has eigenvalues $\lambda_1 = -36$ and $\lambda_2 = -64$ with associated eigenvalues $\mathbf{v}_2 = [2 \quad 1]^{\mathrm{T}}$ and $\mathbf{v}_2 = [1 \quad -3]^{\mathrm{T}}$. Hence a general solution is given by

$$x(t) = 2a_1 \cos 6t + 2a_2 \sin 6t + b_1 \cos 8t + b_2 \sin 8t,$$
$$y(t) = a_1 \cos 6t + a_2 \sin 6t - 3b_1 \cos 8t - 3b_2 \sin 8t.$$

The natural frequencies are $\omega_1 = 6$ and $\omega_2 = 8$. In mode 1 the two masses oscillate in the same direction with frequency $\omega_1 = 6$ and with the amplitude of motion of m_1 being twice that of m_2. In mode 2 the two masses oscillate in opposite directions with frequency $\omega_2 = 8$ and with the amplitude of motion of m_2 being 3 times that of m_1.

(b)   Substitution of the trial solution $x = c_1 \cos 7t$, $y = c_2 \cos 7t$ in the system

$$x'' = -40x + 8y - 195\cos 7t, \quad y'' = 12x - 60y - 195\cos 7t$$

yields $c_1 = 19$, $c_2 = 3$, so a general solution is given by

$$x(t) = 2a_1 \cos 6t + 2a_2 \sin 6t + b_1 \cos 8t + b_2 \sin 8t + 19 \cos 7t,$$
$$y(t) = a_1 \cos 6t + a_2 \sin 6t - 3b_1 \cos 8t - 3b_2 \sin 8t + 3 \cos 7t.$$

Imposition of the initial conditions $x(0) = 19$, $x'(0) = 12$, $y(0) = 3$, $y'(0) = 6$ now yields $a_1 = 0$, $a_2 = 1$, $b_1 = 0$, $b_2 = 0$. The resulting particular solution is

$$x(t) = 2 \sin 6t + 19 \cos 7t,$$
$$y(t) = \sin 6t + 3 \cos 7t.$$

Thus the expected oscillation with frequency $\omega_2 = 8$ is missing, and we have a superposition of (only two) oscillations, in which the two masses move

- in the same direction with frequency $\omega_1 = 6$ and with the amplitude of motion of m_1 being twice that of m_2;
- in the same direction with frequency $\omega_3 = 7$ and with the amplitude of motion of m_1 being 19/7 times that of m_2.

13. The coefficient matrix $\mathbf{A} = \begin{bmatrix} -4 & 2 & 0 \\ 2 & -4 & 2 \\ 0 & 2 & -4 \end{bmatrix}$ has characteristic polynomial

$$-\lambda^3 - 12\lambda^2 - 40\lambda - 32 = -(\lambda + 4)(\lambda^2 + 8\lambda + 8).$$

Its eigenvalues $\lambda_1 = -4$, $\lambda_2 = -4 - 2\sqrt{2}$, $\lambda_3 = -4 + 2\sqrt{2}$ have associated eigenvectors $\mathbf{v}_1 = [1 \quad 0 \quad -1]^T$, $\mathbf{v}_2 = [1 \quad -\sqrt{2} \quad 1]^T$, $\mathbf{v}_3 = [1 \quad \sqrt{2} \quad 1]^T$. Hence the system's three natural modes of oscillation have

- Natural frequency $\omega_1 = 2$ with amplitude ratios $1 : 0 : -1$.
- Natural frequency $\omega_2 = \sqrt{4 + 2\sqrt{2}}$ with amplitude ratios $1 : -\sqrt{2} : 1$.
- Natural frequency $\omega_2 = \sqrt{4 - 2\sqrt{2}}$ with amplitude ratios $1 : \sqrt{2} : 1$.

15. First we need the general solution of the homogeneous system $\mathbf{x}'' = \mathbf{A}\mathbf{x}$ with

$$\mathbf{A} = \begin{bmatrix} -50 & 25/2 \\ 50 & -50 \end{bmatrix}$$

The eigenvalues of $\mathbf{A}$ are $\lambda_1 = -25$ and $\lambda_2 = -75$, so the natural frequencies of the system are $\omega_1 = 5$ and $\omega_2 = 5\sqrt{3}$. The associated eigenvectors are $\mathbf{v}_1 = [1 \quad 2]^T$ and $\mathbf{v}_2 = [1 \quad -2]^T$, so the complementary solution $\mathbf{x}_c(t)$ is given by

$$x_1(t) = a_1 \cos 5t + a_2 \sin 5t + b_1 \cos 5\sqrt{3}t + b_2 \sin 5\sqrt{3}t,$$
$$x_2(t) = 2a_1 \cos 5t + 2a_2 \sin 5t - 2b_1 \cos 5\sqrt{3}t - 2b_2 \sin 5\sqrt{3}t.$$

When we substitute the trial solution $\mathbf{x}_p(t) = [c_1 \quad c_2]^T \cos 10t$ in the nonhomogeneous system, we find that $c_1 = 4/3$ and $c_2 = -16/3$, so a particular solution $\mathbf{x}_p(t)$ is described by

$$x_1(t) = (4/3)\cos 10t, \qquad x_2(t) = -(16/3)\cos 10t.$$

Finally, when we impose the zero initial conditions on the solution $\mathbf{x}(t) = \mathbf{x}_c(t) + \mathbf{x}_p(t)$ we find that $a_1 = 2/3$, $a_2 = 0$, $b_1 = -2$, and $b_2 = 0$. Thus the solution we seek is described by

$$x_1(t) = (2/3)\cos 5t - 2\cos 5\sqrt{3}t + (4/3)\cos 10t$$

$$x_2(t) = (4/3)\cos 5t + 4\cos 5\sqrt{3}t + (16/3)\cos 10t.$$

We have a superposition of two oscillations with the natural frequencies $\omega_1 = 5$ and $\omega_2 = 5\sqrt{3}$ and a forced oscillation with frequency $\omega = 10$. In each of the two natural oscillations the amplitude of motion of m_2 is twice that of m_1, while in the forced oscillation the amplitude of motion of m_2 is four times that of m_1.

17. With $c_1 = c_2 = 2$, it follows from Problem 16 that the natural frequencies and associated eigenvectors are $\omega_1 = 0$, $\mathbf{v}_1 = [1 \quad 1]^T$ and $\omega_2 = 2$, $\mathbf{v}_2 = [1 \quad -1]^T$. Hence Theorem 1 gives the general solution

$$x_1(t) = a_1 + b_1 t + a_2 \cos 2t + b_2 \sin 2t$$
$$x_2(t) = a_1 + b_1 t - a_2 \cos 2t - b_2 \sin 2t.$$

The initial conditions $x_1'(0) = v_0$, $x_1(0) = x_2(0) = x_2'(0) = 0$ yield $a_1 = a_2 = 0$ and $b_1 = v_0/2$, $b_2 = v_0/4$, so

$$x_1(t) = (v_0/4)(2t + \sin 2t)$$
$$x_2(t) = (v_0/4)(2t - \sin 2t)$$

while $x_2 - x_1 = (v_0/4)(-2\sin 2t) < 0$, that is, until $t = \pi/2$. Finally, $x_1'(\pi/2) = 0$ and $x_2'(\pi/2) = v_0$.

19. With $c_1 = 1$ and $c_2 = 3$, it follows from Problem 16 that the natural frequencies and associated eigenvectors are $\omega_1 = 0$, $\mathbf{v}_1 = [1 \quad 1]^T$ and $\omega_2 = 2$, $\mathbf{v}_2 = [1 \quad -3]^T$. Hence Theorem 1 gives the general solution

$$x_1(t) = a_1 + b_1 t + a_2 \cos 2t + b_2 \sin 2t$$

$$x_2(t) = a_1 + b_1 t - 3a_2 \cos 2t - 3b_2 \sin 2t.$$

The initial conditions $x_1'(0) = v_0$, $x_1(0) = x_2(0) = x_2'(0) = 0$ yield $a_1 = a_2 = 0$ and $b_1 = 3v_0/4$, $b_2 = v_0/8$, so

$$x_1(t) = (v_0/8)(6t + \sin 2t)$$

$$x_2(t) = (v_0/8)(6t - 3\sin 2t)$$

while $x_2 - x_1 = (v_0/8)(-4 \sin 2t) < 0$; that is, until $t = \pi/2$. Finally, $x_1'(\pi/2) = v_0/2$ and $x_2'(\pi/2) = 3v_0/2$.

21. (a) The matrix

$$\mathbf{A} = \begin{bmatrix} -160/3 & 320/3 \\ 8 & -116 \end{bmatrix}$$

has eigenvalues $\lambda_1 \approx -41.8285$ and $\lambda_2 \approx -127.5049$, so the natural frequencies are

$$\omega_1 \approx 6.4675 \text{ rad/sec} \approx 1.0293 \text{ Hz}$$
$$\omega_2 \approx 11.2918 \text{ rad/sec} \approx 1.7971 \text{ Hz}.$$

(b) Resonance occurs at the two critical speeds

$$v_1 = 20\omega_1/\pi \approx 41 \text{ ft/sec} \approx 28 \text{ mi/h}$$
$$v_2 = 20\omega_2/\pi \approx 72 \text{ ft/sec} \approx 49 \text{ mi/h}.$$

In Problems 23-25 we substitute the given physical parameters into the equations in (42):

$$mx'' = -(k_1 + k_2)x + (k_1 L_1 - k_2 L_2)\theta$$

$$I\theta'' = (k_1 L_1 - k_2 L_2)x - (k_1 L_1^2 + k_2 L_2^2)\theta$$

As in Problem 21, a critical frequency of ω rad/sec yields a critical velocity of $v = 20\omega/\pi$ ft/sec.

23. $100 x'' = -4000 x$, $8000\theta'' = 1000000\theta$

Obviously the matrix $\mathbf{A} = \begin{bmatrix} -40 & 0 \\ 0 & -125 \end{bmatrix}$ has eigenvalues $\lambda_1 = -40$ and $\lambda_2 = -125$.

Up-and-down: $\qquad \omega_1 = \sqrt{40}$, $\qquad v_1 \approx 40.26$ ft/sec ≈ 27 mph
Angular: $\qquad \omega_2 = \sqrt{125}$, $\qquad v_2 \approx 71.18$ ft/sec ≈ 49 mph

25.
$$100\,x'' = -3000\,x - 5000\,\theta$$
$$800\,\theta'' = -5000\,x - 75000\,\theta$$

The matrix $\mathbf{A} = \begin{bmatrix} -30 & -50 \\ -25/4 & -375/4 \end{bmatrix}$ has eigenvalues $\lambda_1, \lambda_2 = \dfrac{5}{8}\left(-99 \pm \sqrt{3401}\right)$.

$\omega_1 \approx 5.0424$, $\qquad v_1 \approx 32.10$ ft/sec ≈ 22 mph
$\omega_2 \approx 9.9158$, $\qquad v_2 \approx 63.13$ ft/sec ≈ 43 mph

SECTION 5.4

MULTIPLE EIGENVALUE SOLUTIONS

In each of Problems 1-6 we give first the characteristic equation with repeated (multiplicity 2) eigenvalue λ. In each case we find that $(\mathbf{A} - \lambda\mathbf{I})^2 = \mathbf{0}$. Then $\mathbf{w} = \begin{bmatrix} 1 & 0 \end{bmatrix}^T$ is a generalized eigenvector and $\mathbf{v} = (\mathbf{A} - \lambda\mathbf{I})\mathbf{w} \neq \mathbf{0}$ is an ordinary eigenvector associated with λ. We give finally the scalar component functions $x_1(t)$, $x_2(t)$ of the general solution

$$\mathbf{x}(t) = c_1\mathbf{v}e^{\lambda t} + c_2(\mathbf{v}t + \mathbf{w})e^{\lambda t}$$

of the given system $\mathbf{x}' = \mathbf{A}\mathbf{x}$.

1. Characteristic equation $\qquad \lambda^2 + 6\lambda + 9 = 0$
Repeated eigenvalue $\qquad \lambda = -3$
Generalized eigenvector $\qquad \mathbf{w} = \begin{bmatrix} 1 & 0 \end{bmatrix}^T$

$$\mathbf{v} = (\mathbf{A} - \lambda\mathbf{I})\mathbf{w} = \begin{bmatrix} 1 & 1 \\ -1 & -1 \end{bmatrix}\begin{bmatrix} 1 \\ 0 \end{bmatrix} = \begin{bmatrix} 1 \\ -1 \end{bmatrix}$$

$$x_1(t) = (c_1 + c_2 + c_2t)e^{-3t}$$
$$x_2(t) = (-c_1 \quad - c_2t)e^{-3t}.$$

3. Characteristic equation $\qquad \lambda^2 - 6\lambda + 9 = 0$
Repeated eigenvalue $\qquad \lambda = 3$
Generalized eigenvector $\qquad \mathbf{w} = \begin{bmatrix} 1 & 0 \end{bmatrix}^T$

$$v = (A - \lambda I)w = \begin{bmatrix} -2 & -2 \\ 2 & 2 \end{bmatrix}\begin{bmatrix} 1 \\ 0 \end{bmatrix} = \begin{bmatrix} -2 \\ 2 \end{bmatrix}$$

$$x_1(t) = (-2c_1 + c_2 - 2c_2 t)e^{3t}$$

$$x_2(t) = (2c_1 + 2c_2 t)e^{3t}.$$

5.　　Characteristic equation　　$\lambda^2 - 10\lambda + 25 = 0$
　　　Repeated eigenvalue　　　$\lambda = 5$
　　　Generalized eigenvector　　$w = [1 \quad 0]^T$

$$v = (A - \lambda I)w = \begin{bmatrix} 2 & 1 \\ -4 & -2 \end{bmatrix}\begin{bmatrix} 1 \\ 0 \end{bmatrix} = \begin{bmatrix} 2 \\ -4 \end{bmatrix}$$

$$x_1(t) = (2c_1 + c_2 + 2c_2 t)e^{5t}$$

$$x_2(t) = (-4c_1 - 4c_2 t)e^{5t}.$$

In each of Problems 7-10 the characteristic polynomial is easily calculated by expansion along the row or column of **A** that contains two zeros. The matrix **A** has only two distinct eigenvalues, so we write $\lambda_1, \lambda_2, \lambda_3$ with either $\lambda_1 = \lambda_2$ or $\lambda_2 = \lambda_3$. Nevertheless, we find that it has 3 linearly independent eigenvectors $v_1, v_2,$ and v_3. We list also the scalar components $x_1(t), x_2(t), x_3(t)$ of the general solution $x(t) = c_1 v_1 e^{\lambda_1 t} + c_2 v_2 e^{\lambda_2 t} + c_3 v_3 e^{\lambda_3 t}$ of the system.

7.　　Characteristic equation　　$-\lambda^3 + 13\lambda^2 - 40\lambda + 36 = -(\lambda - 2)^2(\lambda - 9)$
　　　Eigenvalues　　　　　　　$\lambda = 2, 2, 9$
　　　Eigenvectors　　　　　　　$[1 \quad 1 \quad 0]^T, [1 \quad 0 \quad 1]^T, [0 \quad 1 \quad 0]^T$

$$x_1(t) = c_1 e^{2t} + c_2 e^{2t}$$

$$x_2(t) = c_1 e^{2t} + c_3 e^{9t}$$

$$x_3(t) = c_1 e^{2t}$$

9.　　Characteristic equation　　$-\lambda^3 + 19\lambda^2 - 115\lambda + 225 = -(\lambda - 5)^2(\lambda - 9)$
　　　Eigenvalues　　　　　　　$\lambda = 5, 5, 9$
　　　Eigenvectors　　　　　　　$[1 \quad 2 \quad 0]^T, [7 \quad 0 \quad 2]^T, [3 \quad 0 \quad 1]^T$

$$x_1(t) = c_1 e^{5t} + 7c_2 e^{5t} + 3c_3 e^{9t}$$

$$x_2(t) = 2c_1 e^{5t}$$

$$x_3(t) = 2c_2 e^{5t} + c_3 e^{9t}$$

In each of Problems 11-14, the characteristic equation is $-\lambda^3 - 3\lambda^2 - 3\lambda - 1 = -(\lambda+1)^3$.
Hence $\lambda = -1$ is a triple eigenvalue of defect 2, and we find that $(\mathbf{A} - \lambda\mathbf{I})^3 = \mathbf{0}$. In each
problem we start with $\mathbf{v}_3 = [1 \ \ 0 \ \ 0]^T$ and then calculate $\mathbf{v}_2 = (\mathbf{A} - \lambda\mathbf{I})\mathbf{v}_3$ and
$\mathbf{v}_1 = (\mathbf{A} - \lambda\mathbf{I})\mathbf{v}_2 \neq \mathbf{0}$. It follows that $(\mathbf{A} - \lambda\mathbf{I})\mathbf{v}_1 = (\mathbf{A} - \lambda\mathbf{I})^2\mathbf{v}_2 = (\mathbf{A} - \lambda\mathbf{I})^3\mathbf{v}_3 = \mathbf{0}$, so $\mathbf{v}_1$ is an
ordinary eigenvector associated with the triple eigenvalue λ. Hence $\{\mathbf{v}_1, \mathbf{v}_2, \mathbf{v}_3\}$ is a length 3
chain of generalized eigenvectors, and the corresponding general solution is described by

$$\mathbf{x}(t) = e^{-t}[c_1\mathbf{v}_1 + c_2(\mathbf{v}_1\, t + \mathbf{v}_2) + c_3(\mathbf{v}_1\, t^2/2 + \mathbf{v}_2\, t + \mathbf{v}_3)].$$

We give the scalar components $x_1(t)$, $x_2(t)$, $x_3(t)$ of $\mathbf{x}(t)$.

11. $\mathbf{v}_1 = [0 \ \ 1 \ \ 0]^T$, $\mathbf{v}_2 = [-2 \ \ -1 \ \ 1]^T$, $\mathbf{v}_3 = [1 \ \ 0 \ \ 0]^T$

$x_1(t) = e^{-t}(-2c_2 + c_3 - 2c_3\, t)$

$x_2(t) = e^{-t}(c_1 - c_2 + c_2\, t - c_3\, t + c_3\, t^2/2)$

$x_3(t) = e^{-t}(c_2 + c_3\, t)$

13. $\mathbf{v}_1 = [1 \ \ 0 \ \ 0]^T$, $\mathbf{v}_2 = [0 \ \ 2 \ \ 1]^T$, $\mathbf{v}_3 = [1 \ \ 0 \ \ 0]^T$

$x_1(t) = e^{-t}(c_1 + c_2\, t + c_3\, t^2/2)$

$x_2(t) = e^{-t}(2c_2 + c_3 + 2c_3\, t)$

$x_3(t) = e^{-t}(c_2 + c_3\, t)$

In each of Problems 15-18, the characteristic equation is $-\lambda^3 + 3\lambda^2 - 3\lambda + 1 = -(\lambda-1)^3$.
Hence $\lambda = 1$ is a triple eigenvalue of defect 1, and we find that $(\mathbf{A} - \lambda\mathbf{I})^2 = \mathbf{0}$. First we find
the two linearly independent (ordinary) eigenvectors $\mathbf{u}_1$ and $\mathbf{u}_2$ associated with λ. Then we
start with $\mathbf{v}_2 = [1 \ \ 0 \ \ 0]^T$ and calculate $\mathbf{v}_1 = (\mathbf{A} - \lambda\mathbf{I})\mathbf{v}_2 \neq \mathbf{0}$. It follows that
$(\mathbf{A} - \lambda\mathbf{I})\mathbf{v}_1 = (\mathbf{A} - \lambda\mathbf{I})^2\mathbf{v}_2 = \mathbf{0}$, so $\mathbf{v}_1$ is an ordinary eigenvector associated with λ. However,
$\mathbf{v}_1$ is a linear combination of $\mathbf{u}_1$ and $\mathbf{u}_2$, so $\mathbf{v}_1 e^t$ is a linear combination of the independent
solutions $\mathbf{u}_1 e^t$ and $\mathbf{u}_2 e^t$. But $\{\mathbf{v}_1, \mathbf{v}_2\}$ is a length 2 chain of generalized eigenvectors
associated with λ, so $(\mathbf{v}_1 t + \mathbf{v}_2)e^t$ is the desired third independent solution. The corresponding
general solution is described by

$$\mathbf{x}(t) = e^t[c_1\mathbf{u}_1 + c_2\mathbf{u}_2 + c_3(\mathbf{v}_1\, t + \mathbf{v}_2)]$$

We give the scalar components $x_1(t)$, $x_2(t)$, $x_3(t)$ of $\mathbf{x}(t)$.

15. $\mathbf{u}_1 = [3 \ \ -1 \ \ 0]^T$ $\mathbf{u}_2 = [0 \ \ 0 \ \ 1]^T$

$\quad\quad\ \ \mathbf{v}_1 = [-3 \ \ 1 \ \ 1]^T$ $\mathbf{v}_2 = [1 \ \ 0 \ \ 0]^T$

$$x_1(t) = e^t(3c_1 + c_3 - 3c_3\,t)$$

$$x_2(t) = e^t(-c_1 + c_3\,t)$$

$$x_3(t) = e^t(c_2 + c_3\,t)$$

17. $\mathbf{u}_1 = [2\ \ 0\ \ -9]^T$ $\mathbf{u}_2 = [1\ \ -3\ \ 0]^T$

$\mathbf{v}_1 = [0\ \ 6\ \ -9]^T$ $\mathbf{v}_2 = [0\ \ \ 1\ \ \ 0]^T$

(Either $\mathbf{v}_2 = [1\quad 0\quad 0]^T$ or $\mathbf{v}_2 = [0\quad 0\quad 1]^T$ can be used also, but they yield different forms of the solution than given in the book's answer section.)

$$x_1(t) = e^t(2c_1 + c_2)$$

$$x_2(t) = e^t(-3c_2 + c_3 + 6c_3\,t)$$

$$x_3(t) = e^t(-9c_1 - 9c_3\,t)$$

19.   Characteristic equation $\lambda^4 - 2\lambda^2 + 1 = 0$

Double eigenvalue $\lambda = -1$ with eigenvectors

$$\mathbf{v}_1 = [1\ \ 0\ \ 0\ \ 1]^T \ \ \text{and} \ \ \mathbf{v}_2 = [0\ \ 0\ \ 1\ \ 0]^T.$$

Double eigenvalue $\lambda = +1$ with eigenvectors

$$\mathbf{v}_3 = [0\ \ 1\ \ 0\ \ -2]^T \ \ \text{and} \ \ \mathbf{v}_4 = [1\ \ 0\ \ 3\ \ 0]^T.$$

General solution

$$\mathbf{x}(t) = e^{-t}(c_1\mathbf{v}_1 + c_2\mathbf{v}_2) + e^t(c_3\mathbf{v}_3 + c_4\mathbf{v}_4)$$

Scalar components

$$x_1(t) = c_1 e^{-t} + c_4 e^t$$

$$x_2(t) = c_3 e^t$$

$$x_3(t) = c_2 e^{-t} + 3c_4 e^t$$

$$x_4(t) = c_1 e^{-t} - 2c_3 e^t$$

21.   Characteristic equation $\lambda^4 - 4\lambda^3 + 6\lambda^2 - 4\lambda + 1 = (\lambda - 1)^4 = 0$

Eigenvalue $\lambda = 1$ with multiplicity 4 and defect 2.

We find that $(\mathbf{A} - \lambda\mathbf{I})^2 \neq 0$ but $(\mathbf{A} - \lambda\mathbf{I})^3 = 0$. We therefore start with $\mathbf{v}_3 = [1\ \ 0\ \ 0\ \ 0]^T$ and define $\mathbf{v}_2 = (\mathbf{A} - \lambda\mathbf{I})\mathbf{v}_3$ and $\mathbf{v}_1 = (\mathbf{A} - \lambda\mathbf{I})\mathbf{v}_2 \neq 0$, thereby obtaining the length 3 chain $\{\mathbf{v}_1,\ \mathbf{v}_2,\ \mathbf{v}_3\}$ with

$$\mathbf{v}_1 = [0\ \ 0\ \ 0\ \ 1]^T, \quad \mathbf{v}_2 = [-2\ 1\ 1\ 0]^T, \quad v3 = [1\ \ 0\ \ 0\ \ 0]^T.$$

Then we find the second ordinary eigenvector $\mathbf{v}_4 = [0 \quad 0 \ 1 \ 0]^T$. The corresponding general solution

$$\mathbf{x}(t) = e^t [c_1\mathbf{v}_1 + c_2(\mathbf{v}_1 t + \mathbf{v}_2) + c_3(\mathbf{v}_1 t^2/2 + \mathbf{v}_2 t + \mathbf{v}_3) + c_4\mathbf{v}_4]$$

has scalar components

$$x_1(t) = e^t(-2c_2 + c_3 - 2c_3 t)$$
$$x_2(t) = e^t(c_2 + c_3 t)$$
$$x_3(t) = e^t(c_2 + c_4 + c_3 t).$$
$$x_4(t) = e^t(c_1 + c_2 t + c_3 t^2/2.)$$

In Problems 23 and 24 there are only two distinct eigenvalues λ_1 and λ_2. However, the eigenvector equation $(\mathbf{A} - \lambda\mathbf{I})\mathbf{v} = 0$ yields the three linearly independent eigenvectors $\mathbf{v}_1$, $\mathbf{v}_2$, and $\mathbf{v}_3$ that are given. We list the scalar components of the corresponding general solution $\mathbf{x}(t) = c_1\mathbf{v}_1 e^{\lambda_1 t} + c_2\mathbf{v}_2 e^{\lambda_2 t} + c_3\mathbf{v}_3 e^{\lambda_2 t}$.

23. $\lambda_1 = -1$: $\{\mathbf{v}_1\}$ with $\mathbf{v}_1 = [1 \quad -1 \quad 2]^T$
        $\lambda_2 = 3$: $\{\mathbf{v}_2\}$ with $\mathbf{v}_2 = [4 \quad 0 \quad 9]^T$ and
                   $\{\mathbf{v}_3\}$ with $\mathbf{v}_3 = [0 \quad 2 \quad 1]^T$

Scalar components

$$x_1(t) = c_1 e^{-t} + 4c_2 e^{3t}$$
$$x_2(t) = -c_1 e^{-t} \qquad\quad + 2c_3 e^{3t}$$
$$x_3(t) = 2c_1 e^{-t} + 9c_2 e^{3t} + c_3 e^{3t}$$

In Problems 25, 26, and 28 there is given a single eigenvalue λ of multiplicity 3. We find that $(\mathbf{A} - \lambda\mathbf{I})^2 \neq 0$ but $(\mathbf{A} - \lambda\mathbf{I})^3 = 0$. We therefore start with $\mathbf{v}_3 = [1 \ 0 \ 0]^T$ and define $\mathbf{v}_2 = (\mathbf{A} - \lambda\mathbf{I})\mathbf{v}_3$ and $\mathbf{v}_1 = (\mathbf{A} - \lambda\mathbf{I})\mathbf{v}_2 \neq 0$, thereby obtaining the length 3 chain $\{\mathbf{v}_1, \mathbf{v}_2, \mathbf{v}_3\}$ of generalized eigenvectors based on the ordinary eigenvector $\mathbf{v}_1$. We list the scalar components of the corresponding general solution

$$\mathbf{x}(t) = c_1\mathbf{v}_1 e^{\lambda t} + c_2(\mathbf{v}_1 t + \mathbf{v}_2) e^{\lambda t} + c_3(\mathbf{v}_1 t^2/2 + \mathbf{v}_2 t + \mathbf{v}_3) e^{\lambda t}.$$

25. $\{\mathbf{v}_1, \mathbf{v}_2, \mathbf{v}_3\}$ with
$$\mathbf{v}_1 = [-1 \quad 0 \ -1]^T, \quad \mathbf{v}_2 = [-4 \ -1 \ 0]^T, \quad \mathbf{v}_3 = [1 \ 0 \ 0]^T$$

Scalar components

$$x_1(t) = e^{2t}(-c_1 - 4c_2 + c_3 - c_2 t - 4c_3 t - c_3 t^2 / 2)$$
$$x_2(t) = e^{2t}(-c_2 - c_3 t)$$
$$x_3(t) = e^{2t}(-c_1 - c_2 t - c_3 t^2 / 2)$$

27. We find that the triple eigenvalue $\lambda = 2$ has the two linearly independent eigenvectors $[1 \quad 1 \quad 0]^T$ and $[-1 \quad 0 \quad 1]^T$. Next we find that $(\mathbf{A} - \lambda\mathbf{I}) \neq 0$ but $(\mathbf{A} - \lambda\mathbf{I})^2 = 0$. We therefore start with $\mathbf{v}_2 = [1 \quad 0 \quad 0]^T$ and define

$$\mathbf{v}_1 = (\mathbf{A} - \lambda\mathbf{I})\mathbf{v}_2 = [-5 \quad 3 \quad 8]^T \neq \mathbf{0},$$

thereby obtaining the length 2 chain $\{\mathbf{v}_1, \mathbf{v}_2\}$ of generalized eigenvectors based on the ordinary eigenvector $\mathbf{v}_1$. If we take $\mathbf{v}_3 = [1 \quad 1 \quad 0]^T$, then the general solution $\mathbf{x}(t) = e^{2t}[c_1\mathbf{v}_1 + c_2(\mathbf{v}_1 t + \mathbf{v}_2) + c_3\mathbf{v}_3]$ has scalar components

$$x_1(t) = e^{2t}(-5c_1 + c_2 + c_3 - 5c_2 t)$$
$$x_2(t) = e^{2t}(3c_1 + 3c_2 t)$$
$$x_3(t) = e^{2t}(8c_1 + 8c_2 t).$$

In Problems 29 and 30 the matrix $\mathbf{A}$ has two distinct eigenvalues λ_1 and λ_2 each having multiplicity 2 and defect 1. First, we select $\mathbf{v}_2$ so that $\mathbf{v}_1 = (\mathbf{A} - \lambda_1\mathbf{I})\mathbf{v}_2 \neq \mathbf{0}$ but $(\mathbf{A} - \lambda_1\mathbf{I})\mathbf{v}_1 = \mathbf{0}$, so $\{\mathbf{v}_1, \mathbf{v}_2\}$ is a length 2 chain based on $\mathbf{v}_1$. Next, we select $\mathbf{u}_2$ so that $\mathbf{u}_1 = (\mathbf{A} - \lambda_1\mathbf{I})\mathbf{u}_2 \neq \mathbf{0}$ but $(\mathbf{A} - \lambda_1\mathbf{I})\mathbf{u}_1 = \mathbf{0}$, so $\{\mathbf{u}_1, \mathbf{u}_2\}$ is a length 2 chain based on $\mathbf{u}_1$. We give the scalar components of the corresponding general solution

$$\mathbf{x}(t) = e^{\lambda_1 t}[c_1\mathbf{v}_1 + c_2(\mathbf{v}_1 t + \mathbf{v}_2)] + e^{\lambda_2 t}[c_3\mathbf{u}_1 + c_4(\mathbf{u}_1 t + \mathbf{u}_2)].$$

29. $\lambda = -1$: $\{\mathbf{v}_1, \mathbf{v}_2\}$ with $\mathbf{v}_1 = [1 \; -3 \; -1 \; -2]^T$ and $\mathbf{v}_2 = [0 \quad 1 \quad 0 \quad 0]^T$,
$\lambda = 2$: $\{\mathbf{u}_1, \mathbf{u}_2\}$ with $\mathbf{u}_1 = [0 \; -1 \quad 1 \quad 0]^T$ and $\mathbf{u}_2 = [0 \quad 0 \quad 2 \quad 1]^T$

Scalar components

$$x_1(t) = e^{-t}(c_1 + c_2 t)$$
$$x_2(t) = e^{-t}(-3c_1 + c_2 - 3c_2 t) + e^{2t}(-c_3 - c_4 t)$$
$$x_3(t) = e^{-t}(-c_1 - c_2 t) + e^{2t}(c_3 + 2c_4 + c_4 t)$$
$$x_4(t) = e^{-t}(-2c_1 - 2c_2 t) + e^{2t}(c_4)$$

31. We have the single eigenvalue $\lambda = 1$ of multiplicity 4. Starting with $\mathbf{v}_3 = [1 \ \ 0 \ \ 0 \ \ 0]^T$, we calculate $\mathbf{v}_2 = (\mathbf{A} - \lambda\mathbf{I})\mathbf{v}_3$ and $\mathbf{v}_1 = (\mathbf{A} - \lambda\mathbf{I})\mathbf{v}_2 \neq \mathbf{0}$, and find that $(\mathbf{A} - \lambda\mathbf{I})\mathbf{v}_1 = \mathbf{0}$. Therefore $\{\mathbf{v}_1, \mathbf{v}_2, \mathbf{v}_3\}$ is a length 3 chain based on the ordinary eigenvector $\mathbf{v}_1$. Next, the eigenvector equation $(\mathbf{A} - \lambda\mathbf{I})\mathbf{v} = \mathbf{0}$ yields the second linearly independent eigenvector $\mathbf{v}_4 = [0 \ \ 1 \ \ 3 \ \ 0]^T$. With

$$\mathbf{v}_1 = [42 \ \ 7 \ \ -21 \ \ -42]^T, \qquad \mathbf{v}_2 = [34 \ \ 22 \ \ -10 \ \ -27]^T,$$
$$\mathbf{v}_3 = [1 \ \ 0 \ \ 0 \ \ 0]^T \quad \text{and} \quad \mathbf{v}_4 = [0 \ \ 1 \ \ 3 \ \ 0]$$

the general solution

$$\mathbf{x}(t) = e^t[c_1\mathbf{v}_1 + c_2(\mathbf{v}_1 t + \mathbf{v}_2) + c_3(\mathbf{v}_1 t^2/2 + \mathbf{v}_2 t + \mathbf{v}_3) + c_4\mathbf{v}_4]$$

has scalar components

$$x_1(t) = e^t(42c_1 + 34c_2 + c_3 + 42c_2 t + 34c_3 t + 21c_3 t^2)$$
$$x_2(t) = e^t(7c_1 + 22c_2 + c_4 + 7c_2 t + 22c_3 t + 7c_3 t^2/2)$$
$$x_3(t) = e^t(-21c_1 - 10c_2 + 3c_4 - 21c_2 t - 10c_3 t - 21c_3 t^2/2)$$
$$x_4(t) = e^t(-42c_1 - 27c_2 - 42c_2 t - 27c_3 t - 21c_3 t^2).$$

33. The chain $\{\mathbf{v}_1, \mathbf{v}_2\}$ was found using the matrices

$$\mathbf{A} - \lambda\mathbf{I} = \begin{bmatrix} 4i & -4 & 1 & 0 \\ 4 & 4i & 0 & 1 \\ 0 & 0 & 4i & -4 \\ 0 & 0 & 4 & 4i \end{bmatrix} \rightarrow \begin{bmatrix} 1 & i & 0 & 0 \\ 0 & 0 & 1 & 0 \\ 0 & 0 & 0 & 1 \\ 0 & 0 & 0 & 0 \end{bmatrix}$$

and

$$(\mathbf{A} - \lambda\mathbf{I})^2 = \begin{bmatrix} -32 & -32i & 8i & -8 \\ 32i & -32 & 8 & 8i \\ 0 & 0 & -32 & -32i \\ 0 & 0 & 32i & -32 \end{bmatrix} \rightarrow \begin{bmatrix} 1 & i & 0 & 0 \\ 0 & 0 & 1 & i \\ 0 & 0 & 0 & 0 \\ 0 & 0 & 0 & 0 \end{bmatrix}$$

where $\rightarrow$ signifies reduction to row-echelon form. The resulting real-valued solution vectors are

$$\mathbf{x}_1(t) = e^{3t}[\ \cos 4t \qquad \sin 4t \qquad 0 \qquad 0 \ ]^T$$
$$\mathbf{x}_2(t) = e^{3t}[-\sin 4t \qquad \cos 4t \qquad 0 \qquad 0 \ ]^T$$
$$\mathbf{x}_3(t) = e^{3t}[\ t\cos 4t \qquad t\sin 4t \qquad \cos 4t \qquad \sin 4t \ ]^T$$
$$\mathbf{x}_4(t) = e^{3t}[-t\sin 4t \qquad t\cos 4t \qquad -\sin 4t \qquad \cos 4t \ ]^T.$$

35. The coefficient matrix

$$\mathbf{A} \;=\; \begin{bmatrix} 0 & 0 & 1 & 0 \\ 0 & 0 & 0 & 1 \\ -1 & 1 & -2 & 1 \\ 1 & -1 & 1 & -2 \end{bmatrix}$$

has eigenvalues

$\lambda = 0$ with eigenvector $\quad \mathbf{v}_1 = [1 \quad 1 \quad 0 \quad 0]^T$
$\lambda = -1$ with eigenvectors $\quad \mathbf{v}_2 = [1 \quad 0 \;-1 \quad 0]^T$ and $\mathbf{v}_3 = [0 \quad 1 \quad 0 \;-1]^T$,
$\lambda = -2$ with eigenvector $\quad \mathbf{v}_4 = [1 \;-1 \;-2 \quad 2]^T$.

When we impose the given initial conditions on the general solution

$$\mathbf{x}(t) \;=\; c_1\mathbf{v}_1 + c_2\mathbf{v}_2 e^{-t} + c_3\mathbf{v}_3 e^{-t} + c_4\mathbf{v}_4 e^{-2t}$$

we find that $c_1 = v_0$, $c_2 = c_3 = -v_0$, $c_4 = 0$. Hence the position functions of the two masses are given by

$$x_1(t) \;=\; x_2(t) \;=\; v_0(1 - e^{-t}).$$

Each mass travels a distance v_0 before stopping.

SECTION 5.5

MATRIX EXPONENTIALS AND LINEAR SYSTEMS

In Problems 1-8 we first use the eigenvalues and eigenvectors of the coefficient matrix $\mathbf{A}$ to find first a fundamental matrix $\Phi(t)$ for the homogeneous system $\mathbf{x}' = \mathbf{A}\mathbf{x}$. Then we apply the formula

$$\mathbf{x}(t) \;=\; \Phi(t)\Phi(0)^{-1}\mathbf{x}_0,$$

to find the solution vector $\mathbf{x}(t)$ that satisfies the initial condition $\mathbf{x}(0) = \mathbf{x}_0$. Formulas (11) and (12) in the text provide inverses of 2-by-2 and 3-by-3 matrices.

1. Eigensystem: $\quad \lambda_1 = 1, \quad \mathbf{v}_1 = [1 \;-1]^T; \qquad \lambda_2 = 3, \quad \mathbf{v}_2 = [1 \quad 1]^T$

$$\Phi(t) \;=\; \left[e^{\lambda_1 t}\mathbf{v}_1 \quad e^{\lambda_2 t}\mathbf{v}_2 \right] = \begin{bmatrix} e^t & e^{3t} \\ -e^t & e^{3t} \end{bmatrix}$$

$$\mathbf{x}(t) = \begin{bmatrix} e^t & e^{3t} \\ -e^t & e^{3t} \end{bmatrix} \cdot \frac{1}{2}\begin{bmatrix} 1 & -1 \\ 1 & 1 \end{bmatrix} \cdot \begin{bmatrix} 3 \\ -2 \end{bmatrix} = \frac{1}{2}\begin{bmatrix} 5e^t + e^{3t} \\ -5e^t + e^{3t} \end{bmatrix}$$

3. Eigensystem: $\lambda = 4i, \quad \mathbf{v} = [1+2i \quad 2]^T$

$$\Phi(t) = \begin{bmatrix} \mathrm{Re}(\mathbf{v}e^{\lambda t}) & \mathrm{Im}(\mathbf{v}e^{\lambda t}) \end{bmatrix} = \begin{bmatrix} \cos 4t - 2\sin 4t & 2\cos 4t + \sin 4t \\ 2\cos 4t & 2\sin 4t \end{bmatrix}$$

$$\mathbf{x}(t) = \begin{bmatrix} \cos 4t - 2\sin 4t & 2\cos 4t + \sin 4t \\ 2\cos 4t & 2\sin 4t \end{bmatrix} \cdot \frac{1}{4}\begin{bmatrix} 0 & 2 \\ 2 & -1 \end{bmatrix} \cdot \begin{bmatrix} 0 \\ 1 \end{bmatrix} = \frac{1}{4}\begin{bmatrix} -5\sin 4t \\ 4\cos 4t - 2\sin 4t \end{bmatrix}$$

5. Eigensystem: $\lambda = 3i, \quad \mathbf{v} = [-1+i \quad 3]^T$

$$\Phi(t) = \begin{bmatrix} \mathrm{Re}(\mathbf{v}e^{\lambda t}) & \mathrm{Im}(\mathbf{v}e^{\lambda t}) \end{bmatrix} = \begin{bmatrix} -\cos 3t - \sin 3t & \cos 3t - \sin 3t \\ 3\cos 3t & 3\sin 3t \end{bmatrix}$$

$$\mathbf{x}(t) = \begin{bmatrix} -\cos 3t - \sin 3t & \cos 3t - \sin 3t \\ 3\cos 3t & 3\sin 3t \end{bmatrix} \cdot \frac{1}{3}\begin{bmatrix} 0 & 1 \\ 3 & 1 \end{bmatrix} \cdot \begin{bmatrix} 1 \\ -1 \end{bmatrix} = \frac{1}{3}\begin{bmatrix} 3\cos 3t - \sin 3t \\ -3\cos 3t + 6\sin 3t \end{bmatrix}$$

7. Eigensystem:
$\lambda_1 = 0, \quad \mathbf{v}_1 = [6 \quad 2 \quad 5]^T; \quad \lambda_2 = 1, \quad \mathbf{v}_2 = [3 \ 1 \ 2]^T; \quad \lambda_3 = -1, \quad \mathbf{v}_3 = [2 \ 1 \ 2]^T$

$$\Phi(t) = \begin{bmatrix} e^{\lambda_1 t}\mathbf{v}_1 & e^{\lambda_2 t}\mathbf{v}_2 & e^{\lambda_3 t}\mathbf{v}_3 \end{bmatrix} = \begin{bmatrix} 6 & 3e^t & 2e^{-t} \\ 2 & e^t & e^{-t} \\ 5 & 2e^t & 2e^{-t} \end{bmatrix}$$

$$\mathbf{x}(t) = \begin{bmatrix} 6 & 3e^t & 2e^{-t} \\ 2 & e^t & e^{-t} \\ 5 & 2e^t & 2e^{-t} \end{bmatrix} \cdot \begin{bmatrix} 0 & -2 & 1 \\ 1 & 2 & -2 \\ -1 & 3 & 0 \end{bmatrix} \cdot \begin{bmatrix} 2 \\ 1 \\ 0 \end{bmatrix} = \begin{bmatrix} -12 + 12e^t + 2e^{-t} \\ -4 + 4e^t + e^{-t} \\ -10 + 8e^t + 2e^{-t} \end{bmatrix}$$

In each of Problems 9–20 we first solve the given linear system to find two linearly independent solutions $\mathbf{x}_1$ and $\mathbf{x}_2$, then set up the fundamental matrix $\Phi(t) = \begin{bmatrix} \mathbf{x}_1(t) & \mathbf{x}_2(t) \end{bmatrix}$, and finally calculate the matrix exponential $e^{At} = \Phi(t)\,\Phi(0)^{-1}$.

9. Eigensystem: $\lambda_1 = 1, \quad \mathbf{v}_1 = [1 \quad 1]^T; \qquad \lambda_2 = 3, \quad \mathbf{v}_2 = [2 \quad 1]^T$

$$\Phi(t) = \begin{bmatrix} e^{\lambda_1 t}\mathbf{v}_1 & e^{\lambda_2 t}\mathbf{v}_2 \end{bmatrix} = \begin{bmatrix} e^t & 2e^{3t} \\ e^t & e^{3t} \end{bmatrix}$$

$$e^{At} = \begin{bmatrix} e^t & 2e^{3t} \\ e^t & e^{3t} \end{bmatrix}\begin{bmatrix} -1 & 2 \\ 1 & -1 \end{bmatrix} = \begin{bmatrix} -e^t + 2e^{3t} & 2e^t - 2e^{3t} \\ -e^t + e^{3t} & 2e^t - e^{3t} \end{bmatrix}$$

11. Eigensystem: $\lambda_1 = 2$, $\mathbf{v}_1 = [1 \quad 1]^T$; $\qquad \lambda_2 = 3$, $\mathbf{v}_2 = [3 \quad 2]^T$

$$\Phi(t) = \left[e^{\lambda_1 t} \mathbf{v}_1 \quad e^{\lambda_2 t} \mathbf{v}_2 \right] = \begin{bmatrix} e^{2t} & 3e^{3t} \\ e^{2t} & 2e^{3t} \end{bmatrix}$$

$$e^{\mathbf{A}t} = \begin{bmatrix} e^{2t} & 3e^{3t} \\ e^{2t} & 2e^{3t} \end{bmatrix} \begin{bmatrix} -2 & 3 \\ 1 & -1 \end{bmatrix} = \begin{bmatrix} -2e^{2t} + 3e^{3t} & 3e^{2t} - 3e^{3t} \\ -2e^{2t} + 2e^{3t} & 3e^{2t} - 2e^{3t} \end{bmatrix}$$

13. Eigensystem: $\lambda_1 = 1$, $\mathbf{v}_1 = [1 \quad 1]^T$; $\qquad \lambda_2 = 3$, $\mathbf{v}_2 = [4 \quad 3]^T$

$$\Phi(t) = \left[e^{\lambda_1 t} \mathbf{v}_1 \quad e^{\lambda_2 t} \mathbf{v}_2 \right] = \begin{bmatrix} e^{t} & 4e^{3t} \\ e^{t} & 3e^{3t} \end{bmatrix}$$

$$e^{\mathbf{A}t} = \begin{bmatrix} e^{t} & 4e^{3t} \\ e^{t} & 3e^{3t} \end{bmatrix} \begin{bmatrix} -3 & 4 \\ 1 & -1 \end{bmatrix} = \begin{bmatrix} -3e^{t} + 4e^{3t} & 4e^{t} - 4e^{3t} \\ -3e^{t} + 3e^{3t} & 4e^{t} - 3e^{3t} \end{bmatrix}$$

15. Eigensystem: $\lambda_1 = 1$, $\mathbf{v}_1 = [2 \quad 1]^T$; $\qquad \lambda_2 = 2$, $\mathbf{v}_2 = [5 \quad 2]^T$

$$\Phi(t) = \left[e^{\lambda_1 t} \mathbf{v}_1 \quad e^{\lambda_2 t} \mathbf{v}_2 \right] = \begin{bmatrix} 2e^{t} & 5e^{2t} \\ e^{t} & 2e^{2t} \end{bmatrix}$$

$$e^{\mathbf{A}t} = \begin{bmatrix} 2e^{t} & 5e^{2t} \\ e^{t} & 2e^{2t} \end{bmatrix} \begin{bmatrix} -2 & 5 \\ 1 & -2 \end{bmatrix} = \begin{bmatrix} -4e^{t} + 5e^{2t} & 10e^{t} - 10e^{2t} \\ -2e^{t} + 2e^{2t} & 5e^{t} - 4e^{2t} \end{bmatrix}$$

17. Eigensystem: $\lambda_1 = 2$, $\mathbf{v}_1 = [1 \quad -1]^T$; $\qquad \lambda_2 = 4$, $\mathbf{v}_2 = [1 \quad 1]^T$

$$\Phi(t) = \left[e^{\lambda_1 t} \mathbf{v}_1 \quad e^{\lambda_2 t} \mathbf{v}_2 \right] = \begin{bmatrix} e^{2t} & e^{4t} \\ -e^{2t} & e^{4t} \end{bmatrix}$$

$$e^{\mathbf{A}t} = \begin{bmatrix} e^{2t} & e^{4t} \\ -e^{2t} & e^{4t} \end{bmatrix} \cdot \frac{1}{2} \begin{bmatrix} 1 & -1 \\ 1 & 1 \end{bmatrix} = \frac{1}{2} \begin{bmatrix} e^{2t} + e^{4t} & -e^{2t} + e^{4t} \\ -e^{2t} + e^{4t} & e^{2t} + e^{4t} \end{bmatrix}$$

19. Eigensystem: $\lambda_1 = 5$, $\mathbf{v}_1 = [1 \quad -2]^T$; $\qquad \lambda_2 = 10$, $\mathbf{v}_2 = [2 \quad 1]^T$

$$\Phi(t) = \left[e^{\lambda_1 t} \mathbf{v}_1 \quad e^{\lambda_2 t} \mathbf{v}_2 \right] = \begin{bmatrix} e^{5t} & 2e^{10t} \\ -2e^{5t} & e^{10t} \end{bmatrix}$$

$$e^{\mathbf{A}t} = \begin{bmatrix} e^{5t} & 2e^{10t} \\ -2e^{5t} & e^{10t} \end{bmatrix} \cdot \frac{1}{5} \begin{bmatrix} 1 & -2 \\ 2 & 1 \end{bmatrix} = \frac{1}{5} \begin{bmatrix} e^{5t} + 4e^{10t} & -2e^{5t} + 2e^{10t} \\ -2e^{5t} + 2e^{10t} & 4e^{5t} + e^{10t} \end{bmatrix}$$

21. $\mathbf{A}^2 = \mathbf{0}$ so $e^{\mathbf{A}t} = \mathbf{I} + \mathbf{A}t = \begin{bmatrix} 1+t & -t \\ t & 1-t \end{bmatrix}$

23. $\mathbf{A}^3 = \mathbf{0}$ so $e^{\mathbf{A}t} = \mathbf{I} + \mathbf{A}t + \dfrac{1}{2}\mathbf{A}^2t^2 = \begin{bmatrix} 1+t & -t & -t-t^2 \\ t & 1-t & t-t^2 \\ 0 & 0 & 1 \end{bmatrix}$

25. $\mathbf{A} = 2\mathbf{I} + \mathbf{D}$ where $\mathbf{D}^2 = \mathbf{0}$, so $e^{\mathbf{A}t} = e^{2\mathbf{I}t}e^{\mathbf{D}t} = (e^{2t}\mathbf{I})(\mathbf{I} + \mathbf{D}t)$. Hence

$$e^{\mathbf{A}t} = \begin{bmatrix} e^{2t} & 5te^{2t} \\ 0 & e^{2t} \end{bmatrix}, \qquad \mathbf{x}(t) = e^{\mathbf{A}t}\begin{bmatrix} 4 \\ 7 \end{bmatrix} = e^{2t}\begin{bmatrix} 4+35t \\ 7 \end{bmatrix}$$

27. $\mathbf{A} = \mathbf{I} + \mathbf{D}$ where $\mathbf{D}^3 = \mathbf{0}$, so $e^{\mathbf{A}t} = e^{\mathbf{I}t}e^{\mathbf{D}t} = (e^t\mathbf{I})(\mathbf{I} + \mathbf{D}t + \tfrac{1}{2}\mathbf{D}^2t^2)$. Hence

$$e^{\mathbf{A}t} = \begin{bmatrix} e^t & 2te^t & (3t+2t^2)e^t \\ 0 & e^t & 2te^t \\ 0 & 0 & e^t \end{bmatrix}, \qquad \mathbf{x}(t) = e^{\mathbf{A}t}\begin{bmatrix} 4 \\ 5 \\ 6 \end{bmatrix} = e^t\begin{bmatrix} 4+28t+12t^2 \\ 5+12t \\ 6 \end{bmatrix}$$

29. $\mathbf{A} = \mathbf{I} + \mathbf{D}$ where $\mathbf{D}^4 = \mathbf{0}$, so $e^{\mathbf{A}t} = e^{\mathbf{I}t}e^{\mathbf{D}t} = (e^t\mathbf{I})(\mathbf{I} + \mathbf{D}t + \tfrac{1}{2}\mathbf{D}^2t^2 + \tfrac{1}{6}\mathbf{D}^3t^3)$. Hence

$$e^{\mathbf{A}t} = e^t\begin{bmatrix} 1 & 2t & 3t+6t^2 & 4t+6t^2+4t^3 \\ 0 & 1 & 6t & 3t+6t^2 \\ 0 & 0 & 1 & 2t \\ 0 & 0 & 0 & 1 \end{bmatrix}, \qquad \mathbf{x}(t) = e^{\mathbf{A}t}\begin{bmatrix} 1 \\ 1 \\ 1 \\ 1 \end{bmatrix} = e^t\begin{bmatrix} 1+9t+12t^2+4t^3 \\ 1+9t+6t^2 \\ 1+2t \\ 1 \end{bmatrix}$$

33. $e^{\mathbf{A}t} = \mathbf{I}\cosh t + \mathbf{A}\sinh t = \begin{bmatrix} \cosh t & \sinh t \\ \sinh t & \cosh t \end{bmatrix}$, so the general solution of $\mathbf{x}' = \mathbf{A}\mathbf{x}$ is

$$\mathbf{x}(t) = e^{\mathbf{A}t}\mathbf{c} = \begin{bmatrix} c_1\cosh t + c_2\sinh t \\ c_1\sinh t + c_2\cosh t \end{bmatrix}.$$

In Problems 35-40 we give first the linearly independent generalized eigenvectors $\mathbf{u}_1, \mathbf{u}_2, \cdots, \mathbf{u}_n$ of the matrix $\mathbf{A}$ and the corresponding solution vectors $\mathbf{x}_1(t), \mathbf{x}_2(t), \cdots, \mathbf{x}_n(t)$ defined by Eq. (34) in the text, then the fundamental matrix $\Phi(t) = [\mathbf{x}_1(t) \ \ \mathbf{x}_2(t) \ \ \cdots \ \ \mathbf{x}_n(t)]$. Finally we calculate the exponential matrix $e^{\mathbf{A}t} = \Phi(t)\Phi(0)^{-1}$.

35. $\lambda = 3:$ $\mathbf{u}_1 = [4 \quad 0]^T,$ $\mathbf{u}_2 = [0 \quad 1]^T$

$\{\mathbf{u}_1, \mathbf{u}_2\}$ is a length 2 chain based on the ordinary (rank 1) eigenvector $\mathbf{u}_1$, so $\mathbf{u}_2$ is a generalized eigenvector of rank 2.

$$\mathbf{x}_1(t) = e^{\lambda t}\mathbf{u}_1, \quad \mathbf{x}_2(t) = e^{\lambda t}\left(\mathbf{u}_2 + (\mathbf{A} - \lambda\mathbf{I})\mathbf{u}_2 t\right)$$

$$\Phi(t) = [\mathbf{x}_1(t) \quad \mathbf{x}_2(t)] = e^{3t}\begin{bmatrix} 4 & 4t \\ 0 & 1 \end{bmatrix}$$

$$e^{\mathbf{A}t} = e^{3t}\begin{bmatrix} 4 & 4t \\ 0 & 1 \end{bmatrix} \cdot \frac{1}{4}\begin{bmatrix} 1 & 0 \\ 0 & 4 \end{bmatrix} = e^{3t}\begin{bmatrix} 1 & 4t \\ 0 & 1 \end{bmatrix}$$

37. $\lambda_1 = 2:$ $\mathbf{u}_1 = [1 \quad 0 \quad 0]^T,$ $\mathbf{x}_1(t) = e^{\lambda_1 t}\mathbf{u}_1$

$\lambda_2 = 1:$ $\mathbf{u}_2 = [9 \quad -3 \quad 0]^T,$ $\mathbf{u}_3 = [10 \quad 1 \quad -1]^T$

$\{\mathbf{u}_2, \mathbf{u}_3\}$ is a length 2 chain based on the ordinary (rank 1) eigenvector $\mathbf{u}_2$, so $\mathbf{u}_3$ is a generalized eigenvector of rank 2.

$$\mathbf{x}_2(t) = e^{\lambda_2 t}\mathbf{u}_2, \quad \mathbf{x}_3(t) = e^{\lambda_2 t}\left(\mathbf{u}_3 + (\mathbf{A} - \lambda_2\mathbf{I})\mathbf{u}_3 t\right)$$

$$\Phi(t) = [\mathbf{x}_1(t) \quad \mathbf{x}_2(t) \quad \mathbf{x}_3(t)] = \begin{bmatrix} e^{2t} & 9e^t & (10+9t)e^t \\ 0 & -3e^t & (1-3t)e^t \\ 0 & 0 & -e^t \end{bmatrix}$$

$$e^{\mathbf{A}t} = \begin{bmatrix} e^{2t} & 9e^t & (10+9t)e^t \\ 0 & -3e^t & (1-3t)e^t \\ 0 & 0 & -e^t \end{bmatrix} \cdot \frac{1}{3}\begin{bmatrix} 3 & 9 & 13 \\ 0 & -1 & -1 \\ 0 & 0 & -3 \end{bmatrix}$$

$$= \begin{bmatrix} e^{2t} & -3e^t + 3e^{2t} & (-13-9t)e^t + 13e^{2t} \\ 0 & e^t & 3t\,e^t \\ 0 & 0 & e^t \end{bmatrix}$$

39. $\lambda_2 = 1:$ $\mathbf{u}_1 = [3 \quad 0 \quad 0 \quad 0]^T,$ $\mathbf{u}_2 = [0 \quad 1 \quad 0 \quad 0]^T$

$\{\mathbf{u}_1, \mathbf{u}_2\}$ is a length 2 chain based on the ordinary (rank 1) eigenvector $\mathbf{u}_1$, so $\mathbf{u}_2$ is a generalized eigenvector of rank 2.

$$\mathbf{x}_1(t) = e^{\lambda_1 t}\mathbf{u}_1, \quad \mathbf{x}_2(t) = e^{\lambda_1 t}\left(\mathbf{u}_2 + (\mathbf{A} - \lambda_1\mathbf{I})\mathbf{u}_2 t\right)$$

$\lambda_2 = 2:$ $\mathbf{u}_3 = [144 \quad 36 \quad 12 \quad 0]^T,$ $\mathbf{u}_4 = [0 \quad 27 \quad 17 \quad 4]^T$

$\{\mathbf{u}_3, \mathbf{u}_4\}$ is a length 2 chain based on the ordinary (rank 1) eigenvector $\mathbf{u}_3$, so

$\mathbf{u}_4$ is a generalized eigenvector of rank 2.

$$\mathbf{x}_3(t) = e^{\lambda_2 t}\mathbf{u}_3, \quad \mathbf{x}_4(t) = e^{\lambda_2 t}\left(\mathbf{u}_4 + (\mathbf{A} - \lambda_2\mathbf{I})\mathbf{u}_4 t\right)$$

$$\Phi(t) = [\mathbf{x}_1(t) \;\; \mathbf{x}_2(t) \;\; \mathbf{x}_3(t) \;\; \mathbf{x}_4(t)] = \begin{bmatrix} 3e^t & 3t\,e^t & 144e^{2t} & 144t\,e^{2t} \\ 0 & e^t & 36e^{2t} & (27+36t)e^{2t} \\ 0 & 0 & 12e^{2t} & (17+12t)e^{2t} \\ 0 & 0 & 0 & 4e^{2t} \end{bmatrix}$$

$$e^{\mathbf{A}t} = \begin{bmatrix} 3e^t & 3t\,e^t & 144e^{2t} & 144t\,e^{2t} \\ 0 & e^t & 36e^{2t} & (27+36t)e^{2t} \\ 0 & 0 & 12e^{2t} & (17+12t)e^{2t} \\ 0 & 0 & 0 & 4e^{2t} \end{bmatrix} \cdot \frac{1}{48}\begin{bmatrix} 16 & 0 & -192 & 816 \\ 0 & 48 & -144 & 288 \\ 0 & 0 & 4 & -17 \\ 0 & 0 & 0 & 12 \end{bmatrix}$$

$$= \begin{bmatrix} e^t & 3t\,e^t & (-12-9t)e^t+12t\,e^{2t} & (51+18t)e^t+(-51+36t)e^{2t} \\ 0 & e^t & -3e^t+3e^{2t} & 6e^t+(-6+9t)e^{2t} \\ 0 & 0 & e^{2t} & 3t\,e^{2t} \\ 0 & 0 & 0 & e^{2t} \end{bmatrix}$$

SECTION 5.6

NONHOMOGENEOUS LINEAR SYSTEMS

1. Substitution of the trial solution $x_p(t) = a, \; y_p(t) = b$ yields the equations
    $a + 2b + 3 = 0, \; 2a + b - 2 = 0$ with solution $a = 7/3, \; b = -8/3$. Thus we obtain the
    particular solution $x(t) = 7/3, \; y(t) = -8/3$.

3. When we substitute the trial solution

    $$x_p = a_1 + b_1 t + c_1 t^2, \quad y_p = a_2 + b_2 t + c_2 t^2$$

    and collect coefficients, we get the equations

    $$\begin{aligned} 3a_1 + 4a_2 &= b_1 & 3b_1 + 4b_2 &= 2c_1 & 3c_1 + 4c_2 &= 0 \\ 3a_1 + 2a_2 &= b_2 & 3b_1 + 2b_2 &= 2c_2 & 3c_1 + 2c_2 + 1 &= 0. \end{aligned}$$

Working backwards, we solve first for $c_1 = -2/3$, $c_2 = 1/2$, then for $b_1 = 10/9$, $b_2 = -7/6$, and finally for $a_1 = -31/27$, $a_2 = 41/36$. This determines the particular solution $x_p(t)$, $y_p(t)$. Next, the coefficient matrix of the associated homogeneous system has eigenvalues $\lambda_1 = -1$ and $\lambda_2 = 6$ with eigenvectors $\mathbf{v}_1 = [1 \quad -1]^T$ and $\mathbf{v}_2 = [4 \quad 3]^T$, respectively, so the complementary solution is given by

$$x_c(t) = c_1 e^{-t} + 4c_2 e^{6t}, \qquad x_c(t) = -c_1 e^{-t} + 3c_2 e^{6t}.$$

When we impose the initial conditions $x(0) = 0$, $y(0) = 0$ on the general solution $x(t) = x_c(t) + x_p(t)$, $y(t) = y_c(t) + y_p(t)$ we find that $c_1 = 8/7$, $c_2 = 1/756$. This finally gives the desired particular solution

$$x(t) = \frac{1}{756}(864 e^{-t} + 4 e^{6t} - 868 + 840t - 504t^2)$$

$$y(t) = \frac{1}{756}(-864 e^{-t} + 3 e^{6t} + 861 - 882t + 378t^2).$$

5. The coefficient matrix of the associated homogeneous system has eigenvalues $\lambda_1 = -1$ and $\lambda_2 = 5$, so the nonhomogeneous term e^{-t} duplicates part of the complementary solution. We therefore try the particular solution

$$x_p(t) = a_1 + b_1 e^{-t} + c_1 t e^{-t}, \quad y_p(t) = a_2 + b_2 e^{-t} + c_2 t e^{-t}.$$

Upon solving the six linear equations we get by collecting coefficients after substitution of this trial solution into the given nonhomogeneous system, we obtain the particular solution

$$x(t) = \frac{1}{3}(-12 - e^{-t} - 7t e^{-t}), \quad y(t) = \frac{1}{3}(-6 - 7t e^{-t}).$$

7. First we try the particular solution

$$x_p(t) = a_1 \sin t + b_1 \cos t, \qquad y_p(t) = a_2 \sin t + b_2 \cos t.$$

Upon solving the four linear equations we get by collecting coefficients after substitution of this trial solution into the given nonhomogeneous system, we find that $a_1 = -21/82$, $b_1 = -25/82$, $a_2 = -15/41$, $b_2 = -12/41$. The coefficient matrix of the associated homogeneous system has eigenvalues $\lambda_1 = 1$ and $\lambda_2 = -9$ with eigenvectors $\mathbf{v}_1 = [1 \quad 1]^T$ and $\mathbf{v}_2 = [2 \quad -3]^T$, respectively, so the complementary solution is given by

$$x_c(t) = c_1 e^t + 2c_2 e^{-9t}, \qquad y_c(t) = c_1 e^t - 3c_2 e^{-9t}.$$

When we impose the initial conditions $x(0) = 1$, $y(0) = 0$, we find that $c_1 = 9/10$ and $c_2 = 83/410$. It follows that the desired particular solution $x = x_c + x_p$, $y = y_c + y_p$ is given by

$$x(t) = \frac{1}{410}(369e^t + 166e^{-9t} - 125\cos t - 105\sin t)$$

$$y(t) = \frac{1}{410}(369e^t - 249e^{-9t} - 120\cos t - 150\sin t).$$

9.   Here the associated homogeneous system is the same as in Problem 8, so the nonhomogeneous term $\cos 2t$ term duplicates the complementary function. We therefore substitute the trial solution

$$x_p(t) = a_1 \sin 2t + b_1 \cos 2t + c_1 t \sin 2t + d_1 t \cos 2t$$
$$y_p(t) = a_2 \sin 2t + b_2 \cos 2t + c_2 t \sin 2t + d_2 t \cos 2t$$

and use a computer algebra system to solve the system of 8 linear equations that results when we collect coefficients in the usual way. This gives the particular solution

$$x(t) = \frac{1}{4}(\sin 2t + 2t\cos 2t + t\sin 2t), \qquad y(t) = \frac{1}{4}t\sin 2t.$$

11.   The coefficient matrix of the associated homogeneous system has eigenvalues $\lambda_1 = 0$ and $\lambda_2 = 4$, so there is duplication of constant terms. We therefore substitute the particular solution

$$x_p(t) = a_1 + b_1 t, \quad y_p(t) = a_2 + b_2 t$$

and solve the resulting equations for $a_1 = -2$, $a_2 = 0$, $b_1 = -2$, $b_2 = 1$. The eigenvectors of the coefficient matrix associated with the eigenvalues $\lambda_1 = 0$ and $\lambda_2 = 4$ are $\mathbf{v}_1 = [2 \quad -1]^T$ and $\mathbf{v}_2 = [2 \quad 1]^T$, respectively, so the general solution of the given nonhomogeneous system is given by

$$x(t) = 2c_1 + 2c_2 e^{4t} - 2 - 2t, \qquad y(t) = -c_1 + c_2 e^{4t} + t.$$

When we impose the initial conditions $x(0) = 1$, $y(0) = -1$ we find readily that $c_1 = 5/4$, $c_2 = 1/4$. This gives the desired particular solution

$$x(t) = \tfrac{1}{2}(1 - 4t + e^{4t}), \qquad y(t) = \tfrac{1}{4}(-5 + 4t + e^{4t}).$$

13.   The coefficient matrix of the associated homogeneous system has eigenvalues $\lambda_1 = 1$ and $\lambda_2 = 3$, so there is duplication of e^t terms. We therefore substitute the trial solution

$$x_p(t) = (a_1 + b_1 t)e^t, \quad y_p(t) = (a_2 + b_2 t)e^t.$$

This leads readily to the particular solution

$$x(t) = \frac{1}{2}(1 + 5t)e^t, \qquad y(t) = -\frac{5}{2}te^t.$$

In Problems 15 and 16 the amounts $x_1(t)$ and $x_2(t)$ in the two tanks satisfy the equations

$$x_1' = rc_0 - k_1 x_1, \qquad x_2' = k_1 x_1 - k_2 x_2$$

where $k_i = r/V_i$ in terms of the flow rate r, the inflowing concentration c_0, and the volumes V_1 and V_2 of the two tanks.

15. **(a)** We solve the initial value problem

$$x_1' = 20 - x_1/10, \qquad x_1(0) = 0$$
$$x_2' = x_1/10 - x_2/20, \qquad x_2(0) = 0$$

for $x_1(t) = 200(1 - e^{-t/10})$, $x_2(t) = 400(1 + e^{-t/10} - 2e^{-t/20})$.

(b) Evidently $x_1(t) \to 200$ gal and $x_2(t) \to 400$ gal as $t \to \infty$.

(c) It takes about 6 min 56 sec for tank 1 to reach a salt concentration of 1 lb/gal, and about 24 min 34 sec for tank 2 to reach this concentration.

In Problems 17-34 we apply the variation of parameters formula in Eq. (28) of Section 5.6. The answers shown below were actually calculated using the Mathematica code listed in the computing project for Section 5.6. For instance, for Problem 17 we first enter the coefficient matrix

```
A = {{6,   -7},
     {1,   -2}};
```

the initial vector

```
x0 = {{0},
      {0}};
```

and the vector

```
f[t_] := {{60},
           {90}};
```

of nonhomogeneous terms. It simplifies the notation to rename Mathematica's exponential matrix function by defining

```
exp[A_] := MatrixExp[A]
```

Then the integral in the variation of parameters formula is given by

```
integral =
Integrate[exp[-A*s] . f[s], {s, 0, t}] // Simplify
```

$$\begin{bmatrix} -102 + 7e^{-5t} + 95e^{t} \\ -96 + e^{-5t} + 95e^{t} \end{bmatrix}.$$

Finally the desired particular solution is given by

```
solution =
exp[A*t] . (x0 + integral) // Simplify
```

$$\begin{bmatrix} 102 - 7e^{-5t} - 95e^{t} \\ 96 - e^{-5t} - 95e^{t} \end{bmatrix}.$$

(Maple and MATLAB versions of this computation are provided in the computing projects manual that accompanies the textbook.)

In each succeeding problem, we need only substitute the given coefficient matrix **A**, initial vector **x0**, and the vector **f** of nonhomogeneous terms in the above commands, and then re-execute them in turn. We give below only the component functions of the final results.

17. $x_1(t) = 102 - 95e^{-t} - 7e^{5t}, \quad x_2(t) = 96 - 95e^{-t} - e^{5t}$

19. $x_1(t) = -70 - 60t + 16e^{-3t} + 54e^{2t}, \quad x_2(t) = 5 - 60t - 32e^{-3t} + 27e^{2t}$

21. $x_1(t) = -e^{-t} - 14e^{2t} + 15e^{3t}, \quad x_2(t) = -5e^{-t} - 10e^{2t} + 15e^{3t}$

23. $x_1(t) = 3 + 11t + 8t^2, \quad x_2(t) = 5 + 17t + 24t^2$

25. $x_1(t) = -1 + 8t + \cos t - 8\sin t, \quad x_2(t) = -2 + 4t + 2\cos t - 3\sin t$

27. $x_1(t) = 8t^3 + 6t^4$, $x_2(t) = 3t^2 - 2t^3 + 3t^4$

29. $x_1(t) = t\cos t - \ln(\cos t)\sin t$, $x_2(t) = t\sin t - \ln(\cos t)\cos t$

31. $x_1(t) = (9t^2 + 4t^3)e^t$, $x_2(t) = 6t^2 e^t$, $x_3(t) = 6t e^t$

33. $x_1(t) = 15t^2 + 60t^3 + 95t^4 + 12t^5$, $x_2(t) = 15t^2 + 55t^3 + 15t^4$,
$x_3(t) = 15t^2 + 20t^3$, $x_4(t) = 15t^2$

CHAPTER 6

NONLINEAR SYSTEMS AND PHENOMENA

SECTION 6.1

STABILITY AND THE PHASE PLANE

1. The only solution of the homogeneous system $2x - y = 0$, $x - 3y = 0$ is the origin $(0, 0)$. The only figure among Figs. 6.1.11 through 6.1.18 showing a single critical point at the origin is Fig. 6.1.13. Thus the only critical point of the given autonomous system is the saddle point $(0, 0)$ shown in Figure 6.1.13 in the text.

3. The only solution of the system $x - 2y + 3 = 0$, $x - y + 2 = 0$ is the point $(-1, 1)$. The only figure among Figs. 6.1.11 through 6.1.18 showing a single critical point at $(-1, 1)$ is Fig. 6.1.18. Thus the only critical point of the given autonomous system is the stable center $(-1, 1)$ shown in Figure 6.1.18 in the text.

5. The first equation $1 - y^2 = 0$ gives $y = 1$ or $y = -1$ at a critical point. Then the second equation $x + 2y = 0$ gives $x = -2$ or $x = 2$, respectively. The only figure among Figs. 6.1.11 through 6.1.18 showing two critical points at $(-2, 1)$ and $(2, -1)$ is Fig. 6.1.11. Thus the critical points of the given autonomous system are the spiral point $(-2, 1)$ and the saddle point $(2, 1)$ shown in Figure 6.1.11 in the text.

7. The first equation $4x - x^3 = 0$ gives $x = -2$, $x = 0$, or $x = 2$ at a critical point. Then the second equation $x - 2y = 0$ gives $y = -1$, $y = 0$, or $y = 1$, respectively. The only figure among Figs. 6.1.11 through 6.1.18 showing three critical points at $(-2, -1)$, $(0, 0)$, and $(2, 1)$ is Fig. 6.1.14. Thus the critical points of the given autonomous system are the spiral point $(0, 0)$ and the saddle points $(-2, 1)$ and $(2, 1)$ shown in Figure 6.1.14 in the text.

In each of Problems 9–12 we need only set $x' = x'' = 0$ and solve the resulting equation for x.

9. The equation $4x - x^3 = x(4 - x^2) = 0$ has the three solutions $x = 0, \pm 2$. This gives the three equilibrium solutions $x(t) \equiv 0$, $x(t) \equiv 2$, $x(t) \equiv -2$ of the given 2nd-order differential equation.

11. The equation $4 \sin x = 0$ is satisfied by $x = n\pi$ for any integer n. Thus the given 2nd-order equation has infinitely many equilibrium solutions: $x(t) \equiv n\pi$ for any integer n.

In Problems 13-16, the given x- and y-equations are independent exponential differential equations that we can solve immediately by inspection.

13. Solution: $x(t) = x_0 e^{-2t}, \ y(t) = y_0 e^{-2t}$

Then $y = (y_0 / x_0)x = kx$, so the trajectories are straight lines through the origin. Clearly $x(t), y(t) \to 0$ as $t \to +\infty$, so the origin is a stable proper node like the one shown in Figure 6.1.4 in the text.

15. Solution: $x(t) = x_0 e^{-2t}, \ y(t) = y_0 e^{-t}$

Then $x = (x_0 / y_0^2)(y_0 e^{-t})^2 = ky^2$, so the trajectories are parabolas of the form $x = ky^2$, and clearly $x(t), y(t) \to 0$ as $t \to +\infty$. Thus the origin is a stable improper node similar to the one shown in Figure 6.1.5 in the text.

17. Differentiation of the first equation and substitution using the second one gives

$$x'' = y' = x, \quad \text{so} \quad x'' + x = 0.$$

We therefore get the general solution

$$\begin{aligned} x(t) &= A \cos t + B \sin t \\ y(t) &= B \cos t - A \sin t \end{aligned} \qquad (y = x').$$

Then

$$\begin{aligned} x^2 + y^2 &= (A\cos t + B\sin t)^2 + (B\cos t - A\sin t)^2 \\ &= (A^2 + B^2)\cos^2 t + (A^2 + B^2)\sin^2 t = A^2 + B^2. \end{aligned}$$

Therefore the trajectories are clockwise-oriented circles centered at the origin, and the origin is a stable center.

19. Elimination of y as in Problem 17 gives $x'' + 4x = 0$, so we get the general solution

$$\begin{aligned} x(t) &= A \cos 2t + B \sin 2t, \\ y(t) &= B \cos 2t - A \sin 2t \end{aligned} \qquad (y = \tfrac{1}{2}x').$$

Then $x^2 + y^2 = A^2 + B^2$, so the origin is a stable center, and the trajectories are clockwise-oriented circles centered at $(0, 0)$.

21. We want to solve the system

$$\begin{aligned} -ky + x(1 - x^2 - y^2) &= 0 \\ kx + y(1 - x^2 - y^2) &= 0. \end{aligned}$$

If we multiply the first equation by $-y$ and the second one by x, then add the two results, we get $k(x^2 + y^2) = 0$. It therefore follows that $x = y = 0$.

23. The equation $dy/dx = -x/y$ separates to $x\,dx + y\,dy = 0$, so $x^2 + y^2 = C$. Thus the trajectories consist of the origin $(0, 0)$ and the circles $x^2 + y^2 = C > 0$.

25. The equation $dy/dx = -x/4y$ separates to $x\,dx + 4y\,dy = 0$, so $x^2 + 4y^2 = C$. Thus the trajectories consist of the origin $(0, 0)$ and the ellipses $x^2 + 4y^2 = C > 0$.

27. If $\phi(t) = x(t + \gamma)$ and $\psi(t) = y(t + \gamma)$ then

$$\phi'(t) = x'(t + \gamma) = y(t + \gamma) = \psi(t),$$

but

$$\psi(t) = y'(t + \gamma) = x(t + \gamma) \cdot (t + \gamma) = t\,\phi(t) + \gamma\,\phi(t) \neq t\,\phi(t).$$

SECTION 6.2

LINEAR AND ALMOST LINEAR SYSTEMS

In Problems 1-10 we first find the roots λ_1 and λ_2 of the characteristic equation of the coefficient matrix of the given linear system. We can then read the type and stability of the critical point (0,0) from Theorem 1 and the table of Figure 6.2.9 in the text.

1. The roots $\lambda_1 = -1$ and $\lambda_2 = -3$ of the characteristic equation $\lambda^2 + 4\lambda + 3 = 0$ are both negative, so (0,0) is an asymptotically stable node.

3. The roots $\lambda_1 = -1$ and $\lambda_2 = 3$ of the characteristic equation $\lambda^2 - 2\lambda - 3 = 0$ have different signs, so (0,0) is an unstable saddle point.

5. The roots $\lambda_1 = \lambda_2 = -1$ of the characteristic equation $\lambda^2 + 2\lambda + 1 = 0$ are negative and equal, so (0,0) is an asymptotically stable node.

7. The roots $\lambda_1, \lambda_2 = 1 \pm 2\,i$ of the characteristic equation $\lambda^2 - 2\lambda + 5 = 0$ are complex conjugates with positive real part, so (0,0) is an unstable spiral point.

9. The roots $\lambda_1, \lambda_2 = \pm 2\,i$ of the characteristic equation $\lambda^2 + 4 = 0$ are pure imaginary, so (0,0) is a stable (but not asymptotically stable) center.

11. The substitution $u = x - 2$, $v = y - 1$ transforms the given system to the system

$$u' = u - 2v, \qquad v' = 3u - 4v$$

with characteristic roots $\lambda_1 = -1$, $\lambda_2 = -2$ that are both negative. Hence $(2, 1)$ is an asymptotically stable node.

13.   The substitution $u = x - 2$, $v = y - 2$ transforms the given system to the system

$$u' = 2u - v, \qquad v' = 3u - 2v$$

with characteristic roots $\lambda_1 = 1$, $\lambda_2 = -1$ that are real with different signs. Hence $(2, 2)$ is an unstable saddle point.

15.   The substitution $u = x - 1$, $v = y - 1$ transforms the given system to the system

$$u' = u - v, \qquad v' = 5u - 3v$$

with characteristic roots $\lambda_1, \lambda_2 = -1 \pm i$ that are complex conjugates with negative real part. Hence $(1, 1)$ is an asymptotically stable spiral point.

17.   The substitution $u = x - 5/2$, $v = y + 1/2$ transforms the given system to the system

$$u' = u - 5v, \qquad v' = u - v$$

with pure imaginary characteristic roots $\lambda_1, \lambda_2 = \pm 2\, i$. Hence $(5/2, -1/2)$ is a stable (but not asymptotically stable) center.

In each of Problems 19-28 the associated linear system is obtained simply by deleting the nonlinear terms in the given almost linear system. We first find the characteristic roots λ_1 and λ_2 of the coefficient matrix of the associated linear system, and then apply Theorem 2 to determine as much as we can about the type and stability of the critical point $(0,0)$ of the given almost linear system.

19.   The roots $\lambda_1 = -2$ and $\lambda_2 = -3$ of the characteristic equation $\lambda^2 + 5\lambda + 6 = 0$ of the associated linear system are real and both negative. Hence $(0,0)$ is an asymptotically stable node of the given almost linear system.

21.   The roots $\lambda_1 = -3$ and $\lambda_2 = 2$ of the characteristic equation $\lambda^2 + \lambda - 6 = 0$ of the associated linear system are real and have different signs. Hence $(0,0)$ is an unstable saddle point of the given almost linear system.

23.   The roots $\lambda_1, \lambda_2 = -2 \pm 2\, i$ of the characteristic equation $\lambda^2 + 4\lambda + 8 = 0$ of the associated linear system are complex conjugates with negative real part. Hence $(0,0)$ is an asymptotically stable spiral point of the given almost linear system.

25. The roots $\lambda_1 = \lambda_2 = -1$ of the characteristic equation $\lambda^2 + 2\lambda + 1 = 0$ of the associated linear system are real, equal, and negative. Hence $(0,0)$ is an asymptotically stable node or spiral point of the given almost linear system.

27. The roots $\lambda_1, \lambda_2 = \pm i$ of the characteristic equation $\lambda^2 + 1 = 0$ of the associated linear system are pure imaginary. Hence $(0,0)$ is either a center or a spiral point of the given almost linear system, but its stability is not determined by Theorem 2.

29. The critical points of the given system are $(0,0)$ and $(1, 1)$. At $(0,0)$ the characteristic roots are $\lambda_1 = -1, \lambda_2 = 1$ so $(0,0)$ is an unstable saddle point. The substitution $u = x - 1, v = y - 1$ transforms the given system to the almost linear system

$$u' = u - v, \qquad v' = 2u + v + u^2$$

whose linearization has characteristic roots $\lambda_1, \lambda_2 = \pm i$. Hence $(1, 1)$ is either a center or a spiral point, but its stability is indeterminate.

31. The critical points of the given system are $(1, 1)$ and $(-1,-1)$. The substitution $u = x - 1, v = y - 1$ transforms it to the almost linear system

$$u' = 2v + v^2, \qquad v' = 3u - v + 3u^2 + u^3$$

whose linearization has characteristic roots $\lambda_1 = -3, \lambda_2 = 2$. Hence $(1, 1)$ is an unstable saddle point of the given system. The substitution $u = x + 1, v = y + 1$ transforms it to the almost linear system

$$u' = -2v + v^2, \qquad v' = 3u - v - 3u^2 + u^3$$

whose linearization has characteristic roots $\lambda_1, \lambda_2 = (-1 \pm i\sqrt{23})/2$. Hence $(-1,-1)$ is an asymptotically stable spiral point.

33. The characteristic equation of the given linear system is

$$(\lambda - \varepsilon)^2 + 1 = 0$$

with characteristic roots $\lambda_1, \lambda_2 = \varepsilon \pm i$.

(a) So if $\varepsilon < 0$ then λ_1, λ_2 are complex conjugates with negative real part, and hence $(0, 0)$ is an asymptotically stable spiral point.

(b) If $\varepsilon = 0$ then $\lambda_1, \lambda_2 = \pm i$ (pure imaginary), so $(0,0)$ is a stable center.

(c) If $\varepsilon > 0$, the situation is the same as in (a) except that the real part is positive, so $(0, 0)$ is an unstable spiral point.

35. **(a)**   If $h = 0$ we have the familiar system $x' = y$, $y' = -x$ with circular trajectories about the origin, which is therefore a center.

(b)   The change to polar coordinates as in Example 6 of Section 6.1 is routine, yielding $r' = hr^3$ and $\theta' = -1$.

(c)   If $h = -1$, then $r' = -r^3$ integrates to give $2r^2 = 1/(t + C)$ where C is a positive constant, so clearly $r \to 0$ as $t \to +\infty$, and thus the origin is a stable spiral point.

(d)   If $h = +1$, then $r' = r^3$ integrates to give $2r^2 = -1/(t + C)$ where $C = -B$ is a positive constant. It follows that $2r^2 = 1/(B - t)$, so now r increases as t starts at 0 and increases.

37.   The substitution $y = vx$ in the homogeneous first-order equation

$$\frac{dy}{dx} = \frac{y(2x^3 - y^3)}{x(x^3 - 2y^3)}$$

yields

$$x\frac{dv}{dx} = -\frac{v^4 + v}{2v^3 - 1}.$$

Separating the variables and integrating by partial fractions, we get

$$\int\left(-\frac{1}{v} + \frac{1}{v+1} + \frac{2v-1}{v^2 - v + 1}\right)dv = -\int\frac{dx}{x}$$

$$\ln((v+1)(v^2 - v + 1)) = \ln v - \ln x + \ln C$$

$$(v+1)(v^2 - v + 1) = \frac{Cv}{x}$$

$$v^3 + 1 = \frac{Cv}{x}.$$

Finally, the replacement $v = y/x$ yields $x^3 + y^3 = Cxy$.

SECTION 6.3

ECOLOGICAL APPLICATIONS: PREDATORS AND COMPETITORS

1. If $x = u + b/q$, $y = v + a/p$ then $x' = u'$ and $y' = v'$ so the first predator-prey equation in

$$x' = ax - pxy, \quad y' = -by + qxy \tag{1}$$

yields

$$u' = a(u + b/q) - p(u + b/q)(v + a/p)$$
$$= au + ab/q - puv - au - bpv/q - ab/q = -bpv/q - puv.$$

upon cancellation of a couple of pairs of terms. In a quite similar way the second predator-prey equation transforms to $v' = aqu/p + quv$. The coefficient matrix of the linearization of this transformed system is

$$\mathbf{A} = \begin{bmatrix} 0 & -bp/a \\ aq/p & 0 \end{bmatrix}.$$

Its characteristic values $\lambda = \pm i\sqrt{bq}$ are pure imaginary, so the linear system has a stable center at the origin.

3. The effect of using the insecticide is to replace b by $b + f$ and a by $a - f$ in the predator-prey equations, while leaving p and q unchanged. Hence the new harmful population is $(b + f)/q > b/q = x_E$, and the new benign population is $(a - f)/p < a/p = y_E$.

Problems 4-7 deal with the competition system

$$x' = 60x - 4x^2 - 3xy, \quad y' = 42y - 2y^2 - 3xy. \tag{2}$$

In each problem we denote by $\mathbf{A}$ the coefficient matrix of the linearized system.

5. The substitution $x = u$, $y = v + 21$ gives the linearization $u' = -3u$, $v' = -63u - 42v$ at $(0, 21)$. Then the characteristic equation

$$|\mathbf{A} - \lambda \mathbf{I}| = \begin{vmatrix} -3 - \lambda & 0 \\ -63 & -42 - \lambda \end{vmatrix} = (\lambda + 3)(\lambda + 42) = 0$$

has negative roots $\lambda_1 = -3$ and $\lambda_2 = -42$ indicating a nodal sink.

7. The substitution $x = u + 6$, $y = v + 12$ gives the linearization $u' = -24u - 18v$, $v' = -36u - 24v$ at $(6, 12)$. Then the characteristic equation

$$|A - \lambda I| = \begin{vmatrix} -24 - \lambda & -18 \\ -36 & -24 - \lambda \end{vmatrix} = (-24 - \lambda)^2 - 2(18)^2 = 0$$

has real roots $\lambda_1 = -24 + 18\sqrt{2} > 0$, $\lambda_2 = -24 - 18\sqrt{2} < 0$ of opposite sign, indicating a saddle point.

Problems 8-10 deal with the competition system

$$x' = 60x - 3x^2 - 4xy, \quad y' = 42y - 3y^2 - 2xy \tag{3}$$

9. The substitution $x = u + 20$, $y = v$ gives the linearization $u' = -60u - 80v$, $v' = 2v$ at $(20, 0)$. Then the characteristic equation

$$|A - \lambda I| = \begin{vmatrix} -60 - \lambda & -80 \\ 0 & 2 - \lambda \end{vmatrix} = (\lambda + 60)(\lambda - 2) = 0$$

has real roots $\lambda_1 = -60$ and $\lambda_2 = 2$ of opposite sign, indicating a saddle point.

Problems 11-13 deal with the predator-prey system

$$x' = 5x - x^2 - xy, \quad y' = -2y + xy. \tag{4}$$

11. We simply delete the quadratic terms in (4) to linearize at $(0,0)$. Then it is quite obvious that the coefficient matrix $A = \begin{bmatrix} 5 & 0 \\ 0 & -2 \end{bmatrix}$ has real eigenvalues $\lambda_1 = 5$ and $\lambda_2 = -2$ of opposite sign, indicating a saddle point.

13. The substitution $x = u + 2$, $y = v + 3$ gives the linearization $u' = -2u - 2v$, $v' = 3u$. at $(2, 3)$. Then the characteristic equation

$$|A - \lambda I| = \begin{vmatrix} -2 - \lambda & -2 \\ 3 & -\lambda \end{vmatrix} = \lambda^2 + 2\lambda + 6 = 0$$

has complex conjugate roots $\lambda = -1 \pm i\sqrt{5}$ with negative real part, indicating a spiral sink.

Problems 14-17 deal with the predator-prey system

$$x' = x^2 - 2x - xy, \quad y' = y^2 - 4y + xy. \tag{5}$$

15. The substitution $x = u$, $y = v + 4$ gives the linearization $u' = -6u$, $v' = 4u + 4v$ at $(0, 4)$. Then the characteristic equation

$$|A - \lambda I| = \begin{vmatrix} -6 - \lambda & 0 \\ 4 & 4 - \lambda \end{vmatrix} = (\lambda + 6)(\lambda - 4) = 0$$

has negative roots $\lambda_1 = -6$ and $\lambda_2 = 4$ of opposite sign, indicating a saddle point.

17. The substitution $x = u + 3$, $y = v + 1$ gives the linearization $u' = 3u - 3v$, $v' = u + v$ at $(3, 1)$. Then the characteristic equation

$$|A - \lambda I| = \begin{vmatrix} 3 - \lambda & -3 \\ 1 & 1 - \lambda \end{vmatrix} = \lambda^2 - 4\lambda + 6 = 0$$

has complex conjugate roots $\lambda = 2 \pm i\sqrt{2}$ with positive real part, indicating a spiral source.

Problems 18 and 19 deal with the predator-prey system

$$x' = 2x - xy, \quad y' = -5y + xy \tag{7}$$

19. The substitution $x = u + 5$, $y = v + 2$ gives the linearization $u' = -5v$, $v' = 2u$ at $(5, 2)$. Then the characteristic equation

$$|A - \lambda I| = \begin{vmatrix} -\lambda & -5 \\ 2 & -\lambda \end{vmatrix} = \lambda^2 + 10 = 0$$

has pure imaginary roots $\lambda = \pm i\sqrt{10}$, so the origin is a stable center for the linearized system. This is the indeterminate case, but the figure in the text suggests that $(5, 2)$ is also a stable center for the original system in (7).

Problems 20-22 deal with the predator-prey system

$$x' = -3x + x^2 - xy, \quad y' = -5y + xy \tag{8}$$

21. The substitution $x = u + 3$, $y = v$ gives the linearization $u' = 3u - 3v$, $v' = -2v$ at $(3, 0)$. Then the characteristic equation

$$|\mathbf{A} - \lambda \mathbf{I}| = \begin{vmatrix} 3-\lambda & -3 \\ 0 & -2-\lambda \end{vmatrix} = (\lambda - 3)(\lambda + 2) = 0$$

has real roots $\lambda_1 = 3$ and $\lambda_2 = -2$ of opposite sign, indicating a saddle point.

Problems 23-25 deal with the predator-prey system

$$x' = 7x - x^2 - xy, \qquad y' = -5y + xy \tag{9}$$

23.   We simply delete the quadratic terms in (9) to linearize at (0,0). Then it is quite obvious that the coefficient matrix $\mathbf{A} = \begin{bmatrix} 7 & 0 \\ 0 & -5 \end{bmatrix}$ has real eigenvalues $\lambda_1 = 7$ and $\lambda_2 = -5$ of opposite sign, indicating a saddle point.

25.   The substitution $x = u + 5$, $y = u + 2$ gives the linearization $u' = -5u - 5v$, $v' = 2u$ at $(5, 2)$. Then the characteristic equation

$$|\mathbf{A} - \lambda \mathbf{I}| = \begin{vmatrix} -5-\lambda & -5 \\ 2 & -\lambda \end{vmatrix} = \lambda^2 + 5\lambda + 10 = 0$$

has complex conjugate roots $\lambda = \frac{1}{2}\left(-5 \pm i\sqrt{15}\right)$ with negative real part, indicating a spiral sink.

SECTION 6.4

NONLINEAR MECHANICAL SYSTEMS

In each of Problems 1-4 we need only substitute the familiar power series for the exponential, sine, and cosine functions, and then discard all higher-order terms. For each problem we give the corresponding linear system, the eigenvalues λ_1 and λ_2, and the type of this critical point.

1. $x' = 1 - \left(1 + x + \frac{1}{2}x^2 + \cdots\right) + 2y \approx -x + 2y$

   $y' = -x - 4\left(y - \frac{1}{6}y^3 + \cdots\right) \approx -x - 4y$

   The coefficient matrix $\mathbf{A} = \begin{bmatrix} -1 & 2 \\ -1 & -4 \end{bmatrix}$ has negative eigenvalues $\lambda_1 = -2$ and $\lambda_2 = -3$ indicating a stable nodal sink.

3.
$$x' = \left(1+x+\tfrac{1}{2}x^2+\cdots\right)+2y-1 \approx x+2y$$
$$y' = 8x+\left(1+y+\tfrac{1}{2}y^2+\cdots\right)-1 \approx 8x+y$$

The coefficient matrix $\mathbf{A} = \begin{bmatrix} 1 & 2 \\ 8 & 1 \end{bmatrix}$ has real eigenvalues $\lambda_1 = -3$ and $\lambda_2 = 5$ of opposite sign, indicating an unstable saddle point.

5. The critical points are of the form $(0, n\pi)$ where n is an integer, so we substitute $x=u,\ y=v+n\pi$. Then

$$u' = x' = -u+\sin(v+n\pi) = -u+(\cos n\pi)v = -u+(-1)^n v.$$

Hence the linearized system at $(0, n\pi)$ is

$$u' = -u \pm v, \qquad v' = 2u$$

where we take the plus sign if n is even, the minus sign if n is odd. If n is even the eigenvalues are $\lambda_1 = 1$ and $\lambda_2 = -2$, so $(0, n\pi)$ is an unstable saddle point. If n is odd the eigenvalues are $\lambda_1, \lambda_2 = (-1 \pm i\sqrt{7})/2$, so $(0, n\pi)$ is a stable spiral point.

7. The critical points are of the form $(n\pi, n\pi)$ where n is an integer, so we substitute $x=u+n\pi,\ y=v+n\pi$. Then

$$u' = x' = 1-e^{u-v} = 1-\left(1+(u-v)+\tfrac{1}{2}(u-v)^2+\cdots\right) \approx -u+v,$$
$$v' = y' = 2\sin(u+n\pi) = 2\sin u\cos n\pi \approx 2(-1)^n u.$$

Hence the linearized system at $(n\pi, n\pi)$ is

$$u' = -u+v, \qquad v' = \pm 2u$$

and has coefficient matrix $\mathbf{A} = \begin{bmatrix} -1 & 1 \\ \pm 2 & 0 \end{bmatrix}$, where we take the plus sign if n is even, the minus sign if n is odd. With n even, The characteristic equation $\lambda^2+\lambda-2 = 0$ has real roots $\lambda_1 = 1$ and $\lambda_2 = -2$ of opposite sign, so $(n\pi, n\pi)$ is an unstable saddle point. With n odd, the characteristic equation $\lambda^2+\lambda+2 = 0$ has complex conjugate eigenvalues are $\lambda_1, \lambda_2 = (-1 \pm i\sqrt{7})/2$ with negative real part, so $(n\pi, n\pi)$ is a stable spiral point.

For Problems 9-11 the linearization of the damped pendulum system at the critical point $(n\pi, 0)$ is obtained by substituting $x=u+n\pi,\ y=v$. This gives the linear system

$$u' = v,$$

$$v' = -\omega^2 \sin(u+n\pi) - cv = -\omega^2 \sin u \cos n\pi - cv \approx -\omega^2 (-1)^n u - cv$$

with coefficient matrix $\mathbf{A} = \begin{bmatrix} 0 & 1 \\ -(-1)^n\omega^2 & -c \end{bmatrix}$, where we take the plus sign if n is odd, the minus sign if n is even.

9. If n is odd then the characteristic equation $\lambda^2 + c\lambda - \omega^2 = 0$ has real roots

$$\lambda_1, \lambda_2 = \frac{-c \pm \sqrt{c^2 + 4\omega^2}}{2}$$

with opposite signs, so $(n\pi, 0)$ is an unstable saddle point.

11. If $c^2 < 4\omega^2$ then the two eigenvalues

$$\lambda_1, \lambda_2 = \frac{-c \pm \sqrt{c^2 - 4\omega^2}}{2} = -\frac{c}{2} \pm \frac{i}{2}\sqrt{4\omega^2 - c^2}$$

are complex conjugates with negative real part, so $(n\pi, 0)$ is a stable spiral point.

Problems 12-16 call for us to find and classify the critical points of the first order-system $x' = y$, $y' = -f(x, y)$ that corresponds to the given equation $x'' + f(x, x') = 0$.

13. The critical points are $(0, 0)$ and $(\pm 2, 0)$. At $(0, 0)$, the substitution $x = u$, $y = v$ gives the linear system $u' = v$, $v' = -20u - 2v$. The coefficient matrix $\mathbf{A} = \begin{bmatrix} 0 & 1 \\ -20 & -2 \end{bmatrix}$ has complex conjugate eigenvalues $\lambda = -1 \pm i\sqrt{19}$ with negative real part, which indicates a spiral sink.

At $(-2, 0)$, the substitution $x = u - 2$, $y = v$ gives the linear system $u' = v$, $v' = 40u - 2v$. The coefficient matrix $\mathbf{A} = \begin{bmatrix} 0 & 1 \\ 40 & -2 \end{bmatrix}$ has real eigenvalues $\lambda = -1 \pm \sqrt{41}$ of opposite sign, which indicates a saddle point.

At $(2, 0)$, the substitution $x = u + 2$, $y = v$ gives the same linear system $u' = v$, $v' = 40u - 2v$ as at $(-2, 0)$, so a saddle point is indicated here also.

15. The critical points are (0, 0) and (4, 0). At (0, 0), the substitution $x = u$, $y = v$ gives the linear system $u' = v$, $v' = -4u$. The coefficient matrix $\mathbf{A} = \begin{bmatrix} 0 & 1 \\ -4 & 0 \end{bmatrix}$ has pure imaginary eigenvalues $\lambda = \pm 2i$ with opposite signs, which indicates a stable center.

At (4,0), the substitution $x = u + 4$, $y = v$ gives the linear system $u' = v$, $v' = 4u$. The coefficient matrix $\mathbf{A} = \begin{bmatrix} 0 & 1 \\ 4 & 0 \end{bmatrix}$ has real eigenvalues $\lambda = \pm 2$ of opposite sign, which indicates a saddle point.

The statements of Problems 17-22 in the text include their answers and rather fully outline their solutions, which therefore are omitted here.

SECTION 6.5

CHAOS IN DYNAMICAL SYSTEMS

We list here some programs that may be useful in the projects for this section. Further discussion of these projects can be found in the Computing Projects Manual that accompanies this text.

As indicated in Fig. 6.5.1 in the text, you can use the Maple commands

```
r := 1.5:
x = array(1..200):
x[1] := 0.5:
for n from 2 to 200 do
    z := x[n-1]:
    x[n] := r*z*(1-z):
    od:
```

the Mathematica commands

```
r = 1.5;
x = Table[n,{n,1,200}];
x[[1]] = 0.5;
For[n=2, n<=200,
    n=n+1,
    z = x[[n-1]];
    x[[n]] = r*z*(1-z)];
```

or the MATLAB commands

```
r = 1.5;
x = 1:200;
x(1) = 0.5;
for n = 2:200
   z = x(n-1);
   x(n) = r*z*(1-z);
   end
```

to calculate and assemble a list of the successive iterates given by $x_{n+1} = r x_n (1 - x_n)$, as illustrated in Figures 6.5.2 through 6.5.7 in the text. The following BASIC program can be used to investigate periodic cycles for this iteration.

```
100  'Program PERIODS
110  '
120  'The period-doubling iteration
130  '
140  '          x    =     rx(1 - x)
150  '
160  '   r  =  2.75  :   Period  1
170  '   r  =  3.25  :   Period  2
180  '   r  =  3.50  :   Period  4
190  '   r  =  3.55  :   Period  8
200  '   r  =  3.565 :   Period 16
210  '   r  =  3.57  :   CHAOS
220  '   r  =  3.84  :   Period  3
230  '   r  =  3.845 :   Period  6
240  '   r  =  3.848 :   Period 12
250  '
260   DEFDBL R,X
270   INPUT "Value of r"; R
280   INPUT "Print in blocks of k  =  "; K
290   P$  =   "#.####      "
300   X  =  .5                    'Initial seed
310  '
320   FOR I  =  1 TO 500          '500 initial
330      X  =  R*X*(1 - X)        'iterations to
340   NEXT I                      'stabilize.
350  '
360   FOR  I  =  1  TO  K
370      X  =  R*X*(1 - X)        'Final iterations
380      PRINT USING P$; X;
390   NEXT
400   IF K <> 8 THEN PRINT
410  '
420  'Press any key but Q to continue:
430   A$  =   INKEY$
440   IF A$  =   "" THEN GOTO 430
450   IF A$  =  "q" OR A$  =  "Q" THEN END
460   GOTO 360                    'End of loop
470  '
480   END
```

The next BASIC program below can be used to plot pitchfork diagrams as in Figures 6.5.8 and 6.5.9 in the text. As written, it runs well in Borland TurboBasic, but may have to be fine-tuned to run in other dialects of BASIC.

```
100  'Program PICHFORK
110  '
120  'Exhibits the period-doubling toward chaos
130  'generated by the Verhulst iteration
140  '
150  '          x  =  rx(1 - x)
160  '
170  'as the growth parameter  r  is increased
180  'in the range from about  3  to about  4.
190  '
200    DEFDBL H,K,R,X
210    DEFINT I,J,M,N,P,Q
220    INPUT "Rmin,Rmax"; RMIN, RMAX      'Try 2.8 and 4.0
230    INPUT "Xmin,Xmax"; XMIN, XMAX      'Try  0   and  1
240  '
250    KEY OFF  : CLS
260  'SCREEN 1 :  N  =  319              'For med resolution
270    SCREEN 2 :  N  =  639              'For hi  resolution
280    M  =  200                          'Hor rows for either
290    H  =  (RMAX - RMIN)/N
300    K  =  (XMAX - XMIN)/M
310  '
320    LINE (0,0) - (N,0)                 'Draws a box
330    LINE - (N,199)                     'around
340    LINE - (0,199)                     'the screen
350    LINE - (  0,0)
360  '
370    FOR P  =  1 TO 9                   'Tick marks on
380        Q  =  (P*(N+1)/10) - 1         'top and bottom
390          LINE (Q,0) - (Q,5)           'of box
400          LINE (Q,195) - (Q,199)
410    NEXT P
420  '
430    FOR J  =  0 TO  N                  'Jth vertical column
440        R  =  RMIN + J*H               'of pixels on screen
450        X  =  .5
460        FOR P  =  0 TO 1000            'These iterations
470            X  =  R*X*(1-X)            'to settle down.
480        NEXT P
490        FOR Q  =  0 TO 250             'These iterations
500            X  =  R*X*(1-X)            'are recorded.
510            I  =  INT((X - XMIN)/K)
520            I  =  200 - I
530            IF (0< = I) AND (I<200) THEN PSET (J,I)
540        NEXT Q
550    NEXT J
```

```
560 '
570  WHILE INKEY$  =   ""              'Press a key when
580  WEND                             'finished looking.
590  SCREEN 0  :  CLS  :  KEY ON
600  END
```

A more elaborate construction of these pitchfork diagrams is given by the following
Mathematica program, a slight elaboration of one found on page 102 of T. Gray and J. Glynn,
Exploring Mathematics with Mathematica, Addison-Wesley, 1991.

```
g[x_] : =  r x (1 - x);
Clear[r];
a  =  2.8;  b  =  4.0.       (* r-range for Fig 6.5.8 *)
c  =  0;    d  =  1;         (* x-range *)
m  =  250;                        (* no of x-points *)
n  =  500;                        (* no of r-values *)
ListPlot[
   Flatten[Table[
      Transpose[{
         Table[r, {m+1}],
                NestList[g, Nest[q, 0.5, 2m], m] }],
              {r, a, b, (b-a)/n} ],
            1],
      PlotStyle -> PointSize[0.001],
      PlotRange -> {{a,b},{c,d}},
      AspectRatio -> 0.75,
      Frame -> True,
      AxesLabel -> {"r","x"} ]
```

This Mathematica program runs slowly, and requires a fast machine with plenty of memory to
finish within a reasonable waiting time. The following MATLAB program (which was actually
used to construct Figs 6.5.8 and 6.5.9) runs much faster on a comparable computer, and may be
easier to understand.

```
% pitchfork diagram script
% for Figures 6.5.8 and 6.5.9

hold off
m  =  400;                   % no of r-subintervals
n  =  400;                   % no of x-subintervals

a  =  2.8;   b  =  4.0;      % r-range for 6.5.9
dr =  (b - a)/m;
R  =  a+dr/2 : dr : b;       % vector of r-values
c  =  0;      d  =  1;       % x-range
dx =  (d - c)/n
X  =  c+dx/2 : dx : d;       % vector of x-values
```

```
[rr,xx]  =  meshgrid(R,X);        % matrices of r- and x-coords
                                  % of grid points in rx-rect

C = zeros(m,n);
for j  =  1 : m                   % Cycle through r-values
   r  =  a - dr/2 + j*dr;
   x  =  0.5;                      % Initialize x-value
   for k  =  1:1000               % 1000 iterations to stabilize
      x  =  r*x*(1-x);
   end
   for k  =  1:1000               % 1000 more iterations
      x  =  r*x*(1-x);
   i = ceil(x/dx);
      C(i,j) = 1;                  % lattice point to plot
      end
   end

C = C + 1;
C = flipud(C);                    % matrix of points for image
image(R,X,C)
colormap([1 1 1; 0 0 0])         % color them black or white
axis square
```

The following MATLAB function defines the forced Duffing equation for Figures 6.5.13 through 6.5.16.

```
function  yp = ypduffing(t,x)
F0 = 0.80;
yp = x;
y = x(2);    x = x(1);
yp(1) = y;
yp(2) = F0*cos(t)-y+x-x.^3;
```

Then the following MATLAB script can be used to construct Fig. 6.5.16.

```
% fig6_5_16.m script
options = odeset('RelTol',1e-8,'AbsTol',1e-8);
[t,y] = ode45('ypduffing', [0 100], [1;0],options);
n = length(t);
y100 = y(n,:)';
[t,y] = ode45('ypduffing', [100 300], y100,options);
hold off
plot(y(:,1),y(:,2),'b')          % Fig. 6.5.16(a)
axis([-1.5 1.5 -1.5 1.5])
axis square
hold on
plot([-1.5 1.5],[0 0],'k')
plot([0 0],[-1.5 1.5],'k')
```

```
pause
hold off
plot(t,y(:,1),'b')                % Fig. 6.5.16(b)
axis([100 300 -1.5 1.5])
axis square
hold on
plot([100 300],[0 0],'k')
plot([0 0],[-1.5 1.5],'k')
```

CHAPTER 7

LAPLACE TRANSFORM METHODS

SECTION 7.1

LAPLACE TRANSFORMS AND INVERSE TRANSFORMS

The objectives of this section are especially clearcut. They include familiarity with the definition of the Laplace transform $\mathcal{L}\{f(t)\} = F(s)$ that is given in Equation (1) in the textbook, the direct application of this definition to calculate Laplace transforms of simple functions (as in Examples 1-3), and the use of known transforms (those listed in Figure 7.1.2) to find Laplace transforms and inverse transforms (as in Examples 4–6). Perhaps students need to be told explicitly to memorize the transforms that are listed in the short table that appears in Figure 7.1.2.

1. $\mathcal{L}\{t\} = \displaystyle\int_0^\infty e^{-st} t \, dt \qquad (u = -st, \quad du = -s \, dt)$

$$= \int_0^{-\infty} \left[\frac{1}{s^2}\right] u e^u \, du = \frac{1}{s^2}\left[(u-1)e^u\right]_0^{-\infty} = \frac{1}{s^2}$$

3. $\mathcal{L}\{e^{3t+1}\} = \displaystyle\int_0^\infty e^{-st} e^{3t+1} \, dt = e\int_0^\infty e^{-(s-3)t} \, dt = \frac{e}{s-3}$

5. $\mathcal{L}\{\sinh t\} = \frac{1}{2}\mathcal{L}\{e^t - e^{-t}\} = \frac{1}{2}\displaystyle\int_0^\infty e^{-st}\left(e^t - e^{-t}\right)dt = \frac{1}{2}\int_0^\infty \left(e^{-(s-1)t} - e^{-(s+1)t}\right)dt$

$$= \frac{1}{2}\left[\frac{1}{s-1} - \frac{1}{s+1}\right] = \frac{1}{s^2 - 1}$$

7. $\mathcal{L}\{f(t)\} = \displaystyle\int_0^1 e^{-st} \, dt = \left[-\frac{1}{s}e^{-st}\right]_0^1 = \frac{1-e^{-s}}{s}$

9. $\mathcal{L}\{f(t)\} = \displaystyle\int_0^1 e^{-st} t \, dt = \frac{1-e^{-s}-se^{-s}}{s^2}$

11. $\mathcal{L}\{\sqrt{t} + 3t\} = \dfrac{\Gamma(3/2)}{s^{3/2}} + 3\cdot\dfrac{1}{s^2} = \dfrac{\sqrt{\pi}}{2s^{3/2}} + \dfrac{3}{s^2}$

13. $\mathcal{L}\{t - 2e^{3t}\} = \dfrac{1}{s^2} - \dfrac{2}{s-3}$

15. $\mathcal{L}\{1 + \cosh 5t\} = \dfrac{1}{s} + \dfrac{s}{s^2 - 25}$

17. $\mathcal{L}\{\cos^2 2t\} = \dfrac{1}{2}\mathcal{L}\{1 + \cos 4t\} = \dfrac{1}{2}\left(\dfrac{1}{s} + \dfrac{s}{s^2 + 16}\right)$

19. $\mathcal{L}\{(1+t)^3\} = \mathcal{L}\{1 + 3t + 3t^2 + t^3\} = \dfrac{1}{s} + 3\cdot\dfrac{1!}{s^2} + 3\cdot\dfrac{2!}{s^3} + \dfrac{3!}{s^4} = \dfrac{1}{s} + \dfrac{3}{s^2} + \dfrac{6}{s^3} + \dfrac{6}{s^4}$

21. Integration by parts with $u = t$ and $dv = e^{-st}\cos 2t\,dt$ yields

$$\mathcal{L}\{t\cos 2t\} = \int_0^\infty te^{-st}\cos 2t\,dt = -\dfrac{1}{s^2 + 4}\int_0^\infty e^{-st}\left(-s\cos 2t + 2\sin 2t\right)dt$$

$$= -\dfrac{1}{s^2 + 4}\left[-s\mathcal{L}\{\cos 2t\} + 2\mathcal{L}\{\sin 2t\}\right]$$

$$= -\dfrac{1}{s^2 + 4}\left[\dfrac{-s^2}{s^2 + 4} + \dfrac{4}{s^2 + 4}\right] = \dfrac{s^2 - 4}{\left(s^2 + 4\right)^2}.$$

23. $\mathcal{L}^{-1}\left\{\dfrac{3}{s^4}\right\} = \mathcal{L}^{-1}\left\{\dfrac{1}{2}\cdot\dfrac{6}{s^4}\right\} = \dfrac{1}{2}t^3$

25. $\mathcal{L}^{-1}\left\{\dfrac{1}{s} - \dfrac{2}{s^{5/2}}\right\} = \mathcal{L}^{-1}\left\{\dfrac{1}{s} - \dfrac{2}{\Gamma(5/2)}\cdot\dfrac{\Gamma(5/2)}{s^{5/2}}\right\} = 1 - \dfrac{2}{\frac{3}{2}\cdot\frac{1}{2}\sqrt{\pi}}\cdot t^{3/2} = 1 - \dfrac{8t^{3/2}}{3\sqrt{\pi}}$

27. $\mathcal{L}^{-1}\left\{\dfrac{3}{s - 4}\right\} = 3\cdot\mathcal{L}^{-1}\left\{\dfrac{1}{s - 4}\right\} = 3e^{4t}$

29. $\mathcal{L}^{-1}\left\{\dfrac{5 - 3s}{s^2 + 9}\right\} = \dfrac{5}{3}\cdot\mathcal{L}^{-1}\left\{\dfrac{3}{s^2 + 9}\right\} - 3\cdot\mathcal{L}^{-1}\left\{\dfrac{s}{s^2 + 9}\right\} = \dfrac{5}{3}\sin 3t - 3\cos 3t$

31. $\mathcal{L}^{-1}\left\{\dfrac{10s - 3}{25 - s^2}\right\} = -10\cdot\mathcal{L}^{-1}\left\{\dfrac{s}{s^2 - 25}\right\} + \dfrac{3}{5}\cdot\mathcal{L}^{-1}\left\{\dfrac{5}{s^2 - 25}\right\} = -10\cosh 5t + \dfrac{3}{5}\sinh 5t$

33. $\mathcal{L}\{\sin kt\} = \mathcal{L}\left\{\dfrac{e^{ikt} - e^{-ikt}}{2i}\right\} = \dfrac{1}{2i}\left(\dfrac{1}{s - ik} - \dfrac{1}{s + ik}\right)$

$$= \dfrac{1}{2i}\cdot\dfrac{2ik}{(s - ik)(s - ik)} = \dfrac{k}{s^2 + k^2} \qquad \text{(because } i^2 = -1\text{)}$$

35. Using the given tabulated integral with $a = -s$ and $b = k$, we find that

$$\mathcal{L}\{\cos kt\} = \int_0^\infty e^{-st} \cos kt\, dt = \left[\frac{e^{-st}}{s^2+k^2}(-s\cos kt + k\sin kt)\right]_{t=0}^\infty$$

$$= \lim_{t\to\infty}\left(\frac{e^{-st}}{s^2+k^2}(-s\cos kt + k\sin kt)\right) - \frac{e^0}{s^2+k^2}(-s\cdot 1 + k\cdot 0) = \frac{s}{s^2+k^2}.$$

37. $f(t) = 1 - u_a(t) = 1 - u(t-a)$ so $\mathcal{L}\{f(t)\} = \mathcal{L}\{1\} - \mathcal{L}\{u_a(t)\} = \dfrac{1}{s} - \dfrac{e^{-as}}{s}$

39. Use of the geometric series gives

$$\mathcal{L}\{f(t)\} = \sum_{n=0}^\infty \mathcal{L}\{u(t-n)\} = \sum_{n=0}^\infty \frac{e^{-ns}}{s} = \frac{1}{s}\left(1 + e^{-s} + e^{-2s} + e^{-3s} + \cdots\right)$$

$$= \frac{1}{s}\left(1 + (e^{-s}) + (e^{-s})^2 + (e^{-s})^3 + \cdots\right) = \frac{1}{s}\cdot\frac{1}{1-e^{-s}} = \frac{1}{s(1-e^{-s})}.$$

41. By checking values at sample points, you can verify that $g(t) = 2f(t) - 1$ in terms of the square wave function $f(t)$ of Problem 40. Hence

$$\mathcal{L}\{g(t)\} = \mathcal{L}\{2f(t) - 1\} = \frac{2}{s(1+e^{-s})} - \frac{1}{s} = \frac{1}{s}\left(\frac{2}{1+e^{-s}} - 1\right) = \frac{1}{s}\cdot\frac{1-e^{-s}}{1+e^{-s}}$$

$$= \frac{1}{s}\cdot\frac{1-e^{-s}}{1+e^{-s}}\cdot\frac{e^{s/2}}{e^{s/2}} = \frac{1}{s}\cdot\frac{e^{s/2}-e^{-s/2}}{e^{s/2}+e^{-s/2}} = \frac{1}{s}\cdot\frac{\frac{1}{2}\left(e^{s/2}-e^{-s/2}\right)}{\frac{1}{2}\left(e^{s/2}+e^{-s/2}\right)}$$

$$= \frac{1}{s}\cdot\frac{\sinh(s/2)}{\cosh(s/2)} = \frac{1}{s}\tanh\frac{s}{2}.$$

SECTION 7.2

TRANSFORMATION OF INITIAL VALUE PROBLEMS

The focus of this section is on the use of transforms of derivatives (Theorem 1) to solve initial value problems (as in Examples 1 and 2). Transforms of integrals (Theorem 2) appear less frequently in practice, and the extension of Theorem 1 at the end of Section 7.2 may be considered entirely optional (except perhaps for electrical engineering students).

In Problems 1-10 we give first the transformed differential equation, then the transform $X(s)$ of the solution, and finally the inverse transform $x(t)$ of $X(s)$.

1. $[s^2X(s) - 5s] + 4\{X(s)\} = 0$

$$X(s) = \frac{5s}{s^2+4} = 5 \cdot \frac{s}{s^2+4}$$

$x(t) = \mathcal{L}^{-1}\{X(s)\} = 5\cos 2t$

3. $[s^2X(s) - 2] - [sX(s)] - 2[X(s)] = 0$

$$X(s) = \frac{2}{s^2-s-2} = \frac{2}{(s-2)(s+1)} = \frac{2}{3}\left(\frac{1}{s-2} - \frac{1}{s+1}\right)$$

$x(t) = (2/3)(e^{2t} - e^{-t})$

5. $[s^2X(s)] + [X(s)] = 2/(s^2+4)$

$$X(s) = \frac{2}{(s^2+1)(s^2+4)} = \frac{2}{3} \cdot \frac{1}{s^2+1} - \frac{1}{3} \cdot \frac{2}{s^2+4}$$

$x(t) = (2\sin t - \sin 2t)/3$

7. $[s^2X(s) - s] + [X(s)] = s/s^2 + 9)$

$(s^2 + 1)X(s) = s + s/(s^2 + 9) = (s^3 + 10s)/(s^2 + 9)$

$$X(s) = \frac{s^2+10s}{(s^2+1)(s^2+9)} = \frac{9}{9} \cdot \frac{s}{s^2+1} - \frac{1}{8} \cdot \frac{s}{s^2+9}$$

$x(t) = (9\cos t - \cos 3t)/8$

9. $s^2X(s) + 4sX(s) + 3X(s) = 1/s$

$$X(s) = \frac{1}{s(s^2+4s+3)} = \frac{1}{s(s+1)(s+3)} = \frac{1}{3} \cdot \frac{1}{s} - \frac{1}{2} \cdot \frac{1}{s+1} + \frac{1}{6} \cdot \frac{1}{s+3}$$

$x(t) = (2 - 3e^{-t} + e^{-3t})/6$

11. The transformed equations are

$$sX(s) - 1 = 2X(s) + Y(s)$$
$$sY(s) + 2 = 6X(s) + 3Y(s).$$

We solve for the Laplace transforms

$$X(s) = \frac{s-5}{s(s-5)} = \frac{1}{s}$$

$$Y(s) = X(s) = \frac{-2s+10}{s(s-5)} = -\frac{2}{s}.$$

Hence the solution is given by

$$x(t) = 1, \qquad\qquad y(t) = -2.$$

13. The transformed equations are

$$sX(s) + 2[sY(s) - 1] + X(s) = 0$$
$$sX(s) - [sY(s) - 1] + Y(s) = 0,$$

which we solve for the transforms

$$X(s) = -\frac{2}{3s^2 - 1} = -\frac{2}{3} \cdot \frac{1}{s^2 - 1/3} = -\frac{2}{\sqrt{3}} \cdot \frac{1/\sqrt{3}}{s^2 - \left(1/\sqrt{3}\right)^2}$$

$$X(s) = \frac{3s + 1}{3s^2 - 1} = \frac{s + 1/3}{s^2 - 1/3} = \frac{s}{s^2 - \left(1/\sqrt{3}\right)^2} + \frac{1}{\sqrt{3}} \cdot \frac{1/\sqrt{3}}{s^2 - \left(1/\sqrt{3}\right)^2}.$$

Hence the solution is

$$x(t) = -\left(2/\sqrt{3}\right) \sinh\left(t/\sqrt{3}\right)$$
$$y(t) = \cosh\left(t/\sqrt{3}\right) + \left(1/\sqrt{3}\right) \sinh\left(t/\sqrt{3}\right).$$

15. The transformed equations are

$$[s^2 X - s] + [sX - 1] + [sY - 1] + 2X - Y = 0$$
$$[s^2 Y - s] + [sX - 1] + [sY - 1] + 4X - 2Y = 0,$$

which we solve for

$$X(s) = \frac{s^2 + 3s + 2}{s^3 + 3s^2 + 3s} = \frac{1}{3}\left(\frac{2}{s} + \frac{s + 3}{s^2 + 3s + 3}\right) = \frac{1}{3}\left(\frac{2}{s} + \frac{s + 3}{(s + 3/2)^2 + (3/4)}\right)$$

$$= \frac{1}{3}\left(\frac{2}{s} + \frac{s + 3/2}{(s + 3/2)^2 + (\sqrt{3}/2)^2} + \sqrt{3} \cdot \frac{\sqrt{3}/2}{(s + 3/2)^2 + (\sqrt{3}/2)^2}\right)$$

$$Y(s) = \frac{-s^3 - 2s^2 + 2s + 4}{s^3 + 3s^2 + 3s} = \frac{1}{21}\left(\frac{28}{s} - \frac{9}{s - 1} + \frac{2s + 15}{s^2 + 3s + 3}\right)$$

$$= \frac{1}{21}\left(\frac{28}{s} - \frac{9}{s - 1} + \frac{2s + 15}{(s + 3/2)^2 + 3/4}\right)$$

$$= \frac{1}{21}\left(\frac{28}{s} - \frac{9}{s - 1} + 2 \cdot \frac{s + 3/2}{(s + 3/2)^2 + (\sqrt{3}/2)^2} + 8\sqrt{3} \cdot \frac{\sqrt{3}/2}{(s + 3/2)^2 + (\sqrt{3}/2)^2}\right).$$

Here we've used some fairly heavy-duty partial fractions (Section 7.3). The transforms

$$\mathcal{L}\left\{e^{at}\cos kt\right\} = \frac{s-a}{(s-a)^2+k^2}, \qquad \mathcal{L}\left\{e^{at}\sin kt\right\} = \frac{k}{(s-a)^2+k^2}$$

from the inside-front-cover table (with $a=-3/2$, $k=\sqrt{3}/2$) finally yield

$$x(t) = \frac{1}{3}\left\{2+e^{-3t/2}\left[\cos\left(\sqrt{3}t/2\right)+\sqrt{3}\sin\left(\sqrt{3}t/2\right)\right]\right\}$$

$$y(t) = \frac{1}{21}\left\{28-9e^{t}+e^{-3t/2}\left[2\cos\left(\sqrt{3}t/2\right)+8\sqrt{3}\sin\left(\sqrt{3}t/2\right)\right]\right\}.$$

17. $f(t) = \int_0^t e^{3\tau}\,d\tau = \left[\frac{1}{3}e^{3\tau}\right]_{\tau=0}^{t} = \frac{1}{3}\left(e^{3t}-1\right)$

19. $f(t) = \int_0^t \frac{1}{2}\sin 2\tau\,d\tau = \left[-\frac{1}{4}\cos 2\tau\right]_{\tau=0}^{t} = \frac{1}{4}\left(1-\cos 2t\right)$

21. $f(t) = \int_0^t\left[\int_0^\tau \sin t\,dt\right]d\tau = \int_0^t (1-\cos\tau)\,d\tau = \left[\tau-\sin\tau\right]_{\tau=0}^{t} = t-\sin t$

23. $f(t) = \int_0^t\left[\int_0^\tau \sinh t\,dt\right]d\tau = \int_0^t (\cosh\tau-1)\,d\tau = \left[\sinh\tau-\tau\right]_{\tau=0}^{t} = \sinh t-t$

25. With $f(t) = \cos kt$ and $F(s) = s/(s^2+k^2)$, Theorem 1 in this section yields

$$\mathcal{L}\{-k\sin kt\} = \mathcal{L}\{f'(t)\} = sF(s) - 1 = s\cdot\frac{s}{s^2+k^2}-1 = -\frac{k^2}{s^2+k^2},$$

so division by $-k$ yields $\mathcal{L}\{\sin kt\} = k/(s^2+k^2)$.

27. (a) With $f(t) = t^n e^{at}$ and $f'(t) = nt^{n-1}e^{at} + at^n e^{at}$, Theorem 1 yields

$$\mathcal{L}\{nt^{n-1}e^{at} + at^n e^{at}\} = s\,\mathcal{L}\{t^n e^{at}\}$$

so

$$n\,\mathcal{L}\{t^{n-1}e^{at}\} = (s-a)\mathcal{L}\{t^n e^{at}\}$$

and hence

$$\mathcal{L}\{t^n e^{at}\} = \frac{n}{s-a}\mathcal{L}\{t^{n-1}e^{at}\}.$$

(b) $n=1$: $\mathcal{L}\left\{t\,e^{at}\right\} = \dfrac{1}{s-a}\mathcal{L}\left\{e^{at}\right\} = \dfrac{1}{s-a}\cdot\dfrac{1}{s-a} = \dfrac{1}{(s-a)^2}$

$n=2$: $\mathcal{L}\left\{t^2\,e^{at}\right\} = \dfrac{2}{s-a}\mathcal{L}\left\{t\,e^{at}\right\} = \dfrac{2}{s-a}\cdot\dfrac{1}{(s-a)^2} = \dfrac{2!}{(s-a)^3}$

$n=3$: $\mathcal{L}\left\{t^3\,e^{at}\right\} = \dfrac{3}{s-a}\mathcal{L}\left\{t^2\,e^{at}\right\} = \dfrac{3}{s-a}\cdot\dfrac{2!}{(s-a)^3} = \dfrac{3!}{(s-a)^4}$

And so forth.

29.   Let $f(t) = t\sinh kt$, so $f(0) = 0$. Then

$$f'(t) = \sinh kt + kt\cosh kt$$
$$f''(t) = 2k\cosh kt + k^2 t\sinh kt,$$

and thus $f'(0) = 0$, so Formula (5) in this section yields

$$\mathcal{L}\{2k\cosh kt + k^2 t\sinh kt\} = s^2\mathcal{L}\{\sinh kt\},$$

$$2k\cdot\dfrac{s}{s^2-k^2} + k^2 F(s) = s^2 F(s).$$

We readily solve this last equation for

$$\mathcal{L}\{t\cosh kt\} = F(s) = \dfrac{2ks}{\left(s^2-k^2\right)^2}.$$

31.   Using the known transform of $\sin kt$ and the Problem 28 transform of $t\cos kt$, we obtain

$$\mathcal{L}\left\{\dfrac{1}{2k^3}(\sin kt - kt\cos kt)\right\} = \dfrac{1}{2k^3}\cdot\dfrac{k}{s^2+k^2} - \dfrac{k}{2k^3}\cdot\dfrac{s^2-k^2}{\left(s^2+k^2\right)^2}$$

$$= \dfrac{1}{2k^2}\left[\dfrac{1}{s^2+k^2} - \dfrac{s^2-k^2}{\left(s^2+k^2\right)^2}\right] = \dfrac{1}{2k^2}\cdot\dfrac{2k^2}{\left(s^2+k^2\right)^2} = \dfrac{1}{\left(s^2+k^2\right)^2}$$

33. $f(t) = u_a(t) - u_b(t) = u(t-a) - u(t-b)$, so the result of Problem 32 gives

$$\mathcal{L}\{f(t)\} = \mathcal{L}\{u(t-a)\} - \mathcal{L}\{u(t-b)\} = \dfrac{e^{-as}}{s} - \dfrac{e^{-bs}}{s} = \dfrac{e^{-as} - e^{-bs}}{s}.$$

35.   Let's write $g(t)$ for the on-off function of this problem to distinguish it from the square wave function of Problem 34. Then comparison of Figures 7.2.6 and 7.2.7 makes it clear that $g(t) = \frac{1}{2}(1 + f(t))$, so (using the result of Problem 34) we obtain

$$G(s) = \frac{1}{2s} + \frac{1}{2}F(s) = \frac{1}{2s} + \frac{1}{2s}\tanh\frac{s}{2} = \frac{1}{2s}\left(1 + \frac{e^{s/2} - e^{-s/2}}{e^{s/2} + e^{-s/2}} \cdot \frac{e^{-s/2}}{e^{-s/2}}\right)$$

$$= \frac{1}{2s}\left(1 + \frac{1 - e^{-s}}{1 + e^{-s}}\right) = \frac{1}{2s} \cdot \frac{2}{1 + e^{-s}} = \frac{1}{s(1 + e^{-s})}.$$

37. We observe that $f(0) = 0$ and that the sawtooth function has jump -1 at each of the points $t_n = n = 1, 2, 3, \cdots$. Also, $f'(t) \equiv 1$ wherever the derivative is defined. Hence Eq. (21) in this section gives

$$\frac{1}{s} = sF(s) + \sum_{n=1}^{\infty}e^{-ns} = sF(s) - 1 + \sum_{n=0}^{\infty}e^{-ns} = sF(s) - 1 + \frac{1}{1 - e^{-ns}},$$

using the geometric series $\sum_{n=0}^{\infty}x^n = 1/(1-x)$ with $x = e^{-s}$. Solution for $F(s)$ gives

$$F(s) = \frac{1}{s^2} + \frac{1}{s} - \frac{1}{s(1 - e^{-s})} = \frac{1}{s^2} - \frac{e^{-s}}{s(1 - e^{-s})}.$$

SECTION 7.3

TRANSLATION AND PARTIAL FRACTIONS

This section is devoted to the computational nuts and bolts of the staple technique for the inversion of Laplace transforms — partial fraction decompositions. If time does not permit going further in this chapter, Sections 7.1-7.3 provide a self-contained introduction to Laplace transforms that suffices for the most common elementary applications.

1. $\mathcal{L}\{t^4\} = \dfrac{24}{s^5}$, so $\mathcal{L}\{t^4 e^{\pi t}\} = \dfrac{24}{(s - \pi)^5}$

3. $\mathcal{L}\{\sin 3\pi t\} = \dfrac{3\pi}{s^2 + 9\pi^2}$, so $\mathcal{L}\{e^{-2t}\sin 3\pi t\} = \dfrac{3\pi}{(s + 2)^2 + 9\pi^2}$.

5. $F(s) = \dfrac{3}{2s - 4} = \dfrac{3}{2} \cdot \dfrac{1}{s - 2}$, so $f(t) = \dfrac{3}{2}e^{2t}$

7. $F(s) = \dfrac{1}{(s + 2)^2}$, so $f(t) = t e^{-2t}$

9. $F(s) = 3 \cdot \dfrac{s-3}{(s-3)^2+16} + \dfrac{7}{2} \cdot \dfrac{4}{(s-3)^2+16}$, so $f(t) = e^{3t}[3\cos 4t + (7/2)\sin 4t]$

11. $F(s) = \dfrac{1}{4} \cdot \dfrac{1}{s-2} - \dfrac{1}{4} \cdot \dfrac{1}{s+2}$, so $f(t) = \dfrac{1}{4}\left(e^{2t} - e^{-2t}\right) = \dfrac{1}{2}\sinh 2t$

13. $F(s) = 3 \cdot \dfrac{1}{s+2} - 5 \cdot \dfrac{1}{s+5}$, so $f(t) = 3e^{-2t} - 5e^{-5t}$

15. $F(s) = \dfrac{1}{25}\left(-1 \cdot \dfrac{1}{s} - 5 \cdot \dfrac{1}{s^2} + \dfrac{1}{s-5}\right)$, so $f(t) = \dfrac{1}{25}\left(-1 - 5t + e^{5t}\right)$

17. $F(s) = \dfrac{1}{8}\left(\dfrac{1}{s^2-4} - \dfrac{1}{s^2+4}\right) = \dfrac{1}{16}\left(\dfrac{2}{s^2-4} - \dfrac{2}{s^2+4}\right)$

$f(t) = \dfrac{1}{16}\left(\sinh 2t - \sin 2t\right)$

19. $F(s) = \dfrac{s^2-2s}{(s^2+1)(s^2+4)} = \dfrac{1}{3}\left(\dfrac{-2s-1}{s^2+1} + \dfrac{2s+4}{s^2+4}\right)$

$f(t) = \dfrac{1}{3}\left(-2\cos t - \sin t + 2\cos 2t + 2\sin 2t\right)$

21. First we need to find A, B, C, D so that

$$\frac{s^2+3}{(s^2+2s+2)^2} = \frac{As+B}{s^2+2s+2} + \frac{Cs+D}{(s^2+2s+2)^2}.$$

When we multiply both sides by the quadratic factor s^2+2s+2 and collect coefficients, we get the linear equations

$$-2B - D + 3 = 0$$
$$-2A - 2B - C = 0$$
$$-2A - B + 1 = 0$$
$$-A = 0$$

which we solve for $A=0$, $B=1$, $C=-2$, $D=1$. Thus

$$F(s) = \frac{1}{(s+1)^2 +1} + \frac{-2s+1}{\left[(s+1)^2 +1\right]^2} = \frac{1}{(s+1)^2 +1} - 2 \cdot \frac{s+1}{\left[(s+1)^2 +1\right]^2} + 3 \cdot \frac{1}{\left[(s+1)^2 +1\right]^2}.$$

We now use the inverse Laplace transforms given in Eq. (16) and (17) of Section 7.3 — supplying the factor e^{-t} corresponding to the translation $s \to s+1$ — and get

$$f(t) = e^{-t}\left[\sin t - 2 \cdot \frac{1}{2} t \sin t + 3 \cdot \frac{1}{2}(\sin t - t \cos t)\right] = \frac{1}{2} e^{-t}(5\sin t - 2t\sin t - 3t\cos t).$$

23. $$\frac{s^3}{s^4 +4a^4} = \frac{1}{2}\left(\frac{s-a}{s^2 -2as +2a^2} + \frac{s+a}{s^2 +2as +2a^2}\right),$$

and $s^2 \pm 2as + 2a^2 = (s \pm a)^2 + a^2$, so it follows that

$$\mathcal{L}^{-1}\left\{\frac{s^3}{s^4 +4a^4}\right\} = \frac{1}{2}\left(e^{at} + e^{-at}\right)\cos at = \cosh at \cos at.$$

25. $$\frac{s}{s^4 +4a^4} = \frac{1}{4a}\left(\frac{s}{s^2 -2as +2a^2} - \frac{s}{s^2 +2as +2a^2}\right)$$

$$= \frac{1}{4a}\left(\frac{s-a}{s^2 -2as +2a^2} + \frac{a}{s^2 -2as +2a^2} - \frac{s+a}{s^2 +2as +2a^2} + \frac{a}{s^2 +2as +2a^2}\right),$$

and $s^2 \pm 2as + 2a^2 = (s \pm a)^2 + a^2$, so it follows that

$$\mathcal{L}^{-1}\left\{\frac{s}{s^4 +4a^4}\right\} = \frac{1}{4a}\left[e^{at}(\cos at + \sin at) - e^{-at}(\cos at - \sin at)\right]$$

$$= \frac{1}{2a}\left[\frac{1}{2}\left(e^{at} + e^{-at}\right)\sin at + \frac{1}{2}\left(e^{at} - e^{-at}\right)\cos at\right]$$

$$= \frac{1}{2a}(\cosh at \sin at + \sinh at \cos at).$$

In Problems 27-40 we give first the transformed equation, then the Laplace transform $X(s)$ of the solution, and finally the desired solution $x(t)$.

27. $[s^2 X(s) - 2s - 3] + 6[sX(s) - 2] + 25X(s) = 0$

$$X(s) = \frac{2s+15}{s^2 +6s +25} = 2 \cdot \frac{s+3}{(s+3)^2 +16} + \frac{9}{4} \cdot \frac{4}{(s+3)^2 +16}$$

$x(t) = e^{-3t}[2\cos 4t + (9/4)\sin 4t]$

29. $s^2 X(s) - 4X(s) = \dfrac{3}{s^2}$

$$X(s) = \frac{3}{s^2(s^2-4)} = \frac{3}{4}\left(\frac{1}{s^2-4} - \frac{1}{s^2}\right)$$

$$x(t) = \frac{3}{8}\sinh 2t - \frac{3}{4}t = \frac{3}{8}\left(\sinh 2t - 2t\right)$$

31. $[s^3 X(s) - s - 1] + [s^2 X(s) - 1] - 6[sX(s)] = 0$

$$X(s) = \frac{s+2}{s^3 + s^2 - 6s} = \frac{1}{15}\left(-\frac{5}{s} - \frac{1}{s+3} + \frac{6}{s-2}\right)$$

$$x(t) = \frac{1}{15}\left(-5 - e^{-3t} + 6e^{2t}\right)$$

33. $[s^4 X(s) - 1] + X(s) = 0$

$$X(s) = \frac{1}{s^4+1}$$

It therefore follows from Problem 26 with $a = \sqrt[4]{1/4} = 1/\sqrt{2}$ that

$$x(t) = \frac{1}{\sqrt{2}}\left(\cosh\frac{t}{\sqrt{2}}\sin\frac{t}{\sqrt{2}} - \sinh\frac{t}{\sqrt{2}}\cos\frac{t}{\sqrt{2}}\right).$$

35. $\left[s^4 X(s) - 1\right] + 8s^2 X(s) + 16X(s) = 0$

$$X(s) = \frac{1}{s^4 + 8s^2 + 16} = \frac{1}{\left(s^2+4\right)^2}$$

$$x(t) = \frac{1}{16}\left(\sin 2t - 2t\cos 2t\right) \qquad \text{(by Eq. (17) in Section 7.3)}$$

37. $\left[s^2 X(s) - 2\right] + 4sX(s) + 13X(s) = \dfrac{1}{(s+1)^2}$

$$X(s) = \frac{2 + 1/(s+1)^2}{s^2 + 4s + 13} = \frac{2s^2 + 4s + 13}{(s+1)^2\left(s^2 + 4s + 13\right)}$$

$$= \frac{1}{50}\left[-\frac{1}{s+1} + \frac{5}{(s+1)^2} + \frac{s+98}{(s+2)^2 + 9}\right]$$

$$= \frac{1}{50}\left[-\frac{1}{s+1}+\frac{5}{(s+1)^2}+\frac{s+2}{(s+2)^2+9}+32\cdot\frac{3}{(s+2)^2+9}\right]$$

$$x(t) = \frac{1}{50}\left[(-1+5t)e^{-t}+e^{-2t}(\cos 3t+32\sin 3t)\right]$$

39. $x''+9x = 6\cos 3t, \quad x(0)=x'(0)=0$

$$s^2 X(s)+9X(s) = \frac{6s}{s^2+9}$$

$$X(s) = \frac{6s}{\left(s^2+9\right)^2}$$

$$x(t) = 6\cdot\frac{1}{2\cdot 3}t\sin 3t = t\sin 3t \qquad \text{(by Eq. (16) in Section 7.3)}$$

SECTION 7.4

DERIVATIVES, INTEGRALS, AND PRODUCTS OF TRANSFORMS

This section completes the presentation of the standard "operational properties" of Laplace transforms, the most important one here being the convolution property $\mathcal{L}\{f*g\} = \mathcal{L}\{f\}\cdot\mathcal{L}\{g\}$, where the **convolution** $f*g$ is defined by

$$f * g(t) = \int_0^t f(x)g(t-x)\,dx.$$

Here we use x rather than τ as the variable of integration; compare with Eq. (3) in Section 7.4 of the textbook

1. With $f(t)=t$ and $g(t)=1$ we calculate

$$t*1 = \int_0^t x\cdot 1\,dx = \left[\frac{1}{2}x^2\right]_{x=0}^{x=t} = \frac{1}{2}t^2.$$

3. To compute $(\sin t)*(\sin t) = \int_0^t \sin x\sin(t-x)\,dx$, we first apply the identity $\sin A \sin B = [\cos(A - B) - \cos(A + B)]/2$. This gives

$$(\sin t) * (\sin t) = \int_0^t \sin x \sin(t-x)\, dx$$

$$= \frac{1}{2}\int_0^t [\cos(2x-t) - \cos t]\, dx$$

$$= \frac{1}{2}\left[\frac{1}{2}\sin(2x-t) - x\cos t\right]_{x=0}^{x=t}$$

$$(\sin t) * (\sin t) = \frac{1}{2}(\sin t - t\cos t).$$

5. $$e^{at} * e^{at} = \int_0^t e^{ax}e^{a(t-x)}\, dx = \int_0^t e^{at}\, dx = e^{at}\,[x]_{x=0}^{x=t} = t\, e^{at}$$

7. $$f(t) = 1 * e^{3t} = e^{3t} * 1 = \int_0^t e^{3x}\cdot 1\, dx = \frac{1}{3}\left(e^{3t}-1\right)$$

9. $$f(t) = \frac{1}{9}\sin 3t * \sin 3t = \frac{1}{9}\int_0^t \sin 3x \sin 3(t-x)\, dx$$

$$= \frac{1}{9}\int_0^t \sin 3x\,[\sin 3t \cos 3x - \cos 3t \sin 3x]\, dx$$

$$= \frac{1}{9}\sin 3t \int_0^t \sin 3x \cos 3x\, dx - \frac{1}{9}\cos 3t \int_0^t \sin^2 3x\, dx$$

$$= \frac{1}{9}\sin 3t\left[\frac{1}{6}\sin^2 3x\right]_{x=0}^{x=t} - \frac{1}{9}\cos 3t\left[\frac{1}{2}\left(x-\frac{1}{6}\sin 6x\right)\right]_{x=0}^{x=t}$$

$$f(t) = \frac{1}{54}(\sin 3t - 3t\cos 3t)$$

11. $$f(t) = \cos 2t * \cos 2t = \int_0^t \cos 2x \cos 2(t-x)\, dx$$

$$= \int_0^t \cos 2x \left(\cos 2t \cos 2x + \sin 2t \sin 2x\right)\, dx$$

$$= (\cos 2t)\int_0^t \cos^2 2x\, dx + (\sin 2t)\int_0^t \cos 2x \sin 2x\, dx$$

$$= (\cos 2t)\left[\frac{1}{2}\left(x+\frac{1}{4}\sin 4x\right)\right]_{x=0}^{x=t} + (\sin 2t)\left[\frac{1}{4}\sin^2 2x\right]_{x=0}^{x=t}$$

$$f(t) = \frac{1}{4}(\sin 2t + 2t\cos 2t)$$

13. $$f(t) = e^{3t} * \cos t = \int_0^t (\cos x)e^{3(t-x)}\, dx$$

$$= e^{3t}\int_0^t e^{-3x}\cos x\, dx$$

$$= e^{3t} \left[\frac{e^{-3x}}{10} (-3\cos x + \sin x) \right]_{x=0}^{x=t} \qquad \text{(by integral formula \#50)}$$

$$f(t) = \frac{1}{10} \left(3e^{3t} - 3\cos t + \sin t \right)$$

15. $\quad \mathcal{L}\{t \sin t\} = -\dfrac{d}{ds} (\mathcal{L}\{\sin t\}) = -\dfrac{d}{ds} \left(\dfrac{3}{s^2 + 9} \right) = \dfrac{6s}{\left(s^2 + 9 \right)^2}$

17. $\quad \mathcal{L}\{e^{2t} \cos 3t\} = (s - 2)/(s^2 - 4s + 13)$

$\quad \mathcal{L}\{te^{2t} \cos 3t\} = -(d/ds)[(s - 2)/(s^2 - 4s + 13)] = (s^2 - 4s - 5)/(s^2 - 4s + 13)^2$

19. $\quad \mathcal{L}\left\{ \dfrac{\sin t}{t} \right\} = \displaystyle\int_s^\infty \dfrac{ds}{s^2 + 1} = \left[\tan^{-1} s \right]_s^\infty = \dfrac{\pi}{2} - \tan^{-1} s = \tan^{-1} \left(\dfrac{1}{s} \right)$

21. $\quad \mathcal{L}\left\{ e^{3t} - 1 \right\} = \dfrac{1}{s-3} - \dfrac{1}{s}, \quad$ so

$$\mathcal{L}\left\{ \dfrac{e^{3t} - 1}{t} \right\} = \int_s^\infty \left(\dfrac{1}{s-3} - \dfrac{1}{s} \right) ds = \left[\ln \left(\dfrac{s-3}{s} \right) \right]_s^\infty = \ln \left(\dfrac{s}{s-3} \right)$$

23. $\quad f(t) = -\dfrac{1}{t} \mathcal{L}^{-1}\{F'(s)\} = -\dfrac{1}{t} \mathcal{L}^{-1}\left\{ \dfrac{1}{s-2} - \dfrac{1}{s+2} \right\} = -\dfrac{1}{t} \left(e^{2t} - e^{-2t} \right) = -\dfrac{2 \sinh 2t}{t}$

25. $\quad f(t) = -\dfrac{1}{t} \mathcal{L}^{-1}\{F'(s)\} = -\dfrac{1}{t} \mathcal{L}^{-1}\left\{ \dfrac{2s}{s^2+1} - \dfrac{1}{s+2} - \dfrac{1}{s-3} \right\} = \dfrac{1}{t} \left(e^{-2t} + e^{3t} - 2\cos t \right)$

27. $\quad f(t) = -\dfrac{1}{t} \mathcal{L}^{-1}\{F'(s)\} = -\dfrac{1}{t} \mathcal{L}^{-1}\left\{ \dfrac{-2/s^3}{1 + 1/s^2} \right\}$

$$= \dfrac{2}{t} \mathcal{L}^{-1}\left\{ \dfrac{1}{s^3+s} \right\} = \dfrac{2}{t} \mathcal{L}^{-1}\left\{ \dfrac{1}{s} - \dfrac{s}{s^2+1} \right\} = \dfrac{2}{t} (1 - \cos t)$$

29. $\quad -[s^2 X(s) - x'(0)]' - [s X(s)]' - 2[s X(s)] + X(s) = 0$

$\quad s(s + 1)X'(s) + 4s\, X(s) = 0 \qquad$ (separable)

$$X(s) = \dfrac{A}{(s+1)^4} \quad \text{with } A \neq 0$$

$\quad x(t) = Ct^3 e^{-t} \text{ with } C \neq 0$

31. $-[s^2X(s) - x'(0)]' + 4[s\,X(s)]' - [s\,X(s)] - 4[X(s)]' + 2X(s) = 0$

$(s^2 - 4s + 4)X'(s) + (3s - 6)X(s) = 0$ (separable)

$(s - 2)X'(s) + 3X(s) = 0$

$X(s) = \dfrac{A}{(s-2)^3}$ with $A \neq 0$

$x(t) = Ct^2 e^{2t}$ with $C \neq 0$

33. $-[s^2X(s) - x(0)]' - 2[s\,X(s)] - [X(s)]' = 0$

$(s^2 + 1)X'(s) + 4s\,X(s) = 0$ (separable)

$X(s) = \dfrac{A}{(s^2 + 1)^2}$ with $A \neq 0$

$x(t) = C(\sin t - t\cos t)$ with $C \neq 0$

35. $\mathcal{L}^{-1}\left\{\dfrac{1}{(s-1)\sqrt{s}}\right\} = e^t * \dfrac{1}{\sqrt{\pi t}} = \displaystyle\int_0^t \dfrac{1}{\sqrt{\pi x}} \cdot e^{t-x}\,dx$

$\qquad = \dfrac{e^t}{\sqrt{\pi}} \displaystyle\int_0^{\sqrt{t}} \dfrac{1}{u} \cdot e^{-u^2} \cdot 2u\,du = \dfrac{2e^t}{\sqrt{\pi}} \displaystyle\int_0^{\sqrt{t}} e^{-u^2}\,du = e^t \operatorname{erf}\left(\sqrt{t}\right)$

37. $s^2 X(s) + 2sX(s) + X(s) = F(s)$

$X(s) = F(s) \cdot \dfrac{1}{(s+1)^2}$

$x(t) = te^{-t} * f(t) = \displaystyle\int_0^t \tau e^{-\tau} f(t-\tau)\,d\tau$

SECTION 7.5

PERIODIC AND PIECEWISE CONTINUOUS FORCING FUNCTIONS

1. $F(s) = e^{-3s}\mathcal{L}\{t\}$ so Eq. (3b) in Theorem 1 gives

$$f(t) = u(t-3)\cdot(t-3) = \begin{cases} 0 & \text{if } t < 3, \\ t-3 & \text{if } t \geq 3. \end{cases}$$

The graph of f is shown below.

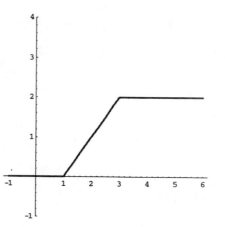

3. $F(s) = e^{-s}\mathcal{L}\{e^{-2t}\}$ so $f(t) = u(t-1)\cdot e^{-2(t-1)} = \begin{cases} 0 & \text{if } t<1, \\ e^{-2(t-1)} & \text{if } t\geq 1. \end{cases}$

5. $F(s) = e^{-\pi s}\mathcal{L}\{\sin t\}$ so

$$f(t) = u(t-\pi)\cdot\sin(t-\pi) = -u(t-\pi)\sin t = \begin{cases} 0 & \text{if } t<\pi, \\ -\sin t & \text{if } t\geq\pi. \end{cases}$$

7. $F(s) = \mathcal{L}\{\sin t\} - e^{-2\pi s}\mathcal{L}\{\sin t\}$ so

$$f(t) = \sin t - u(t-2\pi)\sin(t-2\pi) = \left[1 - u(t-2\pi)\right]\sin t = \begin{cases} \sin t & \text{if } t < 2\pi, \\ 0 & \text{if } t \geq 2\pi. \end{cases}$$

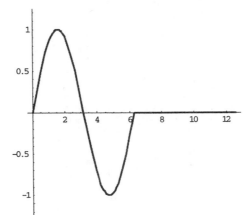

9. $F(s) = \mathcal{L}\{\cos \pi t\} + e^{-3s}\mathcal{L}\{\cos \pi t\}$ so

$$f(t) = \cos \pi t + u(t-3)\cos \pi(t-3) = \left[1 - u(t-3)\right]\cos \pi t = \begin{cases} \cos \pi t & \text{if } t < 3, \\ 0 & \text{if } t \geq 3. \end{cases}$$

11. $f(t) = 2 - u(t-3)\cdot 2$ so $F(s) = \dfrac{2}{s} - e^{-3s}\dfrac{2}{s} = \dfrac{2}{s}\left(1 - e^{-3s}\right).$

13. $f(t) = [1 - u(t-2\pi)]\sin t = \sin t - u(t-2\pi)\sin(t-2\pi)$ so

$$F(s) = \frac{1}{s^2+1} - e^{-2\pi s}\cdot\frac{1}{s^2+1} = \frac{1 - e^{-2\pi s}}{s^2+1}.$$

15. $f(t) = [1 - u(t-3\pi)]\sin t = \sin t + u(t-3\pi)]\sin(t-3\pi)$ so

$$F(s) = \frac{1}{s^2+1} + \frac{e^{-3\pi s}}{s^2+1} = \frac{1 + e^{-3\pi s}}{s^2+1}.$$

17. $f(t) = [u(t-2) - u(t-3)]\sin \pi t = u(t-2)\sin \pi(t-2) + u(t-3)\sin \pi(t-3)$ so

$$F(s) = \left(e^{-2s} + e^{-3s}\right)\cdot\frac{\pi}{s^2+\pi^2} = \frac{\pi\left(e^{-2s} + e^{-3s}\right)}{s^2+\pi^2}.$$

19. If $g(t) = t+1$ then $f(t) = u(t-1)\cdot t = u(t-1)\cdot g(t-1)$ so

$$F(s) = e^{-s}G(s) = e^{-s}L\{t+1\} = e^{-s}\cdot\left(\frac{1}{s^2} + \frac{1}{s}\right) = \frac{e^{-s}(s+1)}{s^2}.$$

21. If $g(t) = t+1$ and $h(t) = t+2$ then

$$
\begin{aligned}
f(t) &= t\left[1-u(t-1)\right]+(2-t)\left[u(t-1)-u(t-2)\right] \\
&= t - 2t\,u(t-1) + 2u(t-1) - 2u(t-2) + t\,u(t-2) \\
&= t - 2u(t-1)g(t-1) + 2u(t-1) - 2u(t-2) + u(t-2)h(t-2)
\end{aligned}
$$

so

$$
F(s) = \frac{1}{s^2} - 2e^{-s}\left(\frac{1}{s^2}+\frac{1}{s}\right) + \frac{2e^{-s}}{s} - \frac{2e^{-2s}}{s} + e^{-2s}\left(\frac{1}{s^2}+\frac{2}{s}\right) = \frac{\left(1-e^{-s}\right)^2}{s^2}.
$$

23. With $f(t) = 1$ and $p = 1$, Formula (12) in the text gives

$$
\mathcal{L}\{1\} = \frac{1}{1-e^{-s}}\int_0^1 e^{-st}\cdot 1\,dt = \frac{1}{1-e^{-s}}\left[-\frac{e^{-st}}{s}\right]_{t=0}^{t=1} = \frac{1}{s}.
$$

25. With $p = 2a$ and $f(t) = 1$ if $0 \le t \le a$, $f(t) = 0$ if $a < t \le 2a$, Formula (12) gives

$$
\begin{aligned}
\mathcal{L}\{f(t)\} &= \frac{1}{1-e^{-2as}}\int_0^a e^{-st}\cdot 1\,dt = \frac{1}{1-e^{-2as}}\left[-\frac{e^{-st}}{s}\right]_{t=0}^{t=a} \\
&= \frac{1-e^{-as}}{s\left(1-e^{-as}\right)\left(1+e^{-as}\right)} = \frac{1}{s\left(1+e^{-as}\right)}.
\end{aligned}
$$

27. $G(s) = \mathcal{L}\{t/a - f(t)\} = (1/as^2) - F(s)$. Now substitution of the result of Problem 26 in place of $F(s)$ immediately gives the desired transform.

29. With $p = 2\pi/k$ and $f(t) = \sin kt$ for $0 \le t \le \pi/k$ while $f(t) = 0$ for $\pi/k \le t \le 2\pi/k$, Formula (12) the integral formula

$$
\int e^{at}\sin bt\,dt = e^{at}\left[\frac{a\sin bt - b\cos bt}{a^2+b^2}\right]+C
$$

give

$$
\begin{aligned}
\mathcal{L}\{f(t)\} &= \frac{1}{1-e^{-2\pi s/k}}\int_0^{\pi/k} e^{-st}\cdot \sin kt\,dt \\
&= \frac{1}{1-e^{-2\pi s/k}}\left[e^{-st}\left(\frac{-s\sin kt - k\cos kt}{s^2+k^2}\right)\right]_{t=0}^{t=\pi/k} \\
&= \frac{1}{1-e^{-2\pi s/k}}\left[\frac{e^{-\pi s/k}(k)-(-k)}{s^2+k^2}\right]
\end{aligned}
$$

$$= \frac{k\left(1+e^{-\pi s/k}\right)}{\left(1-e^{-\pi s/k}\right)\left(1+e^{-\pi s/k}\right)\left(s^2+k^2\right)} = \frac{k}{\left(s^2+k^2\right)\left(1-e^{-\pi s/k}\right)}.$$

In Problems 31-42, we first write and transform the appropriate differential equation. Then we solve for the transform of the solution, and finally inverse transform to find the desired solution.

31. $x'' + 4x = 1 - u(t - \pi)$

$$s^2 X(s) + 4X(s) = \frac{1-e^{-\pi s}}{s}$$

$$X(s) = \frac{1-e^{-\pi s}}{s\left(s^2+4\right)} = \frac{1}{4}\left(1-e^{-\pi s}\right)\left(\frac{1}{s} - \frac{s}{s^2+4}\right)$$

$x(t) = (1/4)[1 - u(t - \pi)][1 - \cos 2(t - \pi)] = (1/2)[1 - u(t - \pi)]\sin^2 t$

33. $x'' + 9x = [1 - u(t - 2\pi)]\sin t$

$$X(s) = \frac{1-e^{-2\pi s}}{\left(s^2+1\right)\left(s^2+4\right)} = \frac{1}{8}\left(1-e^{-2\pi s}\right)\left(\frac{1}{s^2+1} - \frac{1}{s^2+9}\right)$$

$$x(t) = \frac{1}{8}[1-u(t-2\pi)]\left(\sin t - \frac{1}{3}\sin 3t\right)$$

35. $x'' + 4x' + 4x = [1 - u(t - 2)]t = t - u(t - 2)g(t - 2)$ where $g(t) = t + 2$

$$(s+2)^2 X(s) = \frac{1}{s^2} - e^{-2s}\left(\frac{2}{s} + \frac{1}{s^2}\right)$$

$$X(s) = \frac{1}{s^2\left(s+2\right)^2} - e^{-2s}\frac{2s+1}{s^2\left(s+2\right)^2}$$

$$= \frac{1}{4}\left(-\frac{1}{s} + \frac{1}{s^2} + \frac{1}{s+2} + \frac{1}{\left(s+2\right)^2}\right) - \frac{1}{4}e^{-2s}\left(\frac{1}{s} + \frac{1}{s^2} - \frac{1}{s+2} - \frac{3}{\left(s+2\right)^2}\right)$$

$x(t) = (1/4)\{-1 + t + (1 + t)e^{-2t} + u(t-2)[1 - t + (3t - 5)e^{-2(t-2)}]\}$

37. $i'(t) + 10^4 \int i(t)\, dt = 100[1 - u(t - 2\pi)]$

$$s I(s) + 10^4 \frac{I(s)}{s} = 100\frac{1-e^{-2\pi s}}{s}$$

$$I(s) = \frac{100\left(1-e^{-2\pi s}\right)}{s^2+10^4} = \left(1-e^{-2\pi s}\right)\mathcal{L}\{\sin 100t\}$$

$$i(t) = \sin 100t - u(t-2\pi)\sin 100(t-2\pi) = [1 - u(t-2\pi)]\sin 100t$$

39. $i'(t) + 150\,i(t) + 5000\int i(t)\,dt = 100t[1 - u(t-1)]$

$$sI(s)+150I(s)+5000\frac{I(s)}{s} = \frac{100}{s^2}-100e^{-s}\left(\frac{1}{s}+\frac{1}{s^2}\right)$$

$$I(s) = \frac{100}{s(s+50)(s+100)} - e^{-s}\cdot\frac{100(s+1)}{s(s+50)(s+100)}$$

$$= \frac{1}{50}\left(\frac{1}{s}-\frac{2}{s+50}+\frac{1}{s+100}\right) - \frac{1}{50}e^{-s}\left(\frac{1}{s}+\frac{98}{s+50}-\frac{99}{s+100}\right)$$

$$i(t) = (1/50)[1 - 2e^{-50t} + e^{-100t}] - (1/50)u(t-1)[1 + 98e^{-50(t-1)} - 99e^{-100(t-1)}]$$

41. $x'' + 4x = f(t), \qquad x(0) = x'(0) = 0$

$$\left(s^2+4\right)X(s) = \frac{4\left(1-e^{-\pi s}\right)}{s\left(1+e^{-\pi s}\right)} \qquad \text{(by Example 6 of Section 7.5)}$$

$$\left(s^2+4\right)X(s) = \frac{4}{s}+\frac{8}{s}\sum_{n=1}^{\infty}(-1)^n e^{-n\pi s} \qquad \text{(as in Eq. (16) of Section 7.5)}$$

Now let

$$g(t) = \mathcal{L}^{-1}\left\{\frac{4}{s(s^2+4)}\right\} = 1-\cos 2t = 2\sin^2 t.$$

Then it follows that

$$x(t) = g(t)+2\sum_{n=1}^{\infty}(-1)^n u_{n\pi}(t)g(t-n\pi) = 2\sin^2 t+4\sum_{n=1}^{\infty}(-1)^n u_{n\pi}(t)\sin^2 t.$$

Hence

$$x(t) = \begin{cases} 2\sin^2 t & \text{if } 2n\pi \le t < (2n+1)\pi, \\ -2\sin^2 t & \text{if } (2n-1)\pi \le t < 2n\pi. \end{cases}$$

Consequently the complete solution

$$x(t) = 2|\sin t|\sin t$$

is periodic, so the transient solution is zero.

SECTION 7.6

IMPULSES AND DELTA FUNCTIONS

Among the several ways of introducing delta functions, we consider the physical approach of the first two pages of this section to be the most tangible one for elementary students. Whatever the approach, however, the practical consequences are the same — as described in the discussion associated with equations (11)-(19) in the text. That is, in order to solve a differential equation of the form

$$ax''(t) + bx'(t) + cx(t) \ = \ f(t)$$

where $f(t)$ involves delta functions, we transform the equation using the operational principle $\mathcal{L}\{\delta_a(t)\} \ = \ e^{-as}$, then solve for $X(s)$, and finally invert as usual to find the formal solution $x(t)$.

1. $\quad s^2 X(s) + 4X(s) \ = \ 1$

$$X(s) \ = \ \frac{1}{s^2 + 4}$$

$$x(t) \ = \ \frac{1}{2}\sin 2t$$

3. $\quad s^2 X(s) + 4sX(s) + 4X(s) \ = \ \frac{1}{s} + e^{-2s}$

$$X(s) \ = \ \frac{1}{s(s+2)^2} + \frac{e^{-2s}}{(s+2)^2} \ = \ \frac{1}{4}\left(\frac{1}{s} - \frac{1}{s+2} - \frac{2}{(s+2)^2}\right) + \frac{e^{-2s}}{(s+2)^2}$$

$$x(t) \ = \ \frac{1}{4}\left[1 - e^{-2t} - 2t\,e^{-2t}\right] + u(t-2)(t-2)e^{-2(t-2)}$$

5. $\quad (s^2 + 2s + 2)X(s) \ = \ 2e^{-\pi s}$

$$X(s) \ = \ \frac{2e^{-\pi s}}{(s+1)^2 + 1}$$

$$x(t) \ = \ 2u(t-\pi)e^{-(t-\pi)}\sin(t-\pi) \ = \ \begin{cases} 0 & \text{if} \quad 0 \le t \le \pi, \\ -2e^{-(t-\pi)}\sin t & \text{if} \quad t \ge \pi. \end{cases}$$

The graph of $x(t)$ is shown at the top of the next page.

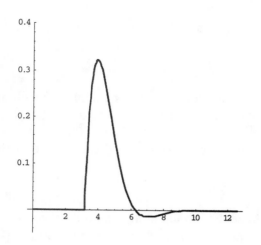

7. $[s^2X(s) - 2] + 4sX(s) + 5X(s) = e^{-\pi s} + e^{-2\pi s}$

$$X(s) = \frac{2 + e^{-\pi s} + e^{-2\pi s}}{(s+2)^2 + 1}$$

$x(t) = 2e^{-2t}\sin t + u_\pi(t)e^{-2(t-\pi)}\sin(t - \pi) + u_{2\pi}(t)e^{-2(t-2\pi)}\sin(t - 2\pi)$

$\quad = [2 - e^{2\pi}u(t - \pi) + e^{4\pi}u(t - 2\pi)]\, e^{-2t}\sin t$

9. $s^2X(s) + 4X(s) = F(s)$

$$X(s) = \frac{1}{s^2 + 4} \cdot F(s)$$

$x(t) = \frac{1}{2}\int_0^t (\sin 2u)\, f(t - u)\, du$

11. $(s^2 + 6s + 8)X(s) = F(s)$

$$X(s) = \frac{1}{(s+3)^2 - 1} \cdot F(s)$$

$$x(t) = \int_0^t e^{-3u}(\sinh u)f(t-u)\,du$$

13. (a) $mx\varepsilon''(t) = (p/\varepsilon)[u_0(t) - u_\varepsilon(t)]$

$ms^2X_\varepsilon(s) = (p/\varepsilon)[1/s - e^{-\varepsilon s}/s]$

$mX_\varepsilon(s) = (p/\varepsilon)[(1 - e^{-\varepsilon s})/s^3]$

$mx_\varepsilon(t) = (p/2\varepsilon)[t^2 - u_\varepsilon(t)(t - \varepsilon)^2]$

(b) If $t > \varepsilon$ then

$$mx_\varepsilon(t) = (p/2\varepsilon)[t^2 - (t^2 - 2\varepsilon t + \varepsilon^2)] = (p/2\varepsilon)(2\varepsilon t - \varepsilon^2).$$

Hence $mx_\varepsilon(t) \to pt$ as $\varepsilon \to 0$.

(c) $mv = (mx)' = (pt)' = p.$

15. Each of the two given initial value problems transforms to

$$(ms^2 + k)X(s) = mv_0 = p_0.$$

17. (b) $i' + 100i = \delta_1(t) - \delta_2(t), \quad i(0) = 0$

$$I(s) = \frac{e^{-s} - e^{-2s}}{s + 100}I(s)$$

$$i(t) = u_1(t)e^{-100(t-1)} - u_2(t)e^{-100(t-2)}$$

19. $\left(s^2 + 100\right)I(s) = 10\sum_{n=0}^{\infty}(-1)^n e^{-n\pi s/10}$

$$I(s) = \frac{10\sum\limits_{n=0}^{\infty}(-1)^n e^{-n\pi s/10}}{s^2 + 100} = \sum_{n=0}^{\infty}\left((-1)^n e^{-n\pi s/10} \cdot \frac{10}{s^2 + 100}\right)$$

$$i(t) = \sum_{n=0}^{\infty} (-1)^n u_{n\pi/10}(t) \sin 10(t - n\pi/10) = \sum_{n=0}^{\infty} u(t - n\pi/10) \sin 10t$$

because $\sin(10t - n\pi) = (-1)^n \sin 10t$. Hence

$$i(t) = (n+1)\sin 10t$$

if $n\pi/10 < t < (n+1)\pi/10$.

21. $\left(s^2 + 60s + 1000\right)I(s) = 10\sum_{n=0}^{\infty}(-1)^n e^{-n\pi s/10}$

$$I(s) = \frac{10\sum_{n=0}^{\infty}(-1)^n e^{-n\pi s/10}}{s^2 + 60s + 1000} = \sum_{n=0}^{\infty}\left((-1)^n e^{-n\pi s/10} \cdot \frac{10}{(s+30)^2 + 100}\right)$$

$i(t) = \Sigma\,(-1)^n u_{n\pi/10}(t)\,g(t - n\pi/10)$

where $g(t) = e^{-30t}\sin 10t$, and so

$$g(t - n\pi/10) = \exp[-30(t - n\pi/10)]\sin 10(t - n\pi/10)$$
$$= e^{3n\pi}e^{-30t}\cdot(-1)^n \sin 10t$$

Therefore

$$i(t) = \sum_{n=0}^{\infty}u(t - n\pi/10)\,e^{3n\pi}e^{-30t}\sin t.$$

If $n\pi/10 < t < (n+1)\pi/10$ then it follows that

$$i(t) = (1 + e^{3\pi} + \cdots + e^{3n\pi})e^{-30t}\sin 10t = \frac{e^{(3n+1)\pi} - 1}{e^{3\pi} - 1}e^{-30t}\sin 10t.$$

CHAPTER 8

POWER SERIES METHODS

SECTION 8.1

INTRODUCTION AND REVIEW OF POWER SERIES

The power series method consists of substituting a series $y = \Sigma c_n x^n$ into a given differential equation in order to determine what the coefficients $\{c_n\}$ must be in order that the power series will satisfy the equation. It might be pointed out that, if we find a recurrence relation in the form $c_{n+1} = \phi(n)c_n$, then we can determine the radius of convergence ρ of the series solution directly from the recurrence relation,

$$\rho = \lim_{n \to \infty} \left| \frac{c_n}{c_{n+1}} \right| = \lim_{n \to \infty} \left| \frac{1}{\phi(n)} \right|.$$

In Problems 1-10 we give first that recurrence relation that can be used to find the radius of convergence and to calculate the succeeding coefficients $c_1, c_2, c_3, \cdots$ in terms of the arbitrary constant c_0. Then we give the series itself

1. $c_{n+1} = \dfrac{c_n}{n+1};$ it follows that $c_n = \dfrac{c_0}{n!}$ and $\rho = \lim_{n \to \infty}(n+1) = \infty$.

$$y(x) = c_0 \left(1 + x + \frac{x^2}{2} + \frac{x^3}{6} + \frac{x^4}{24} + \cdots \right) = c_0 \left(1 + \frac{x}{1!} + \frac{x^2}{2!} + \frac{x^3}{3!} + \frac{x^4}{4!} + \cdots \right) = c_0 e^x$$

3. $c_{n+1} = -\dfrac{3c_n}{2(n+1)};$ it follows that $c_n = \dfrac{(-1)^n 3^n c_0}{2^n n!}$ and $\rho = \lim_{n \to \infty} \dfrac{2(n+1)}{3} = \infty$.

$$y(x) = c_0 \left(1 - \frac{3x}{2} + \frac{9x^2}{8} - \frac{9x^3}{16} + \frac{27x^4}{128} - \cdots \right)$$

$$= c_0 \left(1 - \frac{3x}{1!2} + \frac{3^2 x^2}{2!2^2} - \frac{3^3 x^3}{3!2^3} + \frac{3^4 x^4}{4!2^4} - \cdots \right) = c_0 e^{-3x/2}$$

5.   When we substitute $y = \Sigma c_n x^n$ into the equation $y' = x^2 y$, we find that

$$c_1 + 2c_2 x + \sum_{n=0}^{\infty} \left[(n+3)c_{n+3} - c_n \right] x^{n+1} = 0.$$

Hence $c_1 = c_2 = 0$ — which we see by equating constant terms and x-terms on the two sides of this equation — and $c_3 = \dfrac{c_n}{n+3}$. It follows that

$$c_{3k+1} = c_{3k+2} = 0 \quad \text{and} \quad c_{3k} = \frac{c_0}{3 \cdot 6 \cdots (3k)} = \frac{c_0}{k!\,3^k}.$$

Hence

$$y(x) = c_0\left(1 + \frac{x^3}{3} + \frac{x^6}{18} + \frac{x^9}{162} + \cdots\right) = c_0\left(1 + \frac{x^3}{1!\,3} + \frac{x^6}{2!\,3^2} + \frac{x^9}{3!\,3^3} + \cdots\right) = c_0 e^{(x^3/3)}.$$

and $\rho = \infty$.

7. $\quad c_{n+1} = 2c_n;$ it follows that $c_n = 2^n c_0$ and $\rho = \lim\limits_{n\to\infty} \dfrac{1}{2} = \dfrac{1}{2}.$

$$y(x) = c_0\left(1 + 2x + 4x^2 + 8x^3 + 16x^4 + \cdots\right)$$
$$= c_0\left[1 + (2x) + (2x)^2 + (2x)^3 + (2x)^4 + \cdots\right] = \frac{c_0}{1 - 2x}$$

9. $\quad c_{n+1} = \dfrac{(n+2)c_n}{n+1};$ it follows that $c_n = (n+1)c_0$ and $\rho = \lim\limits_{n\to\infty} \dfrac{n+1}{n+2} = 1.$

$$y(x) = c_0\left(1 + 2x + 3x^2 + 4x^3 + 5x^4 + \cdots\right)$$

Separation of variables gives $\quad y(x) = \dfrac{c_0}{(1-x)^2}.$

In Problems 11-14 the differential equations are second-order, and we find that the two initial coefficients c_0 and c_1 are both arbitrary. In each case we find the even-degree coefficients in terms of c_0 and the odd-degree coefficients in terms of c_1. The solution series in these problems are all recognizable power series that have infinite radii of convergence.

11. $\quad c_{n+1} = \dfrac{c_n}{(n+1)(n+2)};$ it follows that $c_{2k} = \dfrac{c_0}{(2k)!}$ and $c_{2k+1} = \dfrac{c_1}{(2k+1)!}.$

$$y(x) = c_0\left(1 + \frac{x^2}{2!} + \frac{x^4}{4!} + \frac{x^6}{6!} + \cdots\right) + c_1\left(x + \frac{x^3}{3!} + \frac{x^5}{5!} + \frac{x^7}{7!} + \cdots\right) = c_0 \cosh x + c_1 \sinh x$$

13. $\quad c_{n+1} = -\dfrac{9c_n}{(n+1)(n+2)};$ it follows that $c_{2k} = \dfrac{(-1)^k 3^{2k} c_0}{(2k)!}$ and $c_{2k+1} = \dfrac{(-1)^k 3^{2k} c_1}{(2k+1)!}.$

$$y(x) = c_0\left(1 - \frac{9x^2}{2} + \frac{27x^4}{8} - \frac{81x^6}{80} + \cdots\right) + c_1\left(x - \frac{3x^3}{2} + \frac{27x^5}{40} - \frac{81x^7}{560} + \cdots\right)$$
$$= c_0\left(1 - \frac{(3x)^2}{2!} + \frac{(3x)^4}{4!} - \frac{(3x)^6}{6!} + \cdots\right) + \frac{c_1}{3}\left((3x) - \frac{(3x)^3}{3!} + \frac{(3x)^5}{5!} - \frac{(3x)^7}{7!} + \cdots\right)$$

$$= c_0 \cos 3x + \frac{c_1}{3} \sin x$$

15. Assuming a power series solution of the form $y = \Sigma c_n x^n$, we substitute it into the differential equation $xy' + y = 0$ and find that $(n+1)c_n = 0$ for all $n \geq 0$. This implies that $c_n = 0$ for all $n \geq 0$, which means that the only power series solution of our differential equation is the trivial solution $y(x) \equiv 0$. Therefore the equation has no *non-trivial* power series solution.

17. Assuming a power series solution of the form $y = \Sigma c_n x^n$, we substitute it into the differential equation $x^2 y' + y = 0$. We find that $c_0 = c_1 = 0$ and that $c_{n+1} = -nc_n$ for $n \geq 1$, so it follows that $c_n = 0$ for all $n \geq 0$. Just as in Problems 15 and 16, this means that the equation has no *non-trivial* power series solution.

In Problems 19-22 we first give the recurrence relation that results upon substitution of an assumed power series solution $y = \Sigma c_n x^n$ into the given second-order differential equation. Then we give the resulting general solution, and finally apply the initial conditions $y(0) = c_0$ and $y'(0) = c_1$ to determine the desired particular solution.

19. $c_{n+2} = -\dfrac{2^2 c_n}{(n+1)(n+2)}$ for $n \geq 0$, so $c_{2k} = \dfrac{(-1)^k 2^{2k} c_0}{(2k)!}$ and $c_{2k+1} = \dfrac{(-1)^k 2^{2k} c_1}{(2k+1)!}$.

$$y(x) = c_0 \left(1 - \frac{2^2 x^2}{2!} + \frac{2^4 x^4}{4!} - \frac{2^6 x^6}{6!} + \cdots \right) + c_1 \left(x - \frac{2^2 x^3}{3!} + \frac{2^4 x^5}{5!} - \frac{2^6 x^7}{7!} + \cdots \right)$$

$c_0 = y(0) = 0$ and $c_1 = y'(0) = 3$, so

$$y(x) = 3 \left(x - \frac{2^2 x^3}{3!} + \frac{2^4 x^5}{5!} - \frac{2^6 x^7}{7!} + \cdots \right)$$

$$= \frac{3}{2} \left[(2x) - \frac{(2x)^3}{3!} + \frac{(2x)^5}{5!} - \frac{(2x)^7}{7!} + \cdots \right] = \frac{3}{2} \sin 2x.$$

21. $c_{n+1} = \dfrac{2nc_n - c_{n-1}}{n(n+1)}$ for $n \geq 1$; with $c_0 = y(0) = 0$ and $c_1 = y'(0) = 1$, we obtain

$$c_2 = 1, \ c_3 = \frac{1}{2}, \ c_4 = \frac{1}{6} = \frac{1}{3!}, \ c_5 = \frac{1}{24} = \frac{1}{4!}, \ c_6 = \frac{1}{120} = \frac{1}{5!}. \text{ Evidently } c_n = \frac{1}{(n-1)!}, \text{ so}$$

$$y(x) = x + x^2 + \frac{x^3}{2!} + \frac{x^4}{3!} + \frac{x^5}{4!} + \cdots = x \left(1 + x + \frac{x^2}{2!} + \frac{x^3}{3!} + \frac{x^4}{4!} + \cdots \right) = xe^x.$$

23. $c_0 = c_1 = 0$ and the recursion relation

$$(n^2 - n + 1)c_n + (n-1)c_{n-1} = 0$$

for $n \geq 2$ imply that $c_n = 0$ for $n \geq 0$. Thus any assumed power series solution $y = \Sigma c_n x^n$ must reduce to the trivial solution $y(x) \equiv 0$.

25. This problem is pretty fully outlined in the textbook. The only hard part is squaring the power series:

$$\left(1 + c_3 x^3 + c_5 x^5 + c_7 x^7 + c_9 x^9 + c_{11} x^{11} + \cdots\right)^2$$
$$= x^2 + 2c_3 x^4 + \left(c_3^2 + 2c_5\right)x^6 + \left(2c_3 c_5 + 2c_7\right)x^8 +$$
$$\left(c_5^2 + 2c_3 c_7 + 2c_9\right)x^{10} + \left(2c_5 c_7 + 2c_3 c_9 + 2c_{11}\right)x^{12} + \cdots$$

SECTION 8.2

SERIES SOLUTIONS NEAR ORDINARY POINTS

Instead of deriving in detail the recurrence relations and solution series for Problems 1 through 15, we indicate where some of these problems and answers originally came from. Each of the differential equations in Problems 1-10 is of the form

$$(Ax^2 + B)y'' + Cxy' + Dy = 0$$

with selected values of the constants A, B, C, D. When we substitute $y = \Sigma c_n x^n$, shift indices where appropriate, and collect coefficients, we get

$$\sum_{n=0}^{\infty}\left[An(n-1)c_n + B(n+1)(n+2)c_{n+2} + Cnc_n + Dc_n\right]x^n = 0.$$

Thus the recurrence relation is

$$c_{n+2} = -\frac{An^2 + (C - A)n + D}{B(n+1)(n+2)}c_n \qquad \text{for } n \geq 0.$$

It yields a solution of the form

$$y = c_0\, y_{\text{even}} + c_1\, y_{\text{odd}}$$

where y_{even} and y_{odd} denote series with terms of even and odd degrees, respectively. The even-degree series $c_0 + c_2 x^2 + c_4 x^4 + \cdots$ converges (by the ratio test) provided that

$$\lim_{n \to \infty}\left|\frac{c_{n+2}x^{n+2}}{c_n x^n}\right| = \left|\frac{Ax^2}{B}\right| < 1.$$

Hence its radius of convergence is at least $\rho = \sqrt{|B/A|}$, as is that of the odd-degree series $c_1 x + c_3 x^3 + c_5 x^4 + \cdots$. (See Problem 6 for an example in which the radius of convergence is, surprisingly, greater than $\sqrt{|B/A|}$.)

In Problems 1-15 we give first the recurrence relation and the radius of convergence, then the resulting power series solution.

1. $\quad c_{n+2} = c_n; \qquad \rho = 1; \qquad c_0 = c_2 = c_4 = \cdots; \qquad c_1 = c_3 = c_4 = \cdots$

$$y(x) = c_0 \sum_{n=0}^{\infty} x^{2n} + c_1 \sum_{n=0}^{\infty} x^{2n+1} = \frac{c_0 + c_1 x}{1 - x^2}$$

3. $\quad c_{n+2} = -\dfrac{c_n}{(n+2)}; \qquad \rho = \infty;$

$$c_{2n} = \frac{(-1)^n c_0}{(2n)(2n-2)\cdots\cdot 4 \cdot 2} = \frac{(-1)^n c_0}{n! 2^n}; \qquad c_{2n+1} = \frac{(-1)^n c_1}{(2n+1)(2n-1)\cdots\cdot 5 \cdot 3} = \frac{(-1)^n c_1}{(2n+1)!!}$$

$$y(x) = c_0 \sum_{n=0}^{\infty} (-1)^n \frac{x^{2n}}{n! 2^n} + c_1 \sum_{n=0}^{\infty} (-1)^n \frac{x^{2n+1}}{(2n+1)!!}$$

5. $\quad c_{n+2} = \dfrac{nc_n}{3(n+2)}; \qquad \rho = 3; \qquad c_2 = c_4 = c_6 = \cdots = 0$

$$c_{2n+1} = \frac{2n-1}{3(2n+1)} \cdot \frac{2n-3}{3(2n-1)} \cdots \cdot \frac{3}{3(5)} \cdot \frac{1}{3(3)} c_1 = \frac{c_1}{(2n+1)3^n}$$

$$y(x) = c_0 + c_1 \sum_{n=0}^{\infty} \frac{x^{2n+1}}{(2n+1)3^n}$$

7. $\quad c_{n+2} = -\dfrac{(n-4)^2}{3(n+1)(n+2)} c_n; \qquad \rho \geq \sqrt{3}$

The factor $(n-4)$ yields $c_6 = c_8 = c_{10} = \cdots = 0$, so y_{even} is a 4th-degree polynomial.

We find first that $c_3 = -c_1/2$ and $c_5 = c_1/120$, and then for $n \geq 3$ that

$$c_{2n+1} = \left(-\frac{(2n-5)^2}{3(2n)(2n+1)} \right)\left(-\frac{(2n-7)^2}{3(2n-2)(2n-1)} \right)\cdots\left(-\frac{1^2}{3(6)(7)} \right) c_5 =$$

$$= (-1)^{n-2} \frac{[(2n-5)!!]^2}{3^{n-2}(2n+1)(2n-1)\cdots\cdot 7 \cdot 6} \cdot \frac{c_1}{120} = 9 \cdot (-1)^n \frac{[(2n-5)!!]^2}{3^n (2n+1)!} c_1$$

$$y(x) = c_0\left(1 - \frac{8}{3}x^2 + \frac{8}{27}x^4\right) + c_1\left[x - \frac{1}{2}x^3 + \frac{1}{120}x^5 + 9\sum_{n=3}^{\infty}\frac{[(2n-5)!!]^2(-1)^n}{(2n+1)!\,3^n}x^{2n+1}\right]$$

9. $\qquad c_{n+2} = \dfrac{(n+3)(n+4)}{(n+1)(n+2)}c_n; \qquad \rho = 1$

$$c_{2n} = \frac{(2n+1)(2n+2)}{(2n-1)(2n)}\cdot\frac{(2n-1)(2n)}{(2n-3)(2n-2)}\cdots\cdot\frac{3\cdot 4}{1\cdot 2}c_0 = \frac{1}{2}(n+1)(2n+1)c_0$$

$$c_{2n+1} = \frac{(2n+2)(2n+3)}{(2n)(2n+1)}\cdot\frac{(2n)(2n+1)}{(2n-2)(2n-1)}\cdots\cdot\frac{4\cdot 5}{2\cdot 3}c_1 = \frac{1}{3}(n+1)(2n+3)c_1$$

$$y(x) = c_0\sum_{n=0}^{\infty}(n+1)(2n+1)x^{2n} + \frac{1}{3}c_1\sum_{n=0}^{\infty}(n+1)(2n+3)x^{2n+1}$$

11. $\qquad c_{n+2} = \dfrac{2(n-5)}{5(n+1)(n+2)}c_n; \qquad \rho = \infty$

The factor $(n-5)$ yields $c_7 = c_9 = c_{11} = \cdots = 0$, so y_{odd} is a 5th-degree polynomial.
We find first that $c_2 = -c_1$, $c_4 = c_0/10$ and $c_6 = c_0/750$, and then for $n \ge 4$ that

$$c_{2n} = \frac{2(2n-7)}{5(2n)(2n-1)}\cdot\frac{2(2n-5)}{5(2n-2)(2n-3)}\cdots\cdot\frac{2(1)}{5(8)(7)}c_6$$

$$= \frac{2^{n-3}(2n-7)!!}{5^{n-3}(2n)(2n-1)\cdots(8)(7)}\cdot\frac{c_0}{750} =$$

$$= \frac{5^3\cdot 6!}{2^3\cdot 750}\cdot\frac{2^n(2n-7)!!}{5^n(2n)(2n)\cdots(8)(7)\cdot 6!}\cdot c_1 = 15\cdot\frac{2^n(2n-7)!!}{5^n(2n)!}c_0$$

$$y(x) = c_1\left(x - \frac{4x^3}{15} + \frac{4x^5}{375}\right) + c_0\left[1 - x^2 + \frac{x^4}{10} + \frac{x^6}{750} + 15\sum_{n=4}^{\infty}\frac{(2n-7)!!\,2^n}{(2n)!\,5^n}x^{2n}\right]$$

13. $\qquad c_{n+3} = -\dfrac{c_n}{n+3}; \qquad \rho = \infty$

When we substitute $y = \Sigma c_n x^n$ into the given differential equation, we find first that
$c_2 = 0$, so the recurrence relation yields $c_5 = c_8 = c_{11} = \cdots = 0$ also.

$$y(x) = c_0\sum_{n=0}^{\infty}\frac{(-1)^n x^{3n}}{n!\,3^n} + c_1\sum_{n=0}^{\infty}\frac{(-1)^n x^{3n+1}}{1\cdot 4\cdots(3n+1)}$$

15. $\qquad c_{n+4} = -\dfrac{c_n}{(n+3)(n+4)}; \qquad \rho = \infty$

When we substitute $y = \Sigma c_n x^n$ into the given differential equation, we find first that

$c_2 = c_3 = 0$, so the recurrence relation yields $c_6 = c_{10} = \cdots = 0$ and $c_7 = c_{11} = \cdots = 0$ also. Then

$$c_{4n} = \frac{-1}{(4n)(4n-1)} \cdot \frac{-1}{(4n-4)(4n-5)} \cdots\cdots \frac{-1}{4 \cdot 3} c_0 = \frac{(-1)^n c_0}{4^n n!\,(4n-1)(4n-5)\cdots\cdots 5 \cdot 3},$$

$$c_{3n+1} = \frac{-1}{(4n+1)(4n)} \cdot \frac{-1}{(4n-3)(4n-4)} \cdots\cdots \frac{-1}{5 \cdot 4} c_1 = \frac{(-1)^n c_1}{4^n n!\,(4n+1)(4n-3)\cdots\cdots 9 \cdot 5}.$$

$$y(x) = c_0\left[1 + \sum_{n=1}^{\infty} \frac{(-1)^n x^{4n}}{4^n n!\,3 \cdot 7 \cdots\cdots (4n-1)}\right] + c_1\left[x + \sum_{n=1}^{\infty} \frac{(-1)^n x^{4n+1}}{4^n n!\,5 \cdot 9 \cdots\cdots (4n+1)}\right]$$

17. The recurrence relation

$$c_{n+2} = -\frac{(n-2)c_n}{(n+1)(n+2)}$$

yields $c_2 = c_0 = y(0) = 1$ and $c_4 = c_6 = \cdots = 0$. Because $c_1 = y'(0) = 0$, it follows also that $c_1 = c_3 = c_5 = \cdots = 0$. Thus the desired particular solution is $y(x) = 1 + x^2$.

19. The substitution $t = x - 1$ yields $(1 - t^2)y'' - 6ty' - 4y = 0$, where primes now denote differentiation with respect to t. When we substitute $y = \Sigma c_n t^n$ we get the recurrence relation

$$c_{n+2} = \frac{n+4}{n+2}c_n.$$

for $n \geq 0$, so the solution series has radius of convergence $\rho = 1$, and therefore converges if $-1 < t < 1$. The initial conditions give $c_0 = 0$ and $c_1 = 1$, so $c_{\text{even}} = 0$ and

$$c_{2n+1} = \frac{2n+3}{2n+1} \cdot \frac{2n+1}{2n-1} \cdots\cdots \frac{7}{5} \cdot \frac{5}{3} c_1 = \frac{2n+3}{3}.$$

Thus

$$y = \frac{1}{3}\sum_{n=0}^{\infty}(2n+3)t^{2n+1} = \frac{1}{3}\sum_{n=0}^{\infty}(2n+3)(x-1)^{2n+1},$$

and the x-series converges if $0 < x < 2$.

21. The substitution $t = x + 2$ yields $(4t^2 + 1)y'' = 8y$, where primes now denote differentiation with respect to t. When we substitute $y = \Sigma c_n t^n$ we get the recurrence relation

$$c_{n+2} = -\frac{4(n-2)}{(n+2)}c_n$$

for $n \geq 0$. The initial conditions give $c_0 = 1$ and $c_1 = 0$. It follows that $c_{\text{odd}} = 0$, $c_2 = 4$ and $c_4 = c_6 = \cdots = 0$, so the solution reduces to

$$y = 2 + 4t^2 = 1 + 4(x+2)^2.$$

In Problems 23-26 we first derive the recurrence relation, and then calculate the solution series $y_1(x)$ with $c_0 = 1$ and $c_1 = 0$, the solution series $y_2(x)$ with $c_0 = 0$ and $c_1 = 1$.

23.   Substitution of $y = \Sigma c_n x^n$ yields

$$c_0 + 2c_2 + \sum_{n=1}^{\infty}\left[c_{n-1} + c_n + (n+1)(n+2)c_{n+2}\right]x^n = 0,$$

so

$$c_2 = -\frac{1}{2}c_0, \qquad c_{n+2} = -\frac{c_{n-1}+c_n}{(n+1)(n+2)} \quad \text{for} \quad n \geq 1.$$

$$y_1(x) = 1 - \frac{x^2}{2} - \frac{x^3}{6} + \frac{x^4}{24} + \cdots; \qquad y_2(x) = x - \frac{x^3}{6} - \frac{x^4}{12} + \frac{x^5}{120} + \cdots$$

25.   Substitution of $y = \Sigma c_n x^n$ yields

$$2c_2 + 6c_3 x + \sum_{n=2}^{\infty}\left[c_{n-2} + (n-1)c_{n-1} + (n+1)(n+2)c_{n+2}\right]x^n = 0,$$

so

$$c_2 = c_3 = 0, \qquad c_{n+2} = -\frac{c_{n-2}+(n-1)c_{n-1}}{(n+1)(n+2)} \quad \text{for} \quad n \geq 2.$$

$$y_1(x) = 1 - \frac{x^4}{12} + \frac{x^7}{126} + \frac{x^8}{672} + \cdots; \qquad y_2(x) = x - \frac{x^4}{12} - \frac{x^5}{20} + \frac{x^7}{126} + \cdots$$

27.   Substitution of $y = \Sigma c_n x^n$ yields

$$c_0 + 2c_2 + (2c_1 + 6c_3)x + \sum_{n=2}^{\infty}\left[2c_{n-2} + (n+1)c_n + (n+1)(n+2)c_{n+2}\right]x^n = 0,$$

so

$$c_2 = -\frac{c_0}{2}, \qquad c_3 = -\frac{c_1}{3}, \qquad c_{n+2} = -\frac{2c_{n-2}+(n+1)c_n}{(n+1)(n+2)} \quad \text{for} \quad n \geq 2.$$

With $c_0 = y(0) = 1$ and $c_1 = y'(0) = -1$, we obtain

$$y(x) = 1 - x - \frac{x^2}{2} + \frac{x^3}{3} - \frac{x^4}{24} + \frac{x^5}{30} + \frac{29x^6}{720} - \frac{13x^7}{630} - \frac{143x^8}{40320} + \frac{31x^9}{22680} + \cdots.$$

Finally, $x = 0.5$ gives

$$y(0.5) = 1 - 0.5 - 0.125 + 0.041667 - 0.002604 + 0.001042$$
$$+ 0.000629 - 0.000161 - 0.000014 + 0.000003 + \cdots$$
$$y(0.5) \approx 0.415562 \approx 0.4156.$$

29. When we substitute $y = \Sigma c_n x^n$ and $\cos x = \sum (-1)^n x^{2n}/(2n)!$ and then collect coefficients of the terms involving $1, x, x^2, \cdots, x^6$, we obtain the equations

$$c_0 + 2c_2 = 0, \quad c_1 + 6c_3 = 0, \quad 12c_4 = 0, \quad -2c_3 + 20c_5 = 0,$$

$$\frac{1}{12}c_2 - 5c_4 + 30c_6 = 0, \quad \frac{1}{4}c_3 - 9c_5 + 42c_6 = 0,$$

$$-\frac{1}{360}c_2 + \frac{1}{2}c_4 - 14c_6 + 56c_8 = 0.$$

Given c_0 and c_1, we can solve easily for $c_2, c_3, \cdots, c_8$ in turn. With the choices $c_0 = 1, \ c_1 = 0$ and $c_0 = 0, \ c_1 = 1$ we obtain the two series solutions

$$y_1(x) = 1 - \frac{x^2}{2} + \frac{x^6}{720} + \frac{13x^8}{40320} + \cdots \quad \text{and} \quad y_2(x) = x - \frac{x^3}{6} - \frac{x^5}{60} - \frac{13x^7}{5040} + \cdots.$$

SECTION 8.3

REGULAR SINGULAR POINTS

1. Upon division of the given differential equation by x we see that $P(x) = 1 - x^2$ and $Q(x) = (\sin x)/x$. Because both are analytic at $x = 0$ — in particular, $(\sin x)/x \to 1$ as $x \to 0$ because

$$\frac{\sin x}{x} = \frac{1}{x}\sum_{n=0}^{\infty} \frac{(-1)^n x^{2n+1}}{(2n+1)!} = \sum_{n=1}^{\infty} \frac{(-1)^n x^{2n}}{(2n+1)!} = 1 - \frac{x^2}{3!} + \frac{x^4}{5!} - \frac{x^6}{7!} + \cdots$$

— it follows that $x = 0$ is an ordinary point.

3. When we rewrite the given equation in the standard form of Equation (3) in this section, we see that $p(x) = (\cos x)/x$ and $q(x) = x$. Because $(\cos x)/x \to \infty$ as $x \to 0$ it follows that $p(x)$ is not analytic, so $x = 0$ is an irregular singular point.

5. In the standard form of Equation (3) we have $p(x) = 2/(1 + x)$ and $q(x) = 3x^2/(1 + x)$. Both are analytic, so $x = 0$ is a regular singular point. The indicial equation is

$$r(r - 1) + 2r = r^2 + r = r(r + 1) = 0,$$

so the exponents are $r_1 = 0$ and $r_2 = -1$.

7. In the standard form of Equation (3) we have $p(x) = (6 \sin x)/x$ and $q(x) = 6$, so $x = 0$ is a regular singular point with $p_0 = q_0 = 6$. The indicial equation is $r^2 + 5r + 6 = 0$, so the exponents are $r_1 = -2$ and $r_2 = -3$.

9. The only singular point of the differential equation $y'' + \dfrac{x}{1-x}y' + \dfrac{x^2}{1-x}y = 0$ is $x = 1$.

Upon substituting $t = x - 1$, $x = t + 1$ we get the transformed equation

$y'' - \dfrac{t+1}{t}y' - \dfrac{(t+1)^2}{t}y = 0$, where primes now denote differentiation with respect to t.

In the standard form of Equation (3) we have $p(t) = -(1+t)$ and $q(t) = -t(1+t)^2$. Both these functions are analytic, so it follows that $x = 1$ is a regular singular point of the original equation.

11. The only singular points of the differential equation $y'' - \dfrac{2x}{1-x^2}y' + \dfrac{12}{1-x^2}y = 0$ are

$x = +1$ and $x = -1$.

$x = +1$: Upon substituting $t = x - 1$, $x = t + 1$ we get the transformed equation

$y'' + \dfrac{2(t+1)}{t(t+2)}y' - \dfrac{12}{t(t+2)}y = 0$, where primes now denote differentiation with respect to

t. In the standard form of Equation (3) we have $p(t) = \dfrac{2(t+1)}{t+2}$ and $q(t) = -\dfrac{12t}{t+2}$.

Both these functions are analytic at $t = 0$, so it follows that $x = +1$ is a regular singular point of the original equation.

$x = -1$: Upon substituting $t = x + 1$, $x = t - 1$ we get the transformed equation

$y'' + \dfrac{2(t-1)}{t(t-2)}y' - \dfrac{12}{t(t-2)}y = 0$, where primes now denote differentiation with respect to

t. In the standard form of Equation (3) we have $p(t) = \dfrac{2(t-1)}{t-2}$ and $q(t) = -\dfrac{12t}{t-2}$.

Both these functions are analytic at $t = 0$, so it follows that $x = -1$ is a regular singular point of the original equation.

13. The only singular points of the differential equation $y'' + \dfrac{1}{x-2}y' + \dfrac{1}{x+2}y = 0$ are

$x = +2$ and $x = -2$.

$x = +2$: Upon substituting $t = x - 2$, $x = t + 2$ we get the transformed equation

$y'' + \dfrac{1}{t+4}y' + \dfrac{1}{t}y = 0$, where primes now denote differentiation with respect to t. In the

standard form of Equation (3) we have $p(t) = \dfrac{t}{t+4}$ and $q(t) = t$. Both these

functions are analytic at $t = 0$, so it follows that $x = +2$ is a regular singular point of the original equation.

$x = -2$: Upon substituting $t = x + 2$, $x = t - 2$ we get the transformed equation

$y'' + \dfrac{1}{t} y' + \dfrac{1}{t-4} y = 0$, where primes now denote differentiation with respect to t. In the

standard form of Equation (3) we have $p(t) \equiv 1$ and $q(t) = \dfrac{t^2}{t-4}$. Both these

functions are analytic at $t = 0$, so it follows that $x = -2$ is a regular singular point of the original equation.

15. The only singular point of the differential equation $y'' - \dfrac{x^2 - 4}{(x-2)^2} y' + \dfrac{x+2}{(x-2)^2} y = 0$ is

$x = 2$. Upon substituting $t = x - 2$, $x = t + 2$ we get the transformed equation

$y'' - \dfrac{t+4}{t} y' + \dfrac{t+4}{t^2} y = 0$, where primes now denote differentiation with respect to t. In

the standard form of Equation (3) we have $p(t) = -(t+4)$ and $q(t) = t + 4$. Both these functions are analytic, so it follows that $x = 2$ is a regular singular point of the original equation.

Each of the differential equations in Problems 17-20 is of the form

$$Axy'' + By' + Cy = 0$$

with indicial equation $Ar^2 + (B - A)r = 0$. Substitution of $y = \Sigma c_n x^{n+r}$ into the differential equation yields the recurrence relation

$$c_n = -\dfrac{C c_{n-1}}{A(n+r)^2 + (B-A)(n+r)}$$

for $n \geq 1$. In these problems the exponents $r_1 = 0$ and $r_2 = (A - B)/A$ do *not* differ by an integer, so this recurrence relation yields two linearly independent Frobenius series solutions when we apply it separately with $r = r_1$ and with $r = r_2$.

17. With exponent $r_1 = 0$: $c_n = -\dfrac{c_{n-1}}{4n^2 - 2n}$

$$y_1(x) = x^0 \left(1 - \dfrac{x}{2} + \dfrac{x^2}{24} - \dfrac{x^3}{720} + \cdots \right) = \sum_{n=0}^{\infty} \dfrac{(-1)^n \left(\sqrt{x} \right)^{2n}}{(2n)!} = \cos \sqrt{x}$$

With exponent $r_2 = \dfrac{1}{2}$: $c_n = -\dfrac{c_{n-1}}{4n^2 + 2n}$

$$y_2(x) = x^{1/2} \left(1 - \dfrac{x}{6} + \dfrac{x^2}{120} - \dfrac{x^3}{5040} + \cdots \right) = \sum_{n=0}^{\infty} \dfrac{(-1)^n \left(\sqrt{x} \right)^{2n+1}}{(2n+1)!} = \sin \sqrt{x}$$

19.   With exponent $r_1 = 0$: $c_n = \dfrac{c_{n-1}}{2n^2 - 3n}$

$$y_1(x) = x^0\left(1 - x - \frac{x^2}{2} - \frac{x^3}{18} - \frac{x^4}{360} - \cdots\right) = 1 - x - \sum_{n=2}^{\infty}\frac{x^n}{n!(2n-3)!!}$$

With exponent $r_2 = \dfrac{3}{2}$: $c_n = \dfrac{c_{n-1}}{2n^2 + 3n}$

$$y_2(x) = x^{3/2}\left(1 + \frac{x}{5} + \frac{x^2}{70} + \frac{x^3}{1890} + \frac{x^4}{83160} + \cdots\right) = x^{3/2}\left[1 + 3\sum_{n=1}^{\infty}\frac{x^n}{n!(2n+3)!!}\right]$$

The differential equations in Problems 21-24 are all of the form

$$Ax^2 y'' + Bxy' + (C + Dx^2)y = 0 \tag{1}$$

with indical equation

$$\phi(r) = Ar^2 + (B - A)r + C = 0. \tag{2}$$

Substitution of $y = \Sigma c_n x^{n+r}$ into the differential equation yields

$$\phi(r)c_0 x^r + \phi(r+1)c_1 x^{r+1} + \sum_{n=2}^{\infty}\left[\phi(r+n)c_n + Dc_{n-2}\right]x^{n+r} = 0. \tag{3}$$

In each of Problems 21-24 the exponents r_1 and r_2 do *not* differ by an integer. Hence when we substitute either $r = r_1$ or $r = r_2$ into Equation (*) above, we find that c_0 is arbitrary because $\phi(r)$ is then zero, that $c_1 = 0$ — because its coefficient $\phi(r+1)$ is then nonzero — and that

$$c_n = -\frac{Dc_{n-2}}{\phi(r+n)} = -\frac{Dc_{n-2}}{A(n+r)^2 + (B-A)(n+r) + C} \tag{4}$$

for $n \geq 2$. Thus this recurrence formula yields two linearly independent Frobenius series solutions when we apply it separately with $r = r_1$ and with $r = r_2$.

21.   With exponent $r_1 = 1$: $c_1 = 0$, $c_n = \dfrac{2c_{n-2}}{n(2n+3)}$

$$y_1(x) = x^1\left(1 + \frac{x^2}{7} + \frac{x^4}{154} + \frac{x^6}{6930} + \cdots\right) = x\left[1 + \sum_{n=1}^{\infty}\frac{x^{2n}}{n! \cdot 7 \cdot 11 \cdots (4n+3)}\right]$$

With exponent $r_2 = -\dfrac{1}{2}$: $c_1 = 0$, $c_n = \dfrac{2c_{n-2}}{n(2n-3)}$

$$y_2(x) = x^{-1/2}\left(1 + x^2 + \frac{x^4}{10} + \frac{x^6}{270} + \cdots\right) = \frac{1}{\sqrt{x}}\left[1 + \sum_{n=1}^{\infty}\frac{x^{2n}}{n! \cdot 1 \cdot 5 \cdots (4n-3)}\right]$$

23.   With exponent $r_1 = \dfrac{1}{2}$: $c_1 = 0$, $c_n = \dfrac{c_{n-2}}{n(6n+7)}$

$$y_1(x) = x^{1/2}\left(1 + \frac{x^2}{38} + \frac{x^4}{4712} + \frac{x^6}{1215696} + \cdots\right) = \sqrt{x}\left[1 + \sum_{n=1}^{\infty}\frac{x^{2n}}{2^n n! \cdot 19 \cdot 31 \cdots (12n+7)}\right]$$

With exponent $r_2 = -\frac{2}{3}$: $c_1 = 0$, $c_n = \frac{c_{n-2}}{n(6n-7)}$

$$y_2(x) = x^{-2/3}\left(1 + \frac{x^2}{10} + \frac{x^4}{680} + \frac{x^6}{118320} + \cdots\right) = x^{-2/3}\left[1 + \sum_{n=1}^{\infty}\frac{x^{2n}}{2^n n! \cdot 5 \cdot 17 \cdots (12n-7)}\right]$$

25. With exponent $r_1 = \frac{1}{2}$: $c_n = -\frac{c_{n-1}}{2n}$

$$y_1(x) = x^{1/2}\left(1 - \frac{x}{2} + \frac{x^2}{8} - \frac{x^3}{48} + \frac{x^4}{384} - \cdots\right) = \sqrt{x}\sum_{n=0}^{\infty}\frac{(-1)^n x^n}{n! 2^n} = \sqrt{x}\,e^{-x/2}$$

With exponent $r_2 = 0$: $c_n = -\frac{c_{n-1}}{2n-1}$

$$y_2(x) = x^0\left(1 - x + \frac{x^2}{3} - \frac{x^3}{15} + \frac{x^4}{105} - \cdots\right) = 1 + \sum_{n=1}^{\infty}\frac{(-1)^n x^n}{(2n-1)!!}$$

The differential equations in Problems 27-29 (after multiplication by x) and the one in Problem 31 are of the same form (1) above as those in Problems 21-24. However, now the exponents r_1 and $r_2 = r_1 - 1$ *do* differ by an integer. Hence when we substitute the smaller exponent $r = r_2$ into Equation (3), we find that c_0 and c_1 are *both* arbitrary, and that c_n is given (for $n \geq 2$) by the recurrence relation in (4). Thus the *smaller* exponent r_2 yields the general solution $y(x) = c_0 y_1(x) + c_1 y_2(x)$ in terms of the two linearly independent Frobenius series solutions $y_1(x)$ and $y_2(x)$.

27. Exponents $r_1 = 0$ and $r_2 = -1$; with $r = -1$: $c_n = -\frac{9c_{n-2}}{n(n-1)}$

$$y(x) = \frac{c_0}{x}\left(1 - \frac{9x^2}{2} + \frac{27x^4}{8} - \frac{81x^6}{80} + \cdots\right) + \frac{c_1}{x}\left(x - \frac{3x^3}{2} + \frac{27x^5}{40} - \frac{81x^7}{560} + \cdots\right)$$

$$= \frac{c_0}{x}\left(1 - \frac{9x^2}{2} + \frac{81x^4}{24} - \frac{729x^6}{720} + \cdots\right) + \frac{c_1}{3x}\left(3x - \frac{27x^3}{6} + \frac{243x^5}{120} - \frac{2187x^7}{5040} + \cdots\right)$$

$$y(x) = c_0\frac{\cos 3x}{x} + \frac{1}{3}c_1\frac{\sin 3x}{x}$$

29. Exponents $r_1 = 0$ and $r_2 = -1$; with $r = -1$: $c_n = -\frac{c_{n-2}}{4n(n-1)}$

$$y(x) = \frac{c_0}{x}\left(1 - \frac{x^2}{8} + \frac{x^4}{384} - \frac{x^6}{46080} + \cdots\right) + \frac{c_1}{x}\left(x - \frac{x^3}{24} + \frac{x^5}{1920} - \frac{x^7}{322560} + \cdots\right)$$

$$= \frac{c_0}{x}\left(1-\frac{x^2}{2^2\cdot 2}+\frac{x^4}{2^4\cdot 24}-\frac{x^6}{2^6\cdot 720}+\cdots\right)+\frac{2c_1}{x}\left(\frac{x}{2}-\frac{x^3}{2^3\cdot 6}+\frac{x^5}{2^5\cdot 120}-\frac{x^7}{2^7\cdot 5040}+\cdots\right)$$

$$y(x) = \frac{c_0}{x}\cos\frac{x}{2}+\frac{2c_1}{x}\sin\frac{x}{2}$$

31. The given differential equation $4x^2y''-4xy'+(3-4x^2)y=0$ has indicial equation $4r^2-8r+3 = (2r-3)(2r-1) = 0$, so its exponents are $r_1 = 3/2$ and $r_2 = 1/2$. With $r = 3/2$, the recurrence relation $c_n = c_{n-2}/n(n-1)$ yields the general solution

$$y(x) = c_0 x^{1/2}\left(1+\frac{x^2}{2}+\frac{x^4}{24}+\frac{x^6}{720}+\cdots\right)+c_1 x^{1/2}\left(x+\frac{x^3}{6}+\frac{x^5}{120}+\frac{x^7}{5040}+\cdots\right)$$

$$y(x) = c_0\sqrt{x}\cosh x+c_1\sqrt{x}\sinh x.$$

33. Exponents $r_1 = 1/2$ and $r_2 = -1$. With each exponent we find that c_0 is arbitrary and we can solve recursively for c_n in terms of c_{n-1}.

$$y_1(x) = \sqrt{x}\left(1+\frac{11x}{20}-\frac{11x^2}{224}+\frac{671x^3}{24192}-\frac{9577x^4}{387072}+\cdots\right)$$

$$y_2(x) = \frac{1}{x}\left(1+10x+5x^2+\frac{10x^3}{9}-\frac{7x^4}{18}+\cdots\right)$$

35. Substitution of $y=x^r\sum c_n x^n$ into the differential equation yields a result of the form

$$-rc_0 x^{r-1}+(\cdots)x^r+(\cdots)x^{r+1}+\cdots = 0,$$

so we see immediately that $c_0 \neq 0$ implies that $r = 0$. Then substitution of the power series $y=\sum c_n x^n$ yields

$$(c_0-c_1)+(4c_1-2c_2)x+(9c_2-3c_3)x^2+(16c_3-4c_4)x^4+\cdots = 0$$

Evidently $c_n = nc_{n-1}$, so if $c_0 = 1$ it follows that $c_n = n!$ for $n \geq 1$. But the series $\sum n!x^n$ has zero radius of convergence, and hence converges only if $x = 0$. We therefore conclude that the given differential equation has *no* nontrivial Frobenius series solution.

37. Substitution of $y=x^r\sum c_n x^n$ into the differential equation $x^3y''-y'+y=0$ yields a result of the form

$$(r-1)^2 c_0 x^r+(\cdots)x^{r+1}+(\cdots)x^{r+2}+\cdots = 0,$$

so it follows that $r = 1$. But then substitution of $y = x \sum c_n x^n$ into the differential equation yields

$$c_1 x^2 + 4c_2 x^3 + 9c_3 x^4 + 16c_4 x^5 + 25c_5 x^6 + \cdots = 0,$$

so it follows that $c_1 = c_2 = c_3 = c_4 = \cdots = 0$. Hence $y(x) = c_0 x$,

39. Exponents $r_1 = 1$ and $r_2 = -1$; with $r = +1$: $c_1 = 0$, $c_n = -\dfrac{c_{n-2}}{n(n+2)}$

$$y(x) = c_0 x \left(1 - \frac{x^2}{8} + \frac{x^4}{192} - \frac{x^6}{9216} + \frac{x^8}{737280} - \cdots \right)$$

$$= c_0 x \left(1 - \frac{x^2}{2^2 1!2!} + \frac{x^4}{2^4 2!3!} - \frac{x^6}{2^6 3!4!} + \frac{x^8}{2^8 4!5!} - \cdots \right)$$

If $c_0 = 1/2$, then

$$y(x) = J_1(x) = \frac{x}{2} \sum_{n=0}^{\infty} \frac{(-1)^n}{n!(n+1)} \left(\frac{x}{2} \right)^{2n}.$$

Now, consider the smaller exponent $r_2 = -1$. A Frobenius series with $r = -1$ is of the form $y = x^{-1} \sum_{n=0}^{\infty} c_n x^n$ with $c_0 \neq 0$. However, substitution of this series into Bessel's equation of order 1 gives

$$-c_1 + c_0 x + (c_1 + 3c_3)x^2 + (c_2 + 8c_4)x^3 + (c_3 + 15c_5)x^5 + \cdots = 0,$$

so it follows that $c_0 = 0$, after all. Thus Bessel's equation of order 1 does not have a Frobenius series solution with leading term $c_0 x^{-1}$. However, there is a little more here that meets the eye. We see further that c_2 is arbitrary and that $c_1 = 0$ and $c_n = c_{n-2}/n(n-2)$ for $n > 2$. It follows that our assumed Frobenius series

$y = x^{-1} \sum_{n=0}^{\infty} c_n x^n$ actually reduces to

$$y(x) = c_2 x \left(1 - \frac{x^2}{8} + \frac{x^4}{192} - \frac{x^6}{9216} + \frac{x^8}{737280} - \cdots \right).$$

But this is the same as our series solution obtained above using the larger exponent $r = +1$ (calling the arbitrary constant c_2 rather than c_0).

SECTION 8.4

METHOD OF FROBENIUS — THE EXCEPTIONAL CASES

Each of the differential equations in Problems 1-6 is of (or can be written in) the form

$$xy'' + (A + Bx)y' + Cy = 0.$$

The origin is a regular singular point with exponents $r = 0$ and $r = 1 - A$, so if A is an integer then we have an exceptional case of the method of Frobenius. When we substitute $y = \Sigma c_n x^{n+r}$ in the differential equation we find that the coefficient of x^{n+r} is

$$[(n + r)^2 + (A - 1)(n + r)]c_n + [B(n + r) + C - B]c_{n-1} = 0. \qquad (*)$$

Case 1:   In each of Problems 1-4 we have $A \geq 2$ and $B = C$, so the larger exponent $r_1 = 0$ and the smaller exponent $r_2 = 1 - A = -N$ differ by a positive integer. When we substitute the smaller exponent $r = -N$ in Equation (*) above, it simplifies to

$$n(n - N)c_n + B(n - N)c_{n-1} = 0. \qquad (1)$$

This equation determines $c_1, c_2, \cdots, c_{N-1}$ in terms of c_0, thereby yielding the solution

$$y_1(x) = x^{-N}(c_0 + c_1 x + \cdots + c_{N-1}x^{n-1}),$$
(2)

provided it is possible to choose $c_N = 0$. But when $n = N$, Equation (1) reduces to

$$0 \cdot c_N + 0 \cdot c_{N-1} = 0,$$

so c_N may be chosen arbitrarily. With $C_N = 0$ we get the terminating Frobenius series solution in (2). For $n > N$, Equation (1) yields the recurrence formula $c_n = -Bc_{n-1}/n$, which if $C_N \neq 0$ gives a second (non-terminating) Frobenius series solution of the form

$$y_2(x) = c_N + c_{N+1}x + c_{N+2}x^2 + \cdots. \qquad (3)$$

Case 2:   If $A \leq 0$ then the larger exponent $r_1 = 1 - A = N$ and the smaller exponent $r_2 = 0$ again differ by a positive integer. In Problems 5 and 6 we have this case with $B = -1$. When we substitute the smaller exponent $r = 0$ in Equation (*), it simplifies to

$$n(n - N)c_n - (n - C - 1)c_{n-1} = 0. \qquad (4)$$

This equation determines $c_1, c_2, \cdots, c_{N-1}$ in terms of c_0. When $n = N$ it reduces to

$$0 \cdot c_N - (N - C - 1)c_{N-1} = 0. \qquad (5)$$

If either $N - C - 1 = 0$ or $c_{N-1} = 0$ (the latter happens in Problem 5) then c_N can be chosen arbitrarily, and finally $c_{N+1}, c_{N+2}, \cdots$ are determined in terms of c_N. Thus we get *two* Frobenius series solutions

$$y_1 = c_0 + c_1 x + \cdots + c_{N-1} x^{N-1}, \qquad \text{(terminating)}$$

$$y_2 = c_N x^N + c_{N+1} x^{N+1} + \cdots . \qquad \text{(not terminating)}$$

On the other hand, if (as in Problem 6) neither $N - C - 1 = 0$ nor $c_{N-1} = 0$, then c_N cannot be chosen so as to satisfy Equation (5), and hence there is no Frobenius series solution corresponding to the smaller exponent $r_2 = 0$. We therefore find the *single* Frobenius series solution by substituting the larger exponent $r_1 = N$ in Equation (*) and using the resulting recurrence relation to determine $c_1, c_2, c_3, \cdots$ in terms of c_0.

Problems 1-4 correspond to case 1 above. We give first the indicial roots and the critical index N, then the recurrence relation that defines c_n in terms of c_{n-1}, for both the N-term solution $y_1(x)$ in (2) and the non-terminating series solution $y_2(x)$ in (3).

1. $r_1 = 0, \ r_2 = -2, \ N = 2, \ c_n = \dfrac{c_{n-1}}{n};$ $\qquad y_1(x) = x^{-2}(1+x);$

$$y_2(x) = 1 + \frac{x}{3} + \frac{x^2}{3 \cdot 4} + \frac{x^3}{3 \cdot 4 \cdot 5} + \cdots = 1 + 2 \sum_{n=1}^{\infty} \frac{x^n}{(n+2)!}$$

3. $r_1 = 0, \ r_2 = -4, \ N = 4, \ c_n = -\dfrac{3c_{n-1}}{n};$ $\qquad y_1(x) = x^{-4}\left(1 - 3x + \frac{9}{2}x^2 - \frac{9}{2}x^3\right)$

$$y_2(x) = 1 - \frac{3x}{5} + \frac{3^2 x^2}{5 \cdot 6} - \frac{3^3 x^3}{5 \cdot 6 \cdot 7} + \cdots = 1 + 24 \sum_{n=1}^{\infty} \frac{(-1)^n 3^n x^n}{(n+4)!}$$

Problems 5 and 6 correspond to case 2 described above.

5. $r_1 = 5, \ r_2 = 0, \ N = 5, \ c_n = \dfrac{(n-4)c_{n-1}}{n(n-5)}$ for $n \neq 5$

$$y_1(x) = 1 + \frac{3}{4}x + \frac{1}{4}x^2 + \frac{1}{24}x^3$$

With $n = 5$ the recurrence relation is $0 \cdot c_5 - c_4 = 0$. Because $c_4 = 0$ we can choose $c_5 = 1$ arbitrarily and proceed:

$$y_2(x) = x^5 + \frac{2x^6}{6} + \frac{3x^7}{6 \cdot 7} + \frac{4x^8}{6 \cdot 7 \cdot 8} + \cdots = x^5\left[1 + 120 \sum_{n=1}^{\infty} \frac{(n+1)x^n}{(n+5)!}\right]$$

7. The indicial exponents are $r = -2, 1$. Substitution of $y = x^{-2}\sum_{n=0}^{\infty} c_n x^n$ in the differential equation leads to the recurrence relation

$$n(n-3)c_n + 3(n-3)c_{n-1} = 0$$

that reduces to $0 \cdot c_3 + 0 \cdot c_2 = 0$ when $n = 3$ so — having found c_1 and c_2 — c_3 can be chosen arbitrarily. With $c_0 = 2$ and $c_3 = 0$ we get the terminating Frobenius series

$$y_1(x) = x^{-2}(2 - 6x + 9x^2).$$

Starting afresh with $c_3 = 3/3! = 1/2$, the recurrence relation $c_n = -3c_{n-1}/n$ for $n > 3$ yields the second Frobenius series solution

$$y_2(x) = x^{-2}\left(\frac{3x^3}{3!} - \frac{3^2 x^4}{4!} + \frac{3^3 x^5}{5!} - \cdots\right) = \sum_{n=1}^{\infty} \frac{(-1)^{n-1} 3^n x^n}{(n+2)!}.$$

In Problems 11-15, we give first the Frobenius series solution $y_1(x)$ corresponding to the larger indicial exponent r_1 of the given differential equation. Then, writing the equation in the form $y'' + P(x)y' + Q(x)y = 0$, we apply the reduction of order formula

$$y_2(x) = \int \frac{\exp\left(-\int P(x)\,dx\right)}{y_1(x)^2}\,dx$$

to derive a second independent solution $y_2(x)$.

9. $r_1 = r_2 = 0$

$$y_1 = 1 + \frac{x^2}{4} + \frac{x^4}{64} + \frac{x^6}{2304} + \frac{x^8}{147456} + \cdots$$

$$P(x) = 1/x; \qquad \exp\left(-\int P(x)\,dx\right) = 1/x$$

$$y_2 = y_1 \int x^{-1} \cdot \left(1 + \frac{x^2}{4} + \frac{x^4}{64} + \frac{x^6}{2304} + \frac{x^8}{147456} + \cdots\right)^{-2} dx$$

$$= y_1 \int x^{-1}\left(1 + \frac{x^2}{2} + \frac{3x^4}{32} + \frac{5x^6}{576} + \frac{35x^8}{73728} + \cdots\right)^{-1} dx$$

$$= y_1 \int x^{-1}\left(1 - \frac{x^2}{2} + \frac{5x^4}{32} - \frac{23x^6}{576} + \frac{677x^8}{73728} + \cdots\right) dx$$

$$y_2 = y_1\left(\ln x - \frac{x^2}{4} + \frac{5x^4}{128} - \frac{23x^6}{3456} + \frac{677x^6}{589824} - \cdots\right)$$

11. $r_1 = r_2 = 2$

$$y_1 = x^2\left(1 - 2x + \frac{3x^2}{2} - \frac{2x^3}{3} + \frac{5x^4}{24} - \cdots\right)$$

$$P(x) = 1 - 3/x; \qquad \exp\left(-\int P(x)\,dx\right) = x^3 e^{-x}$$

$$y_2 = y_1 \int x^3 e^{-x} \cdot x^{-4}\left(1 - 2x + \frac{3x^2}{2} - \frac{2x^3}{3} + \frac{5x^4}{24} - \cdots\right)^{-2} dx$$

$$= y_1 \int x^{-1} e^{-x}\left(1 - 4x + 7x^2 - \frac{22x^3}{3} + \frac{16x^4}{3} - \cdots\right)^{-1} dx$$

$$= y_1 \int x^{-1}\left(1 - x + \frac{x^2}{2} - \frac{x^3}{6} + \frac{x^4}{24} - \cdots\right)\left(1 + 4x + 9x^2 + \frac{46x^3}{3} + \frac{67x^4}{3} + \cdots\right) dx$$

$$= y_1 \int x^{-1}\left(1 + 3x + \frac{11x^2}{2} + \frac{49x^3}{6} + \frac{87x^4}{8} + \cdots\right) dx$$

$$y_2 = y_1\left(\ln x + 3x + \frac{11x^2}{4} + \frac{49x^3}{18} + \frac{87x^4}{32} + \cdots\right)$$

13. $r_1 = 3, \quad r_2 = 1$

$$y_1 = x^3\left(1 - 2x + 2x^2 - \frac{4x^3}{3} + \frac{2x^4}{3} - \cdots\right)$$

$$P(x) = 2 - 3/x; \qquad \exp\left(-\int P(x)\,dx\right) = x^3 e^{-2x}$$

$$y_2 = y_1 \int x^3 e^{-2x} \cdot x^{-6}\left(1 - 2x + 2x^2 - \frac{4x^3}{3} + \frac{2x^4}{3} - \cdots\right)^{-2} dx$$

$$= y_1 \int x^{-3} e^{-2x}\left(1 - 4x + 8x^2 - \frac{32x^3}{3} + \frac{32x^4}{3} - \cdots\right)^{-1} dx$$

$$= y_1 \int x^{-3}\left(1 - 2x + 2x^2 - \frac{4x^3}{3} + \frac{2x^4}{3} - \cdots\right)\left(1 + 4x + 8x^2 + \frac{32x^3}{3} + \frac{32x^4}{3} + \cdots\right) dx$$

$$= y_1 \int x^{-3}\left(1 + 2x + 2x^2 + \frac{4x^3}{3} + \frac{2x^4}{3} + \cdots\right) dx$$

$$y_2 = y_1\left(2\ln x - \frac{1}{2x^2} - \frac{2}{x} + \frac{4x}{3} + \frac{x^2}{3} + \cdots\right)$$

15. $r_1 = r_2 = 0$

$$J_0(x) = 1 - \frac{x^2}{4} + \frac{x^4}{64} - \frac{x^6}{2304} + \frac{x^8}{147456} - \cdots$$

$$P(x) = 1/x; \qquad \exp\left(-\int P(x)\,dx\right) = 1/x$$

$$y_2(x) = J_0(x) \int x^{-1} \cdot \left(1 - \frac{x^2}{4} + \frac{x^4}{64} - \frac{x^6}{2304} + \frac{x^8}{147456} - \cdots\right)^{-2} dx$$

$$= J_0(x) \int x^{-1}\left(1 - \frac{x^2}{2} + \frac{3x^4}{32} - \frac{5x^6}{576} + \frac{35x^8}{73728} - \cdots\right)^{-1} dx$$

$$= J_0(x) \int x^{-1}\left(1 + \frac{x^2}{2} + \frac{5x^4}{32} + \frac{23x^6}{576} + \frac{677x^8}{73728} + \cdots\right) dx$$

$$= J_0(x)\left(\ln x + \frac{x^2}{4} + \frac{5x^4}{128} + \frac{23x^6}{3456} + \frac{677x^6}{589824} - \cdots\right)$$

$$= J_0(x)\ln x +$$

$$\left(1 - \frac{x^2}{4} + \frac{x^4}{64} - \frac{x^6}{2304} + \frac{x^8}{147456} - \cdots\right)\left(\frac{x^2}{4} + \frac{5x^4}{128} + \frac{23x^6}{3456} + \frac{677x^6}{589824} - \cdots\right)$$

$$y_2(x) = J_0(x)\ln x + \frac{x^2}{4} - \frac{3x^4}{128} + \frac{11x^6}{13284} - \cdots$$

17. The given first solution

$$y_1(x) = xe^x = x\left(1 + x + \frac{x^2}{2} + \frac{x^3}{6} + \frac{x^4}{24} + \frac{x^5}{120} + \cdots\right)$$

can be derived by starting with the single exponent $r = 1$, substituting $y = x\sum_{n=0}^{\infty} c_n x^n$ into the differential equation, and calculating successive coefficient recursively as usual. We can verify the alleged second solution by applying the method of reduction of order as in Problems 9-14:

$$P(x) = -1 - 1/x; \qquad \exp\left(-\int P(x)\,dx\right) = xe^x$$

$$y_2 = y_1 \int xe^x \cdot \left(xe^x\right)^{-2} dx = y_1 \int x^{-1} e^{-x}\, dx$$

$$= y_1 \int x^{-1}\left(1 - x + \frac{x^2}{2} - \frac{x^3}{6} + \frac{x^4}{24} - \frac{x^5}{120} + \cdots\right) dx$$

$$= y_1\left(\ln x - x + \frac{x^2}{4} - \frac{x^3}{18} + \frac{x^4}{96} - \frac{x^5}{600} + \cdots\right)$$

$$= y_1 \ln x + \left(1 - x + \frac{x^2}{2} - \frac{x^3}{6} + \frac{x^4}{24} - \frac{x^5}{120} + \cdots\right)\left(-x + \frac{x^2}{4} - \frac{x^3}{18} + \frac{x^4}{96} - \frac{x^5}{600} + \cdots\right)$$

$$= y_1 \ln x - \left(x^2 + \frac{3x^3}{4} + \frac{11x^4}{36} + \frac{25x^5}{288} + \frac{137x^6}{7200} + \cdots\right)$$

$$y_2(x) = xe^x \ln x - \sum_{n=1}^{\infty} \frac{H_n x^{n+1}}{n!}$$

SECTION 8.5

BESSEL'S EQUATION

Of course Bessel's equation is the most important special ordinary differential equation in mathematics, and every student should be exposed at least to Bessel functions of the first kind. Though Bessel functions of integral order can be treated without the gamma function, the subsection on the gamma function is also needed for Chapter 7 on Laplace transforms. The final subsections on Bessel function identities and the parametric Bessel equation will not be needed until Section 10.4, and therefore may be considered optional at this point in the course.

1. $$J_0'(x) = D_x\left(1 + \sum_{m=1}^{\infty} \frac{(-1)^m x^{2m}}{2^{2m}(m!)^2}\right) = \sum_{m=1}^{\infty} \frac{(-1)^m 2m \, x^{2m-1}}{2^{2m}(m!)^2}$$

$$= \sum_{m=1}^{\infty} \frac{(-1)^m x^{2m-1}}{2^{2m-1}(m-1)!(m!)} = \sum_{m=0}^{\infty} \frac{(-1)^{m+1} x^{2m+1}}{2^{2m+1}(m)!(m+1)!}$$

$$= -\sum_{m=0}^{\infty} \frac{(-1)^m x^{2m+1}}{2^{2m+1}(m)!(m+1)!} = -J_1(x)$$

3.   **(a)** $$\Gamma\left(m + \frac{2}{3}\right) = \Gamma\left(\frac{3m+2}{3}\right) = \frac{3m-1}{3} \cdot \frac{3m-4}{3} \cdot \Gamma\left(\frac{3m-4}{3}\right)$$

$$= \frac{3m-1}{3} \cdot \frac{3m-4}{3} \cdots \cdots \frac{5}{3} \cdot \frac{2}{3} \cdot \Gamma\left(\frac{2}{3}\right) = \frac{2 \cdot 5 \cdot 8 \cdots (3m-1)}{3^m} \Gamma\left(\frac{2}{3}\right)$$

(b) $$J_{-1/3}(x) = \sum_{m=0}^{\infty} \frac{(-1)^m}{m! \Gamma(m+2/3)}\left(\frac{x}{2}\right)^{2m-1/3} = \frac{(x/2)^{-1/3}}{\Gamma(2/3)} \sum_{m=0}^{\infty} \frac{(-1)^m 3^m x^{2m}}{m! \cdot 2 \cdot 3 \cdot 8 \cdots (3m-1)}$$

5.   Starting with $p = 3$ in Equation (26) we get

$$J_4(x) = \frac{6}{x} J_3(x) - J_2(x) = \frac{6}{x}\left[\frac{4}{x} J_2(x) - J_1(x)\right] - J_2(x)$$

$$= \left(\frac{24}{x^2} - 1\right)\left[\frac{2}{x}J_1(x) - J_0(x)\right] - \frac{6}{x}J_1(x)$$

$$= \frac{x^2 - 24}{x^2}J_0(x) + \frac{8(6 - x^2)}{x^3}J_1(x)$$

11. $\Gamma(p + m + 1) = (p + m)(p + m - 1)\cdots(p + 2)(p + 1)\Gamma(p + 1)$, so

$$J_p(x) = \sum_{m=0}^{\infty}\frac{(-1)^m}{m!\,\Gamma(p+m+1)}\left(\frac{x}{2}\right)^{2m+p}$$

$$= \frac{(x/2)^p}{\Gamma(p+1)}\sum_{m=0}^{\infty}\frac{(-1)^m}{m!(p+1)(p+2)\cdots(p+m)}\left(\frac{x}{2}\right)^{2m}.$$

In Problems 13-21 we use a conspicuous dot • to indicate our choice of u and dv in the integration by parts formula $\int u\cdot dv = uv - \int v\,du$. We use repeatedly the facts (from Example 1) that $\int xJ_0(x)\,dx = xJ_1(x) + C$ and $\int J_1(x)\,dx = -J_0(x) + C$.

13. $\displaystyle\int x^2 J_0(x)\,dx = \int x\cdot xJ_0(x)\,dx$

$$= x^2 J_1(x) - \int x\cdot J_1(x)\,dx$$

$$= x^2 J_1(x) - \left(-xJ_0(x) + \int J_0(x)\,dx\right)$$

$$= x^2 J_1(x) + xJ_0(x) - \int J_0(x)\,dx + C$$

15. $\displaystyle\int x^4 J_0(x)\,dx = \int x^3\cdot xJ_0(x)\,dx$

$$= x^4 J_1(x) - 3\int x^3\cdot J_1(x)\,dx$$

$$= x^4 J_1(x) - 3\left(-x^3 J_0(x) + 3\int x\cdot xJ_0(x)\,dx\right)$$

$$= x^4 J_1(x) + 3x^3 J_0(x) - 9\left(x^2 J_1(x) - \int x\cdot J_1(x)\,dx\right)$$

$$= x^4 J_1(x) + 3x^3 J_0(x) - 9x^2 J_1(x) + 9\left(-xJ_0(x) + \int J_0(x)\,dx\right)$$

$$= (x^4 - 9x^2)J_1(x) + (3x^3 - 9x)J_0(x) + 9\int J_0(x)\,dx + C$$

17. $\displaystyle\int x^2 J_1(x)\,dx = \int x^2\cdot J_1(x)\,dx$

$$= -x^2 J_0(x) + 2\int xJ_0(x)\,dx = -x^2 J_0(x) + 2xJ_1(x) + C$$

19. $\displaystyle\int x^4 J_1(x)\,dx = \int x^4\cdot J_1(x)$

$$= -x^4 J_0(x) + 4\int x^2\cdot xJ_0(x)\,dx$$

$$= -x^4 J_0(x) + 4\left(x^3 J_1(x) - 2\int x^2 \cdot J_1(x)\, dx\right)$$
$$= -x^4 J_0(x) + 4x^3 J_1(x) - 8\left(-x^2 J_0(x) + 2\int x J_0(x)\, dx\right)$$
$$= (-x^4 + 8x^2)J_0(x) + (4x^3 - 16x)J_1(x) + C$$

21. With $p = 2$, Eq. (23) in the text gives $\int x^{-2} J_3(x)\, dx = -x^{-2} J_2(x) + C$. Hence

$$\int J_3(x)\, dx = \int x^2 \cdot x^{-2} J_3(x)\, dx$$
$$= x^2 \left(-x^{-2} J_2(x)\right) + 2\int x^{-1} J_2(x)\, dx$$
$$= -J_2(x) - \frac{2}{x} J_1(x) + C \qquad \text{(by Example 3)}$$
$$= -\left(\frac{2}{x} J_1(x) - J_0(x)\right) - \frac{2}{x} J_1(x) + C \qquad \text{(By Eq. (26) with } p = 1)$$
$$= J_0(x) - \frac{4}{x} J_1(x) + C.$$

23. This is a special case of the discussion below in Problem 24.

24. Given an integer $n \geq 1$, let us define

$$g_n(x) = \int_0^\pi \cos(n\theta - x\sin\theta)\, d\theta.$$

Differentiation yields

$$g_n'(x) = \int_0^\pi \sin(n\theta - x\sin\theta)\sin\theta\, d\theta.$$

Integration by parts with $u = \sin(n\theta - x\sin\theta)$ and $dv = \sin\theta\, d\theta$ yields

$$g_n'(x) = n\int_0^\pi \cos\theta\, \cos(n\theta - x\sin\theta)\, d\theta - x\int_0^\pi \cos^2\theta\, \cos(n\theta - x\sin\theta)\, d\theta.$$

But differentiation of the first equation for $g_n'(x)$ yields

$$g_n''(x) = -\int_0^\pi \sin^2\theta\, \cos(n\theta - x\sin\theta)\, d\theta.$$

It follows that

$$g_n''(x) + \frac{1}{x} g_n'(x) = -g_n(x) + \frac{n}{x}\int_0^\pi \cos\theta\, \cos(n\theta - x\sin\theta)\, d\theta$$
$$= -g_n(x) - \frac{n}{x^2}\int_0^\pi \left[(n - x\cos\theta) - n\right]\cos(n\theta - x\sin\theta)\, d\theta$$
$$= -g_n(x) - \frac{n}{x^2}\left[\sin(n\theta - x\sin\theta)\right]_0^\pi + \frac{n^2}{x^2} g_n(x) = -\left(1 - \frac{n^2}{x^2}\right)g_n(x).$$

Upon equating the first and last members of this continued inequality and multiplying by x^2, we see that $y = g_n(x)$ satisfies Bessel's equation of order $n \geq 1$. The initial values of $g_n(x)$ are

$$g_n(0) = \int_0^\pi \cos(n\theta)\, d\theta = 0 \quad \text{and} \quad g_n'(0) = \int_0^\pi \sin(\theta)\sin(n\theta)\, d\theta = 0.$$

If $n = 1$ then $g_1'(0) = \pi/2$, whereas $g_n'(0) = 0$ if $n \geq 1$. In either case the values of $g_n(0)$ and $g_n'(0)$ are π times those of $J_n(0)$ and $J_n'(0)$, respectively. Now we know from the general solution of Bessel's equation that $g_n(x) = c\, J_n(x)$ for some constant c. If $n = 1$ than the fact that

$$\pi/2 = g_n'(0) = c\, J_1'(0) = c/2$$

implies that $c = \pi$, as desired. But if $n > 1$ the fact that

$$0 = g_n'(0) = c\, J_n'(0) = c \cdot 0$$

does not suffice to determine c.

SECTION 8.6

APPLICATIONS OF BESSEL FUNCTIONS

Problems 1-12 are routine applications of the theorem in this section. In each case it is necessary only to identify the coefficients A, B, C and the exponent q in the differential equation

$$x^2 y'' + Axy' + (B + Cx^q)y = 0. \tag{1}$$

Then we can calculate the values

$$\alpha = \frac{1-A}{2}, \quad \beta = \frac{q}{2}, \quad k = \frac{2\sqrt{C}}{q}, \quad p = \frac{\sqrt{(1-A)^2 - 4B}}{q} \tag{2}$$

and finally write the general solution

$$y(x) = x^\alpha \left[c_1 J_p(kx^\beta) + c_2 J_{-p}(kx^\beta) \right] \tag{3}$$

specified in Theorem 1 of this section. This is a "template procedure" that we illustrate only in a couple of problems.

1.   We have $A = -1, B = 1, C = 1, q = 2$ so

$$\alpha = \frac{1-(-1)}{2} = 1, \quad \beta = \frac{2}{2} = 1, \quad k = \frac{2\sqrt{1}}{2} = 1, \quad p = \frac{\sqrt{(1-(-1))^2 - 4(1)}}{2} = 0,$$

so our general solution is $y(x) = x[c_1 J_0(x) + c_2 Y_0(x)]$, using $Y_0(x)$ because $p = 0$ is an integer.

3. $y(x) = x[c_1 J_{1/2}(3x^2) + c_2 J_{-1/2}(3x^2)]$

5. To match the given equation with Eq. (1) above, we first divide through by the leading coefficient 16 to obtain the equation

$$x^2 y'' + \frac{5}{3} xy' + \left(-\frac{5}{36} + \frac{1}{4} x^3\right) y = 0$$

with $A = 5/3, B = -5/36, C = 1/4$, and $q = 3$. Then

$$\alpha = \frac{1 - 5/3}{3} = -\frac{1}{3}, \quad \beta = \frac{3}{2}, \quad k = \frac{2\sqrt{1/4}}{3} = \frac{1}{3}, \quad p = \frac{\sqrt{(1 - 5/3)^2 - 4(-5/36)}}{3} = \frac{1}{3},$$

so our general solution is $y(x) = x^{-1/3}[c_1 J_{1/3}(x^{3/2}/3) + c_2 J_{-1/3}(x^{3/2}/3)]$.

7. $y(x) = x^{-1}[c_1 J_0(x) + c_2 Y_0(x)]$

9. $y(x) = x^{1/2}[c_1 J_{1/2}(2x^{3/2}) + c_2 J_{-1/2}(2x^{3/2})]$

11. $y(x) = x^{1/2}[c_1 J_{1/6}(x^3/3) + c_2 J_{-1/6}(x^3/3)]$

13. We want to solve the equation $xy'' + 2y' + xy = 0$. If we rewrite it as

$$x^2 y'' + 2xy' + x^2 y = 0$$

then we have the form in Equation (1) with $A = 2, B = 0, C = 1$, and $q = 2$. Then Equation (2) gives $\alpha = -1/2, \beta = 1, k = 1$, and $p = 1/2$, so by Equation (3) the general solution is

$$y(x) = x^{-1/2}\left[c_1 J_{1/2}(x) + c_1 J_{-1/2}(x)\right]$$
$$= x^{-1/2}\left[c_1 \sqrt{\frac{2}{\pi x}} \cos x + c_2 \sqrt{\frac{2}{\pi x}} \sin x\right] = \frac{1}{x}(a_1 \cos x + a_2 \sin x),$$

(with $a_i = c_i \sqrt{2/\pi}$) using Equations (19) in Section 3.5.

15. The substitution

$$y = -\frac{u'}{u}, \quad y' = \frac{(u')^2}{u^2} - \frac{u''}{u}$$

immediately transforms $y' = x^2 + y^2$ to $u'' + x^2 u = 0$. The equivalent equation

$$x^2 u'' + x^4 u = 0$$

is of the form in (1) with $A = B = 0$, $C = 1$, and $q = 4$. Equations (2) give $\alpha = 1/2$, $\beta = 2$, $k = 1/2$, and $p = 1/4$, so the general solution is

$$u(x) = x^{1/2}[c_1 J_{1/4}(x^2/2) + c_2 J_{-1/4}(x^2/2)].$$

To compute $u'(x)$, let $z = x^2/2$ so $x = 2^{1/2} z^{1/2}$. Then Equation (22) in Section 8.5 with $p = 1/4$ yields

$$\frac{d}{dx}\left(x^{1/2} J_{1/4}(x^2/2)\right) = \frac{d}{dz}\left(2^{1/4} z^{1/4} J_{1/4}(z)\right) \cdot \frac{dz}{dx}$$

$$= 2^{1/4} z^{1/4} J_{-3/4}(z) \cdot \frac{dz}{dx}$$

$$= 2^{1/4} \cdot \frac{x^{1/2}}{2^{1/4}} J_{-3/4}(x^2/2) \cdot x = x^{3/2} J_{-3/4}(x^2/2).$$

Similarly, Equation (23) in Section 8.5 with $p = -1/4$ yields

$$\frac{d}{dx}\left(x^{1/2} J_{-1/4}(x^2/2)\right) = \frac{d}{dz}\left(2^{1/4} z^{1/4} J_{-1/4}(z)\right) \cdot \frac{dz}{dx} = -x^{3/2} J_{3/4}(x^2/2).$$

Therefore

$$u'(x) = x^{3/2}[c_1 J_{-3/4}(x^2/2) - c_2 J_{3/4}(x^2/2)].$$

It follows finally that the general solution of the Riccati equation $y' = x^2 + y^2$ is

$$y(x) = -\frac{u'}{u} = x \cdot \frac{J_{3/4}(\tfrac{1}{2}x^2) - c J_{-3/4}(\tfrac{1}{2}x^2)}{c J_{1/4}(\tfrac{1}{2}x^2) + J_{-1/4}(\tfrac{1}{2}x^2)}$$

where the arbitrary constant is $c = c_1/c_2$.

17. If we write the equation $x^4 y'' + \gamma^2 y = 0$ in the form

$$x^2 y'' + \gamma^2 x^{-2} y = 0,$$

then we see that it is of the form in Equation (3) of this section with $A = B = 0$, $C = \gamma^2$, and $q = -2$. Then Equations (5) give $\alpha = 1/2$, $\beta = -1$, $k = \gamma$, and $p = -1/2$, so the theorem yields the general solution

$$y(x) = x^{1/2}[c_1 J_{1/2}(\gamma/x) + c_2 J_{-1/2}(\gamma/x)] = x[A \cos(\gamma/x) + B \sin(\gamma/x)],$$

using Equations (19) in Section 8.5 for $J_{1/2}(x)$ and $J_{-1/2}(x)$. With a and b both nonzero, the initial conditions $y(a) = y(b) = 0$ yield the equations

$$A \cos(\gamma/a) + B \sin(\gamma/a) = 0$$

$$A \cos(\gamma/b) + B \sin(\gamma/b) = 0.$$

These equations have a nontrivial solution for A and B only if the coefficient determinant

$$\Delta = \sin(\gamma/b) \cos(\gamma/a) - \sin(\gamma/a) \cos(\gamma/b)$$

$$= \sin(\gamma/b - \gamma/a) = \sin(\gamma L/ab)$$

is nonzero. Hence $\gamma L/ab$ must be an integral multiple $n\pi$ of π, and then the nth buckling force is

$$P_n = \frac{EI_0 \gamma_n^2}{b^4} = \frac{EI_0}{b^4} \left(\frac{n\pi ab}{L} \right)^2 = EI_0 \left(\frac{n\pi}{L} \right)^2 \left(\frac{a}{b} \right)^2.$$

CHAPTER 9

FOURIER SERIES METHODS

SECTION 9.1

PERIODIC FUNCTIONS AND TRIGONOMETRIC SERIES

The basic trigonometric functions $\cos(t)$ and $\sin(t)$ have period $P = 2\pi$, so the sine or cosine of ωt (as in Problems 1-4) completes its first period when $\omega t = 2\pi$; hence $P = 2\pi / \omega$.

1.   Smallest period $P = 2\pi/3$

3.   Smallest period $P = 4\pi/3$

However, the basic tangent and cotangent functions have period π (instead of 2π), so $P = \pi / \omega$ in Problems 5 and 6.

5.   Smallest period $P = \pi$

The hyperbolic sine and cosine functions of Problems 7 and 8 are steadily increasing (for $t > 0$), and hence are not periodic.

7.   Not periodic

9.   Smallest period $P = \pi$

11.   With $f(t) = 1$ the integral formulas of Eqs. (16) and (17) in the text give $a_0 = 2$ and $a_n = b_n = 0$ for $n \geq 0$. Thus the Fourier series of f is the single term series $f(t) = 1$.

In Problems 12-13, 18-19, 23, and 26 the function $f(t)$ is defined by one formula on the interval $(-\pi, 0)$ and by another formula on $(0, \pi)$. The coefficient integrals must therefore be split accordingly, and the appropriate formula substituted in each integral:

$$a_0 = \frac{1}{\pi} \int_{-\pi}^{0} f(t)\,dt + \frac{1}{\pi} \int_{0}^{\pi} f(t)\,dt,$$

$$a_n = \frac{1}{\pi} \int_{-\pi}^{0} f(t) \cos nt\,dt + \frac{1}{\pi} \int_{0}^{\pi} f(t) \cos nt\,dt, \qquad (n > 0)$$

$$b_n = \frac{1}{\pi} \int_{-\pi}^{0} f(t) \sin nt\,dt + \frac{1}{\pi} \int_{0}^{\pi} f(t) \sin nt\,dt.$$

13. $a_0 = \dfrac{1}{\pi}\displaystyle\int_{-\pi}^{0}(0)\,dt + \dfrac{1}{\pi}\int_{0}^{\pi}(1)\,dt = 1$

$a_n = \dfrac{1}{\pi}\displaystyle\int_{-\pi}^{0}(0)\cos nt\,dt + \dfrac{1}{\pi}\int_{0}^{\pi}(1)\cos nt\,dt = \dfrac{\sin n\pi}{n\pi} = 0$

$b_n = \dfrac{1}{\pi}\displaystyle\int_{-\pi}^{0}(0)\sin nt\,dt + \dfrac{1}{\pi}\int_{0}^{\pi}(1)\sin nt\,dt =$

$\quad = \dfrac{1-\cos n\pi}{n\pi} = \begin{cases} 0 & \text{for } n \text{ even} \\ 2/n\pi & \text{for } n \text{ odd} \end{cases}$

$f(t) \sim \dfrac{1}{2} + \dfrac{2}{\pi}\left[\dfrac{\sin t}{1} + \dfrac{\sin 3t}{3} + \dfrac{\sin 5t}{5} + \dfrac{\sin 7t}{7} + \cdots \right]$

15. $a_0 = \dfrac{1}{\pi}\displaystyle\int_{-\pi}^{\pi} t\,dt = 0, \qquad a_n = \dfrac{1}{\pi}\displaystyle\int_{-\pi}^{\pi} t\cos nt\,dt = 0$

$b_n = \dfrac{1}{\pi}\displaystyle\int_{-\pi}^{\pi} t\sin nt\,dt = \dfrac{2\sin n\pi - 2n\pi\cos n\pi}{n^2\pi} = \begin{cases} -2/n & \text{for } n \text{ even} \\ +2/n & \text{for } n \text{ odd} \end{cases}$

$f(t) \sim 2\left[\dfrac{\sin t}{1} - \dfrac{\sin 2t}{2} + \dfrac{\sin 3t}{3} - \dfrac{\sin 4t}{4} + \cdots \right]$

17. $a_0 = \dfrac{1}{\pi}\displaystyle\int_{-\pi}^{0}(-t)\,dt + \dfrac{1}{\pi}\int_{0}^{\pi}(t)\,dt = \pi$

$a_n = \dfrac{1}{\pi}\displaystyle\int_{-\pi}^{0}(-t)\cos nt\,dt + \dfrac{1}{\pi}\int_{0}^{\pi}(t)\cos nt\,dt$

$\quad = \dfrac{2(\cos n\pi + n\pi\sin n\pi - 1)}{n^2\pi} = \begin{cases} 0 & \text{for } n \text{ even} \\ -4/n^2\pi & \text{for } n \text{ odd} \end{cases}$

$b_n = \dfrac{1}{\pi}\displaystyle\int_{-\pi}^{0}(-t)\sin nt\,dt + \dfrac{1}{\pi}\int_{0}^{\pi}(t)\sin nt\,dt = 0$

$f(t) \sim \dfrac{\pi}{2} - \dfrac{4}{\pi}\left[\dfrac{\cos t}{1} + \dfrac{\cos 3t}{9} + \dfrac{\cos 5t}{25} + \dfrac{\cos 7t}{49} + \cdots \right]$

19. $a_0 = \dfrac{1}{\pi}\displaystyle\int_{-\pi}^{0}(\pi+t)\,dt + \dfrac{1}{\pi}\int_{0}^{\pi}(0)\,dt = \dfrac{\pi}{2}$

$a_n = \dfrac{1}{\pi}\displaystyle\int_{-\pi}^{0}(\pi+t)\cos nt\,dt + \dfrac{1}{\pi}\int_{0}^{\pi}(0)\cos nt\,dt$

$\quad = \dfrac{1-\cos n\pi}{n^2\pi} = \begin{cases} 0 & \text{for } n \text{ even} \\ 2/n^2\pi & \text{for } n \text{ odd} \end{cases}$

$b_n = \dfrac{1}{\pi}\displaystyle\int_{-\pi}^{0}(\pi+t)\sin nt\,dt + \dfrac{1}{\pi}\int_{0}^{\pi}(0)\sin nt\,dt = \dfrac{\sin n\pi - n\pi}{n^2\pi} = -\dfrac{1}{n}$

$f(t) \sim \dfrac{\pi}{4} + \dfrac{2}{\pi}\left[\dfrac{\cos t}{1} + \dfrac{\cos 3t}{9} + \dfrac{\cos 5t}{25} + \dfrac{\cos 7t}{49} + \cdots \right] - \left[\dfrac{\sin t}{1} + \dfrac{\sin 2t}{2} + \dfrac{\sin 3t}{3} + \dfrac{\sin 4t}{4} + \cdots \right]$

21. $a_0 = \dfrac{1}{\pi}\displaystyle\int_{-\pi}^{\pi} t^2\, dt = \dfrac{2\pi^2}{3}$

$a_n = \dfrac{1}{\pi}\displaystyle\int_{-\pi}^{\pi} t^2 \cos nt\, dt = \dfrac{4n\pi \cos n\pi - 2(n^2\pi^2 - 2)\sin n\pi}{n^3\pi} = \begin{cases} +4/n^2 & \text{for } n \text{ even} \\ -4/n^2 & \text{for } n \text{ even} \end{cases}$

$b_n = \dfrac{1}{\pi}\displaystyle\int_{-\pi}^{\pi} t^2 \sin nt\, dt = 0$

$f(t) \sim \dfrac{\pi^2}{3} - 4\left[\dfrac{\cos t}{1} - \dfrac{\cos 2t}{4} + \dfrac{\cos 3t}{9} - \dfrac{\cos 4t}{16} + \cdots\right]$

23. $a_0 = \dfrac{1}{\pi}\displaystyle\int_{0}^{\pi} t^2\, dt = \dfrac{\pi^2}{3}$

$a_n = \dfrac{1}{\pi}\displaystyle\int_{0}^{\pi} t^2 \cos nt\, dt = \dfrac{2n\pi \cos n\pi + (n^2\pi^2 - 2)\sin n\pi}{n^3\pi} = \dfrac{2(-1)^n}{n^2}$

$b_n = \dfrac{1}{\pi}\displaystyle\int_{0}^{2\pi} t^2 \sin nt\, dt$

$\quad = \dfrac{(2 - n^2\pi^2)\cos n\pi + 2n\pi \sin n\pi - 2}{n^3\pi} = \begin{cases} -\pi/n & \text{for } n \text{ even} \\ (n^2\pi^2 - 4)/\pi n^3 & \text{for } n \text{ odd} \end{cases}$

$f(t) \sim \dfrac{\pi^2}{6} - 2\left[\dfrac{\cos t}{1} - \dfrac{\cos 2t}{4} + \dfrac{\cos 3t}{9} - \dfrac{\cos 4t}{16} + \cdots\right]$

$\quad + \pi\left[\dfrac{\sin t}{1} - \dfrac{\sin 2t}{2} + \dfrac{\sin 3t}{3} - \dfrac{\sin 4t}{4} + \cdots\right] - \dfrac{4}{\pi}\left[\dfrac{\sin t}{1} + \dfrac{\sin 3t}{27} + \dfrac{\sin 5t}{125} + \dfrac{\sin 7t}{343} + \cdots\right]$

The trigonometric identities

$$2 \cos A \cos B = \cos(A + B) + \cos(A - B)$$
$$2 \sin A \cos B = \sin(A + B) + \sin(A - B)$$
$$2 \sin A \sin B = \cos(A - B) - \cos(A + B)$$

are needed to evaluate the integrals that appear in Problems 24-26.

25. In order to evaluate the coefficient integrals in Eqs. (16) and (17) of the text we would need the trigonometric identity

$$\cos^2 2t = \dfrac{1}{2}(1 + \cos 4t)$$

which, however, tells us in advance that the coefficients in the Fourier series of $f(t) = \cos^2 2t$ are given by $a_0 = 1$, $a_4 = 1/2$, $a_n = 0$ otherwise, and $b_n = 0$ for all $n \geq 1$.

26. $a_0 = \dfrac{1}{\pi}\displaystyle\int_0^\pi (\sin t)\, dt = \dfrac{2}{\pi}$

$a_1 = \dfrac{1}{\pi}\displaystyle\int_0^\pi \sin t \cos t \, dt = 0$

$a_n = \dfrac{1}{\pi}\displaystyle\int_0^\pi (\sin t) \cos nt \, dt = \dfrac{1+\cos n\pi}{\pi(1-n^2)} = \begin{cases} -2/\pi(n^2-1) & \text{for } n \text{ even} \\ 0 & \text{for } n>1 \text{ odd} \end{cases}$

$b_1 = \dfrac{1}{\pi}\displaystyle\int_0^\pi \sin^2 t \, dt = \dfrac{1}{2}$

$b_n = \dfrac{1}{\pi}\displaystyle\int_0^\pi (\sin t) \sin nt \, dt = \dfrac{\sin n\pi}{\pi(1-n^2)} = 0 \text{ for } n>1$

$f(t) \sim \dfrac{1}{\pi} + \dfrac{1}{2}\sin t - \dfrac{2}{\pi}\left[\dfrac{\cos 2t}{1} + \dfrac{\cos 4t}{15} + \dfrac{\cos 6t}{35} + \dfrac{\cos 8t}{63} + \cdots \right]$

Note that $f(t) = \tfrac{1}{2}\left(\sin t + |\sin t|\right)$, so this answer agrees with the answer to Problem 24.

SECTION 9.2

GENERAL FOURIER SERIES AND CONVERGENCE

1. $a_0 = \dfrac{1}{3}\displaystyle\int_{-3}^0 (-2)\, dt + \dfrac{1}{3}\displaystyle\int_0^3 (2)\, dt = 0$

$a_n = \dfrac{1}{3}\displaystyle\int_{-3}^0 (-2)\cos\dfrac{n\pi t}{3}\, dt + \dfrac{1}{3}\displaystyle\int_0^3 (2)\cos\dfrac{n\pi t}{3}\, dt = 0$

$b_n = \dfrac{1}{3}\displaystyle\int_{-3}^0 (-2)\sin\dfrac{n\pi t}{3}\, dt + \dfrac{1}{3}\displaystyle\int_0^3 (2)\sin\dfrac{n\pi t}{3}\, dt = \dfrac{4(1-\cos n\pi)}{n\pi} = \dfrac{4}{n\pi}\left[1-(-1)^n\right]$

$f(t) = \dfrac{8}{\pi}\left[\sin\dfrac{\pi t}{3} + \dfrac{1}{3}\sin\dfrac{3\pi t}{3} + \dfrac{1}{5}\sin\dfrac{5\pi t}{3} + \dfrac{1}{7}\sin\dfrac{7\pi t}{3} + \cdots \right]$

$2\int_{-2n}^0 dt \quad : \quad [T]_{-2T}^0 \quad : \quad 2\pi$

3. $a_0 = \dfrac{1}{2\pi}\displaystyle\int_{-2\pi}^0 (2)\, dt + \dfrac{1}{2\pi}\displaystyle\int_0^{2\pi} (-1)\, dt = 1$

$a_n = \dfrac{1}{2\pi}\displaystyle\int_{-2\pi}^0 (2)\cos\dfrac{nt}{2}\, dt + \dfrac{1}{2\pi}\displaystyle\int_0^{2\pi} (-1)\cos\dfrac{nt}{2}\, dt = \dfrac{\sin n\pi}{n\pi} = 0$

$b_n = \dfrac{1}{2\pi}\displaystyle\int_{-2\pi}^0 (2)\sin\dfrac{nt}{2}\, dt + \dfrac{1}{2\pi}\displaystyle\int_0^{2\pi} (-1)\sin\dfrac{nt}{2}\, dt = \dfrac{3(\cos n\pi - 1)}{n\pi} = \dfrac{3}{n\pi}\left[(-1)^n - 1\right]$

$f(t) = \dfrac{1}{2} - \dfrac{6}{\pi}\left[\sin\dfrac{t}{2} + \dfrac{1}{3}\sin\dfrac{3t}{2} + \dfrac{1}{5}\sin\dfrac{5t}{2} + \dfrac{1}{7}\sin\dfrac{7t}{2} + \cdots \right]$

$\dfrac{\cos n\pi - 1}{n\pi}$

5.
$$a_0 = \frac{1}{2\pi} \int_{-2\pi}^{2\pi} t\, dt = 0, \qquad\qquad a_n = \frac{1}{2\pi} \int_{-2\pi}^{2\pi} t \cos\frac{nt}{2}\, dt = 0$$

$$b_n = \frac{1}{2\pi} \int_{-2\pi}^{2\pi} t \sin\frac{nt}{2}\, dt = \frac{4(\sin n\pi - n\pi \cos n\pi)}{n^2\pi} = \frac{4(-1)^{n+1}}{n}$$

$$f(t) = 4\left[\sin\frac{t}{2} - \frac{1}{2}\sin\frac{2t}{2} + \frac{1}{3}\sin\frac{3t}{2} - \frac{1}{4}\sin\frac{4t}{2} + \cdots \right]$$

7.
$$a_0 = \int_{-1}^{0} (-t)\, dt + \int_{0}^{1} (t)\, dt = 1$$

$$a_n = \int_{-1}^{0} (-t)\cos n\pi t\, dt + \int_{0}^{1} t \cos n\pi t\, dt = \frac{2\left[\cos n\pi + n\pi \sin n\pi - 1\right]}{n^2\pi^2} = \frac{2}{n^2\pi^2}\left[(-1)^n - 1\right]$$

$$b_n = \int_{-1}^{0} (-t)\sin n\pi t\, dt + \int_{0}^{1} t \sin n\pi t\, dt = 0$$

$$f(t) = \frac{1}{2} - \frac{4}{\pi^2}\left[\cos\pi t + \frac{1}{9}\cos 3\pi t + \frac{1}{25}\cos 5\pi t + \frac{1}{49}\cos 7\pi t + \cdots \right]$$

9.
$$a_0 = \int_{-1}^{1} t^2\, dt = \frac{2}{3}$$

$$a_n = \int_{-1}^{1} t^2 \cos n\pi t\, dt = \frac{4n\pi \cos n\pi + 2(n^2\pi^2 - 2)\sin n\pi}{n^3\pi^3} = \frac{4(-1)^n}{n^2\pi^2}$$

$$b_n = \int_{-1}^{1} t^2 \sin n\pi t\, dt = 0$$

$$f(t) = \frac{1}{3} - \frac{4}{\pi^2}\left[\cos\pi t - \frac{1}{4}\cos 2\pi t + \frac{1}{9}\cos 3\pi t - \frac{1}{16}\cos 4\pi t + \cdots \right]$$

To calculate the Fourier coefficients in Problems 11–14 we use the trigonometric identities for $\sin A \cos B$ and $\sin A \sin B$ that are listed above in Section 9.1 (prior to Problems 24-26 there).

11.
$$a_0 = \int_{-1}^{1} \cos\frac{\pi t}{2}\, dt = \frac{4}{\pi}$$

$$a_n = \int_{-1}^{1} \cos\frac{\pi t}{2}\cos n\pi t\, dt = -\frac{4\cos n\pi}{\pi(4n^2 - 1)} = \frac{4(-1)^{n+1}}{\pi(4n^2 - 1)}$$

$$b_n = \int_{-1}^{1} \cos\frac{\pi t}{2}\sin n\pi t\, dt = 0$$

$$f(t) = \frac{2}{\pi} + \frac{4}{\pi}\left[\frac{1}{3}\cos\pi t - \frac{1}{15}\cos 2\pi t + \frac{1}{35}\cos 3\pi t - \frac{1}{63}\cos 4\pi t + \cdots \right]$$

13.
$$a_0 = \int_{0}^{1} \sin\pi t\, dt = \frac{2}{\pi}$$

$$a_n = \int_{0}^{1} \sin\pi t \cos n\pi t\, dt = -\frac{1+\cos n\pi}{\pi(n^2 - 1)} = -\frac{1+(-1)^n}{\pi(n^2 - 1)} \quad \text{for } n > 1$$

$$a_1 = \int_0^1 \sin \pi t \cos \pi t \, dt = 0$$

$$b_n = \int_0^1 \sin \pi t \sin n\pi t \, dt = -\frac{\sin n\pi}{\pi(n^2 - 1)} = 0 \text{ for } n > 1$$

$$b_1 = \int_0^1 \sin^2 \pi t \, dt = \frac{1}{2}$$

$$f(t) = \frac{1}{\pi} + \frac{1}{2}\sin \pi t - \frac{2}{\pi}\left[\frac{1}{3}\cos 2\pi t + \frac{1}{15}\cos 4\pi t + \frac{1}{35}\cos 6\pi t + \frac{1}{63}\cos 8\pi t + \cdots\right]$$

15. **(a)** $\quad a_0 = \dfrac{1}{\pi}\displaystyle\int_0^{2\pi} t^2 \, dt = \dfrac{8\pi^2}{3}$

$$a_n = \frac{1}{\pi}\int_0^{2\pi} t^2 \cos nt \, dt = \frac{4n\pi \cos 2n\pi + 2(2n^2\pi^2 - 1)\sin 2n\pi}{\pi n^3} = \frac{4}{n^2}$$

$$b_n = \frac{1}{\pi}\int_0^{2\pi} t^2 \sin nt \, dt = \frac{(2 - 4n^2\pi^2)\cos 2n\pi + 4n\pi \sin 2n\pi - 2}{\pi n^3} = -\frac{4\pi}{n}$$

$$f(t) = \frac{4\pi^2}{3} + 4\sum_{n=1}^{\infty}\frac{\cos nt}{n^2} - 4\pi\sum_{n=1}^{\infty}\frac{\sin nt}{n}$$

(b) If we substitute $t = 0$ in the Fourier series of part (a) and note that
$f(0) = \frac{1}{2}[f(0-) + f(0+)] = \frac{1}{2}[(2\pi)^2 + (0)^2] = 2\pi^2$, we get

$$2\pi^2 = \frac{4\pi^2}{3} + 4\sum_{n=1}^{\infty}\frac{1}{n^2}, \quad \text{so} \quad \sum_{n=1}^{\infty}\frac{1}{n^2} = \frac{\pi^2}{6}.$$

When we substitute $t = \pi$ and $f(\pi) = \pi^2$ in the series of part (a) we get

$$\pi^2 = \frac{4\pi^2}{3} + 4\sum_{n=1}^{\infty}\frac{(-1)^n}{n^2}, \quad \text{so} \quad \sum_{n=1}^{\infty}\frac{(-1)^{n+1}}{n^2} = \frac{\pi^2}{12}.$$

17. **(a)** $\quad a_0 = \displaystyle\int_0^2 t \, dt = 2$

$$a_n = \int_0^2 t \cos n\pi t \, dt = \frac{\cos 2n\pi + 2n\pi \sin 2n\pi - 1}{n^2\pi^2} = 0$$

$$b_n = \int_0^2 t \sin n\pi t \, dt = \frac{\sin 2n\pi - 2n\pi \cos 2n\pi}{n^2\pi^2} = -\frac{2}{n\pi}$$

$$f(t) = 1 - \frac{2}{\pi}\sum_{n=1}^{\infty}\frac{\sin n\pi t}{n}$$

(b) Substitution of $t = 1/2$, $f(t) = 1/2$ in this series gives

$$\frac{1}{2} = 1 - \frac{2}{\pi}\left(1 - \frac{1}{3} + \frac{1}{5} - \frac{1}{7} + \cdots\right), \quad \text{so} \quad 1 - \frac{1}{3} + \frac{1}{5} - \frac{1}{7} + \cdots = \frac{\pi}{4}.$$

The most efficient approach to Problems 18 and 20 is to derive first the expansions

$$t = \pi - 2\left[\sin t + \frac{\sin 2t}{2} + \frac{\sin 3t}{3} + \frac{\sin 4t}{4} + \cdots\right],$$

$$t^2 = \frac{4\pi^2}{3} + 4\left[\cos t + \frac{\cos 2t}{4} + \frac{\cos 3t}{9} + \frac{\cos 4t}{16} + \cdots\right]$$
$$- 4\pi\left[\sin t + \frac{\sin 2t}{2} + \frac{\sin 3t}{3} + \frac{\sin 4t}{4} + \cdots\right].$$

for $0 < t < 2\pi$, as the Fourier series of the functions $f(t)$ and $g(t)$ of period 2π defined for $0 < t < 2\pi$ by $f(t) = t$ and $g(t) = t^2$. The first series above yields the series in Problem 18, and a combination of the two yields the series in Problem 20.

The expansions in Problems 19 and 21 are valid on the interval $-\pi < t < \pi$ rather than the interval $0 < t < 2\pi$. When we calculate the Fourier series of the functions $f(t)$ and $g(t)$ of period 2π defined for $-\pi < t < \pi$ by $f(t) = t$ and $g(t) = t^2$, we find that

$$t = 2\left[\sin t - \frac{\sin 2t}{2} + \frac{\sin 3t}{3} - \frac{\sin 4t}{4} + \cdots\right],$$

$$t^2 = \frac{\pi^2}{3} - 4\left[\cos t - \frac{\cos 2t}{4} + \frac{\cos 3t}{9} - \frac{\cos 4t}{16} + \cdots\right]$$

if $-\pi < t < \pi$.

19. $a_0 = \frac{1}{\pi}\int_{-\pi}^{\pi}\frac{t}{2}\,dt = 0,$ $a_n = \frac{1}{\pi}\int_{-\pi}^{\pi}\frac{t}{2}\cos nt\,dt = 0$

$b_n = \frac{1}{\pi}\int_{-\pi}^{\pi}\frac{t}{2}\sin nt\,dt = \frac{\sin n\pi - n\pi\cos n\pi}{n^2\pi} = \frac{(-1)^{n+1}}{n}$

$\frac{t}{2} = \sum_{n=1}^{\infty}\frac{(-1)^{n+1}\sin nt}{n}$ $(-\pi < t < \pi)$

21. $a_0 = \frac{1}{\pi}\int_{-\pi}^{\pi}t^2\,dt = \frac{\pi^2}{3},$

$a_n = \frac{1}{\pi}\int_{-\pi}^{\pi}t^2\cos nt\,dt = \frac{4n\pi\cos n\pi + 2(n^2\pi^2 - 1)\sin n\pi}{n^3\pi} = \frac{4(-1)^n}{n^2}$

$b_n = \frac{1}{\pi}\int_{-\pi}^{\pi}t^2\sin nt\,dt = 0$

$$t^2 = \frac{\pi^2}{3} + 4\sum_{n=1}^{\infty} \frac{(-1)^n \cos nt}{n^2} \qquad (-\pi < t < \pi)$$

$$\frac{\pi^2 - 3t^2}{12} = \frac{\pi^2}{12} - \frac{1}{4}\left(\frac{\pi^2}{3} + 4\sum_{n=1}^{\infty} \frac{(-1)^n \cos nt}{n^2}\right) = \sum_{n=1}^{\infty} \frac{(-1)^{n+1} \cos nt}{n^2}$$

25.   Now we want to sum the alternating series

$$1 - \frac{1}{3^3} + \frac{1}{5^3} - \frac{1}{7^3} + \frac{1}{9^3} + \cdots$$

of reciprocals of odd cubes. Having used a Fourier series of t^4 in Problem 24 to evaluate $\Sigma(1/n^4)$, it is natural to look at a Fourier series of t^3. Let $f(t)$ be the period 2π function with $f(t) = t^3$ if $-\pi < t < \pi$. We calculate the Fourier coefficients of $f(t)$, and get

$$a_0 = \frac{1}{\pi}\int_{-\pi}^{\pi} t^3 \, dt = 0, \qquad a_n = \frac{1}{\pi}\int_{-\pi}^{\pi} t^3 \cos nt \, dt = 0$$

$$b_n = \frac{1}{\pi}\int_{-\pi}^{\pi} t^3 \sin nt \, dt = -\frac{2n\pi\left(n^2\pi^2 - 6\right)\cos n\pi - 6(n^2\pi^2 - 2)\sin n\pi}{n^4\pi} = 2\left(\frac{6}{n^3} - \frac{\pi^2}{n}\right)$$

$$t^3 = 2\pi^2 \sum_{n=1}^{\infty} (-1)^{n+1} \frac{\sin nt}{n} - 12\sum_{n=1}^{\infty} (-1)^{n+1} \frac{\sin nt}{n^3}.$$

If we substitute $t = \pi/2$ and use Leibniz's series $\Sigma(-1)^{n+1}/n = \pi/4$ of Problem 17 we find that

$$1 - \frac{1}{3^3} + \frac{1}{5^3} - \frac{1}{7^3} + \frac{1}{9^3} + \cdots = \frac{\pi^3}{32}.$$

There is *no* value of t whose substitution in the Fourier series of $f(t) = t^3$ yields the series $\Sigma(1/n^3)$ containing the reciprocal cubes of *both* the odd and even integers. Indeed, the summation in "closed form" of the series

$$\sum_{n=1}^{\infty} \frac{1}{n^3} = 1 + \frac{1}{2^3} + \frac{1}{3^3} + \frac{1}{4^3} + \frac{1}{5^3} + \cdots$$

is a problem that has challenged many fine mathematicians since the time of Euler. Only in modern times (by R. Apery in 1978) has it been shown that this sum is an irrational number. For a delightful account of this work, see the article "A Proof that Euler Missed ... An Informal Report" by Alfred van der Poorten in the *The Mathematical Intelligencer*, Volume 1 (1979), pages 195–203.

SECTION 9.3

FOURIER SINE AND COSINE SERIES

1. $\quad a_0 = \dfrac{2}{L}\displaystyle\int_0^L 1\,dt = 2, \qquad a_n = \dfrac{2}{L}\displaystyle\int_0^L \cos\dfrac{n\pi t}{L}\,dt = \dfrac{2\sin n\pi}{n\pi} = 0$

Cosine series: $f(t) = 1$

$\quad b_n = \dfrac{2}{L}\displaystyle\int_0^L \sin\dfrac{n\pi t}{L}\,dt = \dfrac{2(1-\cos n\pi)}{n\pi} = \dfrac{2}{n\pi}\left[1-(-1)^n\right]$

Sine series: $\quad f(t) = \dfrac{4}{\pi}\left(\sin\dfrac{\pi t}{L} + \dfrac{1}{3}\sin\dfrac{3\pi t}{L} + \dfrac{1}{5}\sin\dfrac{5\pi t}{L} + \dfrac{1}{7}\sin\dfrac{7\pi t}{L} + \cdots\right)$

3. $\quad a_0 = \displaystyle\int_0^2 (1-t)\,dt = 0$

$\quad a_n = \displaystyle\int_0^2 (1-t)\cos\dfrac{n\pi t}{2}\,dt = \dfrac{4-4\cos n\pi - 2n\pi\sin n\pi}{n^2\pi^2} = \dfrac{4}{n^2\pi^2}\left[1-(-1)^2\right]$

Cosine series: $f(t) = \dfrac{8}{\pi^2}\left(\cos\dfrac{\pi t}{2} + \dfrac{1}{3^2}\cos\dfrac{3\pi t}{2} + \dfrac{1}{5^2}\cos\dfrac{5\pi t}{2} + \dfrac{1}{7^2}\cos\dfrac{7\pi t}{2} + \cdots\right)$

$\quad b_n = \displaystyle\int_0^2 (1-t)\sin\dfrac{n\pi t}{2}\,dt = \dfrac{2n\pi(1+\cos n\pi) - 2\sin n\pi}{n^2\pi^2} = \dfrac{2}{n\pi}\left[1+(-1)^n\right]$

Sine series: $\quad f(t) = \dfrac{4}{\pi}\left(\dfrac{\sin\pi t}{2} + \dfrac{\sin 2\pi t}{4} + \dfrac{\sin 3\pi t}{6} + \dfrac{\sin 4\pi t}{8} + \cdots\right)$

5. $\quad a_0 = \dfrac{2}{3}\displaystyle\int_1^2 1\,dt = \dfrac{2}{3}$

$\quad a_n = \dfrac{2}{3}\displaystyle\int_1^2 \cos\dfrac{n\pi t}{3}\,dt = \dfrac{2}{n\pi}\left(\sin\dfrac{2n\pi}{3} - \sin\dfrac{n\pi}{3}\right) = \begin{cases} -2\sqrt{3}/n\pi & \text{if } n = 2, 8, 14, \cdots \\ +2\sqrt{3}/n\pi & \text{if } n = 4, 10, 16, \cdots \\ \quad 0 & \text{otherwise} \end{cases}$

Cosine series: $\quad f(t) = \dfrac{1}{3} - \dfrac{2\sqrt{3}}{\pi}\left[\dfrac{1}{2}\cos\dfrac{2\pi t}{3} - \dfrac{1}{4}\cos\dfrac{4\pi t}{3} + \dfrac{1}{8}\cos\dfrac{8\pi t}{3} - \dfrac{1}{10}\cos\dfrac{10\pi t}{3} + \cdots\right]$

$\quad b_n = \dfrac{2}{3}\displaystyle\int_1^2 \sin\dfrac{n\pi t}{3}\,dt = \dfrac{2}{n\pi}\left(\cos\dfrac{n\pi}{3} - \cos\dfrac{2n\pi}{3}\right) = \begin{cases} \quad 0 \text{ for } n \text{ even} \\ +2/n\pi & \text{if } n = 1, 7, 13, \cdots \\ -4/n\pi & \text{if } n = 3, 9, 15, \cdots \\ +2/n\pi & \text{if } n = 5, 11, 17, \cdots \end{cases}$

Sine series:

$\quad f(t) = \dfrac{2}{\pi}\left[\sin\dfrac{\pi t}{3} - \dfrac{2}{3}\sin\dfrac{3\pi t}{3} + \dfrac{1}{5}\sin\dfrac{5\pi t}{3} + \dfrac{1}{7}\sin\dfrac{7\pi t}{3} - \dfrac{2}{9}\sin\dfrac{9\pi t}{3} + \dfrac{1}{11}\sin\dfrac{11\pi t}{3} + \cdots\right]$

7.

$$a_0 = \frac{2}{\pi}\int_0^\pi t(\pi - t)\, dt = \frac{\pi^2}{3},$$

$$a_n = \frac{2}{\pi}\int_0^\pi t(\pi - t)\cos nt\, dt = -\frac{2\left[n\pi\cos n\pi + n\pi - 2\sin n\pi\right]}{n^3\pi} = -\frac{2}{n^2}\left[1+(-1)^n\right]$$

Cosine series: $f(t) = \frac{\pi^2}{6} - 4\left(\frac{\cos 2t}{2^2} + \frac{\cos 4t}{4^2} + \frac{\cos 6t}{6^2} + \frac{\cos 8t}{8^2} + \cdots\right)$

$$a_n = \frac{2}{\pi}\int_0^\pi t(\pi - t)\sin nt\, dt = \frac{2\left[2 - 2\cos n\pi - 2n\pi\sin n\pi\right]}{n^3\pi} = \frac{4}{\pi n^3}\left[1-(-1)^n\right]$$

Sine series: $f(t) = \frac{8}{\pi}\left(\sin t + \frac{\sin 3t}{3^3} + \frac{\sin 5t}{5^3} + \frac{\sin 7t}{7^3} + \cdots\right)$

9.

$$a_0 = \frac{2}{\pi}\int_0^\pi \sin t\, dt = \frac{4}{\pi},$$

$$a_n = \frac{2}{\pi}\int_0^\pi \sin t\cos nt\, dt = \frac{2\left[1+\cos n\pi\right]}{\pi(1-n^2)} = \frac{2\left[1+(-1)^n\right]}{\pi(1-n^2)} \text{ if } n > 1$$

$$a_1 = \frac{2}{\pi}\int_0^\pi \sin t\cos t\, dt = 0$$

Cosine series: $f(t) = \frac{2}{\pi} - \frac{4}{\pi^2}\left(\frac{\cos 2t}{3} + \frac{\cos 4t}{15} + \frac{\cos 6t}{35} + \frac{\cos 8t}{63} + \cdots\right)$

$$b_n = \frac{2}{\pi}\int_0^\pi \sin t\sin nt\, dt = \frac{2\sin n\pi}{\pi(1-n^2)} = 0 \text{ if } n > 1$$

$$a_1 = \frac{2}{\pi}\int_0^\pi \sin^2 t\, dt = 1$$

Sine series: $f(t) = \sin t$

11.   In order to satisfy the endpoint conditions $x(0) = x(\pi) = 0$ we substitute the sine series

$x(t) = \sum_{n=1}^\infty b_n \sin nt$ and $1 = \frac{4}{\pi}\sum_{n\text{ odd}}\frac{\sin nt}{n}$ (from Example 1 in Section 9.1) into the

differential equation $x'' + 2x = 1$. This gives

$$-\sum_{n=1}^\infty n^2 b_n \sin nt + 2\sum_{n=1}^\infty b_n \sin nt = \frac{4}{\pi}\sum_{n\text{ odd}}\frac{\sin nt}{n}.$$

We therefore choose $b_n = 4/\pi n(2-n^2)$ for n odd, $b_n = 0$ for n even. This gives the formal series solution

$$x(t) = \frac{4}{\pi}\sum_{n\text{ odd}}\frac{\sin nt}{n(2-n^2)} = \frac{4}{\pi}\left(\sin t - \frac{\sin 3t}{21} - \frac{\sin 5t}{115} - \frac{\sin 7t}{329} - \cdots\right).$$

13. In order to satisfy the endpoint conditions $x(0) = x(1) = 0$ we substitute the sine series

$$x(t) = \sum_{n=1}^{\infty} b_n \sin n\pi t \quad \text{and} \quad t = \frac{2}{\pi} \sum_{n=1}^{\infty} \frac{(-1)^{n+1} \sin n\pi t}{n} \quad \text{(from Example 1 in Section 9.3, with}$$

$L = 1$) into the differential equation $x'' + x = t$. This gives

$$-\sum_{n=1}^{\infty} n^2 \pi^2 b_n \sin n\pi t + \sum_{n=1}^{\infty} b_n \sin n\pi t = \frac{2}{\pi} \sum_{n=1}^{\infty} \frac{(-1)^{n+1} \sin n\pi t}{n}.$$

We therefore choose $b_n = 2(-1)^{n+1} / \pi n(1 - n^2 \pi^2)$. This gives the formal series solution

$$x(t) = \frac{2}{\pi} \sum_{n=1}^{\infty} \frac{(-1)^n \sin n\pi t}{n(n^2 \pi^2 - 1)} \quad \text{of our endpoint value problem.}$$

15. In order to satisfy the endpoint conditions $x'(0) = x'(2) = 0$ we substitute the cosine

series $x(t) = \frac{a_0}{2} + \sum_{n=1}^{\infty} a_n \cos nt \quad \text{and} \quad t = \frac{\pi}{2} - \frac{4}{\pi} \sum_{n \text{ odd}} \frac{\cos nt}{n^2} \quad \text{(from Example 1 in Section}$

9.3, with $L = \pi$) into the differential equation $x'' + 2x = t$. This gives

$$-\sum_{n=1}^{\infty} n^2 a_n \cos nt + a_0 + 2 \sum_{n=1}^{\infty} a_n \cos nt = \frac{\pi}{2} - \frac{4}{\pi} \sum_{n \text{ odd}} \frac{\cos nt}{n^2}.$$

We therefore choose $a_0 = \pi/2$, $a_n = 0$ for $n > 0$ even, and $a_n = 4/\pi n^2 (n^2 - 2)$ for n odd. This gives the formal series solution

$$x(t) = \frac{\pi}{4} + \frac{4}{\pi} \sum_{n \text{ odd}} \frac{\cos nt}{n^2 (n^2 - 2)} = \frac{\pi}{4} + \frac{4}{\pi} \left(-\cos t + \frac{\cos 3t}{63} + \frac{\cos 5t}{575} + \frac{\cos 7t}{2303} + \cdots \right)$$

of our endpoint value problem.

17. *Suggestion*: Substitute $u = -t$ in the left-hand integral.

19. The first termwise integration yields

$$\frac{t^2}{2} = 2 \sum_{n=1}^{\infty} \frac{(-1)^n \cos nt}{n^2} + C_1,$$

and substitution of $t = 0$ gives $C_1 = 2 \sum_{n=1}^{\infty} (-1)^{n+1} / n^2 = \pi^2 / 6$, so

$$\frac{t^2}{2} = 2 \sum_{n=1}^{\infty} \frac{(-1)^n \cos nt}{n^2} + \frac{\pi^2}{6}.$$

A second termwise integration gives

$$\frac{t^3}{6} = 2\sum_{n=1}^{\infty} \frac{(-1)^n \sin nt}{n^3} + \frac{\pi^2 t}{6} + C_2,$$

and substitution of $t = 0$ gives $C_2 = 0$. The final termwise integration gives

$$\frac{t^4}{24} = -2\sum_{n=1}^{\infty} \frac{(-1)^n \cos nt}{n^4} + \frac{\pi^2 t^2}{12} + C_3,$$

and substitution of $t = 0$ yields $C_3 = 2\sum_{n=1}^{\infty} (-1)^n / n^4$.

21. We want to calculate the coefficients in the period $4L$ Fourier sine series

$$F(t) = \sum_{n=1}^{\infty} b_n \sin \frac{n\pi t}{2L}$$

which agrees with $f(t)$ if $0 < t < L$. Then

$$b_n = \frac{2}{2L}\int_0^L f(t)\sin\frac{n\pi t}{2L}\,dt + \frac{2}{2L}\int_L^{2L} f(2L-t)\sin\frac{n\pi t}{2L}\,dt.$$

The substitution $u = 2L - t$ yields

$$b_n = \frac{1}{L}\int_0^L f(t)\sin\frac{n\pi t}{2L}\,dt - \frac{1}{L}\int_L^0 f(u)\sin\frac{n\pi(2L-u)}{2L}\,du$$

$$= \frac{1}{L}\int_0^L f(t)\sin\frac{n\pi t}{2L}\,dt - \frac{(-1)^n}{L}\int_0^L f(u)\sin\frac{n\pi u}{2L}\,du.$$

Now it is clear that

$$b_n = \frac{2}{L}\int_0^L f(t)\cos\frac{n\pi t}{2L}\,dt$$

if n is odd, whereas $b_n = 0$ if n is even.

23. $\quad b_n = \dfrac{2}{\pi}\displaystyle\int_0^{\pi} t\sin\frac{nt}{2}\,dt = \frac{4}{\pi n^2}\left(2\sin\frac{n\pi}{2} - n\pi\cos\frac{n\pi}{2}\right) = \frac{8(-1)^{(n-1)/2}}{\pi n^2}$ for n odd

$$f(t) = \frac{8}{\pi^2}\left(\sin\frac{t}{2} - \frac{1}{3^2}\sin\frac{3t}{2} + \frac{1}{5^2}\sin\frac{5t}{2} - \frac{1}{7^2}\sin\frac{7t}{2} + \cdots\right)$$

SECTION 9.4

APPLICATIONS OF FOURIER SERIES

1. We substitute the sine series $x(t) = \sum_{n=1}^{\infty} b_n \sin nt$ and $F(t) = \frac{12}{\pi} \sum_{n \text{ odd}} \frac{\sin nt}{n}$ (from Example 1 in Section 9.1) into the differential equation $x'' + 5x = F(t)$. This gives

$$-\sum_{n=1}^{\infty} n^2 b_n \sin nt + 5 \sum_{n=1}^{\infty} b_n \sin nt = \frac{12}{\pi} \sum_{n \text{ odd}} \frac{\sin nt}{n}.$$

We therefore choose $b_n = 0$ for $n > 0$ even, and $b_n = 12/\pi n(5-n^2)$ for n odd. This gives the formal series solution

$$x_{sp}(t) = \frac{12}{\pi} \sum_{n \text{ odd}} \frac{\sin nt}{n(5-n^2)} = \frac{12}{\pi}\left(\frac{\sin t}{4} - \frac{\sin 3t}{12} - \frac{\sin 5t}{100} - \frac{\sin 7t}{308} - \cdots\right).$$

3. We substitute the sine series $x(t) = \sum_{n=1}^{\infty} b_n \sin nt$ and $F(t) = 2\sum_{n=1}^{\infty} \frac{(-1)^{n-1} \sin nt}{n}$ (from Example 1 in Section 9.3, with $L = \pi$) into the differential equation $x'' + 3x = F(t)$. This gives

$$-\sum_{n=1}^{\infty} n^2 b_n \sin nt + 3 \sum_{n=1}^{\infty} b_n \sin nt = 4\sum_{n=1}^{\infty} \frac{(-1)^{n-1} \sin nt}{n}.$$

We therefore choose $b_n = 4(-1)^{n-1}/n(3-n^2)$. This gives the formal series solution

$$x_{sp}(t) = 4\sum_{n=1}^{\infty} \frac{(-1)^{n-1} \sin nt}{n(3-n^2)} = 4\left(\frac{\sin t}{2} + \frac{\sin 2t}{2} - \frac{\sin 3t}{18} + \frac{\sin 4t}{52} - \cdots\right).$$

5. We substitute the sine series $x(t) = \sum_{n=1}^{\infty} b_n \sin n\pi t$ and $F(t) = \frac{8}{\pi^3} \sum_{n \text{ odd}} \frac{\sin n\pi t}{n^3}$ into the differential equation $x'' + 10x = F(t)$. This gives

$$-\sum_{n=1}^{\infty} n^2 \pi^2 b_n \sin n\pi t + 10 \sum_{n=1}^{\infty} b_n \sin n\pi t = \frac{8}{\pi^3} \sum_{n \text{ odd}} \frac{\sin n\pi t}{n^3}.$$

We therefore choose $b_n = 8/n^3 \pi^3 (10 - n^2\pi^2)$. This gives the formal series solution

$$x_{sp}(t) = \frac{8}{\pi^3} \sum_{n \text{ odd}} \frac{\sin n\pi t}{n^3(10-n^2\pi^2)}.$$

In Problems 7-12 we are dealing with the equation $mx'' + kx = F(t)$ where $F(t)$ is the external periodic force. The natural frequency is $\omega_0 = \sqrt{k/m}$. If the Fourier series of $F(t)$ contains a term of the form $\cos(N\pi t/L)$ or $\sin(N\pi t/L)$ with $\omega_0 = N\pi/L$, then pure resonance occurs. Otherwise, it does not.

7. The natural frequency is $\omega_0 = 3$, and

$$F(t) = \frac{4}{\pi}\left(\sin t + \frac{\sin 3t}{3} + \frac{\sin 5t}{5} + \frac{\sin 7t}{7} + \cdots\right).$$

Thus the Fourier series of $F(t)$ contains a $\sin 3t$ term, so resonance does occur.

9. The natural frequency is $\omega_0 = 2$, and

$$F(t) = \frac{4}{\pi}\left(\sin t + \frac{\sin 3t}{3} + \frac{\sin 5t}{5} + \frac{\sin 7t}{7} + \cdots\right).$$

Because the $\sin 2t$ term is missing from the Fourier series of $F(t)$, resonance will not occur.

11. The natural frequency is $\omega_0 = 4$. From Equation (15) in Section 9.3 we see that

$$F(t) = \frac{\pi}{2} - \frac{4}{\pi}\left(\cos t + \frac{\cos 3t}{3^2} + \frac{\cos 5t}{5^2} + \cdots\right).$$

Because the $\cos 4t$ term is missing, we see that resonance will not occur.

Problems 13-18 are based on Equations (14)-(16) in the text, according to which the steady periodic solution of

$$mx'' + cx' + kx = \sum_{n=1}^{\infty} B_n \sin\frac{n\pi t}{L}$$

is given by

$$x_{sp}(t) = \sum_{n=1}^{\infty} b_n \sin(\omega_n t - \alpha_n),$$

where

$$\omega_n = \frac{n\pi}{L},$$

$$\alpha_n = \tan^{-1}\frac{c\omega_n}{k - m\omega_n^2} \quad \text{in the interval } [0, \pi],$$

$$b_n = \frac{B_n}{\sqrt{\left(k - m\omega_n^2\right)^2 + \left(c\omega_n\right)^2}}.$$

This calculation is readily automated. The following MATLAB script was written to calculate the coefficients $\{b_n\}$ for Problem 13. Only the values of m, c, k, L and the calculation of the force function coefficients $\{B_n\}$ need to be changed for Problems 14–18.

```
m = 1;    c = 0.1;    k = 4;
L = pi;
results = ones(0,4);
for n = 1:9
   w = n*pi/L;
   alpha = atan(c*w/(k-m*w^2));
   if k-m*w^2<0
      alpha = pi + alpha;
   end
   B = 12/(pi*n);          % force function coeffs
   if floor(n/2)==n/2      % are nonzero if n is odd,
      B = 0;               % zero if n is even
   end
   b = B/sqrt((k-m*w^2)^2+(c*w)^2);
   results = [results; n, b, w, alpha];
end
results
```

13. $B_n = 12/\pi n$ for n odd, $B_n = 0$ for n even

$x_{sp}(t) \approx 1.2725 \sin(t - 0.0333) + 0.2542 \sin(3t - 3.0817) + 0.0364 \sin(5t - 3.1178) + \cdots$

15. $B_n = 8/n^3\pi^3$ for n odd, $B_n = 0$ for n even

$x_{sp}(t) \approx 0.08150 \sin(\pi t - 1.44692) + 0.00004 \sin(3\pi t - 3.10176) + \cdots$

17. $B_n = 60/n\pi$ for n odd, $B_n = 0$ for n even

$x_{sp}(t) \approx 0.5687 \sin(\pi t - 0.0562) + 0.4271 \sin(3\pi t - 0.3891)$
$\qquad\qquad + 0.1396 \sin(5\pi t - 2.7899) + 0.0318 \sin(7\pi t - 2.9874) + \cdots$

$x_{sp}(5) \approx 0.248$ ft ≈ 2.98 in.

SECTION 9.5

HEAT CONDUCTION AND SEPARATION OF VARIABLES

1.   From Equation (31) in the text, with $L = \pi$ and $k = 3$, we get

$$u(x,t) = \sum_{n=1}^{\infty} b_n \exp(-3n^2 t) \sin nx.$$

With $b_2 = 4$ and $b_n = 0$ otherwise we get the solution

$$u(x, t) = 4e^{-12t} \sin 2x.$$

3. With $L = 1$ and $k = 2$ in Equation (31), we take $b_1 = 5$, $b_3 = -1/5$, and $b_n = 0$ otherwise. The result is the solution

$$u(x,t) = 5e^{-2\pi^2 t} \sin \pi x - \frac{1}{5} e^{-18\pi^2 t} \sin 3\pi x.$$

5. From Equation (40) in the text, with $k = 2$ and $L = 3$ we get,

$$u(x,t) = \frac{a_0}{2} + \sum_{n=1}^{\infty} a_n \exp\left(-\frac{2n^2\pi^2 t}{9}\right) \cos\frac{n\pi x}{3}.$$

With $a_0 = 0$, $a_2 = 4$, $a_4 = -2$, and $a_n = 0$ otherwise, and $a_n = 0$ we get the solution

$$u(x,t) = 4\exp\left(-\frac{8\pi^2 t}{9}\right) \cos\frac{2\pi x}{3} - 2\exp\left(-\frac{32\pi^2 t}{9}\right) \cos\frac{4\pi x}{3}.$$

7. From Equation (40) in the text, with $k = 1/3$ and $L = 2$ we get,

$$u(x,t) = \frac{a_0}{2} + \sum_{n=1}^{\infty} a_n \exp\left(-\frac{n^2\pi^2 t}{12}\right) \cos\frac{n\pi x}{2}.$$

Because of the identity $\cos^2 2\pi x = (1 + \cos 4\pi x)/2$, we choose $a_0 = 1$, $a_8 = 1/2$, and $a_n = 0$ otherwise. This gives the solution

$$u(x,t) = \frac{1}{2} + \frac{1}{2}\exp\left(-\frac{16\pi^2 t}{3}\right) \cos 4\pi x.$$

9. Because of the zero endpoint conditions $u(0,t) = u(5,t) = 0$, we use the Fourier sine series expansion

$$u(x,0) = \frac{100}{\pi} \sum_{n\,\text{odd}} \frac{1}{n} \sin\frac{n\pi x}{5}$$

of $u(x,0) = 25$ on the interval $0 < x < 5$. When we supply the exponential factors in Eq. (31) with $k = 1/10$ and $L = 5$, we get the solution

$$u(x,t) = \frac{100}{\pi} \sum_{n\,\text{odd}} \frac{1}{n} \exp\left(\frac{-n^2\pi^2 t}{250}\right) \sin\frac{n\pi x}{5}$$

11. Because of the zero-derivative endpoint conditions $u_x(0,t) = u_x(10,t) = 0$, we use the Fourier cosine series expansion

$$u(x,0) = 20 - \frac{160}{\pi^2} \sum_{n\,\text{odd}} \frac{1}{n^2} \cos\frac{n\pi x}{10}$$

of $u(x,0) = 4x$ on the interval $0 < x < 10$ (from Eq. (15) in Section 9.3). When we supply the exponential factors in Eq. (40) here with $k = 1/5$ and $L = 10$, we get

$$u(x,t) = 20 - \frac{160}{\pi^2} \sum_{n\,\text{odd}} \frac{1}{n^2} \exp\left(\frac{-n^2\pi^2 t}{500}\right) \cos\frac{n\pi x}{10}$$

13. **(a)** The boundary value problem is

$$u_t = ku_{xx} \quad (0 < x < 40),$$
$$u_x(0, t) = u_x(40, t) = 0,$$
$$u(x, 0) = 100.$$

By Equation (31) in the text (with $L = 40$) the solution is of the form

$$u(x,t) = \sum_{n=1}^{\infty} b_n \exp\left(-\frac{n^2\pi^2 kt}{1600}\right) \sin\frac{n\pi x}{40}.$$

We use the Fourier sine coefficients $b_n = 400/\pi n$ for n odd, $b_n = 0$ otherwise, of the initial value function $f(x) = 100$ on the interval $0 < x < 100$. This gives

$$u(x,t) = \frac{400}{\pi} \sum_{n\,\text{odd}} \frac{1}{n} \exp\left(\frac{-n^2\pi^2 kt}{1600}\right) \sin\frac{n\pi x}{40}.$$

(b) With $k = 1.15$ for copper we find that

$$u(20,300) \approx 15.1591 - 0.000000204 + \cdots \approx 15.16°C.$$

(c) With $k = 0.005$ for concrete, the first term of the series gives

$$u(20,t) = \frac{400}{\pi} \exp\left(-\frac{0.00\pi^2 t}{1600}\right) = 15,$$

and we solve for $t \approx 66,342 \text{ sec} \approx 19 \text{ hr } 15 \text{ min } 42 \text{ sec}$. As a check that the first term suffices for this computation, we find that the next term in the series is then approximately 0.00000019.

15. We need only calculate the coefficients in the usual zero-endpoint series

$$u(x,t) = \sum_{n=1}^{\infty} b_n \exp\left(-\frac{n^2\pi^2 kt}{L^2}\right) \sin\frac{n\pi x}{L}.$$

For the function $f(x) \equiv A$ for $0 < x < L/2$, $f(x) \equiv 0$ for $L/2 < x < L$ we calculate the Fourier sine coefficient

$$b_n = \frac{2}{L}\int_0^{L/2} A \sin\frac{n\pi x}{L}\,dx = \frac{4A}{n\pi}\sin^2\frac{n\pi}{4} = \frac{4A}{n\pi}\times\begin{cases} 1/2 \text{ for } n \text{ odd,} \\ 1 \text{ for } n = 2,6,10,\cdots, \\ 0 \text{ for } n = 4,8,12,\cdots. \end{cases}$$

SECTION 9.6

VIBRATING STRINGS AND THE ONE-DIMENSIONAL WAVE EQUATION

Ces

In Problems 1-10 we use the general solution

$$y(x,t) = \sum_{n=1}^{\infty}\left(A_n\cos\frac{n\pi a t}{L} + B_n\sin\frac{n\pi a t}{L}\right)\sin\frac{n\pi x}{L} \qquad (*)$$

of the string equation $y_{tt} = a^2 y_{xx}$ with endpoint conditions $y(0, t) = y(L, t) = 0$. This form of the solution is obtained by superposition of the solutions in Equations (23) and (33) of Problems A and B in this section. It remains only to choose the coefficients $\{A_n\}$ and $\{B_n\}$ so as to satisfy given initial conditions

$$y(x,0) = \sum_{n=1}^{\infty} A_n\sin\frac{n\pi x}{L} = f(x), \text{ thus, } A_n = \frac{2}{L}\int_0^L f(x)\sin\frac{n\pi x}{L}\,dx; \text{ and}$$

$$y_t(x,0) = \sum_{n=1}^{\infty}\frac{n\pi a}{L}B_n\sin\frac{n\pi x}{L} = g(x), \text{ thus, } B_n = \frac{2}{n\pi a}\int_0^L g(x)\sin\frac{n\pi x}{L}\,dx.$$

1.   Here $a = 2$ and $L = \pi$. To satisfy the condition $y(x, 0) = (1/10)\sin 2x$ we choose $A_2 = 1/10$ in Eq. (*) above, and $A_n = 0$ otherwise. To satisfy the condition $y_t(x, 0) = 0$ we choose $B_n = 0$ for all n. Thus

$$y(x, t) = \frac{1}{10}\cos 4t \sin 2x.$$

3.   Here $a = 1/2$ and $L = \pi$. Choosing $A_1 = 1/10$ and $A_n = 0$ otherwise, $B_1 = 1/5$ and $B_n = 0$ otherwise, we get

$$y(x, t) = \frac{1}{10}\left(\cos\frac{t}{2} + 2\sin\frac{t}{2}\right)\sin x.$$

5.   Here $a = 5$ and $L = 3$. Choosing $A_3 = 1/4$ and $A_n = 0$ for $n \ne 3$, $B_6 = 1/\pi$ and $B_n = 0$ for $n \ne 6$, we get

$$y(x, t) = \frac{1}{4}\cos 5\pi t \sin \pi x + \frac{1}{\pi}\sin 10\pi t \sin 2\pi x.$$

7. Here $a = 10$ and $L = 1$. To satisfy the condition $y(x, 0) = 0$ we choose $A_n = 0$ for all n, so

$$y(x, t) = \sum_{n=1}^{\infty} B_n \sin 10n\pi t \sin n\pi x.$$

To satisfy the condition $y_t(x, 0) = x$ we choose

$$B_n = \frac{1}{10n\pi} \cdot \frac{2(-1)^{n+1}}{n\pi} = \frac{(-1)^{n+1}}{5n^2\pi^2}$$

for $n \geq 1$ (see Equation (16) in Section 9.3). This gives

$$y(x, t) = \frac{1}{5\pi^2} \sum_{n=1}^{\infty} \frac{(-1)^{n+1}}{n^2} \sin 10n\pi t \sin n\pi x.$$

9. Here $a = 2$ and $L = 1$. To satisfy the condition $y(x, 0) = 0$ we choose $A_n = 0$ for all n, so

$$y(x, t) = \sum_{n=1}^{\infty} B_n \sin 2n\pi t \sin n\pi x.$$

To satisfy the condition $y_t(x, 0) = x(1 - x)$ we choose

$$B_n = \frac{1}{n\pi} \int_0^1 x(1-x) \sin n\pi x \, dx = \frac{2 - 2\cos n\pi - n\pi \sin n\pi}{n^4\pi^4}.$$

Hence

$$y(x,t) = \frac{4}{\pi^4} \sum_{n \text{ odd}} \frac{\sin 2n\pi t \sin n\pi x}{n^4}.$$

11. Substitution of $L = 2$ ft, $T = 32$ lb, and the *linear* density

$$\rho = \frac{1/32 \, \text{oz}}{2 \, \text{ft}} = \frac{1 \, \text{oz}}{64 \, \text{ft}} \cdot \frac{1 \, \text{lb}}{16 \, \text{oz}} \cdot \frac{1 \, \text{slug}}{32 \, \text{lb}} = \frac{1}{32^3} \frac{\text{slug}}{\text{ft}}$$

in Eqs. (2) and (26) in the text yields the velocity $a = \sqrt{T/\rho} = \sqrt{32^4} = 1024$ ft/sec with which waves move along the string, and its fundamental frequency

$$v_1 = \frac{1}{2L}\sqrt{\frac{T}{\rho}} = \frac{a}{2L} = 256 \, \text{Hz},$$

which is approximately middle C.

13. If $y(x,t) = F(x + at) = F(u)$ with $u = x + at$, then the chain rule gives

$$\frac{\partial y}{\partial x} = \frac{dF}{du}\frac{\partial u}{\partial x} = F'(u)\cdot 1 = F'(x+at);$$

$$\frac{\partial y}{\partial t} = \frac{dF}{du}\frac{\partial u}{\partial t} = F'(u)\cdot a = a\,F'(x+at) = a\frac{\partial y}{\partial x};$$

$$\frac{\partial^2 y}{\partial x^2} = \frac{dF'}{du}\frac{\partial u}{\partial x} = F''(u)\cdot 1 = F''(x+at);$$

$$\frac{\partial^2 y}{\partial t^2} = a\frac{dF'}{du}\frac{\partial u}{\partial t} = a\cdot F''(u)\cdot a = a^2 F''(x+at) = a^2\frac{\partial^2 y}{\partial x^2}.$$

15. If $y(x,0)=0$ then the fundamental theorem of calculus gives

$$y(x,t) = y(x,t) - y(x,0) = \int_0^t y_t(x,\tau)\,d\tau = \int_0^t \frac{1}{2}\big[G(x+a\tau)+G(x-a\tau)\big]\,d\tau.$$

19. The general solution of the second-order ordinary differential equation $a^2 y'' = g$ is a second-order polynomial in x with leading coefficient $g/2a^2$. But the polynomial $\phi(x) = gx(x-L)/2a^2$ has this leading coefficient and satisfies the endpoint conditions $y(0) = y(L) = 0$.

23. If $\pi/4 \le x \le 3\pi/4$ then

$$\frac{\pi}{2} \le x+\frac{\pi}{4} \le \pi \quad \text{and} \quad 0 \le x-\frac{\pi}{4} \le \frac{\pi}{2},$$

so

$$y(x,\,\pi/4) = \frac{1}{2}[F(x+\pi/4) + F(x-\pi/4)]$$

$$= \frac{1}{2}[1 - \cos 2(x+\pi/4) + 1 - \cos 2(x-\pi/4)]$$

$$= \frac{1}{2}[1 - \cos(2x+\pi/2) + 1 - \cos(2x-\pi/2)]$$

$$= \frac{1}{2}[2 + \sin 2x - \sin 2x]$$

$$y(x,\,\pi/4) = 1$$

SECTION 9.7

STEADY-STATE TEMPERATURE AND LAPLACE'S EQUATION

1. Because $Y(0) = Y(b) = 0$ we take our separation of variables in the form

$$X'' - \lambda X = 0 = Y'' + \lambda Y$$

with $\lambda > 0$. Then it follows that

$$Y_n(y) = \sin\frac{n\pi y}{b}, \qquad \lambda_n = \frac{n^2\pi^2}{b^2}$$

and thence that

$$X_n(x) = A_n \cosh\frac{n\pi x}{b} + B_n \sinh\frac{n\pi x}{b}.$$

The condition that $X(0) = 0$ implies that $A_n = 0$ so $X_n(x) = B_n \cosh n\pi x/b$, and hence

$$u(x, y) = \sum_{n=1}^{\infty} C_n \sinh\frac{n\pi x}{b}\sin\frac{n\pi y}{b}.$$

Finally we satisfy the condition $u(a, y) = g(y)$ by choosing $C_n = b_n/(\sinh n\pi a/b)$, where the $\{b_n\}$ are the Fourier sine coefficients of $g(y)$ on $0 \le y \le b$.

3. Just as in Example 1 of Section 9.7 we have $X_n(x) = \sin n\pi x/a$ and

$$Y_n(y) = A_n \cosh\frac{n\pi y}{a} + B_n \sinh\frac{n\pi y}{a}.$$

The condition $Y(0) = 0$ now yields $A_n = 0$ so $Y_n(y) = B_n \sinh n\pi y/a$, and hence

$$u(x, y) = \sum_{n=1}^{\infty} C_n \sin\frac{n\pi x}{a}\sinh\frac{n\pi y}{a}.$$

Finally we satisfy the condition $u(x, b) = f(x)$ by choosing $C_n = b_n/(\sinh n\pi b/a)$, where the $\{b_n\}$ are the Fourier sine coefficients of $f(x)$ on $0 \le x \le a$.

5. Now $Y'(0) = Y'(b) = 0$, so we work with the separation of variables

$$X'' - \lambda X = 0 = Y'' + \lambda Y.$$

The eigenvalue problem

$$Y'' + \lambda Y = 0, \qquad Y'(0) = Y'(b) = 0,$$

has eigenvalues and eigenfunctions $\lambda_0 = 0$, $Y_0(y) = 1$ and

$$\lambda_n = \frac{n^2\pi^2}{b^2}, \qquad Y_n(y) = \cos\frac{n\pi y}{b}$$

for $n = 1, 2, 3, \cdots$. When $n = 0$, $X_0''(x) \equiv 0$ yields $X_0(x) = Ax + B$. Then $X_0(a) = 0$ is satisfied by $X_0(x) = a - x$. For $n > 0$ we have

$$X_n(x) = A_n \cosh \frac{n\pi x}{b} + B_n \sinh \frac{n\pi x}{b},$$

and $X_n(a) = 0$ is satisfied by the particular linear combination

$$X_n(x) = C_n \sinh \frac{n\pi(a-x)}{b},$$

of $\cosh n\pi x/b$ and $\sinh n\pi x/b$. Therefore

$$u(x, y) = C_0(a-x) + \sum_{n=1}^{\infty} C_n \sinh \frac{n\pi(a-x)}{b} \cos \frac{n\pi y}{b}.$$

Finally we satisy the condition $u(0, y) = g(y)$ by choosing

$$C_0 = \frac{a_0}{2a} \quad \text{and} \quad C_n = \frac{b_n}{\sinh n\pi a/b},$$

where the $\{a_n\}$ are the Fourier cosine coefficients of $g(y)$ on $0 \le y \le b$.

7.   The eigenvalue problem

$$X'' + \lambda X = 0, \qquad X(0) = X(a) = 0$$

yields the eigenvalues and eigenfunctions

$$\lambda_n = \frac{n^2\pi^2}{a^2}, \qquad X_n(x) = \sin \frac{n\pi x}{a}$$

for $n = 1, 2, 3, \cdots$. Then

$$Y_n'' + \lambda_n Y_n = 0$$

yields

$$Y_n(y) = A_n e^{n\pi y/a} + B_n e^{-n\pi y/a}.$$

In order that $Y(y) \to 0$ as $y \to \infty$ we take $A_n = 0$, so

$$u(x, y) = \sum_{n=1}^{\infty} B_n e^{-n\pi y/a} \sin \frac{n\pi x}{a}.$$

Finally we satisfy the condition $u(x,0) = f(x)$ by choosing the constants $\{B_n\}$ as the Fourier sine coefficients of $f(x)$ on $0 \le x \le a$.

9.   If in Problem 8 we have $f(x) = 10x$ on $0 < x < 10$, then

$$a_0 = \frac{2}{10} \int_0^{10} 10x \, dx = 100,$$

$$a_n = \frac{2}{10}\int_0^{10} 10x\cos\frac{n\pi x}{10}\,dx = \frac{200(\cos n\pi - 1 + n\pi\sin\pi)}{n^2\pi^2},$$

so

$$u(x,y) = 50 - \frac{400}{\pi^2}\sum_{n\text{ odd}}\frac{1}{n^2}e^{-n\pi y/10}\cos\frac{n\pi x}{10}.$$

Then

$$u(0,5) \approx 50 - 8.4250 - 0.0405 - 0.0006 - 0.0000 - \cdots \approx 41.53,$$
$$u(5,5) = 50 - 0 - 0 - 0 - 0 - \cdots = 50,$$
$$u(0,5) \approx 50 + 8.4250 + 0.0405 + 0.0006 + 0.0000 + \cdots \approx 58.47.$$

11. Now the boundary value problem is

$$u_{xx} + u_{yy} = 0 \qquad (0 < x < a,\ 0 < y < b)$$
$$u(a,y) = u_y(x,0) = u(x,b) = 0,$$
$$u(0,y) = g(y).$$

The eigenvalue problem

$$Y'' + \lambda Y = 0, \qquad Y'(0) = Y(b) = 0$$

yields (similar to Example 4 in Section 3.8)

$$\lambda_n = \frac{(2n-1)^2\pi^2}{4b^2}, \qquad Y_n(y) = \cos\frac{(2n-1)\pi y}{2b}$$

for $n = 1, 2, 3, \cdots$. Then

$$X_n'' - \lambda_n X_n = 0$$

yields

$$X_n(x) = A_n\cosh\frac{(2n-1)\pi x}{2b} + B_n\sin\frac{(2n-1)\pi x}{2b}.$$

Now $X_n(a) = 0$ is satisfied by the particular linear combination

$$X_n(x) = C_n\sinh\frac{(2n-1)\pi(a-x)}{2b}$$

of $\cosh(2n-1)\pi x/2b$ and $\sinh(2n-1)\pi x/2b$. Hence

$$u(x,y) = \sum_{n=1}^{\infty} C_n\sinh\frac{(2n-1)\pi(a-x)}{2b}\cos\frac{(2n-1)\pi y}{2b}$$
$$= \sum_{n\text{ odd}} A_n\sinh\frac{n\pi(a-x)}{2b}\cos\frac{n\pi y}{2b}.$$

Finally we satisfy the condition $u(0,y) = g(y)$ by choosing

$$A_n = \frac{a_n}{\sinh n\pi a/2b},$$

where the $\{a_n\}$ are the odd half-multiple cosine coefficients of $g(y)$ on $[0, b]$, as given by Problem 22 in Section 9.3.

13. We start with the periodic polar-coordinate solution

$$u(r,\theta) = \frac{a_0}{2} + \sum_{n=1}^{\infty} r^n (a_n \cos n\theta + b_n \sin n\theta)$$

and choose $a_n \equiv 0$ in order to satisfy the conditions $u(r,0) = u(r,\pi) = 0$. Then

$$u(r,\theta) = \sum_{n=1}^{\infty} r^n c_n \sin n\theta$$

satisfies the nonhomogeneous boundary condition $u(a,\theta) = f(\theta)$ provided that $a^n c_n$ is is the nth Fourier sine coefficient of $f(\theta)$ on the interval $0 < \theta < \pi$, that is,

$$c_n = \frac{2}{\pi a^n} \int_0^\pi f(\theta) \sin n\theta \, d\theta.$$

15. As in the textbook discussion of the polar-coordinate Dirichlet problem, the substitution $u(r,\theta) = R(r)\Theta(\theta)$ in Laplace's equation yields the separated ordinary differential equations

$$r^2 R'' + rR' - \lambda R = 0 \tag{25}$$

and

$$\Theta'' + \lambda\Theta = 0. \tag{26}$$

With $\lambda = \alpha^2$ the general solution of (26) is

$$\Theta(\theta) = A\cos\alpha\theta + B\sin\alpha\theta,$$

and the endpoint condition $\Theta(0) = \Theta'(0) = 0$ yields $A = 0$ and $\theta = (2n-1)/2$, so the nth eigenvalue and eigenfunction are given by

$$\lambda_n = \frac{(2n-1)^2}{4}, \qquad \Theta_n(\theta) = \sin\frac{(2n-1)\theta}{2}.$$

As in the discussion of Eqs. (29) and (30) in the text, the bounded solution of

$$r^2 R_n'' + rR_n' - \frac{(2n-1)^2}{4}R_n = 0$$

is

$$R_n(r) = r^{(2n-1)/2}$$

for $n = 1, 2, 3, \cdots$. We thereby obtain the formal series solution

$$u(r,\theta) = \sum_{n \text{ odd}} c_n r^{n/2} \sin \frac{n\theta}{2}.$$

It remains only to satisfy the nonhomogeneous boundary condition $u(a,\theta) = f(\theta)$ by choosing

$$c_n = \frac{2}{\pi a^{n/2}} \int_0^\pi f(\theta) \sin \frac{n\theta}{2} d\theta,$$

so that (for n odd) $c_n a^{n/2}$ equals the nth odd half-multiple sine coefficient of $f(\theta)$.

17. The substitution $u(r,\theta) = R(r)\Theta(\theta)$ in Laplace's equation yields the same separated solution functions

$$\Theta_0(\theta) = 1, \qquad\qquad R_0(r) = C_0 + D_0 \ln r$$

and

$$\Theta_n(\theta) = A_n \cos n\theta + B_n \sin n\theta, \qquad R_n(r) = C_n r^n + \frac{D_n}{r^n}$$

as in Eqs. (28)-(30) in the text. We choose $B_n \equiv 0$ to satisfy the boundary condition $u(r,\theta) = u(r,-\theta)$, and $n = 1$ with $C_1 = U_0$ to satisfy the given limit condition as $r \to \infty$. Then the condition that $u_r(a,\theta) = 0$ requires that $D_1 = U_0 a^2$, so

$$u(r,\theta) = \frac{U_0}{r}\left(r^2 + a^2\right)\cos\theta.$$

21. **(a)**   Since we cannot simply substitute $r = 0$, we apply continuity of $u(r, t)$ at $r = 0$ and calculate

$$u(0,t) = \lim_{r \to 0} u(r,t)$$

noting that

$$\lim_{r \to 0} \frac{\sin n\pi r/a}{r} = \frac{n\pi}{a} \lim_{r \to 0} \frac{\sin n\pi r/a}{n\pi r/a} = \frac{n\pi}{a} \lim_{r \to 0} \frac{\sin \theta}{\theta} = \frac{n\pi}{a}$$

by the elementary fact that $(\sin\theta)/\theta \to 1$ as $\theta \to 0$.

(b)   With $a = 30$ and $T_0 = 100$ we have

$$u(0,t) = 200 \sum_{n=1}^\infty (-1)^{n+1} \exp\left(-\frac{n^2 \pi^2 kt}{900}\right)$$

If $k = 0.15$ for iron then after 15 minutes = 900 seconds the center temperature is

$$u(0,900) \approx 45.5075 - 0.5361 + 0.0003 - 0.0000 + \cdots \approx 44.97.$$

If $k = 0.005$ for iron then after 15 minutes the center temperature is

$$
\begin{aligned}
u(0,900) \approx\ & 190.37 - 164.174 + 128.276 - 90.8081 + 58.2426 \\
& - 33.8449 + 17.8190 - 8.4998 + 3.6734 - 1.4384 \\
& + 0.5103 - 0.1640 + 0.0478 - 0.0126 + 0.0030 \\
& - 0.0007 + 0.0001 - 0.00002 + 0.00000 - \cdots \\
u(0,900) \approx\ & 100.00
\end{aligned}
$$

Thus the center of the ball has not yet begun to cool. For the center of this concrete ball to reach 45° (as with the iron ball after 15 minutes) would require $(0.15/0.005) \times 15 = 450$ minutes, that is, seven and a half hours!

CHAPTER 10

EIGENVALUES AND BOUNDARY VALUE PROBLEMS

SECTION 10.1

STURM-LIOUVILLE PROBLEMS AND EIGENFUNCTION EXPANSIONS

1. In the notation of Equation (9) in Section 10.1 of the text we have $\alpha_1 = \beta_1 = 0$ and $\alpha_2 = \beta_2 = 1$, so Theorem 1 implies that the eigenvalues are all nonnegative. If $\lambda = 0$, then $y'' = 0$ implies that $y(x) = Ax + B$. Then $y'(x) = A$, so the endpoint conditions yield $A = 0$, but B remains arbitrary. Hence $\lambda_0 = 0$ is an eigenvalue with eigenfunction

$$y_0(x) = 1.$$

If $\lambda = \alpha^2 > 0$, then the equation $y'' + \alpha^2 y = 0$ has general solution

$$y(x) = A \cos \alpha x + B \sin \alpha x,$$

with

$$y'(x) = -A\alpha \sin \alpha x + B\alpha \cos \alpha x.$$

Then $y'(0) = 0$ yields $B = 0$ so $A \neq 0$, and then

$$y'(L) = -A\alpha \sin \alpha L = 0,$$

so αL must be an integral multiple of π. Thus the nth positive eigenvalue is

$$\lambda_n = \alpha_n^2 = \frac{n^2 \pi^2}{L^2},$$

and the associated eigenfunction is

$$y_n(x) = \cos \frac{n \pi x}{L}.$$

3. If $\lambda = 0$ then $y'' = 0$ yields $y(x) = Ax + B$ as usual. But $y'(0) = A = 0$, and then $hy(L) + y'(L) = h(B) + 0 = 0$, so $B = 0$ also. Thus $\lambda = 0$ is not an eigenvalue. If $\lambda = \alpha^2 > 0$ so our equation is $y'' + \alpha^2 y = 0$, then

$$y(x) = A \cos \alpha x + B \sin \alpha x,$$

so
$$y'(x) = -A\alpha \sin \alpha x + B\alpha \cos \alpha x.$$

Now $y'(0) = 0$ yields $B = 0$, so we may write
$$y(x) = \cos \alpha x, \qquad y'(x) = -\alpha \sin \alpha x.$$

The equation
$$hy(L) + y'(L) = h \cos \alpha L - \alpha \sin \alpha L = 0$$
then gives
$$\tan \alpha L = \frac{h}{\alpha} = \frac{hL}{\alpha L},$$

so $\beta_n = \alpha_n L$ is the nth positive root of the equation
$$\tan x = \frac{hL}{x}.$$

Thus
$$\lambda_n = \alpha_n^2 = \frac{\beta_n^2}{L^2}, \qquad y_n(x) = \cos \frac{\beta_n x}{L}.$$

Finally, a sketch of the graphs $y = \tan x$ and $y = hL/x$ indicates that $\beta_n \approx (n-1)\pi$ for n large.

7.   The coefficient c_n in Eq. (23) of this section is given by Formula (25) with $f(x) = r(x) = 1$, $a = 0$, $b = L$, and $y_n(x) = \sin \frac{\beta_n x}{L}$. Using the fact that $\tan \beta_n = -\frac{\beta_n}{hL}$, so $\frac{\sin \beta_n}{\beta_n} = -\frac{\cos \beta_n}{hL}$, we find that

$$\int_0^L \sin^2 \frac{\beta_n x}{L} dx = \int_0^L \frac{1}{2}\left(1 - \cos \frac{2\beta_n x}{L}\right) dx = \frac{1}{2}\left[x - \frac{L}{2\beta_n}\sin \frac{2\beta_n x}{L}\right]_0^L$$

$$= \frac{1}{2}\left(L - L\frac{\sin \beta_n}{\beta_n}\cos \beta_n\right) = \frac{1}{2}\left(L + L\frac{\cos \beta_n}{hL}\cos \beta_n\right) = \frac{hL + \cos^2 \beta_n}{2h}$$

and $\displaystyle\int_0^L \sin \frac{\beta_n x}{L} dx = \frac{L(1 - \cos \beta_n)}{\beta_n}$. Hence the desired eigenfunction expansion i

$$1 = 2hL\sum_{n=1}^{\infty} \frac{1 - \cos \beta_n}{\beta_n\left(hL + \cos^2 \beta_n\right)}\sin \frac{\beta_n x}{L}.$$

for $0 < x < L$.

9.   The coefficient c_n in (23) is given by Formula (25) with $f(x) = r(x) = 1$, $a = 0$, $b = 1$, and $y_n(x) = \sin \beta_n x$. Using the fact that $\tan \beta_n = -\beta_n/h$, so

$h \sin \beta_n = -\beta_n \cos \beta_n$, we find that

$$\int_0^1 \sin^2 \beta_n x \, dx = \int_0^1 \frac{1}{2}(1 - \cos 2\beta_n x)\,dx = \frac{1}{2}\left[x - \frac{\sin 2\beta_n x}{2\beta_n}\right]_0^1$$

$$= \frac{1}{2}\left(1 - \frac{\sin \beta_n}{\beta_n}\cos \beta_n\right) = \frac{1}{2}\left(1 + \frac{\cos^2 \beta_n}{h}\right) = \frac{h + \cos^2 \beta_n}{2h}$$

and

$$\int_0^1 x \sin \beta_n x \, dx = \frac{1}{\beta_n^2}\int_0^1 \beta_n x \sin \beta_n x \cdot \beta_n dx = \frac{1}{\beta_n^2}\int_0^{\beta_n} u \sin u \, du$$

$$= \frac{1}{\beta_n^2}\left[\sin u - u \cos u\right]_0^{\beta_n} = \frac{\sin \beta_n - \beta_n \cos \beta_n}{\beta_n^2}$$

$$= \frac{\sin \beta_n - \beta_n \cos \beta_n}{\beta_n^2} = \frac{(1+h)\sin \beta_n}{\beta_n^2}.$$

It follows that the desired expansion is given by

$$x = 2h(1+h)\sum_{n=1}^{\infty}\frac{\sin \beta_n \sin \beta_n x}{\beta_n^2\left(h + \cos^2 \beta_n\right)}$$

for $0 < x < 1$.

11. If $\lambda = 0$ then $y'' = 0$ implies that $y(x) = Ax + B$. Then $y(0) = 0$ gives $B = 0$, so $y(x) = Ax$. Hence

$$hy(L) - y'(L) = h(AL) - A = A(hL - 1) = 0$$

if and only if $hL = 1$, in which case $\lambda_0 = 0$ has associated eigenfunction $y_0(x) = x$.

13. If $\lambda = +\alpha^2 > 0$, then the general solution of $y'' + \alpha^2 y = 0$ is

$$y(x) = A \cos \alpha x + B \sin \alpha x.$$

But then $y(0) = A = 0$, so we may take $y(x) = \sin \alpha x$. Now the condition $hy(L) = y'(L)$ yields

$$h \sin \alpha L = \alpha \cos \alpha L.$$

It follows that $\beta = \alpha L$ must be a root of the equation

$$\tan x = \frac{x}{hL}.$$

So if β_n is the nth positive root of this equation, then $\lambda_n = \alpha_n^2 = \beta_n^2 / L^2$ and the corresponding eigenfunction is $y_n(x) = \sin \beta_n x / L$.

15.   If $\lambda_0 = 0$, then a general solution of $y'' = 0$ is $y(x) = Ax + B$. The conditions

$$y(0) + y'(0) = B + A = 0, \qquad y(1) = A + B = 0$$

both say that $B = -A$, so we may take $y_0(x) = x - 1$ as the eigenfunction associated with $\lambda_0 = 0$. If $\lambda = +\alpha^2 < 0$, then the general solution of $y'' + \alpha^2 y = 0$ is

$$y(x) = A \cos \alpha x + B \sin \alpha x.$$

But $y(0) + y'(0) = A + B\alpha = 0$, so $A = -B\alpha$, and then

$$y(1) = A \cos \alpha + B \sin \alpha = -B(\alpha \cos \alpha - \sin \alpha) = 0.$$

Thus the possible values of α are the positive roots $\{\beta_n\}$ of the equation $\tan x = x$, and the nth eigenfunction is $y_n(x) = \beta_n \cos \beta_n x - \sin \beta_n x$,

17.   The Fourier sine series of the constant function $f(x) \equiv w$ for $0 < x < L$ is

$$w = \frac{4w}{\pi} \sum_{n \text{ odd}} \frac{1}{n} \sin \frac{n\pi x}{L}.$$

If $y = \sum b_n \sin n\pi x / L$, then

$$EI \, y^{(4)} = EI \sum_{n=1}^{\infty} \frac{n^4 \pi^4 b_n}{L^4} \sin \frac{n\pi x}{L}.$$

Upon equating coefficients in these two series and solving for b_n, we see that

$$y(x) = \frac{4wL^4}{EI\pi^5} \sum_{n \text{ odd}} \frac{1}{n^5} \sin \frac{n\pi x}{L}.$$

19.   With $\lambda = \alpha^4$, the general solution of $y^{(4)} - \alpha^4 y = 0$ is

$$y(x) = A \cosh \alpha x + B \sinh \alpha x + C \cos \alpha x + D \sin \alpha x,$$

and then

$$y'(x) = \alpha(A \sinh \alpha x + B \cosh \alpha x - C \sin \alpha x + D \cos \alpha x).$$

The conditions $y(0) = 0$ and $y'(0) = 0$ yield $C = -A$ and $D = -B$, so now

$$y(x) = A(\cosh \alpha x - \cos \alpha x) + B(\sinh \alpha x - \sin \alpha x).$$

The conditions $y(L) = 0$ and $y'(L) = 0$ yield the two linear equations

$$A(\cosh \alpha L - \cos \alpha L) + B(\sinh \alpha L - \sin \alpha L) = 0,$$

$$A(\sinh \alpha L + \sin \alpha L) + B(\cosh \alpha L - \cos \alpha L) = 0.$$

This linear system can have a non-trivial solution for A and B only if its coefficient determinant vanishes,

$$(\cosh \alpha L - \cos \alpha L)^2 - (\sinh^2 \alpha L - \sin^2 \alpha L) = 0.$$

Using the facts that $\cosh^2 A - \sinh^2 A = 1$ and $\cos^2 A + \sin^2 A = 1$, this equation simplifies to

$$\cosh \alpha L \cos \alpha L - 1 = 0,$$

so $\beta = \alpha L = x$ satisfies the equation

$$\cosh x \cos x = 1.$$

The eigenvalue corresponding to the nth positive root β_n is

$$\lambda_n = \alpha_n^4 = \left(\frac{\beta_n}{L}\right)^4.$$

Finally the first equation in the pair above yields

$$B = -\frac{\cosh \alpha L - \cos \alpha L}{\sinh \alpha L - \sin \alpha L},$$

so we may take

$$y_n(x) = \left(\sinh \beta_n - \sin \beta_n\right)\left(\cosh \frac{\beta_n x}{L} - \cos \frac{\beta_n x}{L}\right)$$
$$- \left(\cosh \beta_n - \cos \beta_n\right)\left(\sinh \frac{\beta_n x}{L} - \sin \frac{\beta_n x}{L}\right)$$

as the eigenfunction associated with the eigenvalue λ_n.

21. As in Problem 19, the solution of $y^{(4)} - \alpha^4 y = 0$ satisfying the left-endpoint conditions $y(0) = 0$ and $y'(0) = 0$ is given by

$$y(x) = A(\cosh \alpha x - \cos \alpha x) + B(\sinh \alpha x - \sin \alpha x).$$

The right-endpoint conditions $y(L) = 0$ and $y''(L) = 0$ yield the two linear equations

$$A(\cosh \alpha L - \cos \alpha L) + B(\sinh \alpha L - \sin \alpha L) = 0,$$

$$A(\cosh \alpha L + \cos \alpha L) + B(\sinh \alpha L + \sin \alpha L) = 0.$$

This linear system can have a non-trivial solution for A and B only if its coefficient determinant vanishes,

$$(\cosh \alpha L - \cos \alpha L)(\sinh \alpha L + \sin \alpha L)$$
$$- (\cosh \alpha L + \cos \alpha L)(\sinh \alpha L - \sin \alpha L) = 0.$$

This equation simplifies to $2\cosh \alpha L \sin \alpha L - 2\cos \alpha L \sinh \alpha L = 0$, which is equivalent to $\tanh \alpha L = \tan \alpha L$. Hence $\beta = \alpha L = x$ satisfies the equation $\tanh x = \tan x$, and the eigenvalue corresponding to the nth positive root β_n is $\lambda_n = \alpha_n^4 = (\beta_n / L)^4$.

SECTION 10.2

APPLICATIONS OF EIGENFUNCTION SERIES

1.   The substitution $u(x,t) = X(x)T(t)$ yields the separated equations

$$X'' + \alpha^2 X = 0 \quad \text{and} \quad T' = -k\lambda T$$

with separation constant $\lambda = \alpha^2$. In Problem 3 of Section 10.1 we saw that the Sturm-Liouville problem

$$X'' + \alpha^2 X = 0, \qquad X'(0) = hX(L) + X'(L) = 0$$

has eigenvalues $\lambda_n = \alpha_n^2 = \beta_n^2 / L^2$ and eigenfunctions

$$X_n(x) = \cos\frac{\beta_n x}{L}$$

for $n = 1, 2, 3, \cdots$, with $\{\beta_n\}$ being the positive roots of the equation $\tan x = hL/x$. The solution of $T_n' = -k\lambda_n T_n$ is then

$$T_n(t) = \exp\left(-\frac{\beta_n^2 kt}{L^2}\right),$$

so the resulting formal series solution is

$$u(x,t) = \sum_{n=1}^{\infty} c_n \exp\left(-\frac{\beta_n^2 kt}{L^2}\right)\cos\frac{\beta_n x}{L}.$$

The coefficients in the eigenfunction expansion are given by

$$c_n = \frac{\int_0^L f(x)\cos\frac{\beta_n x}{L}\,dx}{\int_0^L \cos^2\frac{\beta_n x}{L}\,dx} = \frac{2h}{hL+\sin^2\beta_n}\int_0^L f(x)\cos\frac{\beta_n x}{L}\,dx,$$

because

$$\int_0^L \cos^2\frac{\beta_n x}{L}\,dx = \int_0^L \frac{1}{2}\left(1+\cos\frac{2\beta_n x}{L}\right)dx = \left[\frac{1}{2}\left(x+\frac{L}{2\beta_n}\sin\frac{2\beta_n x}{L}\right)\right]_0^L$$

$$= \frac{1}{2}\left(L+\frac{L}{2\beta_n}\sin 2\beta_n\right) = \frac{1}{2h}\left(hL+\sin\beta_n\cdot\frac{hL\cos\beta_n}{\beta_n}\right)$$

$$= \frac{hL+\sin^2\beta_n}{2h}.$$

In the final step here we use the fact that $(hL\cos\beta_n)/\beta_n = \sin\beta_n$ because $\tan\beta_n = hL/\beta_n$.

3. The substitution $u(x,y) = X(x)Y(y)$ yields the separated equations

$$X'' - \alpha^2 X = 0 \quad \text{and} \quad Y'' + \alpha^2 Y = 0$$

with separation constant $\lambda = \alpha^2$. Problem 3 of Section 10.1 we saw that the Sturm-Liouville problem

$$Y'' + \alpha^2 Y = 0, \qquad Y'(0) = hY(L) + Y'(L) = 0$$

has eigenvalues $\lambda_n = \alpha_n^2 = \beta_n^2/L^2$ and eigenfunctions

$$Y_n(y) = \cos\frac{\beta_n y}{L}$$

for $n = 1, 2, 3, \cdots$, with $\{\beta_n\}$ being the positive roots of the equation $\tan x = hL/x$. The solution of

$$X_n'' - \frac{\beta_n^2}{L^2}X_n = 0, \qquad X(L) = 0$$

is

$$X_n(x) = \sinh\frac{\beta_n(L-x)}{L},$$

so the resulting formal series solution is

$$u(x,y) = \sum_{n=1}^\infty c_n \sinh\frac{\beta_n(L-x)}{L}\cos\frac{\beta_n y}{L}.$$

The coefficients in the eigenfunction expansion are given by

$$c_n = \frac{\int_0^L g(y)\cos\frac{\beta_n y}{L}\,dy}{(\sinh\beta_n)\int_0^L \cos^2\frac{\beta_n y}{L}\,dy} = \frac{2h}{(\sinh\beta_n)\left(hL+\sin^2\beta_n\right)}\int_0^L g(y)\cos\frac{\beta_n y}{L}\,dy,$$

because

$$\int_0^L \cos^2\frac{\beta_n y}{L}\,dy = \int_0^L \frac{1}{2}\left(1+\cos\frac{2\beta_n y}{L}\right)dy = \left[\frac{1}{2}\left(y+\frac{L}{2\beta_n}\sin\frac{2\beta_n y}{L}\right)\right]_0^L$$

$$= \frac{1}{2}\left(L+\frac{L}{2\beta_n}\sin 2\beta_n\right) = \frac{hL+\sin^2\beta_n}{2h}.$$

The final step here is the same as in Problem 1, using the fact that $(hL\cos\beta_n)/\beta_n = \sin\beta_n$ because $\tan\beta_n = hL/\beta_n$.

5.   The substitution $u(x,t) = X(x)T(t)$ yields the separated equations

$$X'' + \alpha^2 X = 0 \quad \text{and} \quad T' = -k\lambda T$$

with separation constant $\lambda = \alpha^2$. In Problem 4 of Section 10.1 we saw that the Sturm-Liouville problem

$$X'' + \alpha^2 X = 0, \qquad hX(0) - X'(0) = X(L) = 0$$

has eigenvalues $\lambda_n = \alpha_n^2 = \beta_n^2/L^2$ and eigenfunctions

$$X_n(x) = \beta_n \cos\frac{\beta_n x}{L} + hL\sin\frac{\beta_n x}{L}$$

for $n = 1, 2, 3, \cdots$, with $\{\beta_n\}$ being the positive roots of the equation $\tan x = -x/hL$. The solution of $T_n' = -k\lambda_n T_n$ is then

$$T_n(t) = \exp\left(-\frac{\beta_n^2 kt}{L^2}\right),$$

so the resulting formal series solution is

$$u(x,t) = \sum_{n=1}^\infty c_n \exp\left(-\frac{\beta_n^2 kt}{L^2}\right)\left(\beta_n \cos\frac{\beta_n x}{L} + hL\sin\frac{\beta_n x}{L}\right).$$

The coefficients in the eigenfunction expansion are given by

$$c_n = \frac{\int_0^L f(x)\left(\beta_n \cos\frac{\beta_n x}{L} + hL\sin\frac{\beta_n x}{L}\right)dx}{\int_0^L \left(\beta_n \cos\frac{\beta_n x}{L} + hL\sin\frac{\beta_n x}{L}\right)^2 dx}.$$

The evaluation of the denominator integral here is elementary, but there seems little point in carrying it out explicitly.

7. The boundary value problem here is

$$u_{xx} + u_{yy} = 0 \quad (0 < x < 1, \quad y > 0)$$
$$u_x(0, y) = u(1, y) + u_x(1, t) = 0,$$
$$u(x, 0) = 100.$$

The substitution $u(x, y) = X(x)Y(y)$ yields the separated equations

$$X'' + \alpha^2 X = 0 \quad \text{and} \quad Y'' - \alpha^2 Y = 0$$

with separation constant $\lambda = \alpha^2$. In Problem 3 of Section 10.1 we saw (taking $h = L = 1$) that the Sturm-Liouville problem

$$X'' + \alpha^2 X = 0, \qquad X'(0) = X(1) + X'(1) = 0$$

has eigenvalues $\lambda_n = \alpha_n^2$ and eigenfunctions

$$X_n(x) = \cos\alpha_n x$$

for $n = 1, 2, 3, \cdots$, with $\{\alpha_n\}$ being the positive roots of the equation $\tan x = 1/x$. The bounded solution of $Y_n'' - \alpha_n^2 Y_n = 0$ is then

$$Y_n(y) = \exp(-\alpha_n y),$$

so the resulting formal series solution is

$$u(x, y) = \sum_{n=1}^{\infty} c_n \cos\alpha_n x \exp(-\alpha_n y).$$

The coefficients in the eigenfunction expansion are given by

$$c_n = \frac{\int_0^L 100\cos\alpha_n x\,dx}{\int_0^L \cos^2\alpha_n x\,dx} = \frac{\left[\dfrac{100}{\alpha_n}\sin\alpha_n x\right]_0^1}{\left[\dfrac{1}{2}\left(x + \dfrac{1}{2\alpha_n}\sin 2\alpha_n x\right)\right]_0^1} = \frac{200\sin\alpha_n}{\alpha_n + \sin\alpha_n \cos\alpha_n},$$

so

$$u(x, y) = 200 \sum_{n=1}^{\infty} \frac{\sin \alpha_n \cos \alpha_n x \exp(-\alpha_n y)}{\alpha_n + \sin \alpha_n \cos \alpha_n}.$$

The first five positive solutions of $\tan x = 1/x$ are $0.8603, 3.4256, 7.4373, 9.5293$, and 12.6453, and we find that

$$u(1,1) \approx 30.8755 + 0.4737 + 0.0074 + 0.0002 + 0.0000 + \cdots \approx 31.4°C.$$

9. (a)   With $\lambda = 0$, the endpoint-value problem in (19) is $X'' = 0$, $X(0) = X'(0) = 0$, which has only the trivial solution $X(x) \equiv 0$. Thus $\lambda = 0$ is not an eigenvalue.

(b)   With $\lambda = -\alpha^2 < 0$, the endpoint-value problem in (19) is

$$X'' - \alpha^2 X = 0, \qquad X(0) = 0, \qquad -m\alpha^2 X(L) = A\delta X'(L).$$

The differential equation and the left-endpoint condition here give $X(x) = \sinh \alpha x$, and substitution in the right-endpoint condition gives

$$-m\alpha^2 \sinh \alpha L = A\delta\alpha \cosh \alpha L, \text{ that is, } \tanh \alpha L = -\frac{k}{\alpha L}$$

with $k = A\delta L/m > 0$. But the graph $y = \tanh x$ lies (aside from the origin) in the first and third quadrants, while the graph $y = -k/x$ lies interior to the second and fourth quadrants. Hence the two cannot intersect, and it follows that there cannot be an eigenvalue of the assumed form $\lambda = -\alpha^2 < 0$, .

11. (a) $a = \sqrt{\dfrac{K}{\delta}} = \sqrt{\dfrac{\lambda p}{m/V}} = \sqrt{\dfrac{\gamma pV}{m}} = \sqrt{\dfrac{\gamma nRT_K}{nm_0}} = \sqrt{\dfrac{\gamma RT_K}{m_0}}$

(b) $a = \sqrt{\dfrac{\gamma RT_K}{m_0}} = \sqrt{\dfrac{1.4 \times 8314(273 + T_C)}{29}} = \sqrt{\dfrac{1.4 \times 8314 \times 273}{29} \left(1 + \dfrac{T_C}{273}\right)}$

$$\approx 331.02 \sqrt{1 + \frac{T_C}{273}} \frac{m}{\sec} \approx 740.47 \sqrt{1 + \frac{T_C}{273}} \frac{\text{miles}}{\text{hour}}$$

$$\approx 740.47 \left[1 + \frac{1}{2}\left(\frac{T_C}{273}\right) + \cdots \right] \approx 740.47 + 1.356 T_C$$

15. $\displaystyle\int_0^L \sin\frac{\beta_m x}{L} \sin\frac{\beta_n x}{L} dx = \frac{L}{2}\left[\frac{\sin(\beta_m - \beta_n)}{\beta_m - \beta_n} - \frac{\sin(\beta_m + \beta_n)}{\beta_m + \beta_n} \right]$

$$= \frac{L}{2(\beta_m^2 - \beta_n^2)}\left[\begin{array}{l} (\beta_m + \beta_n)(\sin\beta_m \cos\beta_n - \sin\beta_n \cos\beta_m) \\ -(\beta_m - \beta_n)(\sin\beta_m \cos\beta_n + \sin\beta_n \cos\beta_m) \end{array} \right]$$

$$= \frac{L}{\beta_m^2 - \beta_n^2} \left[\beta_n \sin \beta_m \cos \beta_n - \beta_m \sin \beta_n \cos \beta_m \right]$$

$$= \frac{L}{\beta_m^2 - \beta_n^2} \left[\beta_n \cdot \frac{M \cos \beta_m}{m \beta_m} \cdot \cos \beta_n - \beta_m \cdot \frac{M \cos \beta_n}{m \beta_n} \cdot \cos \beta_m \right]$$

$$= \frac{LM}{m \left(\beta_m^2 - \beta_n^2 \right)} \cos \beta_m \cos \beta_n \left(\frac{\beta_n}{\beta_m} - \frac{\beta_m}{\beta_n} \right) = -\frac{LM \cos \beta_m \cos \beta_n}{m \beta_m \beta_n} \neq 0$$

19. With the given initial velocity function $g(x)$ with constant value $P/2\rho\varepsilon$ concentrated in the interval $L/2 - \varepsilon < x < L/2 + \varepsilon$, the coefficient formula of Problem 18 gives

$$c_n = \frac{2L}{n^2 \pi^2 a^2} \int_{L/2-\varepsilon}^{L/2+\varepsilon} \frac{P}{2\rho\varepsilon} \sin \frac{n\pi x}{L} \, dx$$

$$= \frac{L^2 P}{n^3 \pi^3 a^2 \rho\varepsilon} \left[\cos \left(\frac{n\pi}{2} - \frac{n\pi\varepsilon}{L} \right) - \cos \left(\frac{n\pi}{2} + \frac{n\pi\varepsilon}{L} \right) \right] = \frac{2L^2 P}{n^3 \pi^3 a^2 \rho\varepsilon} \sin \frac{n\pi}{2} \sin \frac{n\pi\varepsilon}{L}.$$

This gives the ε-dependent solution

$$y(x, t, \varepsilon) = \frac{2L^2 P}{\pi^3 a^2 \rho\varepsilon} \sum_{n=1}^{\infty} \frac{1}{n^3} \sin \frac{n\pi}{2} \sin \frac{n\pi\varepsilon}{L} \sin \frac{n^2 \pi^2 a^2 t}{L^2} \sin \frac{n\pi x}{L}.$$

Because

$$\frac{L}{n\pi\varepsilon} \sin \frac{n\pi\varepsilon}{L} = \frac{\sin(n\pi\varepsilon/L)}{n\pi\varepsilon/L} \to 1 \quad \text{as} \quad \varepsilon \to 0,$$

the limit $y(x, t) = \lim_{\varepsilon \to 0} y(x, t, \varepsilon)$ has the expansion

$$y(x, t) = \frac{2LP}{\pi^2 a^2 \rho} \sum_{n=1}^{\infty} \frac{1}{n^2} \sin \frac{n\pi}{2} \sin \frac{n^2 \pi^2 a^2 t}{L^2} \sin \frac{n\pi x}{L}.$$

SECTION 10.3

STEADY PERIODIC SOLUTIONS AND NATURAL FREQUENCIES

In Problems 1-6 we substitute $u(x, t) = X(x) \cos \omega t$ in

$$u_{tt} = a^2 u_{xx} \qquad (a^2 = E/\delta)$$

and then cancel the factor $\cos \omega t$ to obtain the ordinary differential equation

$$a^2 X'' + \omega^2 X = 0$$

with general solution

$$X(x) = A\cos\frac{\omega x}{a} + B\sin\frac{\omega x}{a}. \qquad\qquad (*)$$

It then remains only to apply the given endpoint conditions to determine the natural (circular) frequencies — the values of ω for which a non-trivial solution exists.

1. Endpoint conditions: $X(0) = X(L) = 0$

    With conditions $X(0) = 0$ in (*) implies that $A = 0$, so $X(x) = \sin(\omega x/a)$. Then $X(L) = \sin(\omega L/a) = 0$ implies that $\omega L/a = n\pi$, an integral multiple of π. Hence the nth natural frequency is $\omega_n = \dfrac{n\pi a}{L} = \dfrac{n\pi}{L}\sqrt{\dfrac{E}{\delta}}$.

3. Endpoint conditions: $X(0) = X'(L) = 0$

    The condition $X(0) = 0$ gives $A = 0$ in (*), so we have

    $$X(x) = \sin\frac{\omega x}{a}, \qquad\text{so}\qquad X'(x) = \frac{\omega}{a}\cos\frac{\omega x}{a}.$$

    Hence the condition $X'(L) = 0$ implies that $\omega L/a$ is an *odd* integral multiple of $\pi/2$. Thus the nth natural frequency is $\omega_n = \dfrac{(2n-1)\pi a}{2L} = \dfrac{(2n-1)\pi}{2L}\sqrt{\dfrac{E}{\delta}}$.

5. Endpoint conditions: $u_x(0, t) = ku(L, t) + AEu_x(L, t) = 0$

    The condition $X'(0) = 0$ gives $B = 0$ in (*), so we have

    $$X(x) = \cos\frac{\omega x}{a}, \qquad\text{so}\qquad u(x,t) = \cos\frac{\omega x}{a}\cos\omega t.$$

    Then

    $$u_x(x,t) = -\frac{\omega}{a}\sin\frac{\omega x}{a}\cos\omega t,$$

    so the other endpoint condition is

    $$k\cos\frac{\omega L}{a}\cos\omega t - AE\frac{\omega}{a}\sin\frac{\omega L}{a}\cos\omega t = 0.$$

    Upon canceling the $\cos\omega t$ factor, we find that

    $$AE\frac{\omega L}{a}\tan\frac{\omega L}{a} = kL.$$

    Thus $\beta = \omega L/a$ is a positive root of the equation $AEx\tan x = kL$, and the nth natural frequency is given by

$$\omega_n = \frac{\beta_n a}{L} = \frac{\beta_n}{L}\sqrt{\frac{E}{\delta}}$$

where β_n is the nth positive root of this equation.

7. Endpoint conditions:

$$u(0, t) = mu_{tt}(L, t) + AEu_x(L, t) + ku(L, t) = 0$$

The condition $u(0, t) = 0$ implies that

$$X(x) = \sin\frac{\omega x}{a}, \quad\text{so}\quad X'(x) = \frac{\omega}{a}\cos\frac{\omega x}{a}.$$

When we substitute $u(x, t) = X(x)\cos \omega t$ in the endpoint condition at $x = L$ and cancel the $\cos \omega t$ factor we get

$$-m\omega^2 X(L) + AEX'(L) + kX(L) = 0.$$

Next we substitute

$$z = \omega L/a, \qquad \omega = az/L, \qquad a^2 = E/\delta,$$

$$X(L) = \sin z, \qquad X'(L) = (z/L)\cos z.$$

The result simplifies readily to the frequency equation

$$(mEz^2 - k\delta L^2)\sin z = MEz \cos z.$$

If β_n is the nth positive root, then the nth natural frequency is $\omega_n = \dfrac{\beta_n a}{L} = \dfrac{\beta_n}{L}\sqrt{\dfrac{E}{\delta}}$.

In Problems 8-14 we substitute $y(x, t) = X(x)\cos \omega t$ in

$$y_{tt} + a^4 y_{xxxx} = 0 \qquad (a^4 = EI/\rho)$$

and then cancel the factor $\cos \omega t$ to obtain the ordinary differential equation

$$a^4 X^{(4)} - \omega^2 X = 0$$

with general solution

$$X(x) = A\cosh\frac{\theta x}{a} + B\sinh\frac{\theta x}{a} + C\cos\frac{\theta x}{a} + D\sin\frac{\theta x}{a} \qquad (**)$$

where $\theta = \sqrt{\omega}$. We then get the natural frequencies of vibration by applying the given endpoint conditions.

9. Endpoint conditions: $y(0, t) = y_x(0, t) = 0, \quad y(L, t) = y_{xx}(L, t) = 0$

Just as in Problem 21 of Section 10.1, the endpoint conditions $X(0) = X'(0) = 0$ and $X(L) = X''(L) = 0$ imply that

$$\lambda_n = \frac{\omega_n^2}{a^4} = \left(\frac{\beta_n}{L}\right)^4$$

where β_n is the nth positive zero of the frequency equation

$$\tanh x = \tan x.$$

Therefore the nth natural frequency ω_n is given by

$$\omega_n = \left(\frac{\beta_n}{L}\right)^2 a^2 = \frac{\beta_n^2}{L^2}\sqrt{\frac{EI}{\rho}}.$$

11. Endpoint conditions: $y(0, t) = y_x(0, t) = 0, \quad y_x(L, t) = y_{xxx}(L, t) = 0$

Here we have the equation

$$X^{(4)} - \lambda X = 0$$

with $\lambda = \omega^2/a^4 = \theta^4/a^4 = \alpha^4$ and endpoint conditions

$$X(0) = X'(0) = X'(L) = X^{(3)}(L) = 0.$$

The left-endpoint conditions readily give $C = -A$ and $D = -B$ in (**), so

$$\begin{aligned} X(x) &= A\cosh\alpha x + B\sinh\alpha x - A\cos\alpha x - B\sin\alpha x. \\ &= A(\cosh\alpha x - \cos\alpha x) + B(\sinh\alpha x - \sin\alpha x). \end{aligned}$$

Then the right-endpoint conditions give

$$\begin{aligned} A(\sinh\alpha L + \sin\alpha L) + B(\cosh\alpha L - \cos\alpha L) &= 0, \\ A(\sinh\alpha L - \sin\alpha L) + B(\cosh\alpha L + \cos\alpha L) &= 0. \end{aligned}$$

The determinant of coefficients of A and B must vanish if there is to be a nontrivial solution, so

$$\begin{aligned} (\sinh\alpha L + \sin\alpha L)&(\cosh\alpha L + \cos\alpha L) \\ -(\sinh\alpha L - \sin\alpha L)&(\cosh\alpha L - \cos\alpha L) = 0. \end{aligned}$$

This equation simplifies to $2\sinh\alpha L\cos\alpha L + 2\cosh\alpha L\sin\alpha L = 0$, which upon division by $\cosh\alpha L\cos\alpha L$ gives the frequency equation

$$\tanh x + \tan x = 0$$

for $\beta = \alpha L$. Then the nth frequency is given as usual by

$$\omega_n = \alpha_n^2 a^2 = \frac{\beta_n^2}{L^2}\sqrt{\frac{EI}{\rho}}.$$

13. This problem is the special case $m = 0$ of Problem 14 below.

14. Endpoint conditions:

$$y(0, t) = y_x(0, t) = y_{xxx}(L, t) = 0$$
$$m y_{tt}(L, t) = EI y_{xxx}(L, t) - k y(L, t)$$

With $p = \theta/a$, $\theta = \sqrt{\omega}$ we may write

$$X(x) = A \cosh px + B \sinh px + C \cos px + D \sin px.$$

The conditions $X(0) = X'(0) = 0$ readily imply that $C = -A$ and $D = -B$, so

$$\begin{aligned}
X &= A(\cosh px - \cos px) + B(\sinh px - \sin px), \\
X' &= pA(\sinh px + \sin px) + pB(\cosh px - \cos px), \\
X'' &= p^2 A(\cosh px + \cos px) + p^2 B(\sinh px + \sin px), \\
X^{(3)} &= p^3 A(\sinh px - \sin px) + p^3 B(\cosh px + \cos px).
\end{aligned}$$

The endpoint conditions at $x = L$ are

$$X''(L) = 0,$$
$$(k - m\omega^2)X(L) - EIX^{(3)}(L) = 0.$$

When we substitute the derivatives above and write $z = pL$ we get

$$A(\cosh z + \cos z) + B(\sinh z + \sin z) = 0,$$

$$\begin{aligned}
&A[(k - m\omega^2)(\cosh z - \cos z) - EIp^3(\sinh z - \sin z)] \\
&+ B[(k - m\omega^2)(\sinh z - \sin z) - EIp^3(\cosh z + \cos z)] = 0.
\end{aligned}$$

If Δ denotes the coefficient determinant of these two linear equations in A and B, then the necessary condition $\Delta = 0$ for a non-trivial solution reduces eventually to the equation

$$EIp^3(1 + \cosh z \cos z) - (k - m\omega^2)(\sinh z \cos z - \cosh z \sin z) = 0.$$

Finally we substitute $p = z/L$, $M = \rho L$, and

$$\omega^2 = p^4 a^4 = (z^4/L^4)(EI/\rho)$$

to get the frequency equation

$$MEIz^3(1 + \cosh z \cos z) = (kML^3 - mEIz^4)(\sinh z \cos z - \cosh z \sin z).$$

We may divide by $\cosh z \cos z$ to write this equation in the form

$$MEIz^3(1 + \operatorname{sech} z \sec z) = (kML^3 - mEIz^4)(\tanh z - \tan z).$$

If β_n denotes the nth positive root of this equation, then as usual the nth natural frequency is

$$\omega_n = \frac{\beta_n^2}{L^2}\sqrt{\frac{EI}{\rho}}.$$

15.   We want to calculate the fundamental frequency of transverse vibration of a cantilever with the numerical parameters

$$L = 400 \text{ cm}$$
$$E = 2 \cdot 10^{12} \text{ gm/cm-sec}^2$$
$$I = (1/12)(30 \text{ cm})(2 \text{ cm})^3 = 20 \text{ cm}^4$$
$$\rho = (7.75 \text{ gm/cm}^3)(60 \text{ cm}^2) = 465 \text{ gm/cm}.$$

When we substitute these values and $\beta_1 = 1.8751$ in the frequency formula

$$\omega_1 = \frac{\beta_1^2}{L^2}\sqrt{\frac{EI}{\rho}},$$

we find that $\omega_1 \approx 6.45$ rad/sec, so the fundamental frequency is $\omega_1/2\pi \approx 1.03$ cycles/sec. Thus the diver should bounce up and down on the end of the diving board about once every second.

17.   When we substitute $y(x, t) = X(x)\cos \omega t$ in the given partial differential equation

$$\rho\frac{\partial^2 y}{\partial t^2} - \frac{I}{A}\frac{\partial^4 y}{\partial x^2 \partial t^2} + EI\frac{\partial^4 y}{\partial x^4} = 0$$

and cancel the factor $\cos \omega t$, we get the ordinary differential equation

$$EIX^{(4)} + PX'' - \lambda X = 0$$

where $P = \lambda I / \rho A$ and $\lambda = \rho\omega^2$. By solving the characteristic equation

$$EI \, r^4 + Pr^2 - \lambda = EI(r^2 - \alpha^2)(r^2 + \beta^2) = 0$$

we find the general solution

$$X(x) = A \cosh \alpha x + B \sinh \alpha x + C \cos \beta x + D \sin \beta x$$

where

$$\alpha^2 = \frac{-P + \sqrt{P^2 + 4\lambda EI}}{2EI}, \qquad \beta^2 = -\frac{-P - \sqrt{P^2 + 4\lambda EI}}{2EI}.$$

The endpoint conditions $X(0) = X''(0) = 0$ imply that $A = C = 0$, so

$$X(x) = B \sinh \alpha x + D \sin \beta x.$$

Then the conditions $X(L) = X''(L) = 0$ yield the equations

$$B \sinh \alpha L + D \sin \beta L = 0,$$

$$\alpha^2 B \sinh \alpha L - \beta^2 D \sin \beta L = 0.$$

The determinant of these two linear equations in B and D must vanish in order that a nontrivial solution exist, so

$$(\alpha^2 + \beta^2) \sinh \alpha L \sin \beta L = 0.$$

It follows that $\sin \beta L = 0$, so βL must be an integral multiple of π. The definitions of α^2 and β^2 imply that

$$\beta^2 - \alpha^2 = \frac{P}{EI} = \frac{\lambda}{\rho AE}, \qquad \alpha^2 \beta^2 = \frac{\lambda}{EI}.$$

Hence if $\beta_n = n\pi/L$, the corresponding value of α_n is given by

$$\alpha_n^2 = \frac{n^2 \pi^2}{L^2} - \frac{\lambda_n}{\rho AE}.$$

Then $\alpha_n^2 \beta_n^2 = \lambda_n / EI$ gives the equation

$$\left(\frac{n^2 \pi^2}{L^2} - \frac{\lambda_n}{\rho AE} \right) \frac{n^2 \pi^2}{L^2} = \frac{\lambda_n}{EI}$$

that we readily solve for λ_n. The resulting value of the nth natural frequency is

$$\omega_n = \sqrt{\frac{\lambda_n}{\rho}} = \frac{n^2 \pi^2}{L^2} \left(1 + \frac{n^2 \pi^2 I}{\rho AL^2} \right)^{-1/2} \sqrt{\frac{EI}{\rho}}.$$

19. Substitution of $y(x,t) = X(x)\sin\omega t$ in the transverse bar problem

$$\frac{\partial^2 y}{\partial t^2} + a^4 \frac{\partial^4 y}{\partial x^4} = 0 \qquad \left(a^4 = \frac{EI}{\rho} \right)$$

$$y(0,t) = y_x(0,t) = 0,$$

$$y_{xx}(L,t) = EI\, y_{xxx}(L,t) + F_0 \sin\omega t = 0$$

yields the endpoint problem

$$X^{(4)} - p^4 X = 0 \qquad (\text{where } p^2 = \omega/a^2),$$

$$X(0) = X'(0) = 0,$$

$$X''(L) = EI\, X'''(L) + F_0 = 0.$$

When we impose the fixed-end conditions $X(0) = X'(0) = 0$ on the general solution

$$X(x) = A\cosh px + B\sinh px + C\cos px + D\sin px$$

we find readily that $C = -A$ and $D = -B$, so

$$X(x) = A(\cosh px - \cos px) + B(\sinh px - \sin px).$$

It remains only to find A and B. But the free-end conditions yield the linear equations

$$A(\cosh pL + \cos pL) + B(\sinh pL + \sin pL) = 0$$

$$A(\sinh pL - \sin pL) + B(\cosh pL + \cos pL) = -F_0/p^3 EI$$

that can be solved for

$$A = K(\sinh pL + \sin pL), \qquad B = -K(\cosh pL + \cos pL)$$

where

$$K = \frac{F_0}{2EIp^3(1+\cosh pL\cos pL)}.$$

SECTION 10.4

CYLINDRICAL COORDINATE PROBLEMS

1. Substitution of $u(r,t) = R(r)T(t)$ in the wave equation

$$\frac{\partial^2 u}{\partial t^2} = a^2 \left(\frac{\partial^2 u}{\partial r^2} + \frac{1}{r}\frac{\partial u}{\partial r} \right)$$

yields the separation

$$\frac{T''}{a^2 T} = \frac{R'' + \frac{1}{r}R'}{R} = \lambda = -\alpha^2.$$

The t-equation has general solution

$$T(t) = A\cos\alpha at + B\sin\alpha at,$$

and we choose $B = 0$, so that $T'(0) = 0$ (because the membrane is initially at rest). The r-equation can be written in the form

$$r^2 R'' + rR' + \alpha^2 r^2 R = 0,$$

which is the parametric Bessel equation of order zero, with continuous solution $R(r) = J_0(\alpha r)$. In order that the fixed boundary condition $R(c) = 0$ be satisfied, we choose $\alpha = \gamma_n / c$, where γ_n is the nth positive solution of $J_0(x) = 0$. At this point we have product functions of the form $J_0(\gamma_n r / c)\cos(\gamma_n at / c)$ that satisfy the wave equation and the homogeneous boundary conditions, so we form the formal series solution

$$u(r,t) = \sum_{n=1}^{\infty} c_n J_0\left(\frac{\gamma_n r}{c}\right)\cos\frac{\gamma_n at}{c}.$$

In order to satisfy the initial position condition $u(r,0) = f(x)$ is suffices that the $\{c_n\}$ be the Fourier-Bessel coefficients of the function $f(x)$ given by

$$c_n = \frac{2}{c^2\left[J_1(\gamma_n)\right]^2}\int_0^c rf(r)J_0\left(\frac{\gamma_n r}{c}\right)dr.$$

3. **(a)**   This is the same as Problem 1, except that the membrane has initial position $u(r,0) = 0$, so in the t-factor $T(t) = A\cos\alpha at + B\sin\alpha at$ we choose $A = 0$ so that $T(0) = 0$. We then get product functions of the form $J_0(\gamma_n r / c)\sin(\gamma_n at / c)$ that satisfy the wave equation and the homogeneous boundary conditions, so we form the formal series solution

$$u(r,t) = \sum_{n=1}^{\infty} c_n J_0\left(\frac{\gamma_n r}{c}\right)\sin\frac{\gamma_n at}{c}.$$

In order to satisfy the given initial condition we must choose

$$
\begin{aligned}
c_n &= \frac{c}{\gamma_n a}\cdot\frac{2}{c^2 J_1(\gamma_n)^2}\int_0^\varepsilon\left(\frac{P_0}{\rho\pi\varepsilon^2}\right)rJ_0\left(\frac{\gamma_n r}{c}\right)dr\\
&= \frac{2P_0 c}{\rho\pi\varepsilon^2\gamma_n^3 a J_1(\gamma_n)^2}\int_0^{\gamma_n\varepsilon/c} xJ_0(x)\,dx \qquad\text{(with } x = \gamma_n r / c)
\end{aligned}
$$

$$= \frac{2P_0 c}{\rho \pi \varepsilon^2 \gamma_n^3 a J_1(\gamma_n)^2} \cdot \frac{\gamma_n \varepsilon}{c} J_1\left(\frac{\gamma_n \varepsilon}{c}\right).$$

$$c_n = \frac{2aP_0}{\pi c \rho a^2 \gamma_n J_1(\gamma_n)^2} \cdot \frac{J_1(\gamma_n \varepsilon / c)}{\gamma_n \varepsilon / c}.$$

(b) The final formula given in the text for $u(r, t)$ now follows because $\rho a^2 = T$ and $J_1(x)/x \to 1/2$ as $x \to 0$.

5. **(a)** We start with the steady-state boundary value problem

$$\frac{\partial^2 u}{\partial r^2} + \frac{1}{r}\frac{\partial u}{\partial r} + \frac{\partial^2 u}{\partial z^2} = 0 \qquad (r < c, \;\; 0 < z < L)$$

$$u(c, z) = 0$$

$$u(r, 0) = 0,$$

$$u(r, L) = u_0.$$

The substitution $u(r, z) = R(r)Z(z)$ yields the equations

$$rR'' + R' + \alpha^2 rR = 0, \qquad Z'' - \alpha^2 Z = 0$$

with separation constant $\lambda = \alpha^2$. The homogeneous endpoint conditions are

$$R(c) = Z(0) = 0.$$

If $\lambda = \alpha^2 = 0$ then $rR'' + R = 0$ implies

$$R(r) = A + B \ln r.$$

We choose $B = 0$ for continuity at $r = 0$, so $R(r) = A$. Then $R(c) = 0$, so $A = 0$ also, and hence 0 is not an eigenvalue.

If $\lambda = \alpha^2 > 0$ then we have the parametric Bessel equation with general solution

$$R(r) = A J_0(\alpha r) + B Y(\alpha r).$$

In order that $R(r)$ be continuous at $r = 0$ we choose $B = 0$, so $R(r) = A J_0(\alpha r)$. Then

$$R(c) = \alpha A J_0(\alpha c) = 0$$

requires that $\gamma = \alpha c$ be a root of the equation

$$J_0(x) = 0.$$

If $\alpha_n = \gamma_n/c$ where γ_n is the nth positive root of this equation, then

$$R_n(r) = J_0\left(\frac{\gamma_n r}{c}\right).$$

The corresponding function $Z(z)$ of z is

$$Z_n(z) = A_n \cosh\frac{\gamma_n z}{c} + B_n \sinh\frac{\gamma_n z}{c},$$

and we choose $A_n = 0$ because $Z(0) = 0$. Thus we get the formal series solution

$$u(r,z) = \sum_{n=1}^{\infty} c_n J_0\left(\frac{\gamma_n r}{c}\right)\sinh\frac{\gamma_n z}{c}$$

where $J_0(\gamma_n) = 0$. To satisfy the condition $u(r, L) = u_0$, we need (by Eq. (22) in the text)

$$c_n = \frac{1}{\sinh(\gamma_n L/c)}\cdot\frac{2}{c^2 J_1(\gamma_n)^2}\int_0^c r u_0 J_0\left(\frac{\gamma_n r}{c}\right)dr$$

$$= \frac{2u_0}{\gamma_n^2 J_1(\gamma_n)^2 \sinh(\gamma_n L/c)}\int_0^{\gamma_n} x J_0(x)\,dx \qquad (\text{with } x = \gamma_n r/c)$$

$$= \frac{2u_0}{\gamma_n^2 J_1(\gamma_n)^2 \sinh(\gamma_n L/c)}\left[x J_1(x)\right]_0^{\gamma_n} = \frac{2u_0}{\gamma_n J_1(\gamma_n)}.$$

This gives the desired solution

$$u(r,t) = 2u_0 \sum_{n=1}^{\infty} \frac{J_0(\gamma_n r/c)\sinh(\gamma_n z/c)}{\gamma_n J_1(\gamma_n)\sinh(\gamma_n L/c)}.$$

7.   We want to solve the boundary value problem

$$\frac{\partial^2 u}{\partial r^2} + \frac{1}{r}\frac{\partial u}{\partial r} + \frac{\partial^2 u}{\partial z^2} = 0 \qquad (r < 1,\ z > 0)$$

$$hu(1, z) + u_r(1, z) = 0$$

$$u(r, z) \text{ bounded as } z \to \infty$$

$$u(r, 0) = u_0.$$

We start with the separation of variables in Problem 5,

$$rR'' + R' + \alpha^2 rR = 0, \qquad Z'' - \alpha^2 Z = 0$$

and readily see that $\alpha = 0$ is not an eigenvalue. When we impose the condition

$$hR(1) + R'(1) = 0$$

on $R(r) = J_0(\alpha r)$, we find that α must satisfy the equation

$$hJ_0(x) + xJ_0'(x) = 0$$

that corresponds to Case 2 with $n = 0$ in Figure 10.4.2 of the text. If $\{\gamma_n\}$ are the positive roots of this equation then

$$R_n(r) = J_0(\gamma_n r).$$

The general solution of $Z'' = \gamma_n^2 Z$ is

$$Z_n(z) = A_n \exp(-\gamma_n z) + B_n \exp(\gamma_n z),$$

and we choose $B_n = 0$ so that $Z_n(z)$ will be bounded as $z \to \infty$. Thus we obtain a solution of the form

$$u(r,z) = \sum_{n=1}^{\infty} c_n \exp(-\gamma_n z) J_0(\gamma_n r)$$

where

$$hJ_0(\gamma_n) + \gamma_n J_0'(\gamma_n) = 0,$$

so $\gamma_n J_1(\gamma_n) = h J_0(\gamma_n)$ because $J_0' = -J_1$. Finally, Eq. (23) in the text gives

$$c_n = \frac{2\gamma_n^2}{c^2 \left(\gamma_n^2 + h^2\right) J_0(\gamma_n)^2} \int_0^c r u_0 J_0\left(\frac{\gamma_n r}{c}\right) dr$$

$$= \frac{2u_0}{\left(\gamma_n^2 + h^2\right) J_0(\gamma_n)^2} \int_0^{\gamma_n} x J_0(x) \, dx \qquad \left(\text{with } x = \gamma_n r / c\right)$$

$$= \frac{2u_0}{\left(\gamma_n^2 + h^2\right) J_0(\gamma_n)^2} \left[x J_1(x) \right]_0^{\gamma_n}$$

$$= \frac{2u_0 \gamma_n J_1(\gamma_n)}{\left(\gamma_n^2 + h^2\right) J_0(\gamma_n)^2} = \frac{2h u_0}{\left(\gamma_n^2 + h^2\right) J_0(\gamma_n)},$$

so

$$u(r,z) = 2h u_0 \sum_{n=1}^{\infty} \frac{\exp(-\gamma_n z) J_0(\gamma_n r)}{\left(\gamma_n^2 + h^2\right) J_0(\gamma_n)}.$$

11. When we substitute $u(r, t) = R(r) \sin \omega t$ in the given partial differential equation and cancel the factor $\sin \omega t$, we get the ordinary differential equation

$$R'' + \frac{1}{r}R' + \left(\frac{\omega}{a}\right)^2 R = -\frac{F_0}{a^2}$$

The associated homogeneous equation is the Bessel equation of order zero with parameter ω/a. Hence it follows readily that the solution that is continuous at $r = 0$ is

$$R(r) = A J_0\left(\frac{\omega r}{a}\right) - \frac{F_0}{\omega^2}.$$

The condition $R(b) = 0$ yields $A = F_0/\omega^2 J_0(\omega b/a)$, so it follows that the desired steady periodic solution is

$$u(r,t) = \frac{F_0}{\omega^2 J_0(\omega b/a)}\left[J_0\left(\frac{\omega r}{a}\right) - J_0\left(\frac{\omega b}{a}\right)\right]\sin \omega t.$$

13. With $w(x) = wx$ and $h(x) = h$ (where w and h on the right are constants) the given partial differential equation

$$\frac{w(x)}{g}\frac{\partial^2 y}{\partial t^2} = \frac{\partial}{\partial x}\left(w(x)h(x)\frac{\partial y}{\partial x}\right) \qquad (*)$$

reduces to

$$x\frac{\partial^2 y}{\partial t^2} = gh\left(\frac{\partial y}{\partial x}+\frac{\partial^2 y}{\partial x^2}\right).$$

When we substitute $y(x, t) = X(x)\cos \omega t$ we get the parametric Bessel equation

$$x^2 X'' + xX' + \frac{\omega^2 x^2}{gh}X = 0$$

with bounded solution

$$X(x) = A J_0\left(\frac{\omega x}{\sqrt{gh}}\right).$$

The condition $X(L) = y_0$ implies that $A = y_0/J_0\left(\omega L/\sqrt{gh}\right)$, so

$$y(x,t) = y_0\frac{J_0\left(\omega x/\sqrt{gh}\right)}{J_0\left(\omega L/\sqrt{gh}\right)}\cos \omega t.$$

15. With $w(x) = wx$ and $h(x) = hx$ (with w and h being constants on the right) the partial differential equation in $(*)$ above reduces to

$$\frac{\partial^2 y}{\partial t^2} = gh\left(2\frac{\partial y}{\partial x}+x\frac{\partial^2 y}{\partial x^2}\right).$$

When we substitute $y(x, t) = X(x)\cos \omega t$ we get the ordinary differential equation

$$x^2 X'' + 2xX' + \frac{\omega^2 x}{gh}X = 0.$$

This has the form of Equation (3) in Section 8.6 with $A = 2$, $B = 0$, $C = \omega^2/gh$, and $q = 1$, so its (bounded) solution is given by

$$X(x) = \frac{A}{\sqrt{x}} J_1\left(2\omega\sqrt{\frac{x}{gh}}\right).$$

The condition $X(L) = y_0$ now implies that $A = y_0\sqrt{L}/J_1\left(2\omega\sqrt{L/gh}\right)$, so

$$y(x,t) = y_0\sqrt{\frac{L}{x}} \frac{J_1\left(2\omega\sqrt{x/gh}\right)}{J_1\left(2\omega\sqrt{L/gh}\right)} \cos\omega t.$$

17. Just as in Problem 1 above, substitution of $u(r,t) = R(r)T(t)$ in the wave equation

$$\frac{\partial^2 u}{\partial t^2} = a^2\left(\frac{\partial^2 u}{\partial r^2} + \frac{1}{r}\frac{\partial u}{\partial r}\right)$$

yields the separation

$$\frac{T''}{a^2 T} = \frac{R'' + \dfrac{1}{r}R'}{R} = \lambda = -\alpha^2.$$

The t-equation has general solution

$$T(t) = A\cos\alpha at + B\sin\alpha at,$$

and we choose $B = 0$, so that $T'(0) = 0$ (assuming, for instance, that the membrane is initially at rest). The r-equation can be written in the form

$$r^2 R'' + rR' + \alpha^2 r^2 R = 0,$$

which is the parametric Bessel equation of order zero. By Problem 16, its solutions satisfying $R(a) = R(b) = 0$ are of the form $R_n(x) = Y_0(\gamma_n a)J_0(\gamma_n x) - J_0(\gamma_n a)Y_0(\gamma_n x)$ with $\alpha = \gamma_n$ being one of the positive roots of the equation

$$J_0(ax)Y_0(bx) - J_0(bx)Y_0(ax) = 0. \tag{#}$$

This leads to a formal series solution of the form

$$u(r,t) = \sum_{n=1}^{\infty} R_n(x)\left(A_n\cos\gamma_n at + B_n\sin\gamma_n at\right),$$

where the frequency of the nth term is $\omega_n = \gamma_n a = \gamma_n\sqrt{T/\rho}$.

19. We want to solve the boundary value problem

$$\frac{\partial^2 u}{\partial r^2} + \frac{1}{r}\frac{\partial u}{\partial r} + \frac{\partial^2 u}{\partial z^2} = 0 \qquad (a < r < 1, \ z > 0)$$

$$u(a,z) = u(b,z) = 0$$

$$u(r,z) \text{ bounded as } z \to \infty$$

$$u(r,0) = f(r).$$

Just as in Problem 5, the substitution $u(r,z) = R(r)Z(z)$ yields the equations

$$rR'' + R' + \alpha^2 rR = 0, \qquad Z'' - \alpha^2 Z = 0$$

with separation constant $\lambda = \alpha^2$. When we impose the conditions $R(a) = R(b) = 0$ on the r-equation here, we have the Sturm-Liouville problem of Problem 16, so $R(r)$ must be one of the eigenfunctions $\{R_n(r)\}$ corresponding to the positive roots $\{\gamma_n\}$ of Equation (#) above. The general solution of $Z'' = \gamma_n^2 Z$ is

$$Z_n(z) = A_n \exp(-\gamma_n z) + B_n \exp(\gamma_n z),$$

and we choose $B_n = 0$ so that $Z_n(z)$ will be bounded as $z \to \infty$. Thus we obtain a solution of the form

$$u(r,z) = \sum_{n=1}^{\infty} c_n \exp(-\gamma_n z) R_n(r)$$

with the coefficients $\{c_n\}$ calculated as in Problem 18.

SECTION 10.5

HIGHER-DIMENSIONAL PHENOMENA

This section provides the interested student with an opportunity to study several applications at greater depth than is afforded by the usual textbook exercises. The problem sets outlined in Section 10.5 can serve as the basis for several fairly substantial computational projects. Because these problem sets and projects are rather heavily annotated in the text, further outlines of solutions are not included in this manual. However, additional discussion — particularly regarding computer implementations — may be found in the *Computing Projects Manual* that accompanies the text.

EXISTENCE AND UNIQUENESS OF SOLUTIONS

In Problems 1-12 we apply the iterative formula

$$y_{n+1} = b + \int_a^x f(t, y_n(t)) \, dt$$

to compute successive approximations $\{y_n(x)\}$ to the solution of the initial value problem

$$y' = f(x, y), \qquad\qquad y(a) = b.$$

starting with $y_0(x) = b$.

1. $y_0(x) = 3$

$y_1(x) = 3 + 3x$

$y_2(x) = 3 + 3x + 3x^2/2$

$y_3(x) = 3 + 3x + 3x^2/2 + x^3/2$

$y_4(x) = 3 + 3x + 3x^2/2 + x^3/2 + x^4/8$

$y(x) = 3 - 3x + 3x^2/2 + x^3/2 + x^4/8 + \cdots = 3e^x$

3. $y_0(x) = 1$

$y_1(x) = 1 - x^2$

$y_2(x) = 1 - x^2 + x^4/2$

$y_3(x) = 1 - x^2 + x^4/2 - x^6/6$

$y_4(x) = 1 - x^2 + x^4/2 - x^6/6 + x^8/24$

$y(x) = 1 - x^2 + x^4/2 - x^6/6 + x^8/24 - \cdots = \exp(-x^2)$

5. $y_0(x) = 0$

$y_1(x) = 2x$

$y_2(x) = 2x + 2x^2$

$y_3(x) = 2x + 2x^2 + 4x^3/3$

$y_4(x) = 2x + 2x^2 + 4x^3/3 + 2x^4/3$

$y(x) = 2x + 2x^2 + 4x^3/3 + 2x^4/3 + \cdots = e^{2x} - 1$

7. $y_0(x) = 0$

$y_1(x) = x^2$

$y_2(x) = x^2 + x^4/2$

$y_3(x) = x^2 + x^4/2 + x^6/6$

$y_4(x) = x^2 + x^4/2 + x^6/6 + x^8/24$

$y(x) = x^2 + x^4/2 + x^6/6 + x^8/24 + \cdots = \exp(x^2) - 1$

9. $y_0(x) = 1$

$y_1(x) = (1 + x) + x^2/2$

$y_2(x) = (1 + x + x^2) + x^3/6$

$y_3(x) = (1 + x + x^2 + x^3/3) + x^4/24$

$y(x) = 1 + x + x^2 + x^3/3 + x^4/12 + \cdots = 2e^x - 1 - x$

11. $y_0(x) = 1$

$y_1(x) = 1 + x$

$y_2(x) = (1 + x + x^2) + x^3/3$

$y_3(x) = (1 + x + x^2 + x^3) + 2x^4/3 + x^5/3 + x^6/9 + x^7/63$

$y(x) = 1 + x + x^2 + x^3 + x^4 + \cdots = 1/(1 - x)$

13.
$$\begin{bmatrix} x_0(t) \\ y_0(t) \end{bmatrix} = \begin{bmatrix} 1 \\ -1 \end{bmatrix}$$

$$\begin{bmatrix} x_1(t) \\ y_1(t) \end{bmatrix} = \begin{bmatrix} 1 + 3t \\ -1 + 5t \end{bmatrix}$$

$$\begin{bmatrix} x_2(t) \\ y_2(t) \end{bmatrix} = \begin{bmatrix} 1 + 3t + \frac{1}{2}t^2 \\ -1 + 5t - \frac{1}{2}t^2 \end{bmatrix}$$

$$\begin{bmatrix} x_3(t) \\ y_3(t) \end{bmatrix} = \begin{bmatrix} 1 + 3t + \frac{1}{2}t^2 + \frac{1}{3}t^3 \\ -1 + 5t - \frac{1}{2}t^2 + \frac{5}{6}t^3 \end{bmatrix}$$